Society and the Social Sciences

An Introduction

Edited by
David Potter
with James Anderson,
John Clarke, Pat Coombes,
Stuart Hall, Laurence Harris,
Clive Holloway
and Tony Walton

for the Social Sciences Foundation Course Team
at the Open University

London
Routledge
in association with
The Open University Press

First published 1981
by Routledge & Kegan Paul

Reprinted in 1983, 1984, 1986 and 1987

Reprinted in 1988
by Routledge
11 New Fetter Lane, London EC4P 4EE
29 West 35th Street, New York, NY 10001

Selection and editorial material copyright © The Open University 1981

Set in IBM Press Roman by
Hope Services, Abingdon, Oxon
and printed in Great Britain by
T. J. Press (Padstow) Ltd, Padstow, Cornwall

British Library Cataloguing in Publication Data

Society and the social sciences.

1. Sociology
I. Potter, David   II. Open University.
Social Sciences Foundation Course Team
301   HM51

ISBN 0-415-03981-9

Library of Congress Cataloging in Publication Data available

Contents

Acknowledgments

We want to thank the six people who agreed to write original papers for this volume – Alan Ryan, Kathleen O'Donnell, Patrick Dunleavy, Doreen Massey, Bob Colenutt and Steven Lukes. Jo Mathieson cheerfully accepted responsibility for the large and swift typing job needed to get the manuscript to the publisher on time; we are grateful for her assistance. We also wish to acknowledge the contribution made by John Taylor for handling arrangements for the manuscript's publication, and by Camilla Raab of Routledge for her judicious and tactful editing.

We as editors are part of a large group of people who planned and produced an introductory course in the social sciences at the Open University. Since this book has grown out of that course, it is theirs as well as ours. We have merely put it together on their behalf. The entire course team is identified in the Appendix, along with a brief indication of the contents of the course.

The Open University and the publishers would like to thank the following for permission to reproduce copyright material. All possible care has been taken to trace ownership of the selections included and to make full acknowledgment for their use.

Reading

2, 7, 14, 20, 23 © The Open University, 1981.
3, 4 By permission of David Higham Associates Limited, 1968.
5, 9 Reprinted by permission of Penguin Books Ltd, 1976, 1979.
6 Copyright © 1952 by Scientific American, Inc. All rights reserved.
8 Copyright © Huw Beynon, 1973.
10 © *Radical America*, 1974.
11 By permission of the author and Cambridge University Press, 1974.
12 © Anthony King, 1976.
13 © David Coates, 1976.
15 Copyright *Naval Research Reviews*, 1973.

16 Reprinted by permission of the author and the University of Chicago Press, 1975.
17 By permission of the author and the American Sociological Association, 1970.
18 © Unesco, 1975.
21, 22 By permission of Macmillan, London and Basingstoke, 1979.
24 By permission of Tower Hamlets Trades Council, 1978.
26 By permission of Inter-Action Inprint, 1978.
27 Copyright © 1959 by Erving Goffman. Reprinted by permission of Doubleday & Company, Inc., and Penguin Books Ltd.
28 © 1972 by Basic Books, Inc., Publishers, New York. Reprinted by permission. Reprinted by permission of Associated Book Publishers Ltd.
29 By permission of the Aristotelian Society, 1978, 1981.
30 Reprinted by permission of Hackett Publishing Company Inc., and Routledge & Kegan Paul Ltd, 1961.
31 Reprinted by permission of Routledge & Kegan Paul Ltd, 1961.
32 By permission of George Allen & Unwin Ltd, 1975.

SECTION 1

Studying Society

1 General introduction

The editors

Our general aim in this book is to provide an introduction to the study of society and the social sciences. As an *introduction*, it is intended for any student who wants to become acquainted with the work of the social sciences; it is also a set book for Open University students taking the Social Sciences Foundation Course (D102). As a study of *society*, it is western industrialized societies with capitalist economies and democratic politics that are singled out for attention, with modern British society providing the main example. As a study of the *social sciences*, five social science disciplines working together, so to speak, are on display – economics, geography, political science, psychology and sociology.

Normally, students starting out in the social sciences take an introductory course in sociology or economics, or in one of the other social science disciplines. Rarely does one find interdisciplinary introductions like this one. We are obliged, therefore, to say why we have adopted this unusual approach. There are a number of reasons, but two perhaps stand out as having had a major impact on the shape and content of this volume.

The first reason is, quite simply, that many of the really important and interesting questions about society are rarely the preserve of any one social science discipline. They tend instead to be the joint concern of several, and we believe that students can and should begin to grapple with such questions at the outset of their studies. Some university lecturers argue that students must first be trained in individual disciplines before finally tackling these important issues. But our objection to that strategy is that students can become submerged in the particular issues of the discipline and never have the time to work on the big questions. One is reminded of A. G. Keller's jibe about the man who is endlessly packing a suitcase for a journey that never takes place.

These reflections (and others) led us to organize this volume (and the D102 course) around one of the biggest and most important issues of all: how does modern capitalist society manage to hold together while changing through time? Take Britain, for example. In the 1970s and early 1980s, British society was constantly changing. The economic

3

crisis was affecting chances of employment and changing standards of living. The decline of particular industries and the effects of planning decisions were altering the social character of whole geographical areas of the country. The coming of the welfare state and the expansion of government led to increased expectations from people about what government could provide; and increasingly there was concern as to whether Parliament and government would be able to cope with the demands made upon them. In addition to these large economic and political changes, there was talk of a general breakdown of family life and morality. All these changes seemed to add up to a profound crisis in British society. Yet at the same time these changes were taking place within a society that remained recognizably British. Many institutions and patterns of life remained stable and familiar. People worked in the same sorts of factories and offices, and spent their earnings on the same sorts of goods. They voted for the same political parties in the same political system. The language altered little, and people seemed to go about their lives in the same familiar ways. The stability of many aspects of British society together with its ability to absorb change without breaking down completely was noteworthy, although there were many problems involved in the process which would not go away. Other industrialized societies, besides Britain, managed the same achievement. But how? The general problem is to explain how the dynamics of a society enable it to change while the conflicts and pressures involved are contained so that it continues to function as a whole instead of falling apart.

That general problem provides the major organizing theme for this volume. We start (in Section 2) with the economy, with the way people are organized in capitalist societies to produce the goods and services they require for their survival and way of life. How does a capitalist economy continue to provide us with goods and services, what are the conditions that assist the process, and what are some of the problems involved? The way the economy operates and co-ordinates many different activities has a major impact on the way society is organized, on its social structure (Section 3). Such structures are made up of different social classes, ethnic groups, genders – all related to each other and giving society some overall coherence. Yet do not such divisions also produce conflict (e.g. class conflict) and threaten to tear society apart? Certainly, but one thing political institutions do is to regulate and contain such conflicts (Section 4). How do political institutions in a liberal democracy operate to perform these functions? Can Britain, for example, be both a class society and a democracy? And does its social order depend on popular consent or on controlling the people? How do individuals conform, how do the family, the educational system and the mass media contribute to the cohesion of the social structure, and what is the role of ideology in all this (Section 5)? Societies cohere, yet they also change. One important way that change occurs is through the decision-making process and the implementation of social policies designed to affect, for example, inner city areas in industrial societies (Section 6). How do policy changes affect such areas and different regions of a country, and who benefits from such changes? In showing how societies change yet cohere, a recurring question is 'how significant are the actions of individuals?' (Section 7). Is it the 'individuals' who change society, or do changes occur primarily as a result of the dynamics of 'society', of relationships between groups and classes?

These are the kinds of questions, in that order, that are pursued in the Open University's Social Sciences Foundation Course (D102), as can be seen from the list of block and unit titles for the course given in the Appendix to this volume. (One 'unit' is equivalent to about one week's work.) The same framework and set of questions are reflected in the arrangement of this volume as indicated in its table of contents. The introductions to each section indicate the particular issues that are examined.

To sum up so far, then, the first reason why this introductory volume is interdisciplinary in approach is because the main problem being considered (how do capitalist societies cohere while changing?) is best examined by using such an approach.

The second main reason for this interdisciplinary approach is that, although individual disciplines look at different aspects of society, they share certain common problems and methods of approach. Two things in particular stand out in this regard, and figure in various places in this volume.

The first is that all disciplines share an interest these days in what can generally be identified as the problem of 'structure and agency'. We referred to it briefly above in outlining the concerns of Section 7 of this volume, but it has a much wider significance for the social sciences as a whole. In showing how society changes yet coheres, a recurring question is 'how significant are the actions of individuals?' How much real freedom of choice have we as individuals within society? For example, what sorts of influences can we exert as voters? Can we bring about changes by acting together in pressure groups on issues that concern us? More generally, to what extent are we as individuals swept along by social forces? Clearly structural forces involving class, occupation, race, gender and so on are important in determining the development of a society. But how important? And, to the extent that actions do have an influence, are these actions to be understood in terms of individuals' choices, in terms of classes or in terms of other social groups? We believe that these questions of structure and agency are central to all the social sciences. The issue crops up in all sorts of places. It appears, for example, in discussions of the relevance of gender contrasted with that of class for women's role in society; at another place it is the role of political elites contrasted with the imperatives imposed by the needs of the social structure; and at another it is the question of whether the profit mechanism would impose its will irrespective of whether workers or capitalists are in control of industry.

The other feature that all the social sciences share is that they are all 'multi-theoretical', that is, they are characterized by major theoretical disputes and controversies. This is perhaps particularly noticeable in the 1980s. It is difficult to identify cleanly, with identical labels for all disciplines, the various positions that are held. But we attempt to distinguish in this volume roughly three competing positions — individualist, pluralist and marxist. Individualist explanations of social change, for example, tend to be stated in terms of individual decisions and the 'human nature' of the decision-makers; pluralist explanations stress institutional factors and the importance of the state 'holding the ring' between conflicting institutions and groups; marxist explanations of social change focus on class structure and struggle between the different classes, particularly employers and workers. Such multi-theoretical disputes between competing explanations figure prominently in this volume. Students are repeatedly faced with the challenge that there is no obvious and straightforward answer to social problems, and that social scientists disagree just as, for example, economists on television disagree over the causes of Britain's economic crisis, and policemen and social workers disagree over the causes of such problems as vandalism. Our general view of this multi-theoretical feature of the social sciences is that, although it means there is no certain or 'one true' explanation of social problems, disagreement between social scientists is a virtue rather than a defect because it is indicative of the relevance of the social sciences to the controversies and dilemmas facing society itself.

We have indicated why this introduction to the study of society is interdisciplinary in construction. The reasons have to do with our belief that students can and should be confronted at the outset of their studies with some of the major questions about how society (and a particular society like Britain) actually works, a question that all disciplines are concerned with, and our view that in the 1980s there are certain problems and methods of approach which all disciplines share; two that stand out and figure in the contents of this volume are the problem of structure and agency and the multi-theoretical character of social science explanations.

It remains to say a word about the social sciences as *sciences*. Some people object to the use of the word 'science' in the social sciences on the ground that such studies do not have the same degree of exactness, certainty and ability to formulate general laws as is found in the physical sciences such as chemistry and physics. One reply to this objection is to say that it is based on a very restricted definition of the word 'science', which actually is derived from the Latin *scientia*, meaning simply knowledge acquired by study. Nevertheless, there is a major question here regarding the extent to which the methods of the social sciences can or ought to resemble in all relevant respects the physical sciences. Can the social scientist provide the kind of knowledge available in the physical sciences? Or is the subject matter of the social sciences so very different that the methods of the physical sciences are simply not applicable to the study of society? These questions are pursued by Alan Ryan in the other essay in this introductory section.

Such questions and issues are frequently raised by people who have a particular interest in the philosophy of the social sciences. But they are not only of concern to them. Such issues are important for all social scientists because the study of society cannot be dissociated from a critical assessment of the character of social science methods and the kinds of knowledge they produce. It is for this reason that we conclude this volume with a consideration of several important issues in the philosophy of the social sciences, including the problem of assessing competing explanations and trying to judge which is the most adequate.

That problem relates back, finally, to what we said about the social sciences being multi-theoretical. From top to bottom, the social sciences are shaped by these divergences of opinion and controversies. We hope that in reading this book, you will find, as we do, that these differences are stimulating rather than irritating, illuminating rather than confusing, and that critical debate is preferable to blind and blinkered certainty. This stimulation, illumination and debate is central to what the social sciences can offer.

2　Is the study of society a science?

Alan Ryan

1　Introduction

There is only one central methodological question about the social sciences, and that is whether they are sciences at all. This is not to say that the question is a perfectly clear one — nothing could be further from the truth. Nor is it to say that it is susceptible of a straightforward answer — nothing could be further from the truth than that. All I am committing myself to is the claim that questions about the success and failure of the social sciences, questions about the sort of knowledge they do, or in principle could, provide us with, ultimately rest on a comparison between our understanding of the natural world and our understanding of the social world. Those who have wanted to put psychology, politics, economics, sociology, geography or history on a 'scientific' basis have always thought of themselves as applying to social events the same sort of investigative standards as apply in the investigation of natural events.

One famous declaration to this effect opens the Sixth Book of John Stuart Mill's *System of Logic* (1843); the first five Books of this treatise had been devoted to a general discussion of such questions as the nature of causal explanation, the relationship between observation and general laws, and so on. The Sixth Book was concerned with what Mill called 'the logic of the moral sciences' — 'moral sciences' having nothing particularly to do with *morals*, but meaning simply all those sciences which deal with the behaviour of creatures with minds — and Mill was quite clear that if the psychological and social sciences are sciences at all, it was because they employ the same methods and reach the same sort of results as other sciences: 'the methods of investigation applicable to moral and social science must have been already described if I have succeeded in enumerating and characterizing those of science in general'.

Mill freely admitted that the social sciences were not as intellectually impressive as physics, chemistry and astronomy had become. This raised the question of[1]

Source: article commissioned for this Reader. Alan Ryan is Reader in Politics, and Fellow of New College, Oxford.

how far the unsatisfactory state of those inquiries is owing to a wrong choice of methods, how far the want of skill in the application of right ones; and what degree of ultimate success may be attained or hoped for by a better choice or more careful employment of logical processes appropriate to the case. In other words, whether moral sciences exist or can exist; to what degree of perfection they are susceptible of being carried; and by what selection or adaptation of the methods brought to view in the previous part of this work that degree of perfection is attainable.

I quote Mill at this length, not because there is no more modern statement of his case — Professor Nagel's *The Structure of Science* is a distinguished successor — but because I want to insist on the length of time during which social scientists, or philosophers on their behalf, have drawn their standards of intellectual respectability from the natural sciences.

It is worth noticing, too, that Mill's view of what the natural sciences were, and of what the social sciences might be, has been immensely influential. When German philosophers such as Wilhelm Dilthey, later in the nineteenth century, wanted to argue that the natural sciences and the social sciences operated along wholly different lines and arrived at quite different kinds of conclusions, their term for the 'moral sciences' was simply a German rendering of Mill's terminology. The *Geisteswissenschaften* are not 'spiritual sciences' any more than the moral sciences are sciences of morals — in both cases, what is being picked out is the special methodological problems raised by the fact that human beings have minds, that when we explain their behaviour we often or almost always invoke what is going on in their minds.

The influence of Mill's assumptions still persists. Twenty years ago, Professor Winch published a striking little book called *The Idea of a Social Science*, the aim of which was to show that the sort of understanding we have of human behaviour is quite different from the sort of understanding we have of (merely) natural events. The target was still Mill's claim that if the social sciences could produce an intellectually respectable account of their subject matter they must do so in the same way as the natural sciences, and it is Mill's version of that claim which comes most continuously under fire.

2 Are the social sciences failures?

The point from which Mill started was the belief that the social sciences were, in some sense, failures. Even in the early nineteenth century it seemed something of an intellectual scandal that the pace at which our knowledge and mastery of the outside world was growing should be so much greater than that at which our knowledge and control of our social existence was growing. As many writers still do, Mill drew a partial exception for the condition of economics, which seemed to him to have achieved scientific respectability, even though the price was extreme abstractness. But, in general, the social sciences lagged a long way behind the natural sciences. At the risk of giving aid and comfort to saloon bar critics of the social sciences whose deeply held belief it is that none but fools and knaves have studied sociology, let us start by looking at the claim that the social sciences have been failures.

I shall set down somewhat more formally the orthodox view of the goals and tactics of the natural sciences a little further on; but I ought now to say that in calling the social sciences 'failures' we are presupposing parts of that account. Among these are the following claims:

1   the aim of science is to produce general laws which are universal, i.e. which apply to all events or things of a certain kind, which are precisely stated, i.e. which say exactly and unequivocally what will happen, and which are of as wide a scope as possible;
2   such laws should enable us to predict and control events, i.e. they should form the basis of a reliable social technology;
3   the search for such laws should be carried on systematically and incrementally, i.e. each generation should be able to inherit the knowledge gained by the previous generation, and should be able to build on it in turn.

Commonsensical complaints against the social sciences seem to take at least these three large claims for granted — the joke that wherever two economists meet you will find three different stories about what's happening to the economy is, in effect, drawing a contrast between the practice of the social sciences and the first and third of the orthodox claims about natural science mentioned above. Equally, the joke that the crime rate rises shortly after any increase in the number of probation officers and social workers is simply an insulting way of drawing attention to the gap between the second test for the success of science and our achievements in the social sciences.

It is, of course, not true that if we know anything we must be scientists. An Australian aborigine who finds his way from one waterhole to the next across a landscape which to strangers is a trackless waste knows a great deal, but he is not a student of scientific geography. Nor is the result of studying anything in a rigorous and careful fashion, perhaps with the aid of a good deal of natural scientific knowledge, always science in the sense of these three claims. It would be foolish to deny that archaeologists study the past in a scientific fashion. They have in recent times been greatly assisted by advances in the natural sciences, as, for instance, by Carbon-14 dating. But, what the archaeologist finds out is not a general law; what he discovers is when a given building was erected or destroyed, what clothes people wore, what sort of language they spoke, and so on. The employment of scientific methods yields information of a sort which direct observation would have yielded had the archaeologist been a contemporary of the people he studies so long after the event. He is not aiming to discover archaeological laws, so much as calling on natural science to remedy the deficiencies of the evidence. He may also call on the findings of social science to interpret his data, though he may need nothing more than the social knowledge we all possess. What he does not do is try to produce laws of the sort which the physicist or chemist would recognize as laws.

It is worth bearing this in mind. There is a tradition in social science which holds that it is quite wrong to suppose that the social sciences have failed; what they have done, on this view, is borrowed the wrong picture of success. If the social sciences are compared with archaeology, they do not at all look like failures — quite bad sociologists can produce more reliable information about living habits in Hackney than very good archaeologists can produce about living habits in Knossos. It is only in the light of the achievements of some of the natural sciences that charges of 'failure' can get off the ground; but, it is also worth recalling that the aim of emulating the natural sciences is not one which was thrust on social scientists by philosophers anxious to discredit them. If nobody has ever claimed to be the Newton of the social sciences, Marx for one was praised as their Darwin.

3   'Laws' in social science

That the social sciences have few generalizations of their own which can stand comparison with anything in the natural sciences seems clear enough. Take the well known branch of traditional economics which explains prices and output in terms of supply and demand. It is a very plausible thought that if the price asked for some good rises, the quantity of it which people will be ready to buy will go down. Again, it is a plausible thought that if the price which people are ready to offer for a good rises, more of that good will be brought to market. This suggests that if the price of a packet of cigarettes is doubled the demand for it ought to fall off (by some unspecified amount). But this economic 'law' is only very broadly true; there are goods which behave as you might say perversely, in the sense that the demand for them increases as the price rises. If the cigarette moves in to a new 'prestige' bracket, it may be more in demand than before. If the good is not one which is immediately (or ever) consumable, a price rise may spark off increased demand, as when a rise in the price of gold triggers off a rush to buy gold, not a rush to sell and buy something else.

Such exceptions to the generalization that a rise in price causes a fall in demand can be handled by restricting the application of the generalization to a narrower class of goods — those which are only used for immediate or final consumption, say, not those which may be used to acquire status or for investment. But, the price of doing this is to restrict the range of the generalization, and perhaps to so restrict it that it becomes useless. We may have *no* way of characterizing the goods which we think the law does apply to except in terms of whether the law applies to them, which is manifestly circular. If cigarettes are employed as a currency, then the relation between their value, or 'price' in terms of other goods and the demand for them may behave much like the relation between the price of gold and the demand for it; it seems that we cannot give any clear *physical* description of the kind of goods to which we wish to confine the operations of the 'law' that rises in price lead to falls in demand.

When the good in question is work there is another familiar paradox to be seen. One might think that if the price offered for work goes up — that is, if wages rise — the amount of work offered will also rise. But, it is a commonplace that employers in societies where there is not much of a market economy find that when they put up wages their workers stay at home more rather than less. This seems also to have been the experience of the National Coal Board in this country from time to time. The explanation of the fact is not very surprising. If a worker has a target income of so much a week, he works whatever hours it takes to get that income and no more. A higher rate of pay allows him to get to his target in a shorter time, so, naturally he works less rather than more. Nonetheless, if the fact is not in the end surprising it certainly is a disturbing one for the aim of producing a wholly general theory of supply and demand. The generalization seems to end up saying that a rise in price will create a rise in the supply of those goods which really are goods of the sort to which the generalization applies — and work sometimes is, and sometimes isn't, one of those.

The condition of other social sciences is no better. Take the generalization that people of low socio-economic status vote for radical or socialist parties. It is true that in Britain there is a strong correlation between membership of one of the lower occupational categories and Labour voting. But it would be very rash to venture from this to any very strong or precise generalization. As a historical summary it's true enough that something like two-thirds of the working class has voted Labour in post-war Britain, but who'd risk a generalization along the lines of 'a rise in price causes a fall in demand'? Would anyone commit himself to 'low socio-economic status brings about "left" voting'? What about the Germany of the Nazis and Mussolini's Italy, what about the way the working-class voter in the USA votes? Would the generalization make any sense in countries where the worst off were largely employed in agriculture?

In other words, do we not have to abandon the search for laws about what makes *all* voters everywhere act in a certain way and go back to the summary of what many voters in a particular country and culture did during a limited historical period? No doubt politics offers many short range and short term generalizations, rules of thumb and local folk wisdom. When you stand for election, your agent may tell you that it's no use bothering with East Ward, since it always and uniquely votes according to whether the candidate is a nonconformist chapel goer; but, just as the Australian aborigine is a good guide to waterholes without relying on geographical 'laws', so your agent is a good guide to the local political eccentricities without relying on anything like a 'law' about voting behaviour.

4   Social technology

The most familiar implication of the absence of general laws on a par with those of the natural scientist is that there is nothing one could properly call social technology. In the areas where there is nothing at stake except the application of natural scientific advances, we see a steady growth in technological achievement. The arrival of effective computers, and advances in metallurgy and fuel technology, let us land men on the moon; but we seem quite unable to land them in secure and stable employment on earth. Marx may or may not have thought that he had discovered the underlying laws which governed the occurrence and non-occurrence of revolutions — his successors certainly claimed this on his behalf — but the history of revolution in the twentieth century is anything but the history of successfully applied technological innovations. Indeed, it is hard to know whether the victors or the vanquished have been more astonished over the past seventy years or so.

One might complain that the analogy between moon landings and revolutions is a bad one; whereas the moon can do nothing to frustrate the machinations of those who wish to land there, the scheduled victims of a revolution can and do try to frustrate the aims of the revolutionaries by all means possible. This certainly makes a considerable difference, but it is not difficult to find examples where there is consensus on the desirability of an outcome, and yet no more success. The socialization of children so that they grow up non-aggressive, non-violent, co-operative and effective members of society is a goal to which even parents who themselves are ineffectual jailbirds are likely to subscribe. All the same, there is no reason to suppose that we shall soon make leaps forward in childrearing techniques like those that have enabled us to move from the horse and buggy to the space shuttle in a matter of a hundred years.

In view of what I shall say later, and in view of what other articles will be saying, I should emphasize that this absence of a technology for social engineering is a factual matter quite independent of the desirability or undesirability of a 'technological' attitude to social and political decision-making. There is a large questionmark over the attraction in principle of social engineering. We may think that to treat other people's behaviour and beliefs as objects for technical manipulation is to dehumanize the people whose behaviour and beliefs they are. This 'squeamish' attitude is, in turn, precisely what B. F. Skinner's *Beyond Freedom and Dignity* deplores in the name of human happiness, arguing, much as the Director in Huxley's *Brave New World* argued, that what we call freedom is no more than submitting to random and ill understood programming by the environment, and that it would be better for everyone if we made that programming rational, controlled, and consciously aimed at maximizing happiness all round. But what this argument presupposes is that some such technology either does exist already, or might without difficulty be created. What I am now urging is that there is no sign that this is true, outside such peculiar conditions that their generalizability to a systematic social programme is a matter of faith not argument.

5   Cumulative growth and 'normal science'

If there are no laws, no technology, it is not surprising that the third feature of the developed natural sciences, the steady, cumulative and accepted growth of knowledge, is also missing. In the natural sciences the picture is one of continuous growth, at any rate during the past three centuries. There are breaks and jumps, 'revolutions' of one sort and another, but they are placeable in a history of ever increasing intellectual mastery of the natural world.

T. S. Kuhn's famous book on *The Structure of Scientific Revolutions* is, as the title implies, concerned with the way in which scientific enquiry gets into a state where 'revolution' — large scale revisions of major theories, occurring with great suddenness — breaks out. But the point of *that* study is that science is generally not in a state of revolutionary ferment. Mostly, what characterizes 'normal science' is the steady addition of new theories to well established ones, the improvement of technique, the filling in of gaps in existing knowledge. Among professional scientists there is agreement on what the current problems are, on what the best available techniques are, on who is good at employing them and who is slipshod, on who shows imagination and who is merely undisciplined — in short, there are agreed answers to all those questions which Mill asked of the social sciences.

It is characteristic of science, seen in this light, that most of the time fundamental questions are neither asked nor answered. 'What is matter?' is a question which a physicist tackles only outside his laboratory for the benefit of laymen and philosophers; inside the laboratory he is too busy solving problems in the measurement of spin in subatomic particles, and neither his problems, nor his techniques, nor his mathematical calculations are at all easily accessible to the layman.

It was not always so in the natural sciences. It is worth noticing this, for it reinforces what we have already had occasion to see, that it is one thing for people to possess a great deal of information about the world, and another for them to have it organized by means of wide ranging theories, and explained by well grounded general laws. In the early seventeenth century, natural scientists sometimes supposed — fewer than some histories suggest but some of them some of the time — that if enough information was collected, then laws of nature would emerge more or less spontaneously. It is much like the frame of mind of those social scientists today who hope that big samples and a good computer will reveal the hidden laws of the social order.

Looking back on the seventeenth century, later scientists are struck by the amount of irrelevant or suspect information that this sort of research strategy yielded. In the absence of clear theoretical guidelines, it is very hard to know what information is revelatory of the secrets of nature and what is merely of anecdotal interest; it is equally hard to know which purported results should be dismissed as simply the result of poor observation. We now know that if I claim to have invented a perpetual motion machine, I am either lying or deluded, but it took the discovery of modern mechanics to show exactly why. The combination of piecemeal information, often in very great quantity, with very general speculation, is characteristic of pre-modern science, and is very reminiscent of the present state of the social sciences.

This, of course, leaves it entirely open whether the social sciences will find their Newton as did the natural sciences, or whether history will refuse to repeat itself. But before we jump to the conclusion that *of course* the social sciences will find their Newton, since the sciences have steadily conquered one domain after another we must recall that not all those areas of 'pre-science' were incorporated in the new sciences – the collected data of astrologists and alchemists went for nothing in the end. It is at least possible that whatever future revolutions there are in the human sciences will show that societies as we now understand them are simply the wrong things to try to find laws for.

A striking thing about 'normal science' is the way it is permeated by the slogan that a dwarf standing on a giant's shoulders sees further than the giant. In the natural sciences, nobody believes he needs to emulate his most eminent predecessors; it is perfectly sensible for somebody to believe both that Newton was far cleverer than any twentieth-century schoolboy scientist and that Newton would have been floored by mathematical puzzles the sixth former takes in his stride. Once Newton discovered the calculus, nobody else had to do so; the wrench of the imagination he needed to get there is not demanded of his successors. This is one way of putting the point that progress in science is a constant process of burying your dead great men. Once they have made their contributions, we can use those contributions without going back to see *how* they were made.

The situation in the social sciences could hardly be more different; nobody would suggest that one does not know what Newtonian mechanics is unless one reads it in Newton's own words, but we constantly do say that there is no substitute for reading Marx in his own words. Marx, Weber and Durkheim are not figures in the *history* of the social sciences as even nineteenth-century scientists like Faraday or Darwin are now figures in the *history* of their subjects rather than in the subjects themselves.

Now, none of this shows that the social sciences discover nothing, teach us nothing, and are of no assistance in practice. All it shows is that not merely have they not so far come to resemble the natural sciences but that they do not seem likely to do so in the near future either. But there are four important, if obvious, reasons why writers like Mill and Nagel, nonetheless, think that the social sciences must in the end come to resemble some branch or other of the natural sciences.

In the first place, there is no ground for general scepticism about the description and up to a point the explanation of individual items of behaviour. Even if it is not always true that men will do more work if they are paid higher wages, there is no very great difficulty about knowing in particular cases whether they will or not – you will find out within a week of making the offer; there is no difficulty in most cases in knowing why they will or will not, for unless they are very inarticulate they will tell you.

In the second place, we constantly make assumptions about the causes of social events which turn out to be correct, and some which we do not test, but certainly believe to be true — as when I refrain from testing the guess that calling you a liar will make you very angry in view of the fact that you are six feet two in your stockinged feet and healthy with it. British Rail do reckon that price rises will cause fewer passengers to use the railways, and they are invariably right; the same obviously goes for most organizations who buy or sell anything or who employ people. If there are no *laws* about supply and demand, there are quite good locally reliable rules of thumb.

Third, even if there is not much one could call social technology, there are a great many cases where we make things happen in a predictable and regular fashion. In general, it is true if we increase the number of police in a given area the number of crimes committed there drops. Each of us spends much of his or her day doing a bit of small scale engineering: we smile to encourage people to go on, drop our glance to indicate that we weren't picking a fight or even trying to pick them up. We make offers to induce people to part with things we want, or turn down offers made by others to see if we can push up the price of our co-operation. There are lots of slips; and the larger the scale on which we practise the more loose ends there will be. Nonetheless, a vast amount of social life would simply not occur if people were unable to get things to happen as they desired.

Fourth, there are some striking regularities in social life, even if they are hard to explain and hard to make any practical use of. The accident rate on the roads, for instance, is very stable from year to year; it is not an ultimate law of nature that it is what it is, but it is reliable enough to plan next year's casualty services against. Durkheim's *Suicide* sprang from the observation that suicide rates in different sorts of society were very different but were very stable in each sort of society, though there too the question of how to interpret this apparent stability has been very much disputed. All these things have made many writers simply *assume* that social science was or soon would be the natural science of social life. Is not the social world in some ways even *more* explicable, *more* predictable, *more* regular than the natural world? How then can it be resistant to being tidily organized under the same sort of natural laws as the outside world?

6   The nature of scientific explanation

It is time we turned to analyse the orthodox view of what it is that a
scientific explanation offers. There are six points which I shall try to
set out briefly. They are not all of the same logical kind, but between
them they sketch in the main logical and methodological points which
need to be made. The first is perhaps the most important: this is the
claim that all genuine explanation is causal, law-governed and deductive,
and operates by subsuming events to be explained under the appropriate
law of nature. When we pick out one event as the cause of another
event, what we are asserting is that the connection between the two
events is an instance of a general law connecting events of that sort.
If we say a man's death was caused by his swallowing two grammes of
cyanide, we are applying a law to the effect that 'anyone who eats two
grammes of cyanide will die'; we must, on this view, appeal to a general
law, since if we want to assert that *this* event caused *that* event, we
have to rule out the possibility that the first event could have occurred
without the second following. The only way this can be secured is if we
can say that *whenever* an event of the first sort occurs an event of the
second sort follows. Thus, all claims about the causes of single events
rely implicitly on some general law to support them. There is much
more to be said about the model, but not here; Professor Hempel's
Aspects of Scientific Explanation goes into the details for the curious.[2]

The second important point is that generalizations or general laws
must not be 'accidental' generalizations. It is easier to point to the
difference between genuinely law-like and merely accidental generalizations than to give precise logical characterization of the difference.
But, contrast 'all the people in this room are called Smith' with 'all
people who eat two grammes of cyanide die of it'. In the case of the
first generalization we cannot draw any counterfactual conclusions,
that is, we cannot say what would have happened if various unfulfilled
conditions had been fulfilled. Thus, it is not true that if Jones *had*
been in the room (which he was not) he would have been called Smith;
we cannot predict that if Jones does enter the room he will be called
Smith. In the second case we can say that if Smith *had* eaten the cyanide
(which he has not) it would have killed him; we can predict that if he
eats the cyanide it will kill him. The only generalizations that explain
anything are of the second sort, and the test of a generalization's law-like
status is its capacity to support counterfactual judgments in this way.

The conviction that what we have is a genuine causal law is obviously
sustained by our ability to guess at a connection between the events
cited, so we can see *how* the first sort of event brings about the second.
Our confidence that the connection between eating cyanide and death

is a causal and not an accidental connection rests partly on the great rapidity with which death follows the consumption of cyanide in conditions where nothing else can readily account for death, and additionally on the development of biological and chemical theories which show what mechanism connects the two events. Much theory in the natural sciences consists of providing models of such mechanisms; it is an interesting question whether theory in the social sciences is of the same sort.

The third basic point about scientific explanation is that it is entirely descriptive. It neither presupposes nor supports any particular views about the goodness or badness of the states of affairs described. It is this that sometimes offends people who look for an answer to the meaning of life; all scientific explanation *can* do is show how things work. There is nothing to be got from science to justify their working this way rather than some other way. It may or may not be a proper task for philosophers to show that the universe ought to run on the general lines it does – Spinoza, Leibniz and Hegel all offered to do something of the sort – but it is not something to be undertaken by the scientist *qua* scientist. This means that at any given moment, much of what science has to say about the world will be flatly final in the sense that once everything that can be explained within a given theory has been explained, explanations have run out, and we are left saying, 'that is how it works' and nothing more.

The fourth point follows from this. It is that there is a distinction between the origin of a theory and a law and its truth or acceptability which must be absolutely respected. It does not matter *who* thought up the theory, nor what prompted him or her to do so; what matters is whether the theory or the hypothesis stands up to testing against the facts. Because explanations are governed by laws, and because the connection between the statements of the law(s) and initial conditions on the one hand and the description of the event to be explained on the other is a deductive one, it *cannot* happen that a true law and a true statement of initial conditions will yield a false statement as a conclusion.

Suppose that we hypothesize that 'whenever anyone eats ginger he or she dies.' The first time we find someone eating ginger and not dying, we have falsified the suggested law. *If* the general statement 'all who eat ginger die' and the statement 'Jones ate ginger' are true, then 'Jones died' has to be true. If 'Jones ate ginger' and 'Jones did *not* die' are both true, then 'all who eat ginger die' must be false.

Those who insist on the four points we have so far outlined do so because they see all of them connecting to provide a theory of what good scientific practice involves. The distinction between the origin and the validity of a law or theory entrenches the need to make sure that nobody can protect a favoured hypothesis from falsification. Equally, it is a way of insisting that no matter what non-factual reasons one may have for believing in a hypothesis, they must be kept out of the process of testing the hypothesis. One may believe, as Einstein did, that 'God does not play dice', and look for deterministic laws governing the behaviour of subatomic particles; all the same, the question whether one has found them is settled by experimental testing. Again, one may think, as Copernicus did, that a rational God would arrange the planets in circular orbits around the Sun, because the circle was a peculiarly perfect figure. But, the facts refused to conform and that's that.

The fifth point is almost a restatement of this, but deserves an independent mention: the sciences are value-free. We may have all sorts of moral or other values which impel us to engage in scientific enquiry, but they make no difference to science's own standards for success and failure. Successful science produces and tests hypotheses about the working of the natural world. It discards its failures in favour of more reliable, more far ranging and more lucid hypotheses. Professor Popper, who believes that the practice of scientific enquiry is one of the glories of the human race, nonetheless insists very fiercely that a condition of science being practised at all is that the distinction between our values and the facts of the world is preserved intact.

Finally, what all this requires is that scientists can agree among themselves about the meaning of the events with which they are presented. That is, it is a practical requirement that there should be either 'objectivity' in scientific descriptions or at any rate 'inter-subjectivity'. Unless we can all agree on what we are seeing, we cannot agree whether we have or have not got a proper test of whatever hypothesis is at issue.

7   Is the explanation of social life 'scientific'?

I have already suggested that we have a great deal of everyday knowledge about social life, and that it really is knowledge; but I have also suggested that the social sciences do not seem to produce general laws or reliable technology in the way that the natural sciences do. It is time to put these two suggestions together, and to show that the everyday knowledge which the social sciences assemble in systematic ways does not and apparently cannot fit into the framework of scientific explanation. Many explanations look rather dubiously causal, many seem not to be backed by generalizations, much explanation seems very localized in its range, value-freedom seems extremely difficult to attain, and it seems equally hard to attain the degree of agreement on the meaning and interpretation of the data that natural scientists regularly achieve.

Take the common explanatory situation in which we overhear a remark in a foreign language. We ask, perhaps, 'Why did he say *bonjour*?' Now, all sorts of responses count as explanations under the circumstances. If we think that what's needed is a simple translation, then '*bonjour* means "good morning"' ends the exchange. Have we given a causal explanation here? That the answer is obviously no is not conclusive. Many explanations in natural science governed areas may be non-causal in just this way. If you look at a car engine and ask 'Why has it got that odd plastic box?' you may just be told 'That's a transistorized contact breaker'. It does not follow that the response is not implicated in a causal explanation. We know why cars have ignition systems, and once we know that *that* is part of an ignition system, we know why it has *that*. If we know why people say 'good morning', we know why they say '*bonjour*' once we know that they mean the same thing.

But suppose we know already what *bonjour* means; we may then be told that the man wanted to greet somebody, i.e. be told what his intentions were; or we may be told that he and the person he is greeting are of some particular social status. We appear in a case like this to be invoking two things, neither of which has any very direct analogy in the natural sciences. One is the notion of *appropriateness*, the other the *intentions* of the people in question, in this case the intention to act appropriately.

Take a much used but illuminating instance: suppose we see a stream of traffic stopping at traffic lights, starting up and driving off again. We may detect quite good regularities. When the light is red the moving vehicle stops. We may be quite convinced that it is a genuinely causal connection, and that the counterfactual 'if the light had been red that car would have stopped' is true. (We should, of course, be pretty puzzled about the mechanism which might link a change of colour and changes of movement; but if we are the visiting Martians beloved of philosophical-example-builders, all we can go on for the moment is regular connection.) But, what we non-Martians know already is that the causal connection between the light turning red and the car stopping is not a mechanical or flatly natural connection. We know that there is a rule to the effect that we *should* stop when the light turns red. And we do not think that an instance where the light turns red and the car does *not* stop overturns the claim that when cars do stop they do so *because* the light has turned red.

This case is one where there is a rule laying down *what to do*, and people (generally) obey that rule. The regularities we see exist only because people know the rule and are generally disposed to obey it. Finding out about the existence of the rule is both like and unlike the chemist finding out about the action of cyanide. It is like it in that it enables us in each case to follow out in a sequential fashion the steps between the beginning and the end of the process we try to explain. It is unlike, in that there is no question of cyanide *obeying* the laws which govern its interaction with organic materials in any sense which suggests that cyanide might disobey those laws. In the human case it is precisely the fact that rules do not govern us unless we allow them to govern us that is at stake. That there is a rule enjoining certain behaviour remains true even when people disobey it — at any rate up to a point — but a straightforward causal connection embodies no such complexity.

The point recurs in innumerable situations. Suppose a friend is standing on the edge of a cliff and you shout 'get back!' To your horror the noise startles him and he falls over the edge. In this case, it is the *noise*, not the meaning of what you said, which has to be invoked to explain the tragedy. If he had heard you, understood you and followed your advice, it would not have been the noise you emitted but the meaning of what you said that made the difference.

This is at the root of the difference between unpredictability in the social sciences and in natural science. There is a well known phenomenon called the self-fulfilling (or self-refuting) prophecy; the financial journalist writes in Sunday's paper that Consolidated Bulldozers will show a rise on Monday morning; punters flock to buy ahead of the rise in order to make a gain, and so the price of Consolidated Bulldozers does rise. Next Sunday, he congratulates himself on his astuteness, except that everyone else sees quite clearly that it was his tip that sent prices up. Self-refuting prophecies are far from rare, too — indeed, many warnings are couched in prophetic terms with precisely the intention that the prophecy should be refuted, as when we tell a child 'You are going to drop that cup' or announce to the friend who is giving us a lift 'You are about to kill us both.'

It is often noticed that this makes a great difference to the reliability of prediction in social science. As people have often said, once Marx tells the capitalists that they are doomed, they are very silly if they don't do something to hold off the predicted disaster. It looks as if prediction in social science is always a prediction of what people would have done if they had not been aware of the prediction.

There are cases in natural science where the activities of the scientist interfere with what he is observing, the most notorious being in sub-atomic physics, where the investigator's observations inevitably disturb the particles he observes. But the difference ought by now to be clear enough: in the social sciences the interference of the prediction with what is predicted is not physical interference. It is not the physical properties of the prediction which alters the behaviour; for the prediction to make a difference, it must be known to and understood by those whose behaviour is in question. Moreover, whereas the natural scientist has no choice about whether his activity interferes with his subject matter's behaviour, the social scientist has. In effect, he may be able to keep his subjects in the dark about something that may matter to them a good deal, and this is at any rate morally a very different situation to be in.

8 Explanation by appropriateness

It would be a mistake to think that all social science explanation involves an appeal to *rules*, as the two examples above may have suggested. Indeed, the example of the rush to buy shares shows that plainly enough. There is no rule which says that we should try to buy cheap shares, or that enjoins us to sell when the price hits forty pence, on a par with the rule that enjoins us to stop when the light turns red. The notion of *appropriateness* is still central, however. Thus, suppose some Grand Master, playing for the world chess championship, plays an absolutely stunningly original move; as a 'rabbit', I cannot suggest what it might be. It is very likely that once the move has been made, other players will quickly see, upon analysis, why it is such a good move. The explanation of the move can hardly rest upon a generalization about what all or most chess players do. By hypothesis, they don't, for this is an original move. Nor does it rest on a generally known and followed rule. It rests on the appropriateness of the move to the goals and aims of the player and the situation on the board. The player perceives 'the logic of his situation' and acts on it.

Professor Popper, to whom the expression 'the logic of the situation' is due, holds that explanations in terms of the logic of the situation are of the same logical category as causal explanations in natural science. The implausibility of this claim can be seen even in the above example. There seems to be *no* causal law that explains the chess player's behaviour. What we have done is show how *he* — and up to this point, he uniquely — follows out a strategy, the properties of which are not causal but logical. What we have done in explaining the chess player's behaviour is demonstrate, first, how it is that the move in question is the *right* move, and then, how it is that it is that fact about it which moves the chess player to action.

The explanation must be in some sense causal since we are saying that what *makes* the chess player make the move is his knowledge of the rightness of the move. We must be saying this when we say that he made the move *because* it was the right one, for we certainly are not saying that he made it by accident or that it 'turned out' that it was the right one. But the belief that there is a causal tie between the rightness of the move and his making it cannot rest on any such generalization as 'chess players always make the right move', since we know already that they do not.

The last feature of the everyday explanation of human social behaviour to which I should draw attention is its lack of value-freedom. This is not simply to draw attention to the obvious fact that we spend a lot of time praising and blaming one another. It is to draw attention to the way in which our practical interest in people's behaviour threatens the agreement on 'neutral' descriptions of our observations and experiments which we identified as one of the necessary features of successful natural science.

The sort of thing I have in mind is illustrated easily enough from recent history. What would a value-free description of the state of affairs at Auschwitz look like? One might say that a description of the murdered and the murderers *could* be given which treated them alike as physical and chemical entities with causal histories, tracks along their own space-time paths. But, the reply to this surely is that this is not so much value-free as the wrong description. To describe my being punched on the nose in terms of the simultaneous occupancy of the same region of space by two objects does not merely leave out the question of whether you did well or badly to punch me on the nose: it leaves out the whole fact that *this* coincidence of two objects in one place *is* your punching me on the nose.

The question then becomes one of how much has to go into the description of the events under discussion if we are to be able to say that we have described them in the right terms for further explanation. It is true that a lot of people died in Auschwitz; but is that the whole truth? It is true that a lot of people were deliberately killed by other people in Auschwitz; is that the whole truth, and is it a value-free description? It seems odd to suppose that it is *wholly* value-free, since if you approach somebody and say, just like that, 'you killed him', it would be taken as an accusation. Of course, it is an accusation which can be fought off in all sorts of ways, from denying it, to redescribing it, to showing that given the nature and intentions of the person who was killed, it is not so much an accusation as praise. But it is *prima facie* an accusation.

The problem is that the question of which is the most apt description is inextricably tied up with the question of where the burden of justification lies. It is therefore unreasonable to expect that the same ready agreement on the description of the facts to be explained will be obtained in the social sciences as in the natural sciences. Again, this is a very large subject on which more elaborate things need to be said. The only simple point I should like to make here is that one should not think that value-freedom can always be achieved just by leaving out more and more of the significance of what is being described. The end of that road is not a neutral description but a thoroughly misleading one.

9   Alternative standards of success

The way the discussion has been organized this far may suggest that it is my case that the social sciences are doing badly in not doing what the natural sciences usually manage to do. This is not the burden of the argument, but before I explain why not, I must take account of two common doubts about the achievements of the natural sciences which both suggest that the weaknesses of the social sciences may be strengths too. In recent years the orthodox view of science which I sketched out has been criticized for its dependence on a naive view of the relation between theory and observation, for its inability to give a persuasive account of what a law of nature is, and for its neglect of the social organization of science. It is often argued that scientific theories are more often accepted because of the authority of those who put them forward and less often because of the authority of the facts that the old story allowed. To the retort that this can hardly be quite true, since the facts must be whatever they are, regardless of authority, the reply has come that what we 'see' or otherwise 'experience' is not a matter of the physical interaction between us and the world but of the interpretation we have put on that interaction. When we 'see the sun rise', we no longer *see* the sun literally coming up over the horizon, because we have been educated – or brainwashed – into thinking that that is just the misleading appearance presented by the true state of affairs. Paul Feyerabend's 'anarchic' essay, *Against Method*, gives an entertaining account of how Galileo simply *bullied* people into seeing the world this way and not seeing it as they had before.

Even the less extreme critics of the orthodox view want us to modify its account of science and its progress. It is held that less emphasis on laws and their testing, and more emphasis on whole research programmes and their development, is needed. Of course, it is flattering to the sociologist to think that it is he who is now in the driving seat, since 'science' itself turns out to be the construction of a social group about whose working it is he who is an expert and not the scientists themselves. In practice is it not quite like that. No philosopher of science goes to the lengths of suggesting that absolutely any theory of the outside world can gain currency if it is imposed with enough vigour. All of them think that the distinction between the accumulation of knowledge in science and its relatively non-cumulative character elsewhere is not much threatened by the 'sociological' view of science. Nor is there any doubt that science does provide the basis for a successful material technology in a way that social science does not provide anything of the sort.

Attention to the social construction of reality has another effect. It draws attention to what science does not tell us, or, at any rate, what science as now practised does not tell us. The argument runs like this. It is no accident that modern science is praised for its technological consequences, in spite of all those scientists who drink toasts to the purity of their disciplines and devoutly hope that their work will never do anyone the least good or harm. For what we have been looking at in studying nature is ways in which we can manipulate nature. The search for causal connections is a search for ways of reliably bringing one thing about by means of another. To say that cyanide causes death is just to say that the way to bring about the event of death is to first bring about the ingestion of cyanide. Even where there is no question of our actually having control over the events in question − if the claim is 'sunspots cause tornadoes', say − the intellectual model with which we approach nature is still a manipulative and technical one. It is not impossible to think of a society which did not 'want' nature to be sorted out along such lines. It might want the world organized by appropriateness in the way our own behaviour is. Aristotelian science, with its thought that things had their proper places, is a partial example of that attitude.

A science which is organized by the technical intellect will never tell us the ultimate point of anything; it has not and cannot have a vision of a world in which all things conspire towards a good end. It just so happens that A will bring about B, under conditions $C_1 \ldots C_n$, and that's how the world is. To ask whether the world could be better organized is an error, and science stops where such questions start. That this is not an entirely happy state of affairs is suggested by Einstein's dismissal of a theory as false because not pretty enough, or Darwin's hankering after a sign that the struggle for survival produced more happiness than misery, and that nature cared more for man than for the more deplorable parasites whose whole career involved tormenting the host in whose guts they dwelled.

It would take us far afield to do more than gesture at the way in which the more philosophically minded marxists have divided among themselves on the question of whether any conceivable revolutionary transformation of society will bring a new sort of science in the wake of a new attitude to the world. What we must note, though, is that if the complaint is that the natural sciences cannot show us the *point* of nature's being organized as it is, the natural sciences cannot do something which the social sciences often do do.

We cannot see the point of the electron's behaviour, and we suppose that is because it has no point; we can see the point of the chess player's behaviour, and explaining that behaviour just is showing its point. It may indeed be said that many of the social sciences are simply systematic attempts to show the point of activities whose point may escape us at first sight. Accounts of revolutionary upheavals in terms of the attempts of an oppressed class to throw off its oppressor's yoke are points providing explanations; but an anti-political explanation of revolutionary outbreaks as escapes from boredom, or from the psychological strains of recognizing our failed status, is just as much a point providing explanation of revolutionary upheavals. Explaining them in quasi-poetic terms as theatrical celebrations of popular hopes and fears is a point providing explanation, too. Showing the point of some event is different from showing how to bring it about. We do the latter with natural events and the former with human events. The result, in one view, is that we must always be less at home in the natural world than the social world.

Still, it cannot be said that this view is the main one to be found among practising social scientists. Until rather recently they have felt that they were being tried by the standards of the natural sciences and that by those standards they had been found wanting. When it was recognized in the 1960s that what scientists possessed was in part a form of social organization and an acceptance of intellectual and professional authority that had no analogy in the social sciences, the response of some social scientists was to wish to impose an intellectual unity on their profession, to copy the social system of natural science in the hope that everything else would follow. It would for many people be very acceptable to be members of an intellectual community with more generally agreed standards of good and bad work, with a clearer pattern of apprenticeship and mastery and so on. Nor ought we to underplay the importance of the practical goals of social science. Three hundred years ago, Thomas Hobbes contrasted the prospects of someone equipped with a *scientific* knowledge of his material with those of a man who only had the knowledge that long experience and prudence gave him — the latter would do well, the first would be infallible. Bacon, too, saw the advance of social science as part and parcel of the grand scientific advance which would lead to 'the achieving of all things possible'.

We might wonder whether the advances of technology have invariably been blessings — advances in medicine mean a long drawn out old age for inhabitants of geriatric hospitals, advances in transport technology mean that we live in noisy, impersonal, ugly commuter towns, and so on. But all these complaints are not complaints against the technology as such so much as complaints against our handling of it. If the human organization is what is deficient, then surely an advance in social science would be an advance towards remedying those deficiencies and a lessening of human misery.

The suggestion is one which many social scientists have accepted. Those who reject it, in order to distinguish between the technical manipulation of nature and the taking of social decisions, reject it largely because they think that there is an important distinction between getting a person to do something and getting a thing to do something. It is possible to get a person consciously to share our purposes and act in a way which furthers them, so it is (it is held) morally intolerable to try to get people to co-operate without getting their uncoerced and undeceived assent. To try to create a social technology implies a division of the world into those who have their own purposes, and decide what goals a society should pursue, and those who are engineered into acquiescence. To the complaint that this squeamishness simply allows social life to go on in an unplanned and unorganized way, the response is that if the price of order is the intellectual and political slavery of the mass of mankind it is too high a price to pay, and that there can be order and organization without slavery only if the right social conditions exist. The work of Jürgen Habermas, for example, is essentially an attempt to spell out the various aspects of this response — to show what the difference is between reasoning with people in search of agreement on the one hand and manipulating them on the other, and to show what conditions of freedom and equality are necessary for the search for agreement to be possible.

10   Are the social sciences simply 'new'?

Even though the views of Habermas and some like-minded thinkers have been relatively popular in the past ten years, the view which I have labelled the orthodox view probably remains the majority view. But so long as we hold it, we have to explain why it is that the social sciences have lagged behind the natural sciences, and why they obstinately seem to depend on kinds of explanation which are not much like those of the natural sciences.

The first and most·popular proposition is that the social sciences are recent arrivals on the scene. It is widely held that they are no more than a hundred or two years old, and that their disarray is no more than the teething troubles to be expected of any healthy infant. It is hard to know just how seriously to take this argument. It is, of course, true that departments of sociology or economics did not appear in universities until the nineteenth century, whereas physics or 'natural philosophy' is a great deal better entrenched. But before the activities of philosophers and of experimental psychologists were as clearly distinct as they nowadays are, the concerns of philosophers or 'students of the mind' overlapped very greatly with those of what we should now call psychologists so that it can hardly be said that all the human sciences are recent. Again, the collection of information about societies and their differences is scarcely less venerable than the collection of information about the motions of the planets and speculation about the composition of matter — both flourished in Greece several hundred years before the birth of Christ. It is not really plausible to claim that social science is simply in its infancy. Political economy goes back to seventeenth- and eighteenth-century writers at the very latest, and that precedes the great leap forward in chemistry which occurred with the discovery of oxygen by Lavoisier. Who, wearing clothes made of synthetic fibres, writing with a ball point pen, watching a television set in a plastic case, could possibly argue that economics has made as much progress as chemistry over the same length of time?

Still, this reply is not conclusive. It does seem foolish to say that the systematic study of society is undeveloped because it is too new, just like that. But if we allow ourselves a somewhat more sympathetic look at the claim, there is a truth hidden in it. In a manner of speaking, what we now call 'chemistry' started with Lavoisier's discovery; the discovery of oxygen turned out to be the crucial breakthrough, which, in conjunction with the application of atomic theory, made the whole subject systematically pursuable. As we have had occasion to remark about the state of affairs before the scientific revolution of the seventeenth century, there is a change of kind when successful theories are discovered. Before that, we have lots of interesting and curious information, and no doubt recipes for producing interesting effects, but afterwards we have real science. If social science is in the same state that natural science once was, then we might say, not that the social sciences have had a short history, but that they have not yet started on their history *at all*. They are not so much new as nascent.

A second explanation of the laggard state of social science takes no particular stand on this first suggestion, but simply points to the horribly difficult nature of the phenomena studied by the social sciences. Nowhere else in nature are there anything like the same problems. Once you have discovered the orbit of a planet you have discovered the orbit as it is for ever; if it should change, there is only a small number of possible disturbing factors which can account for the change, and they are all governed by the same laws that account for the original orbit.

Once you have explained the behaviour of a person or a group, you have to reckon with the possibility that the behaviour will change quite unpredictably. A new idea, a new discovery, a change in the environment, may all disturb the old order. This does not amount to a difficulty of *principle* about the social sciences, but if it is widespread enough, it amounts to such a great difficulty in practice that it would just be silly to expect that the social sciences ever could stand comparison with the natural sciences.

We have mentioned self-fulfilling and self-refuting predictions; this point generalizes from that phenomenon. What people do depends on what they know and what they want; these vary unpredictably. Variations in knowledge are almost in principle unpredictable — since predicted new knowledge would not be new knowledge but old knowledge, and the thought that there will be no more knowledge than what we now have is a very odd one to entertain. Even if one does not get alarmed by these large problems of changeability, the record at lower levels is alarming enough. It used to be orthodox economic theory that a rise in inflation rates would make people spend more and save less, since they would try to anticipate price rises by buying earlier; the new orthodoxy holds that rises in inflation rates make people save more and spend less, as they try to preserve the value of their monetary assets. Each sort of behaviour is rational enough, but how could any economist be expected to anticipate the change from one sort of goal to the other?

The third explanation is the most radical, but extremely difficult to state clearly. It amounts to saying that the way in which we ordinarily explain our own behaviour *is* unassimilable to the scientific pattern of explanation, that explanation by intentions and reasons is not, and cannot be made to be, consistent with explanation by causal laws. It therefore follows that if it is possible to explain human behaviour by scientifically respectable methods, and to derive laws of a reliable kind about how we shall act, the breach with our usual ways of thinking about ourselves must be complete. In effect, the claim is that if there are to be sciences of human behaviour, they will be part of biology, not systematizations of our ordinary ways of explaining ourselves. The development of such an argument is difficult, since it seems to make some very strange claims. One would be that nobody's behaviour is ever truly explained by the reason he or she produces for it, a claim that looks wildly paradoxical when we recall that anyone who accepts such a view presumably does so because he or she finds the reasons for it compelling. To believe that some way round such paradoxes must be found is, for those who hold such a view, less unattractive than the thought that the world is after all divided into two sorts of things, those that can be properly explained and those that cannot.

Two instances from the sociological tradition may clarify what has been said. Durkheim claimed to have set sociology on the scientific road by discovering a method for treating social facts as 'things'; in essence, he thought that social science must be the scientific analysis of social facts, facts which were specifically social. To this end, he recommended that we should not invoke psychological dispositions, intentions and so on. The aim was to show how social causes brought about social effects; the aims and goals of individuals would appear in the explanation only as derivative factors. Yet, as all his critics have said ever since, Durkheim has no hope of following his own instruction; when he analyses suicides, the belief that there *is* such a thing as 'egoistic' or 'anomic' suicide depends on his being able to show that given some plausible assumptions about what people want or what they think morally right, they will find themselves in a situation where killing themselves seems appropriate. That is, although he claims that sociology must be the science of what you might call structural features of a society — or societies generally —, his explanations turn out to be explanations in terms of what we earlier called situational logic.

The same point can equally well be made about Marx. It is, of course, true that Marx's views about the way societies hold together and change are very different from those of various of his contemporaries such as Mill or de Tocqueville, and different again from those of his successors like Weber and Durkheim. But something of the same problem as that which we see in Durkheim faces Marx, too. He evidently saw himself as taking a scientific view of society in insisting on society's organic character; what happened in society is not to be explained by the wishes of this or that individual, but by the fate which awaits a social structure of a given sort. If, however, one looks at the explanation of how this fate is to be known, we find once more that the burden is carried by the thought that we act appropriately to our situation. Capitalists who try to maximize their profits, workers who try to maximize their wages, and so on, are all following out a strategy in the light of what they desire and what they know about the situation.

Now, one thing worth noticing about this is that nothing vital seems to be lost to Marx if it is agreed that the details of Marx's explanation of social and political phenomena rely in the end on what I have called 'everyday explanation' or explanation in terms of the logic of the situation. For what remains distinctively (and contentiously) Marx's own is the view that people are so locked into their situations that what their fate will be can be predicted by him. That is, Marx's views are quite appropriately described as structural and deterministic, not because of his commitment to a view of the nature of social science, but because of his commitment to a view of the actual narrowness of choice, uniformity of aim, and political rigidity which he thought he saw in capitalist societies. He may have held a view of the nature of social science which would have made him extremely unwilling to accept my gloss on his view, though he seems *sometimes* to have held just the view I have suggested, too. All that matters is to notice that anyone who wants to argue that the task of social science is to yield a positive science of the operations of social structures which proceeds independently of anything we discover about individual agents is both going to have to produce some striking evidence of social determinism, and is going to have to solve some philosophically awkward puzzles about the relationship between the accounts of their behaviour given by individuals themselves and the accounts given by social science.

At this vertiginous point, we may reasonably stop and sum up. Three points may plausibly suffice. The first is permissive. Whether or not social science is social *science*, it can certainly be something else, too. That is, it is also an activity which involves giving us the 'feel' of events, providing 'a sense of place' and so on. This is not the time to embark on a full discussion of the claim that the social sciences provide human understanding as well as or instead of scientific explanation. But the claim can be justified at least to the extent of saying that one thing the social scientist *can* do is try to tell us 'what it's like to be ...' whatever it is. Nobody who has ever read Lévi-Strauss's essay on the healer Quesalid could doubt that showing what it's like to be an Indian healer is a serious activity.

The second point is that since what people do depends on what they believe and want, and since beliefs may be mistaken and wants not very well thought out, social phenomena must not be taken at face value. The explanation of an individual person's behaviour may well be that 'he made a mistake'. Whether or not the notion of 'false consciousness', that is, the idea that whole groups suffer from illusions, turns out to be a fruitful one, it certainly points to an important truth. When we explain someone's behaviour, we can always raise the question whether the behaviour is successful or unsuccessful. Indeed, we can hardly help raising such questions, given the extent to which social life is riven with people making claims about the truth and falsity of the information they offer one another. It is not value neutrality to refrain from noticing whether beliefs are true and false, it is leaving out an important part of the explanation.

Third, if it is the case that explaining our own and other people's behaviour involves reference to beliefs and wants and that these are not susceptible to causal explanation in the natural sciences sense, then students of the social sciences should not expect to find themselves in possession of many general laws.

Yet, there is no earthly reason why we should not find ourselves in possession of a great deal of reliable information, together with some general strategies for acquiring more of the same. Social scientists won't exactly be experts in the sense in which the layman cannot be, but they will know a good deal that the layman does not. If this sounds altogether too much like my earlier brief description of the intellectual condition of the forerunners of Sir Isaac Newton, it is perhaps worth reminding ourselves that the intellectual equipment of, say, Francis Bacon is enviable enough.

Notes

1 J. S. Mill, *A System of Logic*, Longman, 1967, pp. 546-7.
2 C. G. Hempel, *Aspects of Scientific Explanation*, New York, Free Press, 1964, ch. 12.

SECTION 2

The Economy: a Social Process

Introduction

Laurence Harris

Britain is a capitalist society. That much is commonplace but, like all commonplace, generally accepted statements, this definition becomes more problematic the more one examines it. I am not going to try to pin down and justify the statement here (Unit 5 of D102 does a much better job than I could of explaining what is meant by Britain being capitalist). However, one point is central to the definition: when we talk of a capitalist *society* we mean that it has a capitalist type of *economy*. Other aspects of the way that British society is arranged – the family, education and religion, for example – may or may not be especially capitalist in nature, but as soon as we say that British society is capitalist it is generally understood that we at least mean that the economy is organized in a capitalist way. It is different from the socialist economic arrangements of the Soviet Union and from the economic system of England in the Middle Ages, before capitalism was established.

The articles we have brought together in this section all relate to the workings of a capitalist economy. The first four concern the way that capitalist economies have developed historically since they were established; the last concerns the theories that economists have developed to explain the way such economies work. Let me say a word or two to put them in context.

The date that capitalism began in England has been a matter of dispute between economic historians. Some have suggested that it had it roots in the mediaeval years with the development of machinery in mining, but it is more generally accepted that its actual onset was in the second half of the eighteenth century. That was the start of almost a century of remarkable developments in the application of machinery to production, and these technical innovations are what we often take to be the distinctive feature of the beginnings of modern industry – hence we christen the period the Industrial Revolution. However, the beginning of capitalist industry in the eighteenth century was not marked only by the start of a series of technical innovations in machinery; it was equally marked by a change in the way that people related to each other in their work and in obtaining the necessities of life — in their economic activity. People produced fewer things for themselves and spent their energies producing things for sale, using the proceeds to buy the necessities. And they received their income not by selling their product themselves — it was the property of their employer, the capitalist, and he sold it — but by receiving wages from the capitalist.

There were, then, two features that marked the beginning of capitalist industry: the rise of modern machinery for men and women to work on, and the widespread development of capitalist factory owners for them to work for. These were new phenomena. So much so that the founders of modern economics, Adam Smith and David Ricardo, wrote at the end of the eighteenth and beginning of the nineteenth century attempting to explain how the new economic system worked. Nowadays we are so accustomed to thinking of production as being organized in factories to make profits for the owners and wages for the workers that it is salutary to read of it as a new phenomenon in Smith's and Ricardo's old tomes. My main point is this, though: although the capitalist economy was new in the eighteenth century its features are still with us (machinery, wages, profits), *but* while retaining its general features, capitalism has gone through some remarkable changes since its inception. Historians studying the capitalist economy of Britain from the eighteenth century to the 1980s are struck by its volatility and rapid changes as much as its continuity. The two articles by Hobsbawm and those by Donaldson and Leontief deal with particular aspects of these historical changes.

Before reading them it is worth bearing in mind this point. Just as there were two distinct aspects of capitalism's foundation, new machinery and new relations between people, so the history of the capitalist economy is marked by developments in each of these elements. On the one hand, new machinery, new techniques of production and, concomitantly, new products have been developed and brought into play. It is trite but still worth remarking that the machinery and techniques used in modern production are quite different from what they were thirty years ago, let alone two centuries ago. On the other hand, the way that the relations between people are organized in the economic sphere of their lives has changed dramatically. A signal illustration of this is that whereas two centuries ago the worker was an individual, a 'hand' employed by another individual, the factory-owner, the capitalist (or a factory manager directly responsible to him), now the worker is typically a member of a powerful organization, a trade unionist rather than an isolated individual, and the employer is a large bureaucracy administered by faceless corporate managers rather than an individual boss. The articles by Hobsbawm and Leontief focus on each of these two aspects of the capitalist economy's history at different points.

The first article by Eric Hobsbawm examines the ways in which both machinery and the economic relations between people changed in Britain between 1750 and the late nineteenth century. Within the first category, Hobsbawm writes of the technical developments in the generation of energy (steam power for most of the period giving way to electricity and the internal combustion engine in the twentieth century); the development of new forms of transport, in particular, the railway boom of the mid-nineteenth century, and the constant improvement in machinery. He also writes, however, of the changes that capitalism wrought in the economic relations between people: the rise of the wage system and the incessant search for markets in which to sell the factories' products.

This paper conveys an impression of the dynamism and growth of the capitalist economy in Britain, but the economy has experienced ups and downs, and some of the downs (crises, depressions or slumps) seemed at the time to throw the whole viability of the economy into doubt. Hobsbawm's second article explains what happened to the economy in the 1920s and 1930s, a period when unemployment and factory closures were so bad that many thought that the capitalist economy was about to break down completely. The author examines here both the technical changes that occurred in production – the development of new machinery and new industrial products – and the changes in relations between the people in the economy. Under the latter heading, he writes particularly of the growth of large firms, giant organizations replacing the individual factory-owner.

The article by Donaldson is a concise piece which concentrates on the growth of large firms. He directly relates this phenomenon in the economic relations between people to the technical phenomenon of the development of modern machinery, using the concept of economies of scale to explain how modern production techniques may require large organizations to exploit them most efficiently.

The article by Wassily Leontief, however, is exclusively concerned with the technical aspects of the history of the capitalist economy. Writing in the 1950s about the American economy, he is concerned with the way in which the application of improved machinery has stimulated productivity and brought general benefits. He concentrates on the benefits that technology has brought and does not emphasize the frictions, unemployment and social costs that accompany new technology. This is exemplified by the prognoses Leontief makes for the new technologies he could see emerging in the 1950s, broadly categorized today as 'automation'. He foresaw the increases in productivity that could result as the basis for a future with vastly increased leisure, but he did not forecast the dislocation that accompanied the introduction of new techniques in the 1970s and 1980s. In the process of adjustment, increased leisure has been enforced by redundancies rather than chosen willingly, and that has been the case, too, in previous periods of rapid changes in industry's machinery and technology.

The final article in the section on the economy is one that we especially commissioned from Kathleen O'Donnell. Whereas the previous papers have been describing as well as analysing economic change, this one is concerned exclusively with a theory, an analysis of the capitalist economy. Reading Hobsbawm, Donaldson or Leontief on the changes that have occurred in the economy, it is natural that one should ask what causes these changes. What is the driving force of the economy? At its most basic, what determines the pattern of production or what is produced? An answer given by many economists is that the ultimate purpose of production is to provide goods that people want to buy, and people want to buy them to use them – or, in other words, consume them – instead of locking them away in vaults. Therefore, it is argued, what people as consumers want to buy determines what is produced: consumers are sovereign. Carried to an extreme, this idea of consumer sovereignty can be used to explain the history of the capitalist economy with its changing pattern of production. O'Donnell examines the idea and the way that it fits into most economists' conception of the economy, but she also shows that it is by no means a self-evident idea and in the view of many economists it is seriously misleading. Thus, she provides an example of the clashes of ideas between social scientists – the disputes acknowledged in Section 1 as being central to the development of ideas.

Altogether, then, this section provides some perspective on the nature of capitalist economies, particularly Britain's, and their historical changes. In compiling this Reader and then producing Course D102, we have taken the view that our economic activities affect all parts of our social lives and therefore are in some ways the most fundamental. The kinds of jobs that we do, whether we have jobs, the cost of living, the prevalence of modern machinery, communications, transport systems and other parts of the economic infrastructure affect our family life, our culture and even our voting behaviour. Because we think that our economic activities are so important we have placed these articles early in the Reader. I hope you will agree that they help you with the whole of your study of society.

3   Industrialization: laying the foundations for the twentieth century

Eric Hobsbawm

[The expansion of the British economy of the middle years of the nineteenth century took place on a much firmer foundation than that of the earlier phase of textile manufacture. It was based on the capital goods industries, on coal, iron and steel and, above all, on railway construction.]

There were two converging reasons for this. The first was the growing industrialization in the rest of the world, which provided a rapidly increasing market for the kind of capital goods which could not be imported in any quantity except from the 'workshop of the world', and which could not yet be produced in sufficient quantity at home. [...]

The second reason, however, has little to do with the growth of demand. It is the pressure of the increasingly vast accumulations of capital for profitable investment, which is best illustrated by the construction of the railways.

Between 1830 and 1850 some six thousand miles of railways were opened in Britain, mostly as the result of two extraordinary bursts of concentrated investment followed by construction, the little 'railway mania' of 1835-7 and the gigantic one of 1845-7. In effect, by 1850 the basic English railway network was already more or less in existence. In every respect this was a revolutionary transformation — more revolutionary, in its way, than the rise of the cotton industry because it represented a far more advanced phase of industrialization and one bearing on the life of the ordinary citizen outside the rather small areas of actual industry. It reached into some of the remotest areas of the countryside and the centres of the greatest cities. It transformed the speed of movement — indeed of human life — from one measured in single miles per hour to one measured in scores of miles per hour, and introduced the notion of a gigantic, nation-wide, complex and exact interlocking routine symbolized by the railway time-table (from which all the subsequent 'time-tables' took their name and inspiration).

Source: *Industry and Empire*, Penguin Books, 1968, extracts from ch. 6, pp. 109-33.

It revealed the possibilities of technical progress as nothing else had done, because it was both more advanced than most other forms of technical activity and omnipresent. The cotton-mills of 1800 were obsolescent by 1840; but by 1850 the railways had reached a standard of performance not seriously improved upon until the abandonment of steam in the mid-twentieth century, their organization and methods were on a scale unparalleled in any other industry, their use of novel and science-based technology (such as the electric telegraph) unprecedented. They appeared to be several generations ahead of the rest of the economy, and indeed 'railway' became a sort of synonym for ultra-modernity in the 1840s, as 'atomic' was to be after the Second World War. Their sheer size and scale staggered the imagination and dwarfed the most gigantic public works of the past. [. . .]

But only a small fraction of the £240 millions invested in railways by 1850 had any such rational justification. Most of it was sunk into the railways, and much of it was sunk without trace, because by the 1830s there were vast accumulations of capital burning holes in their owners' pockets, i.e. seeking any investment likely to yield more than the 3.4 per cent of public stocks. [. . .] In fact, it surged into railways for want of anything equally capital-absorbing, and turned a valuable innovation in transport into a major national programme of capital investment.

As always happens at times of capital glut, much of it was rashly, stupidly, some of it insanely invested. [. . .] Much of it was lost in the slumps which followed the manias. Much of it was perhaps attracted less by rational calculations of profit and loss than by the romantic appeal of technological revolution, which the railway symbolized so marvellously, and which brought out the dreamer (or in economic terms, the speculator, in racing terms, the long-odds punter) in otherwise solid citizens. Still, the money was there to be spent, and if it did not on the whole produce much by way of profit, it produced something more valuable: a new transport system, a new means of mobilizing capital accumulations of all kinds for industrial purposes, and above all, a vast new source of employment and a gigantic and lasting stimulus to the capital goods industries of Britain. [. . .]

The balance sheet of the railway construction of the 1840s is impressive. In Britain: over two hundred millions invested, direct employment — at the peak of construction (1846-8) — of something like 200,000, and an indirect stimulus to employment in the rest of the economy which cannot be calculated.* The railways were largely

* The number of men occupied in mining, metallurgy, machine and vehicle building, etc., which were largely affected by the railway revolution, rose by almost 40 per cent between 1841 and 1851.

responsible for the doubling of British iron output between the middle 1830s and the middle 1840s, and at their peak — 1845-7 — accounted for perhaps forty per cent of the country's entire domestic consumption, settling down thereafter to a steady fifteen per cent of its output. Such a vast economic stimulus, coming at the very moment when the economy was passing through its most catastrophic slump of the century (1841-2), could hardly have been better timed. Outside Britain: a major stimulus to the export of capital goods for the construction of railways abroad. The Dowlais Iron Company, for instance, between 1830 and 1850 supplied twelve British but sixteen foreign railway companies.

Table 3.1 World railway mileage opened, per decade (to nearest thousand miles)

Year	UK	Europe (incl. UK)	America	Rest of world
1840–50	6,000	13,000	7,000	–
1850–60	4,000	17,000	24,000	1,000
1860–70	5,000	31,000	24,000	7,000
1870–80	2,000	39,000	51,000	12,000

But the stimulus was not exhausted with the 1840s. On the contrary, world railway construction continued on an increasingly massive scale, at least until the 1880s, as the above table makes clear; the railways were built to a large extent with British capital, British materials and equipment, and often by British contractors. This remarkable expansion reflected the twin process of industrialization in the 'advanced' countries and economic opening-up of the undeveloped areas, which transformed the world in these mid-Victorian decades, turning Germany* and the USA into major industrial economies soon to be comparable to the British, opening areas like the North American prairies, the South American pampas, the South Russian steppes to export agriculture, breaking down with flotillas of warships the resistance of China and Japan to foreign trade, laying the foundations of tropical and sub-tropical economies based on the export of mines and agrarian products. The consequences of these changes were not felt in Britain until after the crisis of the 1870s. Until then their main effects were patently beneficial to the greatest and in some parts of the world the only exporter of industrial products and capital.

Three consequences of this change in the orientation of the British economy may be noticed.

* Or rather, the area which became Germany in 1871.

The first is the Industrial Revolution in the heavy industries, which for the first time provided the economy with abundant supplies of iron, and more important, steel (which had hitherto been produced by rather old-fashioned methods and in tiny quantities).* In coal this

Table 3.2 Production of pig-iron, steel and coal (in thousand tons)

1850	2,250	49	49,000
1880	7,750	1,440	147,000

increase was achieved substantially by familiar methods, i.e. without any significant labour-saving devices, which meant that the expansion of coal output produced a vast increase in the number of coalminers. In 1850 there were rather more than 200,000 of them in Britain, around 1880 about half a million, and by 1914 well over 1.1 million, working in some three thousand mines, or almost as many as the entire agricultural population and the (male and female) textile workers. This was to be reflected not only in the character of the British labour movement but in national politics, for miners, concentrated in single-industry agglomerations of villages, were one of the few groups of manual workers — and in the countryside almost the only ones — capable of determining the fortunes of parliamentary constituencies. That the British Trades Union Congress committed itself to the socialist slogan of the nationalization of industries as early as the 1890s was largely due to the pressure of the miners, which was in turn due to their general, and amply justified, dissatisfaction, especially with the owners' gross neglect of the men's safety and health in that dark and murderous occupation.†

The vast increase in iron output was also due to unrevolutionary improvements — chiefly a remarkable increase in the capacity productivity of blast-furnaces which, incidentally, tended to keep the capacity of the industry running well ahead of actual output, thus producing a constant tendency to bring down the price of iron though it also suffered wide price fluctuations for other reasons: in the mid-eighties the actual British output was considerably less than half of potential

---

* In 1850 the total steel output of the western world may not have amounted to more than 70,000 tons, of which Britain supplied five-sevenths.

† About 1,000 miners were killed annually in accidents in 1856–86, with occasional giant disasters such as those of High Blantyre (200 dead, 1877), Haydock (189 dead, 1878), Ebbw Vale (268 dead, 1878), Risca (120 dead, 1880), Seaham (164 dead, 1880), Pen-y-Craig (101 dead, 1880).

capacity. Steel production, on the other hand, was revolutionized by the invention of the Bessemer converter in 1850, the open-hearth furnace in the 1860s, and the basic process in the late 1870s. The new ability to mass-produce steel reinforced the general impetus given to the capital goods industries by transport, for as soon as it was available in quantity, a large-scale process of substituting it for the less durable iron began, so that railways, steamships, etc., in effect required two inputs of iron within little more than a generation. Since the productivity per man of these industries rose very sharply, and they never required very much manual labour anyway, their effect on employment was not so great. But like coal, and of course, like the vast expansion of transport which went with iron, steel and coal, they provided jobs for the hitherto unemployed or least employable: unskilled men drawn from the agricultural surplus population (British or Irish). The expansion of these industries was therefore doubly useful: they gave unskilled labour better-paid work, and by drawing off the rural surplus, improved the condition of the remaining farm workers, which began to improve markedly, even dramatically, in the 1850s.*

However, the rise of the capital goods industries provided a comparable stimulus to the employment of skilled labour in the vast expansion of engineering, the building of machines, ships, etc. The number of workers in these industries also just about doubled between 1851 and 1881, and unlike coal and iron they have continued to expand ever since. By 1914 they formed the largest single category of British male workers — considerably more numerous than all workers, male or female, in textiles. They thus greatly reinforced an aristocracy of labour which regarded itself as — and was — much better off than the bulk of the working class.

The second consequence of the new era, it is therefore evident, was a remarkable improvement in employment all round, and a large-scale transfer of labour from worse- to better-paid jobs. This accounts largely for the general sense of improvement in living-standards and the lowering of social tension during the golden years of the mid-Victorians, for the actual wage-rates of many classes of workers did not rise significantly while housing conditions and urban amenities remained shockingly bad.

A third consequence was the remarkable rise in the export of British capital abroad. By 1870 something like £700 million were invested in foreign countries, more than a quarter of it in the rising industrial economy of the USA, so much so that the subsequent and striking growth of British foreign holdings could have been achieved without

* The numbers employed in transport more than doubled in the 1840s, and doubled again between 1851 and 1881, when they stood at almost 900,000.

much further capital export, merely by the reinvestment of the interest and dividend from what was already being held abroad. (Whether this is what actually happened, is another question.) This emigration of capital was, of course, merely one part of the remarkable flow of profits and savings in search of investment; and, thanks to the trans- formations of the capital market in the railway era, prepared to seek it not just in old-fashioned real estate or government stock, but in industrial shares. In turn, businessmen and promoters (contemporaries would probably have said 'unsound businessmen and shady promoters') were now better able to raise capital not only from potential partners or other informed investors, but from a mass of quite uninformed ones looking for a return on their capital anywhere in the golden world economy, and finding it through the agency of family solicitors and stockbrokers, who often paid the solicitors for steering such funds their way. New legislation which made joint stock companies with limited liability possible, encouraged more adventurous investment, for if such a company went bankrupt, the shareholder lost only his investment but not, as he had been liable to, his entire fortune.*

Economically the transformation of the capital market in the railway era — the stock exchanges of Manchester, Liverpool and Glasgow were all the products of the 'mania' of the 1840s — was a valuable, though almost certainly not an essential, means of mobilizing capital for large undertakings beyond the scope of partnerships, or for enterprises in remote parts of the world. Socially, however, it reflected another aspect of the mid-Victorian economy: the growth of a class of *rentiers*, who lived on the profits and savings of the previous two or three generations' accumulations. By 1871 Britain contained 170,000 'persons of rank and property' without visible occupation — almost all of them women, or rather 'ladies'; a surprising number of them un- married ladies.† Stocks and shares, including shares in family firms formed into 'private companies' for this purpose, were a convenient way of providing for widows, daughters and other relatives who could not — and no longer needed to be — associated with the management of property and enterprise. The comfortable avenues of Kensington, the villas of spas and the growing seaside resorts of the middle class, and the environs of Swiss mountains and Tuscan cities welcomed them. The era of railway, iron and foreign investment also provided the economic base for the Victorian spinster and the Victorian aesthete.

* Of course, before the coming of general limited liability special provisions had been made for certain kinds of joint stock investment.

† Of the shareholders in the Bank of Scotland and the Commercial Bank of Scotland in the 1870s about two-fifths were women, and of these in turn almost two-thirds were single.

With the railways Britain therefore entered the period of full industrialization. Its economy was no longer dangerously poised on the narrow platform of two or three pioneer sectors — notably textiles — but broadly based on a foundation of capital goods production, which in turn facilitated the advance of modern technology and organization — or what passed for modern in the mid-nineteenth century — into a wide variety of industries. It had the skills to produce not everything, but anything it chose to produce. It had surmounted the original crisis of the early Industrial Revolution, and not yet begun to feel the crisis of the pioneer industrial country which ceases to be the only 'workshop of the world'.

A fully industrialized industrial economy implies permanence, if only the permanence of further industrialization. One of the most impressive reflections of the new state of affairs — in economics, in social life and in politics — is the new readiness of Britons to accept their revolutionary ways of living as natural or at least irreversible, and to adapt themselves to them. Different classes did so in different ways. We must look briefly at the two most important, the employers and the workers.

Establishing an industrial economy is not the same thing as operating one already in existence, and the very considerable energies of the British 'middle class' in the half-century from Pitt to Peel had been primarily devoted to the first of these objects. Politically and socially this meant a concentrated effort to give themselves confidence and pride in their historic task — the early nineteenth century was the first and last when ladies wrote little pedagogic works on political economy for other ladies to teach to their children, or better still, to the poor* — and a long battle against 'the aristocracy' to reshape the institutions of Britain in a manner suitable to industrial capitalism. The reforms of the 1830s, and the installation of Free Trade in 1846 more or less achieved these objects, at least in so far as this could be done without running the risk of a perhaps uncontrollable mobilization of the labouring masses. By the 'golden years' these battles had been won, though a few actions against the rearguard of the old régime remained to be fought. The very Queen herself was a visible pillar of middle-class respectability, or seemed to be, and the Conservative Party, organ of all that was out

---

* Such as Mrs Marcet, Harriet Martineau and the novelist Maria Edgeworth, much admired by Ricardo and read by the young Princess Victoria. A recent writer observes very acutely that the apparent neglect of the French Revolution and the Napoleonic Wars in the novels of Jane Austen and Maria Edgeworth may have been a deliberate exclusion of subject matter which should be of no interest to the respectable middle class.

of sympathy with industrial Britain, was for several decades a permanent political minority lacking an ideology or a programme. The formidable movement of the labouring poor — Jacobin, Chartist, even in its primitive way socialist — disappeared, leaving foreign exiles like Karl Marx disconsolately trying to make what they could of the liberal-radicalism or the respectable trade unionism which took its place.

But economically the change was quite as striking. The capitalist manufacturers of the first phase of industrial revolution were — or saw themselves as — a pioneering minority seeking to establish an economic system in an environment by no means entirely favourable to it: surrounded by a population deeply distrustful of their efforts, employing a working class unaccustomed to industrialism and hostile to it, struggling — at least initially — to build their factories out of modest initial capital and ploughed-back profits by abstinence, hard work and grinding the faces of the poor. The epics of the rise of the Victorian middle class, as preserved in the works of Samuel Smiles, looked back to an often quite mythical era of heroes of self-help, expelled by the stupid progress-hating multitude yet returning later in triumph and top hats. What is equally to the point, they were themselves men formed by their past — all the more so as they lacked scientific education and prided themselves above all on empiricism. Hence they were only incompletely aware of the most rational way of running their enterprises. It may seem grotesque now that economists could argue, as Nassau Senior did against the Ten Hours Bill of 1847, that the employers' profit was made in the last hour of work, and that therefore a reduction of hours would be fatal to them, but there were plenty of hard-headed men who took the view that the only way to make profits was to pay the lowest money-wages for the longest hours.

The employing class itself was therefore incompletely familiar with the rules of the industrial game, or disinclined to abide by them. These rules decreed that economic transactions were essentially governed by the free play of forces in the market — by all men's unrestricted and competitive pursuit of their economic advantage — which would automatically produce the best results all round. But, quite apart from their own reluctance to compete when it did not suit them,* they did not regard these considerations as applicable to the workers. These were still sometimes bound by long and inflexible contracts, such as the coalminers' 'yearly bond' in the North-east, more often milked for supplementary profit by the non-economic compulsion of 'truck' (payments in kind, or forced purchases in company shops), or fines,

---

* Though cartels, price-fixing arrangements, etc., were at this time rarely lasting or effective, except in such fields as government contracting.

and in general held tight by a law of contract (codified in 1823) which made them liable to imprisonment for breach of employment, while their masters went free or were merely fined for their own breaches. Economic incentives – such as payment by results – were by no means common, except in some industries or for certain kinds of labour, though (as Karl Marx was to argue convincingly) 'piece-work' was at this time the form of wage-payment most suitable to capitalism. The only incentive generally recognized was profit, and those who earned no profits as entrepreneurs or subcontractors of various kinds, were left to work to the pace dictated by the machine, or discipline, or the driving of subcontractors, or – where too skilled to be driven – to their own devices. Though it was already known that higher wages and shorter hours might raise productivity, employers continued to distrust them, seeking instead to depress wages and lengthen hours. Rational cost-accounting or industrial management were rare, and those who recommended them, like the scientist Charles Babbage (pioneer of the computer) were regarded as unpractical eccentrics. Trade unions were seen as either doomed to almost immediate failure, or as engines of economic catastrophe. Though they ceased to be formally illegal in 1824,* every effort was made to destroy them where possible.

In these circumstances it was not surprising that the workers should also refuse to accept capitalism, which, as we have seen, was far from attracting them in the first place. It offered them little in practice. Contrary to the apologists of the system, it offered them little even in theory, at any rate, *so long as they remained workers* – which most of them were destined to do. Until the railway era it did not even offer them its own permanence. It might collapse. It might be overthrown. It might be an episode and not an epoch. It was too young to have established its permanence by sheer duration, for as we have seen, outside a few pioneer areas, even in textiles the main weight of industrialization occurred after the Napoleonic Wars. At the time of the great Chartist general strike of 1842 every adult person in, say, Blackburn could remember the time when the first spinning factory and power-loom had been introduced in the town, less than twenty-five years earlier. And if the 'labouring poor' hesitated to accept the system as permanent, even less were they likely – unless forced, often by extra-economic coercion – to adapt themselves to it, even in their struggles. They might seek to by-pass it, as the early socialists did by free communities of cooperative production. They might seek, in the short run, to evade it, as the early trade unions did by sending their unemployed

---

* Thanks to the efforts of the Philosophic Radicals, who argued that, if legal, their total ineffectiveness must soon become obvious, and the workers would therefore cease to be tempted by them.

members 'on tramp' to some other city, until they discovered that 'bad times' in the new economy were periodic and universal. They might seek to forget about it, dreaming of a return to peasant proprietorship. It is no accident that the greatest mass leader of this era, the Chartist tribune Feargus O'Connor, was an Irishman whose positive economic programme for the masses who swore by him was a plan for land settlement.

Some time in the 1840s all this began to change, and to change rapidly, though by local and unofficial action rather than by any large national legislation or organization. Employers began to abandon 'extensive' methods of exploitation such as lengthening hours and shortening wages for 'intensive' ones, which meant the opposite. The Ten Hours Act of 1847 made this a necessity in the cotton industry, but without any legislative pressure we find the same tendency spreading in the industrial North. What the continentals were to call the 'English week', a free weekend, at all events from Saturday midday — began to spread in Lancashire in the 1840s, in London in the 1850s. Payment by results (i.e. incentive payments to workers) undoubtedly became more popular, while contracts tended to shorten and to become more flexible, though both these developments cannot yet be fully documented. Extra-economic compulsion diminished, the readiness to accept legal supervision of working conditions — as by the admirable Factory Inspectors — increased. These were not so much victories of rationality, or even of political pressure, as relaxations of tension. British industrialists now felt rich and confident enough to be able to afford such changes. It has been pointed out that the employers who advocated policies of relatively high wages and conciliating workers by reforms in the 1850s and 1860s frequently represented old-established and flourishing businesses no longer threatened with bankruptcy by fluctuation of trade. The 'New Model' employers — commoner outside Lancashire than inside — were men like the Bass brothers (brewing), Lord Elcho (coal and iron), Thomas Brassey (railway contracting), Titus Salt, Alfred Illingworth, the Kell Brothers from round Bradford, A. J. Mundella and Samuel Morley (hosiery). Is it an accident that Bradford, which produced several of these, set off the status-competition in the West Riding for municipal monuments by constructing an opulent structure (with a restaurant 'for the accommodation of mercantile men', a hall for 3,100 people, a vast organ and illumination by a continuous line of 1,750 gas jets), thus spurring its rival Leeds to the titanic expenditure of £122,000 on its town hall? Bradford began — like so many other cities — to plan its break with municipal stinginess in 1849.

By the end of the 1860s these changes became more visible, because more formal and official. In 1867 factory legislation was for the first time seriously extended beyond the textile industries, and even began to abandon the fiction that its only purpose was to protect children – adults being theoretically capable of protecting themselves. Even in textiles, where the general business view had been that the Acts of 1833 and 1847 (the Ten Hours Act) were wanton and ruinous interferences with private enterprise, opinion was reconciled to them. No one, wrote the *Economist*, 'had any doubt *now* of the wisdom of those measures'.[1] Progress in the mines was slower, though the yearly bond in the North-east was abolished in 1872 and the right of the miners to check the honesty of their payment by results through an elected 'checkweighman' was theoretically recognized. The unjust Master and Servant code was finally abolished in 1875. More important, trade unions were given what amounted to their modern legal status, i.e. they were henceforth accepted as permanent and not in themselves noxious parts of the industrial scene. This change was all the more startling, because the Royal Commission of 1867 which initiated it was the result of some dramatic, and entirely indefensible acts of terrorism by small craft societies in Sheffield (the 'Sheffield Outrages') which were expected to lead, and twenty years earlier would probably have led, to strong anti-union measures. In fact the Acts of 1871 and 1875 gave the unions a degree of legal freedom which conservative-minded lawyers have since, at intervals, attempted to whittle away.

But the most obvious symptom of the change was political: the Reform Act of 1867 (followed, as we have seen, by a whole crop of important legislative changes) accepted an electoral system dependent on working-class votes. It did not introduce parliamentary democracy, but it implied that the rulers of Britain reconciled themselves to its eventual introduction, which subsequent reforms (in 1884-5, 1918 and 1929) achieved with diminishing amounts of fuss.* Twenty years earlier Chartism had been resisted, because democracy was believed to imply social revolution. Fifty years earlier it would have been unthinkable, except by the masses and a handful of extremist middle-class radicals. George Canning in 1817 had thanked God 'that the House of Commons is not sufficiently identified with the people to catch their every nascent wish . . . According to no principle of our Constitution was it ever meant to be so . . . it never pretended to be so, nor can ever pretend to be so without bringing ruin and misery upon the kingdom.'[2] A Cecil, arguing for the rearguard in those debates of 1866-7 which reveal so much about the attitudes of the British upper classes, still warned his hearers that democracy meant socialism. The rulers of

---

* But *The Times* did not regard democracy as acceptable until 1914.

Britain did not welcome the Reform. On the contrary, but for the mass agitations of the poor, they would not have yielded anything like so much — though their readiness to yield in 1867 contrasts strikingly with their mass mobilization of force against Chartism in 1839, 1842 and 1848. However, they were prepared to accept it, because they no longer regarded the British working class as revolutionary. At all events they now saw it as divided into a policitally moderate aristocracy of labour, ready to accept capitalism, and a politically ineffective, because unorganized and leaderless proletarian plebs, which presented no major danger. For the great mass movements which mobilized all the labouring poor against the employing class, like Chartism, were dead. Socialism had disappeared from the country of its birth.[3]

My sorrowful impressions [wrote an old Chartist in 1870] were confirmed. In our old Chartist time, it is true, Lancashire working men were in rags by the thousands; and many of them often lacked food. But their intelligence was demonstrated wherever you went. You would see them in groups discussing the great doctrine of political justice . . . *Now* you will see no such groups in Lancashire. But you will hear well-dressed working men talking, as they walk with their hands in their pockets, of 'Co-ops' and their shares in them, or in building societies. And you will see others, like idiots leading small greyhound dogs.

Affluence — or what men used to starvation regarded as comfort — had extinguished the fires in hungry bellies. Equally important, the discovery that capitalism was not a temporary catastrophe, but a permanent system which allowed some improvement, had altered the objective of their struggles. There were no Socialists to dream of a new society. There were trade unions, seeking to exploit the laws of political economy in order to create a scarcity of their kind of labour and thus increase their members' wages.

The British middle-class citizen who surveyed the scene in the early 1870s might well have thought that all was for the best in the best of all possible worlds. Nothing very serious was likely to go wrong with the British economy. But it did. Just as phase one of industrialization stumbled into self-made depression and crisis, so phase two bred its own difficulties. The years between 1873 and 1896 are known to economic historians, who have discussed them more eagerly than any other phase of nineteenth-century business conjuncture, as the 'Great Depression'. The name is misleading. So far as the working people are concerned, it cannot compare with the cataclysms of the 1830s and

1840s, or the 1920s and 1930s. But if 'depression' indicates a pervasive — and for the generations since 1850 a new — state of mind of uneasiness and gloom about the prospects of the British economy, the word is accurate. After its glorious advance, the economy stagnated. Though the British boom of the early 1870s did not crash into ruins quite so dramatically as in the USA and Central Europe, amid the débris of bankrupt financiers and cooling blast-furnaces, it drifted inexorably downwards. Unlike in other industrial powers, the British boom would not really revive. Prices, profits and rates of interest fell or stayed puzzlingly low. A few feverish little booms did not really halt this long and frustrating descent, which was not reversed until the middle 1890s. And when the economic sun of inflation once more broke through the prevailing fog, it shone on a very different world. Between 1890 and 1895 both the USA and Germany passed Britain in the production of steel. During the 'Great Depression' Britain ceased to be the 'workshop of the world' and became merely one of its three greatest industrial powers; and in some crucial respects, the weakest of them.

The 'Great Depression' cannot be explained in purely British terms, for it was a world-wide phenomenon, though its effects varied from one country to another and in several — notably the USA, Germany and some new arrivals on the industrial scene such as the Scandinavian countries — it was on balance a period of extraordinary advance rather than stagnation. Yet in all, it marks the end of one phase of economic development — the first, or if we prefer, the 'British' phase of industrialization — and the start of another. Broadly speaking, the mid-century boom was due to the initial — or virtually initial — industrialization of the main 'advanced' economies outside Britain and the opening up of hitherto unexploited, because inaccessible or undeveloped, areas of primary production and agriculture.* So far as the industrial countries were concerned, it was something like an extension of the British Industrial Revolution and the technology on which it was based. So far as the primary producers were concerned, it was the construction of a global system of transport based on the railway and improved — and increasingly steam-driven — shipping, capable of linking regions of relatively easy economic utilization and various mining areas to their markets in the urbanized and industrial sector of the world. Both

---

* This is not to deny the industrial development outside Britain before the 1840s, but its comparability with British industrialization. Thus in 1840 the value of all US and German hardware manufactures was each about one-sixth of the British; the value of all textile manufactures somewhat over one-sixth and one-fifth respectively; the output of pig-iron a little over one-fifth and about one-eighth.

processes immensely stimulated the British economy without as yet doing it any noticeable harm. Yet neither could continue indefinitely.

For one thing, the sharp reduction in costs both in industry and (through the transport revolution) in primary products, was bound to make itself felt sooner or later – when the new plants produced, the new railroads operated, the new farming regions had come under cultivation – as a fall in prices. In fact it took the form of that spectacular twenty-year deflation which reduced the general price-level by about a third and was what most businessmen meant when they talked about persistent depression. Its effects were most dramatic, indeed catastrophic, in parts of agriculture, fortunately a relatively minor part of the British economy though not elsewhere. As soon as the massive flow of cheap foodstuffs converged upon the urbanized areas of Europe – in the 1870s – the bottom fell out of the agricultural market, not only in the receiving areas, but in the competing regions of overseas producers. The flaring discontent of Populist farmers on the North American Continent, the more dangerous rumble of agrarian revolutionism in the Russia of the 1880s and 1890s, not to mention the spurt of agrarian and nationalist unrest in Ireland in the era of Parnellism and Michael Davitt's Land League* testify to its effect on regions of peasant agriculture or family farming, which were at the direct or indirect mercy of world prices. Importing countries ready to protect their farmers by tariffs, as several did after 1879, thought they had some defence. British agriculture was, as we shall see, devastated in so far as it had specialized in grain-crops which now became quite uncompetitive, but was too unimportant to win itself protection, and eventually shifted to products not challenged, or challengeable, by overseas producers.

Again, the immediate benefits of the first phase of industrialization wore off. The possibilities of the technological innovations of the original (British) industrial era tended to exhaust themselves, and most notably so in the countries most completely transformed during this phase. A new phase of technology opened new possibilities in the 1890s, but in the meantime a certain faltering is understandable. It was all the more troubling, because both new and old industrial economies ran into problems of markets and profit-margins analogous to those which had shaken British industry forty years earlier. As the vacuum of demand was filled, markets tended to be glutted, for though they had obviously increased, they had not increased fast enough – at least at home – to keep pace with the multiple expansion of output and

* It had fainter,.because much more localized, echoes in the few peasant regions of Great Britain, notably in the crofter agitation of the Scottish highlands and the analogous movements of the Welsh hill-farmers.

capacity in manufactured goods. As the titanic profits of the industrial pioneers declined, squeezed between the upper millstone of price-reducing competition and the lower of increasingly expensive and mechanized plant, with increasingly large and inelastic overheads, businessmen searched anxiously for a way out. And as they searched, the growing masses of the labouring classes in the industrial economies joined the agrarian population in agitations for improvement and change, as they had done in the corresponding era of British industrialization. The era of the Great Depression was also the era of the emergence of mass socialist (i.e. mainly marxist) working-class parties all over Europe, organized in a marxist International.

In Britain the effect of these global changes was both greater and smaller than elsewhere. The agrarian crises affected this country (but not Ireland) only marginally, and indeed the flood of increasingly cheap imports of food and raw material had its advantages. On the other hand what was elsewhere a mere stumble and change of footing in the progress of industrialization, was much more serious in Britain. In the first instance this was because the British economy had been largely geared to an unbroken expansion abroad, and especially in the USA. The construction of the world network of railways was far from complete in the 1870s; yet the break in the mad construction boom in the early 1870s* had sufficient effect on the British exports of capital in money and goods to make at least one historian explain the Great Depression in the phrase 'What happened when the Railways were Built'.[4] British *rentiers* had got so used to the flow of income back from North America and the undeveloped parts of the world, that the defaults of their foreign debtors in the 1870s − e.g. the collapse of Turkish finance in 1876 − brought the laying up of carriages and the temporary slump of building in places like Bournemouth and Folkestone. (More to the point, it mobilized those militant consortia of foreign bondholders or governments acting for their investors, which were to turn nominally independent governments into virtual or actual protectorates and colonies of the European powers − as in Egypt and Turkey after 1876.)

But the break was not merely temporary. It revealed that other countries were now able to produce for themselves, perhaps even for export, what had hitherto been available in practice only from Britain. And it also revealed that Britain was not ready for all but one of the possible methods of dealing with this situation. Unlike other countries, which now turned to tariffs protecting both their agriculture and their industrial home markets (e.g. France, Germany and the USA), Britain

* Both in the USA and Germany the 1873 crash was largely a crash of railway promotion.

held firmly to free trade. She was equally disinclined to take the path of systematic economic concentration — the formation of trusts, cartels, syndicates, etc. — which was so characteristic of Germany and the USA in the 1880s. She was too deeply committed to the technology and business organization of the first phase of industrialization, which had served her so well, to advance enthusiastically into the field of the new and revolutionary technology and industrial management which came to the fore in the 1890s. This left her with only one major way out — a traditional one for Britain, though one also now adopted by the competing powers — the economic (and increasingly the political) conquest of hitherto unexploited areas of the world. In other words, imperialism.

The era of the Great Depression thus also initiated the era of imperialism; the formal imperialism of the 'partition of Africa' in the 1880s, the semi-formal imperialism of national or international consortia taking over the financial management of weak countries, the informal imperialism of foreign investment. Political historians have professed to find no economic reasons for this virtual division of the world between a handful of west European powers (plus the USA) in the last decades of the nineteenth century. Economic historians have had no such difficulty. Imperialism was not a new thing for Britain. What was new was the end of the virtual British monopoly in the undeveloped world, and the consequent necessity to mark out regions of imperial influence formally against potential competitors; often ahead of any actual prospects of economic benefits, often, it must be admitted, with disappointing economic results.*

One further consequence of the era of the Great Depression, i.e. of the emergence of a *competing group* of industrial and economically advanced powers, must be noted. It is the fusion of political and economical rivalry, the fusion of private enterprise with government backing, which is already visible in the growth of protectionism and imperialist friction. Increasingly business, in one way or another, called on the state not only to give it a free hand, but to save it. A new dimension entered international politics. And, significantly, after a long period of general peace, the great powers moved once again into an age of world wars.

Meanwhile the end of the age of unquestioned expansion, the doubt about the future prospects of the British economy, began a fundamental change in British politics. In 1870 Britain had been

* But even this was not new. British businessmen had great hopes of Latin America in the 1820s, when they hoped to create an informal empire there by the setting up of independent republics. They were, at least initially, disappointed.

Liberal. The bulk of the British bourgeoisie, the bulk of the politically conscious working class, and even the old Whig section of the landed aristocracy, found their political and ideological expression in the party of William Ewart Gladstone, who looked forward to peace, retrenchment and reform, the total abolition of the income tax and national debt. Those who did not had no real alternative programme or perspective. By the middle of the 1890s the great Liberal Party was split, virtually all of its aristocrats and a large section of its capitalists having seceded to the Conservatives or the 'Liberal Unionists' who were to fuse with the Conservatives. The City of London, a Liberal stronghold until 1874, had acquired its Conservative colouring. An independent Labour Party backed by the trade unions and inspired by socialists was about to appear. Already the first cloth-capped proletarian socialist was sitting in the House of Commons. A few years, but a historic era, earlier, a shrewd observer had still (1885) written about the British workers:[5]

> There is less tendency to socialism here than among other nations of the Old World or of the New. The English working man . . . makes none of those extravagant demands upon the protection of the State in the regulation of his daily labour and of the rate of his wages, which are current among the working classes of America and of Germany, and which cause a certain form of socialism to be equally the pest of both countries.

By the end of the Great Depression things had changed.

Notes

1 Quoted in J. H. Clapham, *An Economic History of Modern Britain*, II, p. 41.
2 Quoted in W. Smart, *Econ. Annals of the 19th Century* (1910), I, p. 54.
3 *The Life of Thomas Cooper, Written by Himself* (1872), p. 393.
4 W. W. Rostow, *British Economy in the 19th Century* (1948), p. 88.
5 T. H. S. Escott, *England* (1885 ed.), pp. 135–6.

4   Between the wars

Eric Hobsbawm

The Victorian economy of Britain crashed in ruins between the two world wars. The sun which, as every schoolboy knew, never set on British territory and British trade, went down below the horizon. The collapse of all that Britons had taken for granted since the days of Robert Peel was so sudden, catastrophic and irreversible, that it stunned the incredulous contemporaries. At the very moment when Britain emerged on the victorious side in the first major war since Napoleon, when her chief continental rival Germany was on her knees, when the British Empire, sometimes lightly and unconvincingly disguised as 'mandates', 'protectorates' and satellite Middle Eastern states, covered a greater extent of the world map than ever before, the traditional economy of Britain not only ceased to grow, but contracted. Statistics which had advanced almost without a break for 150 years − not always at equal or satisfactory rates, but still advanced − now retreated. 'Economic decline', something that economists argued about before 1914, now became a palpable fact.

Between 1912 and 1938 the quantity of cotton cloth made in Britain fell from 8,000 million to barely 3,000 million square yards; the amount exported from 7,000 million to less than 1,500 million yards. Never since 1851 had Lancashire exported so little. Between 1854 and 1913 the output of British coal had grown from 65 to 287 million tons. By 1938 it was down to 227 million and still falling. In 1913 twelve million tons of British shipping had sailed the seas, in 1938 there was rather less than eleven million. British shipyards in 1870 built 343,000 tons of vessels for British owners, and in 1913 almost a million tons: in 1938 they built little more than half a million.

In human terms the ruin of the traditional industries of Britain was the ruin of millions of men and women through mass unemployment, and it was this which stamped the years between the wars indelibly with the mark of bitterness and poverty. Industrial areas with a variety of occupations were not wholly devastated. The labour force in cotton

Source: *Industry and Empire*, Penguin Books, 1968, extracts from ch. 11, pp. 207–24.

56

fell by more than half between 1912 and 1938 (from 621,000 to 288,000), but Lancashire had at least some other industries to absorb some of them: its unemployment rate was by no means the worst. The real tragedy was that of areas and towns relying on a single industry, prosperous in 1913, ruined between the wars. In 1913-14 about 3 per cent of the workers in Wales had been unemployed — rather less than the national average. In 1934 — after recovery had begun — 37 per cent of the labour force in Glamorgan, 36 per cent of that in Monmouth, were out of work. Two-thirds of the men of Ferndale, three-quarters of those in Brynmawr, Dowlais and Blaina, 70 per cent of those in Merthyr, had nothing to do except stand at streetcorners and curse the system which put them there. The people of Jarrow, in Durham, lived by Palmers shipyard. When it closed in 1933, Jarrow was derelict, with eight out of every ten of its workers jobless, and having as like as not lost all their savings in the crash of the yard, which had so long been their harsh and noisy universe. It was the concentration of permanent, hopeless unemployment in certain derelict areas, politely renamed 'special areas' by a mealy-mouthed government, which gave the depression its particular character. South Wales, central Scotland, the North-east, parts of Lancashire, parts of Northern Ireland and Cumberland, not to mention smaller enclaves elsewhere, resisted even the modest recovery of the later 1930s. The grimy, roaring, bleak industrial areas of the nineteenth century — in Northern England, Scotland and Wales — had never been very beautiful or comfortable, but they had been active and prosperous. Now all that remained was the grime, the bleakness, and the terrible silence of the factories and mines which did not work, the shipyards which were closed.

At all times between 1921 and 1938 at least one out of every ten citizens of working age was out of a job. In seven out of these eighteen years at least three out of every twenty were unemployed, in the worst years one out of five. In absolute figures unemployment ranged from a minimum of rather over a million to a maximum (1932) of just under three million; at all events, according to the official figures, which for various reasons understated it. In particular industries and regions the record was even blacker. At its peak (1931-2) 34.5 per cent of coalminers, 36.3 per cent of pottery-workers, 43.2 per cent of cotton operatives, 43.8 per cent of pig-iron workers, 47.9 per cent of steelworkers, and 62 per cent — or almost two in three — of shipbuilders and ship-repairers were out of work. Not until 1941 was the back of the problem broken.

The years of slump followed those of world war, and everybody lived in the shadow of these cataclysms. Though their effect varied considerably from one region, industry or social group to another, they had very general consequences. The first was fear: of death or maiming in war, of helplessness and poverty in peace. Such fear does not necessarily correspond to the reality of the danger. In the Second World War the average citizen's chances of death were not in fact very high, and the majority of workers between the wars were not likely to be out of work for very long. Yet even those who knew this, also knew themselves and their relations to be only a hair's breadth from the abyss. Even in peacetime a job lost meant more than a period of uncertainty or poverty. It might mean a family of lives destroyed. This acrid fog of anxiety was the atmosphere which men and women breathed during a generation. Its effect cannot be statistically measured, but equally, it cannot be left out of any account of these years.

It was visibly reflected in the pattern of politics in Britain, which increasingly dominated the life of the citizen through the growing activities of the state. The war and the years of ferment which followed, multiplied the electoral forces of the Labour Party, essentially the class party of the manual workers, over eightfold. Its votes grew from half a million in 1910 to 4½ million in 1922. For the first time in history, a proletarian party became and remained the major alternative government party, and the fear of working-class power and expropriation now haunted the middle classes, not so much because this is what the Labour leaders promised or performed, but because its mere existence as a mass party threw a faint red shadow of potential Soviet revolution across the country. The leaders of the trade unions and the Labour Party were far from revolutionaries. Few of them even trusted themselves in government, which they regarded as essentially, or anyway normally, the function of employers and upper classes, their own being to demand improvements and concessions. But they stood at the head of a vast movement united by the consciousness of class separation and exploitation, and capable of showing its force in such unparalleled acts of solidarity as the General Strike of 1926. Theirs was a movement which had lost confidence in the capacity, perhaps even in the willingness, of capitalism to give labour its modest rights, while at the same time it observed abroad — and perhaps somewhat idealized — the first, and at that time the only, working-class state and socialist economy, Soviet Russia.

The depression produced a further swing to Labour, though the later phase of it was delayed by a temporary stampede of frightened and disoriented citizens to the so-called 'National' government under the impact of the crisis of 1931. The Second World War ended with the first effective Labour government of Britain, and by 1951 the party polled more votes than it had ever done in history. In the prosperous fifties it ceased to advance.

Only one part of the Victorian economy seemed briefly to resist collapse: the City of London, source of the world's capital, nerve-centre of its international trading and financial transactions. Britain was no longer the greatest international lender; indeed, she was now on balance in debt to the USA, which had taken her former place. However, by the middle of the 1920s, British overseas investments earned more than ever before and so, even more strikingly, did her other sources of invisible income — financial and insurance services etc. But the interwar crisis was not merely a British phenomenon, the decline of a former industrial world champion, all the more sudden and sharp for having been delayed for decades. It was the crisis of the entire liberal world of the nineteenth century, and therefore British trade and finance could no longer regain what British industry lost. For the first time since industrialization began the growth of production in *all* the industrial powers faltered. The First World War reduced it by 20 per cent (1913-21), and hardly had it resumed its rise to new heights, when the slump of 1929-32 reduced it temporarily by about a third (largely due to the simultaneous collapse of all the major industrial powers except Japan and the USSR). What is more to the point, the three great international flows of capital, labour and goods, on which the liberal world economy was based, dried up. World trade in manufactured goods only just regained its 1913 level in 1929 and then plummeted by a third. It had not quite recovered by 1939; its value halved in the 1929 slump. World trade in primary products, which was so vital for Britain which sold largely to their producers, fell by considerably more than half after 1929. Though the primary producers desperately sold increased quantities at knock-down prices, they were in 1936-8 unable to buy more than two-thirds of what they had been able to buy in 1913, or much more than a third of what had been within their reach in 1926-9. A network of walls rose along the world's frontiers to prevent the free entry of men and goods and the exit of gold. Britain, the international junction of a flourishing traffic-system, saw the traffic on which she depended disappear, while her investment income from the depressed industrial and the even more hard-hit primary producers fell. Between 1929 and 1932 her foreign dividends fell from £250 to £150 million, her other invisible earnings from £233 million to £86 million. Neither had recovered by the time the Second World War broke out, to reduce her foreign holdings by over a third. When in 1932 Free Trade was finally buried, the Victorian economy went with it. It was only just that the Liberal Party, which had been essentially the party of the liberal world economy, should have finally lost its political prospects with its traditional *raison d'être* in 1931.

Those responsible for the economy were shocked, numbed and

profoundly puzzled by this collapse of all they had taken for granted. The failure of businessmen, politicians and economists to recognize the facts, let alone to know what to do about them, was overwhelming. We are now aware of the unorthodox minority which anticipated the thinking of our own generation, the marxists who actually predicted the great slump and gained prestige both from their prediction and from the immunity of the USSR to it, or J. M. Keynes whose critique of the prevailing economic orthodoxy has in turn become the orthodoxy of a later era. We tend to forget how small and uninfluential a minority they were, until after the economic catastrophe had become so overwhelming — in 1932-3 — as to seem to threaten the very existence of the British, and the world, capitalist system. The businessmen of the 1920s went into it with little more than the conviction that if wages and government spending could be cut savagely enough, British industry would once again be all right, and with indiscriminate calls for protection from the economic hurricane. The politicians — both Conservative and Labour — went into it with little more than the almost equally futile slogans of Richard Cobden or Joseph Chamberlain. The bankers and the officials who were the guardians of 'Treasury orthodoxy' dreamed of a return to the liberal world of 1913, put their confidence in balanced budgets* and the Bank Rate and staked all on the impossible hope of maintaining the City of London as the world's financial centre. The economists, with what can only be described as a quiet heroism worthy of Don Quixote, nailed their flag to the mast of Say's Law which proved that slumps could not actually occur at all. Never did a ship founder with a captain and crew more ignorant of the reasons for its misfortune or more impotent to do anything about it.

Nevertheless, when we compare the interwar depression with the period before 1914, we are inclined to judge it a little less severely. It is hard to find anything positive to say about the Indian summer of the Edwardians, that season of almost deliberately missed opportunities which made certain that the decline of the British economy would be a catastrophe. It had not even achieved that most modest of objectives, the stability of the standard of living of the poor, though it had made the rich a great deal richer. On the other hand — perhaps just because economic catastrophe left very much less scope for complacency — the interwar years were not entirely wasted. By 1939 Britain looked a great deal more like a twentieth-century economy than she had done — in comparison with other industrial states — in 1913. [...] The importance of scientific technology, of mass-production methods, of

* Thus almost certainly making the slump worse by cutting government spending when it would have done most good.

industry producing for the mass market, but above all of economic concentration, 'monopoly capitalism' and state intervention, was very much greater. The interwar years neither modernized the British economy nor made it internationally competitive. It remains old-fashioned and undynamic to this day. But at least certain foundations for modernization were laid, or rather certain major obstacles to it removed.

The reason why the interwar catastrophe had not more fundamental consequences is threefold: the pressure on the economy was not desperate enough, the most efficient — and indeed indispensable — method of modernization, state planning, was used very sparingly, for political reasons, and virtually all economic changes initiated in this period were defensive and negative.

The pressure on the economy was inadequate, partly because the peculiar international position of Britain somewhat blunted the impact of the sharpest spur to action, the great slump of 1929-33. Since the traditional basic industries of Britain were already depressed after 1921, the effect of the slump was less dramatic: those who are already low do not fall so far.* Moreover, while the export industries were battered, the rest of the economy benefited abnormally from the disproportionate fall in the cost of primary products — food and raw material — from the colonial and semi-colonial world. Again, because the Victorian economy had relied so very little on production for the domestic mass market, the scope for a shift into home sales was considerably greater. Britain was in crisis, but she was not faced in the starkest and least avoidable form with the alternative: compete or die.

Second, the state refrained from adequate intervention. Its capacity to intervene effectively was demonstrated in both world wars, but especially the second. When it did, its achievements were sometimes little short of sensational, as in British agriculture, which it transformed between 1940 and 1945. The necessity for its intervention was evident, for several of the basic industries — notably railways and coal-mines — were so run down as to be quite beyond the scope of private restoration, and several others were clearly not capable of rationalizing themselves. Yet after both wars the apparatus of state control was dismantled with nervous speed, and the State's reluctance to interfere with private enterprise remained profound. Its interventions, like the gestures of industry itself in the direction of modernization, were essentially protective in a negative sense.

* For instance, manufacturing production (1913 = 100) in the USA fell from 112.7 in 1929 to 58.4 in 1932, in Germany from 108 to 64.6; but in Britain merely from 109.9 to 90.

This is particularly obvious in the field of economic concentration, for in 1914 Britain was perhaps the least concentrated of the great industrial economies, and in 1939 one of the most. There was of course nothing new about economic concentration. The growth in the scale of productive units and units of ownership, the concentration of a growing share of output, employment, etc., in the hands of a declining number of giant firms, the formal or informal restriction of competition which may reach the point of monopoly or oligopoly: all these are among the best-known tendencies of capitalism. Concentration first became noticeable during the Great Depression — in the 1880s and 1890s — but until 1914 its impact in Britain was strikingly smaller than in Germany and the USA. In its industrial structure Britain was wedded to the small or medium-sized, highly specialized, family-operated and family-financed, and competitive firm, just as in its economic policy it was wedded to Free Trade. There were exceptions, notably in the public utilities and heavy industries (iron and steel, heavy engineering, shipbuilding) which had long required higher initial capital investments than could be raised by individuals and partnerships and, where concentration was fostered by the needs of war. But broadly speaking, the small and disintegrated industry in the open market prevailed, and as it continued to be prosperous, and generally lacked government protection or aid, there was no great reason for it to decline. The average size of plant increased. The public joint-stock company, which hardly existed outside banking and transport before the last quarter of the century, entered industry and multiplied after 1880, and this further increased the size of firms. There were already in 1914 some outstanding examples of great capitalist combinations, and a few which had reached the point of monopoly. The tendency to concentration undoubtedly existed, but it had certainly not transformed the economy.

However, between 1914 and 1939 it did so, accelerated partly by the First World War, partly by the depression (and especially, after 1930, the great slump), and almost invariably fostered by a benevolent government. Unfortunately, it cannot be easily measured, for the statisticians, like the academic economists, did not seriously investigate its quantitative importance or its theoretical implications until after 1930.* Yet there can be no doubt about the broad facts.

Before 1914 there were already a few monopolist products: sewing cotton, Portland cement, wallpaper, flat glass and some others; but in 1935 at an absolute minimum upwards of 170 products were produced substantially by one, two or three firms. In 1914 there had been 130 railway companies; after 1921 there were four giant non-competing

* This is itself a symptom of its growing importance.

monopolies. In 1914 there had been thirty-eight joint-stock banks; in 1924 there were twelve, of whom the 'Big Five' (Midland, National Provincial, Lloyds, Barclays, Westminster) completely dominated the field. In 1914 there had been perhaps fifty trade associations, mainly in iron and steel. By 1925 the Federation of British Industries (founded, like the National Association of Manufacturers in the last years of the war) alone had 250 such associations affiliated to it;* after the Second World War there were perhaps a thousand. In 1907 an expert enquirer could still write: 'Great as is the extent to which industry has passed into the hands of large combinations, greater still is the domain still subject to the individual trader.'[1] By 1939, an expert observer had to note that 'As a feature of industrial and commercial organization free competition has nearly disappeared from the British scene.'[2]

In terms of employment, economic concentration was fairly marked by the middle 1930s. Broadly speaking, there were then in Britain only 519 plants employing more than a thousand workers, out of a total of a little over 140,000 'factories', of which all but some 30,000 were very small establishments of less than twenty-five workers. Yet these few plants then employed about one in five of all workers covered by the Census of Production and in several industries (electrical machinery, motor and cycle manufacture, iron and steel rolling and smelting, silk and artificial silk, newspaper production, shipbuilding, sugar and confectionery) more than 40 per cent. In other words, one-third of one per cent of all factories employed 21.5 per cent of all workers. But since increasingly a single firm owned several plants in the same industry – not to mention in other industries – the actual concentration of employment was even higher. There were thirty-three trades in Britain in which the three largest firms employed seventy per cent or more of all workers.

We cannot compare this precisely with the situation before 1914, but we have some guide in the structure of typical old-fashioned industries which, as one might expect, were less affected than the technologically new ones characteristic of the twentieth century. In 1914 the average coalmine – an unusually large undertaking by contemporary standards – employed some three hundred men; and as late as 1930 the typical cotton-weaving firm was one which employed one to three hundred workers, and almost 40 per cent worked in plants of less than two hundred. In the 'average' British industry in 1935, a little more than a quarter of workers were employed by the

* Out of a sample of a hundred trade associations existing during the Second World War twenty-six had been formed before 1914, thirty-three in 1915–20 and thirty-seven between the wars.

top three firms. In the most highly concentrated industries (chemicals, engineering and vehicles, iron and steel) 40 per cent or more were employed by the top three; in the least concentrated — mines, building, timber — 10 per cent or less. It is fairly certain that before 1914 most of British industry was much more like the last than either of the two others.

But the most striking change was not so much the conversion of Britain into a country of giant corporations, oligopolies, trade associations, etc., but the positive approval of business and government for a change which would have horrified J. S. Mill. It is true that opposition to economic concentration had always been much weaker in practice than in theory. Britain possessed no powerful movement of radical-democratic 'little men' such as that which time and again imposed the (quite ineffective) anti-trust legislation on the USA; and the socialists, though hostile in theory to concentration, were opposed to it because it served private ends rather than at all costs. (In practice, the labour movement was not opposed to it at all.) Nevertheless, the belief in competitive capitalism was almost as firm and dogmatic as that in Free Trade. But what we see between the wars is the systematic effort of governments to *reduce* competition, to foster giant cartels, mergers, combinations and monopolies. The iron and steel industry had been riddled with price-fixing arrangements even before 1914; but it was not, as it became after 1932, a giant restrictionist cartel in open partnership (through the Import Duties Advisory Committee) with the government. The belief in free competition died quickly and painlessly before the belief in Free Trade.

Now economic concentration is not in itself undesirable. Often it is essential, especially in the extreme form of nationalization, to ensure adequate industrial progress. The belief that 'monopoly capitalism' is *ipso facto* less dynamic or technologically progressive than unrestricted competitive enterprise is a myth. Yet the economic concentration which took place between the wars cannot be primarily justified on grounds of efficiency and progress. It was overwhelmingly restrictive, defensive, and protective. It was a blind response to depression, which aimed at maintaining profits high by eliminating competition, or at accumulating great clusters of miscellaneous capital which were in no sense productively more rational than their original independent components, but which provided financiers with investments for surplus capital or with the profits of company promotion. Britain became a non-competing country at home as well as abroad.

In a sense, the strong domestic orientation of British business in this period was also a defensive response to the economy's crisis. Industries like iron and steel frankly fled from the bleak international scene into the protected home market,* though such flights could not save the old, export-oriented industries like cotton from disaster. The government after 1931 systematically protected the home market, and certain industries – notably motor manufacturing – rested entirely on the protection, which in this instance had existed since the First World War. However, it was not mere escapism which made British business turn inwards. It was to a great extent the discovery that the mass consumption of the British working class held unsuspected sales opportunities. The contrast between those branches of the economy which had always looked outwards and those which flourished because they had not, was bound to strike the most superficial observer.

The most startling example of expansion during this depression period was retail distribution. The number of tobacconist shops rose by almost two-thirds between 1911 and 1939, the number of confectionery outlets multiplied two and a half times (1913-38), the number of shops selling medical preparations multiplied more than three times; and shops selling furniture, electrical goods, hardware, etc., grew even faster. And this, while the small shopkeeper lost ground and the larger enterprises – cooperative, department store, but above all the multiple shop – gained ground rapidly. The discovery of the mass market was not new. Certain industries and industrial areas – notably the Midlands – had always concentrated on the domestic consumer, and had done well by this policy. What was new, was the visible contrast between the flourishing home market industries and the despairing exporters, symbolized in the contrast between an expanding Midlands and South-east, and a depressed North and West. In a broad belt stretching between the Birmingham and London regions, industry grew: the new motor manufacture was virtually confined to this zone. The new consumer-goods factories multiplied along the Great West Road out of London, while emigrants from Wales and the North moved to Coventry and Slough. Industrially, Britain was turning into two nations.

The turn to the home market had some connections with the striking expansion of technologically new industries, organized in a new way (mass production). Though some of the 'new' interwar industries had good export sales, fundamentally – and unlike the nineteenth-century staples – they relied on domestic demand, and indeed often on natural or government protection from outside competition. Several – and normally those which relied on a more complex and scientific technology

* Output and domestic consumption of steel (annual average, million tons)

	1910-14	1927-31	1935-8
Output	7.0	7.9	11.3
Domestic consumption	5.0	7.6	10.6

— relied even more directly on government support or backing. The aircraft industry would not have existed otherwise, and the entire buoyant complex of electrical industries benefited more than is measurable from the government monopoly of the wholesaling of power and the construction of the national 'Grid' — a system of power distribution unparalleled at this time anywhere else.

The other side of this picture was, of course, a distinct, and in spite of some patchiness very widespread, improvement in the standard of living of the working classes, which benefited both by the cheapening and widening of the range of goods available, and by their more efficient salesmanship. By 1914 only the food market had been seriously transformed in this manner. The rise of the mass market was somewhat delayed after 1914 both by the effect of the two wars (the first rather more than the efficiently and equitably administered second)* and by the insistence of government and employers that the solution to depression lay in cutting wages and social security payments. Nevertheless, and even allowing for mass unemployment, there was probably some overall improvement. The least sanguine estimates, which spread the losses of unemployment (somewhat unrealistically) over the whole population, still suggest a modest average rise of 5 per cent in real wages, and the more rosy ones (which do not allow for unemployment) of anything up to 40 per cent, though this is very implausible. And there is little doubt that between the wars the new mass production economy really triumphed.

It is true that the mass goods which now came on the market or were decisively cheapened were not yet the expensive 'consumer durables' which few could afford, except perhaps for the bicycle. While by 1939 the USA already provided 150 new refrigerators per year for every 10,000 of its population and Canada 50, Britain in 1935 got only 8. Even the middle class had only begun to buy motor-cars at the modest rate of four per 1,000 consumers (1938). Vacuum cleaners and electric irons were perhaps the only pieces of domestic machinery, apart from the already ubiquitous radio set, which were bought in quantity by the end of the 1930s. The new goods which made the greatest impact were cheap articles of domestic and personal use, of the kind sold in the rapidly multiplying variety of stores of the 'Woolworth' type, the expanding and diversifying 'chemists' (the number of Boots stores rose from 200 in 1900 to 1,180 in 1938) and similar emporia. Cheap cosmetics, for instance, came into use in this

* For instance, food consumption fell by about 10 per cent between 1939 and 1941. Thereafter, thanks to efficient planning, it actually increased a little. In the First World War, food expenditure dropped continuously.

period, and so did fountain pens. Both, incidentally, belonged to the short list of most heavily advertised commodities, with cigarettes, drinks and manufactured foods. For advertising also came of age between the wars and with it the modern national multi-million circulating press, which depended on it.

In one field, however, technological revolution already created an entirely new dimension of life between the wars. In addition to the traditional and declining music-hall and the equally old-fashioned but expanding 'palais-de-danse', two technologically original forms of entertainment triumphed after 1918: radio and cinema. Of these the first was more revolutionary than the second for it brought round-the-clock entertainment ready-made into people's actual homes for the first time in history, though this was not the primary purpose of the uncommercially-minded public corporation which controlled it, the BBC. The cinema took the place of both gin-palace and music-hall as the poor man's dream substitute for luxury. The gigantic and baroque Granadas, Trocaderos and Odeons, their names hinting at exotic languor and luxury hotels, their cushioned seats opening vistas of million-dollar spectacles and huge organs rising to blow out heavy sentiment amid changing coloured lights, rose in the working-class districts with the rate of unemployment. They were probably the most effective dream-producers ever devised, for a visit to them not only cost less and lasted longer than a drink or variety show, but could be —and was — more readily combined with the cheapest of all enjoyments, sex.

The rise in the standard of living remained modest and limited. Much of it was due (at least for those in employment) to the fortunate fact that years of slump also tended to be years of falling costs of living. One pound in 1933 bought four shillings more than it had in 1924, and a man earning £3 a week — the average of employed male workers in 1924 — was still about five shillings better off in 1938.* The improvements which came with full employment in the 1940s and with prosperity in the 1950s would not have seemed so remarkable, if those of the inter-war years had not been so unimpressive. Nevertheless, the paradox that depression, mass unemployment and — at least for very many members of the working class — a rising standard of life went together, reflects the changes in the British economy between the wars.

For a country with Britain's international position, the turn to the internal market was not to be welcomed without qualification. After the Second World War, when governments attempted to encourage the new industries to export, their now established preference for the much easier domestic market was only too obvious. More serious,

* In other words, some of the burden of depression in Britain was transferred to the primary-exporting underdeveloped countries.

even the new British industries remained less technologically dynamic than the best of the foreign ones, and where new innovations came from Britain — as they often did — British industry often proved incapable of developing them commercially, or unwilling to do so. In the pure sciences, Britain's position was eminent, and became even more distinguished after 1933 with the exodus of Germany's best scientific brains; though it depended dangerously on a very small number of men in one or two universities. Britain's place in the development of nuclear physics, of the theory of computers, and in industrially as yet less important branches of science like biochemistry and physiology, was assured. But it is fair to say that between the wars few looked to Britain for the development of new techniques (except in the state-sponsored field of armaments — e.g. radar and the jet engine) and even fewer for a model of what modern industry should be like. Among the very few typical products of our century which were actually developed practically in Britain was television, which was first broadcast here in 1936; but even this — characteristically — owed its advance not merely to a go-ahead private firm (Electric and Musical Industries), but to the dynamism of the state-owned BBC. It is perhaps significant that Britain remained far ahead of all countries except the USA in its use of television; a rare situation.*

To some extent this sluggishness was due to the failure of British business to undertake the systematic and expensive research and development which was increasingly essential for the advance of industries based on scientific technology. The Balfour Committee on Industry and Trade in 1927 bitterly contrasted the 'slow progress made in respect of scientific research generally' with the record of German and American industry.[3] This failure was not so much one of research — for even in the USA, as in Britain, the really major expansion in this field occurred during and after the Second World War under government auspices, and mainly for military purposes — as in 'development', i.e. in the expensive nursing of discovery or invention towards commercial practicability. Few inventions could be *developed* except by some giant: the Calico Printers Association's researchers, who happened on a most valuable artificial fibre (terylene) simply passed it on to Imperial Chemicals in Britain, Dupont in the USA. But the British giants were on the whole less interested in innovation than their opposite numbers abroad.

Nevertheless, when all reservations have been made, the record of British industry between the wars was not unimpressive. The output of *all* British manufacturing industry (including, that is, the declining

* In 1950, Britain had almost 600,000 sets and the rest of Europe none. Even in 1960 well over half all European TV sets were in Britain.

ones) grew considerably faster between 1924 and 1935 than between 1907 and 1924; and this at a time of depression and mass unemployment. Total industrial output per head may have just about doubled between 1850 and 1913, or a little more. It hardly changed between 1913 and 1924. But from then until 1937 it rose by about one-third, i.e. considerably faster than in the heyday of the Victorians. Naturally, this was achieved mainly by the new growth industries. The output of electric goods almost doubled between 1924 and 1935, that of motor-cars more than doubled, as did the supply of electricity. The output of aircraft and silk and rayon (mainly the latter) multiplied five times over in the same brief period. In 1907 the 'growth industries' had produced a mere 6.5 per cent of total output, in 1935 they produced almost one-fifth.

At the outbreak of the Second World War Britain was therefore a very different country economically from 1914. It was a country in which there were fewer agriculturalists but many more government employees; fewer miners but very many more road transport workers; fewer industrial workers but many more shop assistants and office workers; fewer domestic servants but many more entertainers; and within manufacturing industry, fewer textile workers but more in metals and electricity. It was a country with a different industrial geography. Even in 1924 the traditional industrial regions (Lancashire and Cheshire, West Yorkshire, the North-east, South Wales, Central Scotland) had produced half the total net output of industry. In 1935 they only produced 37.6 per cent, barely more than the new industrial regions which had grown rapidly since then: Greater London and the Midlands. And this was natural: South Wales had, even in 1937, 41 per cent of its workers in the declining industries, but the Midlands only 7 per cent; the North-east 35 per cent but London only 1 per cent.

It was a country of two divergent sectors of the economy, the falling and the rising, linked only by three factors: the great accumulations of capital which grasped both, the increasing intervention of government, which spread over both, and the archaism, born of Britain's unusually successful 'fit' into the pattern of nineteenth-century world liberal capitalism, which surrounded both. The liberal world economy was dead by 1939. It died – if we can assign its death a precise date – in 1929–33, and has never revived since. But if its ghost stalked any country, it was Britain which had learned the job of workshop to the world, of its trader, shipper, and financial centre, but did not quite know what to do now that this occupation became redundant. We still do not quite know what to do. But whatever it was, it implied a change in the functions of government, which the nineteenth century would have regarded as inconceivable.

Notes

1 H. W. Macrosty, *The Trust Movement in British Industry* (1907), p. 330.
2 Quoted in S. Pollard, *Development of the British Economy, 1914–50* (1962), p. 168.
3 Committee on Industry and Trade, *Factors in Industrial and Commercial Efficiency* (1927), pp. 38–9.

5 Industrial structure and economies of scale

Peter Donaldson

It is frequently said of the British economy that it lacks the flexibility which is so necessary in a world of rapidly changing techniques and tastes. But although it may have done so insufficiently, the degree to which the economy *has* altered and adapted itself to new conditions during the last few decades is none the less remarkable. By the outbreak of the First World War, British industry had certainly settled into a fossilized pattern from which adjustment was only painfully begun during the inter-war period; the extent to which the process has been completed under the stimulus of the Second World War, technological developments, and growing world trade can be seen if we compare the present pattern of industrial output with that of the pre-1914 period.

It was during this earlier period that Britain enjoyed the fruits of a head-start in the Industrial Revolution. About a third of world industrial exports then came from this country, of which some 70% were coal, iron and steel, or textile products. The prosperity of the economy rested heavily on these three great staple industries, which employed a quarter of the labour force and produced nearly half of British industrial output.

However, being first in the field has its disadvantages, not least of which is the danger of complacency at past progress and a consequent lack of interest in continued innovation. As other nations industrialized, they not only initially concentrated on producing, generally by more up-to-date methods, the basic products with which Britain had previously supplied them; they leapt ahead in the production of new products by new techniques which, although sometimes invented in the UK, had been largely neglected there. The extent to which the world had passed Britain by was revealed in the dreadful decline of the staple industries in the inter-war period.

Today, employment, out of a much expanded labour force, has fallen substantially in the case of coal-mining and drastically in the textile industry. The other old staple, iron and steel, although relatively less

Source: *Guide to the British Economy*, 4th ed., Penguin Books, 1976, pp. 81–90.

important, has recovered under the stimulus of demand from the new industries which have since developed. Nearly a quarter of manufacturing workers are now employed in engineering, electrical goods, and ship-building industries, with their highly variegated output of products which fifty years ago were largely unheard of. A further 10% find employment in the production of vehicles, which, in their greater homogeneity, have the only real claim to being a new staple industry. However, simple comparison of the industrial pattern now with that of earlier periods is hampered by the breakdown of traditional classification of 'industries', which has resulted from the far-reaching technological changes of the past few decades. The developments of petro-chemical products, synthetic fibres, and plastics have all served to blur previous lines of demarcation.

Parallel with these changes in the occupational and output pattern of industry has been a reversal of its earlier geographical distribution. Location was originally heavily concentrated on the coalfields, and it was the development of a new source of energy, electricity, which first released industries to locations closer to the final consumer markets — in particular the London and south-eastern areas. The ties to particular locations have since been loosened further by the immense expansion in the use of oil since 1938, the post-war development of nuclear energy, and the increased use of man-manufactured 'raw materials'.

Structure of industry

Industrial concentration

The majority of British manufacturing establishments still operate on a relatively small scale, employing few more workers than Mr William Lever's Bolton grocery business in the 1880s. But far more significant today are the Unilevers which have developed from such humble origins. Concentration of industrial power has been an outstanding feature of the British economy during the present century. Sometimes it takes the form of a simple union of enterprises producing the same product, who emerge with a single identity. Frequently, however, it is thought prudent to allow old identities to continue in order to retain traditional loyalties of customers and within the firms themselves. It is difficult to remember, as Omo and Surf flash their competing signals across the television screen, that they are both made by the same firm — together, among others, with Sunlight, Lux, Lifebuoy, Vim, Rinso, Pears, Vinolia, Knight's Castile, Persil, Domestos, Sqezy, Stork, Echo, Summer County, Blue Band, Spry, Gibbs, Signal, Pepsodent, Mentasol,

Erasmic, Pin-up, Twink, Icilma, Sunsilk, Atkinson's English Lavender, Walls, Batchelors, Birds-Eye, and Macfisheries products.

A great deal of industrial concentration took place even before the First World War, with a further spurt in face of the intensive foreign competition in the depressed inter-war years. In a classic survey based on the 1935 Census of Production, two investigators, Leak and Maizels, tried to measure the degree of concentration in certain 'trade groups' by calculating the percentage of the total workers occupied in each group who were employed in the three largest business units. The average degree of concentration was 26%. However, we have to treat the conclusions of this and other similar inquiries with a certain amount of caution. If the largest firms in an industry are highly automated, the use of only labour as a yardstick of importance may be very misleading.

Table 5.1 Percentage of total workers occupied in fifteen trade groups employed by the three largest business units

Chemicals	48	Textiles	23
Miscellaneous	47	Paper and printing	22
Public utilities	44	Clay and building materials	22
Engineering and vehicles	43	Leather	15
Iron and steel	39	Clothing	13
Food, drink, and tobacco	32	Mining and quarrying	10
Non-ferrous metals	26	Timber	10
		Building	4

The firm's assets or turnover as a guide to size might give quite different results. Then again, there are difficulties in the definition of 'business unit'. The Leak and Maizels survey almost certainly underestimated the real degree of concentration by not taking into account the significance of minority shareholdings or interlocking directorships.

Looking at individual industries or broader trade groups in this way ignores the fact that many enterprises extend their activities across such boundaries. A marked feature of recent decades has been the development, under the stimulus partly of the petro-chemical and other technological advances, and also of the search for security, of multi-product or joint enterprise firms cutting across the traditional industry demarcations. The example of Unilever has already been quoted. Another is Monsanto Chemicals producing specialist chemical products for the following industries — adhesives, agriculture, aircraft, dental goods, disinfectants, dyestuffs, electrical engineering, food, glass, iron, leather, motors, packaging, paint, paper, perfumery and cosmetics, petrol, pharmaceuticals, plastics, printing and ink, rubber, soaps, textiles, and timber. Joint enterprises, on the other hand, arise where firms from different industries combine resources to exploit new products or processes, e.g. I.C.I. and Courtaulds in the development of nylon (British Nylon Spinners).

In the decade after the war, the process of integration was for the most part quietly unspectacular, only spasmodically exciting public attention as the giants performed their cannibalistic take-over rites. However, during the early sixties a dramatic acceleration took place with annual take-over expenditure averaging £300 million a year – ten times the average for the fifties. By 1967, the figure had risen to above £800 million. This was again *doubled* in 1968 and by 1972 reached a new peak of over £2,500 million. A.E.I. and G.E.C.; B.M.C. and Leyland; Tesco and Victor Value; Radio Rentals and Thorn; Boots and Timothy Whites; Schweppes and Cadbury; Imperial Tobacco and Courage; Unilever and Allied Breweries, are just a few examples of giant enterprises which have become even more mammoth in recent years.

The rate of industrial concentration has undoubtedly increased as a result of this massive transfer of assets. (During 1967-8 alone, some 10% of private industrial assets changed hands.) It is not possible unfortunately, because the presentation of data in successive Censuses of Production has differed, to make a direct comparison with the 1935 position. However, the evidence* suggests an increase in the pace of concentration to the point where, in 1968, the fifty largest firms accounted for no less than 42% of the net output of the economy and 37.8% of employment. And in March 1974, the ten biggest of all, measured by their stock market valuation, were:

		(£m.)
1	British Petroleum	2,011
2	Shell Transport and Trading	1,188
3	I.C.I.	963
4	Burmah Oil	652
5	British American Tobacco	644
6	General Electric	555
7	Unilever	506
8	Rio Tinto-Zinc	470
9	Marks and Spencer	444
10	Barclays Bank	434

* S. Aaronovitch and M. C. Sawyer, 'The Concentration of British Manufacturing', *Lloyds Bank Review*, October 1974.

Economies of large-scale production

In much of this chapter we will be discussing the need for and the difficulties in controlling these concentrations of economic power. At the same time it must be stressed that a major motive behind the process of industrial integration has been the quest for increased efficiency. In many lines of production, the large manufacturing unit enjoys enormous advantages over its smaller competitors which enable it to achieve substantial reductions in costs of production.

Many of these economies arise from the sheer technological superiority of the large firms. This is most obvious when a very high level of output is necessary for the most efficient machines to be used at all, e.g. the automatic loom in the cotton industry which for really economic working requires continuous shiftwork. However, even if the best machines can be produced in either large or small versions, the small firm, while able to enjoy the same quality of input as its larger rival, may find that the cost of producing and maintaining the smaller version is proportionately higher. A ten-ton lorry, for example, both costs relatively less than a five-tonner and requires only the same number of men to operate it. Again, only the large firm may have sufficient demand for its product to be able to afford to *combine* its inputs optimally. Consider, for example, a new entrant to an industry who estimates that his daily sales will be 500 units of a product which is produced by performing three successive manufacturing processes — X, Y, and Z. From the manufacturers, he learns that the best machines available for these three processes have the following capacity:

in process X   300 units per day
in process Y   400 units per day
in process Z   500 units per day

His estimated demand of 500 per day is large enough for him to put in the most efficient machines. But it falls below the level at which he could use them in the most efficient *combination*. Manufacturing 500 units per day, the two machines necessary for the X and Y processes would have surplus capacity of 100 and 300 units per day respectively. Only machine Z would be fully employed. It is not difficult to see that the minimum output which would allow him to work at full capacity would be 6,000 units per day, employing twenty machines in process X, fifteen in Y, and twelve in Z.

So far we have considered large-firm superiority in static terms. In a context of rapid technological progress, of quickly changing consumer preferences, and restriction of many other forms of competition, further benefits accrue to the firms which can successfully undertake research and development of new products and processes. Once again, God seems to favour the big battalions. It may be that the small firm devotes the same proportion of its resources to research activities as its larger rival. But research being primarily a hit-or-miss affair, what tends to count more is the *absolute* level of expenditure. The large firm will enjoy a similar advantage at the stage of translating research into commercial terms. Operating pilot schemes to test commercial viability may be a very expensive business indeed.

The large firm is also likely to be more efficient in its deployment of labour. Adam Smith's famous dictum that 'the division of labour is limited by the extent of the market' sums the position up nicely. The opportunities for labour, on the factory floor or in the board-room, to increase in efficiency through specialization, are clearly enhanced in a firm producing for a mass market. The use of labour in occupations best suited to individual talents, increased dexterity arising from repetition of the same task, saving in time and tools involved in moving from one job to another – these simple and obvious economies are exemplified on the factory floor by the assembly line fitter and also have their counterpart in the board-room.

The application of these superior techniques may be made possible by either integrating or disintegrating the process of manufacture. Sometimes, economies depend on *bringing together* different processes within the same plant, so that substantial savings can be made, for example, in transport and fuel costs. In other lines of production, increased efficiency may chiefly arise from a *separation* of the individual processes to enable specialist plants to deploy standardized, mass-production techniques.

The business of manufacturing industry consists of more than transforming raw materials into final products. The materials have to be purchased, the customers wooed, and the products sold, and capital must be found to make it all possible. In all these commercial activities the large firm enjoys further advantages, and for similar reasons to those already discussed. National Press or television advertising, market research and extensive after-sales service, the raising of capital on the stock exchange – are all examples of facilities which, because they are in some sense indivisible, are not economic for the small firm. And even when the same quality of inputs are available to large and small alike, the big firm may still find that the cost of using them may be relatively less. A million-pound issue on the stock market does not cost twice as much to float as an issue of £500,000; nor need a salesman necessarily take twice as long to take an order twice as large. Moreover, its size may enable a large firm to cut out many of the extra costs involved in passing a product through a number of middlemen; concentration of the whole business of manufacture within a single enterprise may reduce both the level of stocks of semi-finished goods which is required and uncertainty about what that level should be; when manufacturers are large enough to do their own selling, either direct to the public or through their own chain of retail outlets, they can minimize commercial risks by being closely in touch with consumer requirements.

We can conclude, then, that large firms are very frequently able to make considerable economies in production costs. However, these economies of scale do not exist to the same degree in all industries. In some lines of production, the advantages lie more with the smaller units. The benefits of mass production arise primarily from standardization of the product, and, where flexibility, personal service, and a variety of lines is demanded, it may be the small firm which is most suited. Indeed, the very existence of large firms creates the need for smaller enterprises to meet the demand for deviations from their standardized output.

Prices, profits and diseconomies of scale

The argument so far is just that large firms can often cut their average *costs*. For this to be of social as well as private benefit depends on whether the economies are passed on to consumers in the form of lower *prices*. However, firms do not grow only in order to become more efficient; size also gives greater control over the market. Thus, from the point of view of maximizing profits, the output produced by a monopolist may be below that which would be produced by a number of competing producers; a degree of monopolistic control may enable a firm to restrict output and reap exceptional profits — always providing that new entrants to the industry can be kept out. Control over raw materials, or tied markets, the setting up of special 'fighting companies' to eliminate new entrants, and size in itself are among the ways in which potential competition can be stifled. But the fact that the 'new entrant' may not be some puny, inexperienced newcomer, but another industrial giant anxious to extend its empire, or even the State itself, sometimes checks exploitation. So also does ignorance of the precise level of profits which would induce such a response.

The two impulses to integration which we have so far mentioned — the possibilities of reducing costs and increasing prices — both involve the not unreasonable assumption that the firm is interested in making profits. We would beware, however, of generalizing this into the quite different assumption that *entrepreneurs* are concerned *only* with the *maximization* of profits. With site values at present levels, a sole preoccupation with maximizing profits would probably mean that a large number of the smaller firms now operating in the London area would sell out at once. Their directors or proprietors could live happily ever after in Cannes were it not for the fact that in addition to making *some* profits, they also enjoy being businessmen. Similarly, it would be wrong to conclude that large-scale enterprises have developed only because integration was dictated by profit maximization. Security of profits, or the wish for a relatively quiet life, also enter into the picture. But perhaps most significant, with the separation of nominal ownership of the firm from the actual control of its operation by what are often self-perpetuating and internally impregnable Boards, is the possibility that growth of the firm may come to be regarded as an end in itself.

This is not, of course, to argue that firms ignore the effects on profits when deciding whether to expand; however, other considerations may also be thought important and lead to growth of firms which increases total profits but does not *maximize* them. We have shown that integration *can* bring about substantial economies, but it is not true to say that it always does so. First, there are limits to the reductions in costs which can be achieved by increased size. After a certain stage, which will differ from industry to industry, the firm becomes unwieldy and 'diseconomies' may begin to become significant. As the firm becomes bigger so also do the problems of running it effectively. The process of decision-taking becomes more complex as the scope of the firm's activities is extended, and the gap between policy making and execution increases. Bureaucratic delays and waste, the difficulty of achieving just the right delegation of authority — these are functions of size, and as much problems for large private enterprises as for the government departments with which they are more generally associated.

Again, much of the concentration of economic power which has taken place has taken the form of diversification — firms branching out into quite different activities, pharmacists manufacturing jam, beverage producers making pharmaceutical goods or air sweeteners, brewers fishing, and so on. Sometimes such diversification can be justified in terms of commercial if not technical economies. And from the point of view of the firm itself, diversification can nearly always be defended in terms of risk-spreading in volatile market conditions. But it is probable that much integration of this type yields no positive *social* gain. The economies of bulk buying or selling, for example, may be only at the expense of some other intermediary between producer and consumer, the latter enjoying none of the consequent benefits; the spreading of risks is a useful insurance for the firm, but it might be the customer who pays the premium in the form of higher prices to cover the increased management costs.

6 Machines and man

Wassily Leontief

Approximately five hundred years ago the study of nature ceased to be solely a servant of philosophy and became a patron of applied arts and a source of practical invention. The economic development of the Western world has since proceeded at an ever increasing pace; waves of technological change, driven by the surge of scientific discoveries, have followed one another in accelerated succession. The development lag between pure science and engineering application has progressively shortened. It took nearly one hundred years for the steam engine to establish itself as part and parcel of the industrial scene, but electric power took less than fifty years and the internal combustion engine only thirty. The vacuum tube was in almost every American home within fifteen years of its invention, and the numerous progeny of Dr Baekeland's synthetic plastics matured before we learned to pronounce 'polyisobutylene'. At the turn of the twentieth century it was said that 'applied science is pure science twenty years later'; today the interval is much shorter — often only five years and sometimes but one or two.

From the engineering standpoint the era of automatic control has begun. Some of the fully automatic 'factories of the future' are already on paper; they can be described and studied. Engineering, however, is only the first step; what automatic technology will mean to our economic system and our society is still decidedly a thing of the future. In judging its probable impact all we have to go by is tenuous analogy with past experience and theoretical deductions from our very limited information on the new techniques. And it is no help that some of the crucial facts and figures are veiled in secrecy.

Important new inventions are traditionally held to presage the dawn of a new era; they also mark the twilight of an old. For some observers they contain promise; for others, fear. James Hargreaves constructed the first practical multiple spindle machine in 1767, and one year later a mob of spinners invaded his mill and destroyed the new equipment

Source: *Scientific American*, September 1952.

The economists of the time (the golden age of 'classical economics' was about to begin) came to the defense of the machines. They explained to labor that the loss of jobs in spinning would be compensated by new employment in machine-building. And for the next hundred years England did indeed prosper. Its labor force expanded both in textiles and in textile machinery, and wage rates by the end of the nineteenth century were at least three times as high as at its beginning.

But the men-*v.*-machines controversy blazed on. Karl Marx made of 'technological unemployment' the cornerstone of his theory of capitalist exploitation. The conscientious John Stuart Mill came to the conclusion that, while the introduction of machinery might — in most cases would — benefit labor, it would not necessarily do so always. The answer depended on the circumstances of the case. And today that is still the only reasonable point of view one can maintain.

We are hardly in a position to reduce to detailed computation the effects that automatic technology will have on employment, production, or our national standard of living. Aside from the paucity of our information on this new development, our understanding of the structural properties of our economic system itself is still incomplete. We must therefore rely on reasonable conjecture.

The economy of a modern industrial nation — not unlike the feedback mechanisms discussed throughout this issue — must be visualized as a complicated system of interrelated processes. Each industry, each type of activity, consumes the products and services of other sectors of the economy and at the same time supplies its own products and services to them. Just as the operating properties of a servo-mechanism are determined by the technical characteristics of the measuring, communicating, and controlling units of which it is composed, so the operating properties of an economy depend upon the structural characteristics of its component parts and on the way in which they are coupled together. It is not by coincidence that in some advanced phases of his work the modern economist resorts to systems of differential equations similar to those used by the designers of self-regulating machinery.

The services of labor constitute one important set of inputs into the national economy. That it is the largest one is reflected in the fact that labor receives in wages some 73 per cent (in 1950) of the nation's annual net product. But labor is not the only type of input that goes into all other sectors. Certain natural resources, machinery, equipment, and other kinds of productive capital feed into almost every branch of agriculture, manufacture, transportation, and distribution. In Figure 6.1 which depicts the growth of our total national product since 1880, is a breakdown of the share going into salaries and wages on the one hand and into non-labor income (profits, interest, rents, and so on) on the other.

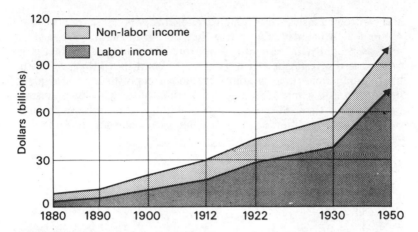

Figure 6.1 Total national income of the U.S., measured in terms of 1940 prices, has increased from $9.2 billion in 1880 to $160 billion in 1950. The ratio between labor income (the compensation of employees) and non-labor income (profits, interest, rent, and so on) is stable, but the share for labor has increased.

The ratio between these two has been generally stable, but labor's share has steadily gained. Behind these figures lie the intricate processes of our economic development, influenced by such factors as population growth, the discovery of new and the exhaustion of old natural resources, the increase in the stock of productive plant and equipment, and last but not least, a steady technological progress.

A better insight into the nature of that progress is given by Figures 6.4, 6.5, 6.6. The number of man-hours required for an average unit of output has gone down steadily since 1880. In the first thirty years of that period the saving of labor seems to have been accompanied by a corresponding increase in capital investment. Between 1880 and 1912 the amount of machinery and of other so-called fixed investment per unit of output rose by 34 per cent, while the man-hour input fell 40 per cent. Then the ratio of investment to output began to drop. We introduced more efficient machinery rather than just a greater quantity of it. That it actually was more efficient can be seen from the fact that labor productivity rose apace. In 1938 a unit of output consumed only about half as many man-hours as would have been spent upon its production in 1918.

Such is the stage which the new technology — the technology of automatic control — has now entered. The best index we have of how far automatization has gone is the annual U.S. production of 'measuring and controlling instruments.' The trend of this production is outlined in Figure 6.3. After hesitation during the depression and the war years, it now rises rapidly. In part this rise mirrors the recent accelerating pace of industrial investment in general, but the chart shows that the instrument production curve is going up more steeply than that of plant investment as a whole. This gain is a measure of the progressive 'instrumentation' of the U.S. economy. A breakdown of the relative progress of automatic operation in individual industries appears in Table 6.1.

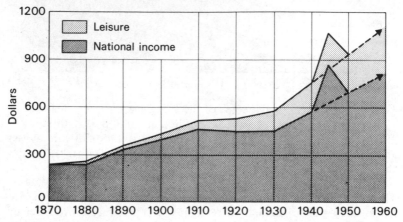

Figure 6.2 Income per capita, measured in terms of 1940 prices and excluding agriculture, increased from $230.60 in 1870 to $706.70 in 1950 (*bottom curve*). If 1870 hours of work had been maintained, the per capita income would be larger (*top curve*). The difference between the two curves shows increase in leisure.

The chemical and machinery industries lead; next come metal processing (mainly in the smelting department) and ceramics. In interpreting this table one must take into account the fact that instrumental control is less costly for some processes than for others (see Table 6.2).

The estimated cost of complete instrumentation of a new modern plant to automatize it as fully as possible today ranges from 1 to 19 per cent (depending on the industry) of the total investment in process equipment. The average for all industries would be about 6 per cent. On this basis, if all the new plants built in 1950 had been automatized, some $600 million would have been spent for measuring and control instruments. Actually the production of such instruments in 1950 totaled only $67 million. In other words, to automatize new plants alone, to say nothing of those already built, would require nearly ten times as great an investment in instruments as we are now making.

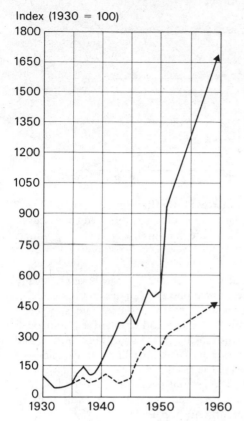

Index (1930 = 100)

Figure 6.3 Sales of instruments for industrial recording and controlling purposes have increased enormously since 1930 (*solid line*) as compared with the total U.S. expenditure for plant and equipment (*broken line*).

Yet 6 per cent is far from a formidable figure. Furthermore, the investment in instruments would not necessarily mean a net increase in the total plant investment per unit of output. On the contrary, the smoother and better-balanced operation of self-regulating plants has already shown that they can function with less capitalization than a non-automatic plant of identical capacity. And much existing equipment can readily be converted from manual to automatic control. It therefore seems that the automatization of our industries, at least to the extent made possible by present technology, is likely to advance rapidly. The mechanization of the nineteenth century required heavy capital investment and proceeded slowly; the new technology, unhampered by such vast capital requirements, can be introduced at a much faster pace.

Index (1880 = 100)

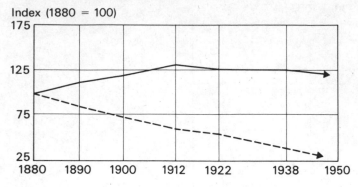

Figure 6.4 U.S. production has increased in efficiency. The solid line plots the decreasing index of plant and equipment required to produce one unit of output; the broken line, the man-hours required to produce one unit.

In transportation and agriculture, machines by now have practically eliminated the need for human muscle power. Man has all but ceased to be a lifter and mover and become primarily a starter and stopper, a setter and assembler and repairer. With the introduction of self-controlled machinery, his direct participation in the process of production will be narrowed even further. The starter and stopper will disappear first, the setter and assembler will go next. The trouble-shooter and repairman of course will keep their jobs for a long time to come; the need for them will even increase, for the delicate and complicated equipment of automatic control will require constant expert care. We shall continue to need inventors and designers, but perhaps not many even of them: the chief engineer of a large electronic equipment firm recently expressed to me his apparently well founded hope that before long he would have circuits designed by an electronic machine, eliminating human errors.

All this inevitably will change the character of our labor force. The proportion of unskilled labor has already declined greatly in recent decades; it is down to less than 20 per cent. Meanwhile the numbers of the semi-skilled have risen, and they now constitute over 22 per cent of the labor force. This trend has slowed down during the past decade, however. Now we shall probably see an accelerated rise in the proportion of skilled workers, clerks, and professional personnel, who already make up 42 per cent of our working population.

In a country with a less fluid and more differentiated social structure than ours, these rapid changes in the occupational composition of the population might have brought about considerable strain. But the

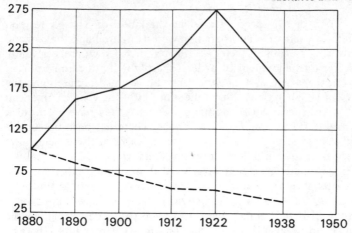

Figure 6.5 Mining and manufacture similarly increased in productivity. Labor savings have been secured largely by expenditure on plant equipment. Increasing efficiency of plant is now reflected in declining capital cost.

celebrated, and often criticized, uniformity of American living renders the effects of such transition almost imperceptible. For example, recent studies indicate that the family of a typical $3000-a-year clerk spends its money in very much the same way as the family, say, of a machine-press operator with a similar income.

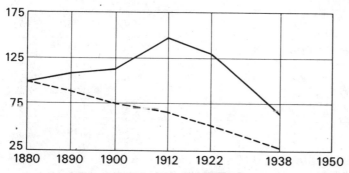

Figure 6.6 Agriculture shows a similar pattern. Here the index of plant and equipment per unit of output is actually lower in 1938 than in 1880, reflecting the enormous increase in the productivity of agricultural machinery.

Will the machine-press operator be able to earn his $3000 when an automatic controlling device takes over his job? The answer must depend in part on the speed with which the labor force is able to train and to retrain itself. If such upgrading were to fall behind the demand of the changing technology, semi-skilled and unskilled workers certainly would suffer unemployment or at least sharply reduced earning power. The experience of the last twenty years, however, has underlined the flexibility of U.S. workmen. Under the stimulus of the general American striving toward social and economic betterment, they have been quick to take to vocational training for new jobs. There has been no surplus of unskilled and semi-skilled labor: indeed, wages in these fields have risen even faster than in skilled and professional work.

But if automatic machines largely take over our production, will there be enough jobs, skilled or otherwise, to go around? Admittedly the possibility of eventual unemployment cannot be excluded on a priori grounds. If the capital investment were to increase rapidly while the need for manpower dropped, the resulting rise in capital's share of the national income could cause drastic unemployment. But as we have seen, the amount of capital needed for each unit of output has actually been reduced in recent years, and the installation of automatic machinery will further reduce it. Therefore labor should be able to maintain or improve its relative share of the national income. The danger of technological unemployment should be even smaller in the foreseeable future than it was at the end of the nineteenth century, when capital requirements were rising.

Table 6.1

Industry	1946	1947	1948	1949	1950	1951
Ceramics	110	113	106	70	102	131
Chemicals	125	110	101	62	117	208
Foods	125	107	96	66	103	107
Machinery	107	112	119	61	105	168
Metals	113	98	106	81	134	249
Petroleum	80	90	140	86	98	132
Textiles	106	105	112	75	129	128
Utilities	72	96	122	111	147	222
Total	100	104	115	82	122	192

Growth of instrumentation in various industries is shown in this table, which lists the sales of instruments to those industries by years. The index of the table: 1946–9 average sales of instruments = 100.

While the increase in productivity need not lead to involuntary idleness, it certainly does result in a steady reduction in the number of years and hours that an average American spends at making his living.

The average work-week has been shortened from 67.2 hours in 1870 to 42.5 hours in 1950. This reflects a deliberate decision by the American people to enjoy an ever-increasing part of their rising standard of living in the form of leisure. If we had kept to the 67-hour week, we would be turning out a considerably greater amount of goods than we actually are. The difference between this hypothetical per capita output, computed on the basis of the well-known Cobb–Douglas formula, and the actual present output is indicated in Figure 6.2. This difference represents the amount of commodities and services which the average American has chosen *not* to produce and consequently not to consume in order to enjoy shorter hours and longer vacations. The spread between the two curves has steadily increased: in other words, we have chosen to spend more and more of our ever increasing production potential on leisure. The temporary shift to a high output of material goods during the last war only emphasizes this tendency, for we returned to the long-run trend immediately after the war. In the future, even more than in the past, the increased productivity of the American economy will be enjoyed as additional leisure.

Table 6.2

Industry	per cent
Meat packing	19
Pharmaceuticals	15
Textile plants	5–12
Soap	3.2–8.6
Dry ice	6.3
Equipment manufacture for the chemical and oil refining industry	.5–6
Paper mill	5
Rubber	5
Petroleum refining	3–5
Packaged foods	3–5
Mining and processing of ores	2–5
Chlor-alkali electrolytic plants	3.25
Sulfuric acid (*contact method*)	3
Pulp mill	3
Carpets	2–3
Rayon and rayon yarn	1–2

Relative cost of instrumental control in various industries is given by per cent of total equipment cost.

Looking back, one can see that 1910 marked the real turning point in this country's economic and social development. That was the year when the last wave of immigration reached its crest; the year, also, when our rural population began to decline in absolute terms. Between 1890 and 1910 our national input of human labor had shot up from 28.3 million standard man-years to 42.5 million. Then in 1909 the model-T Ford began to roll off the first continuous production line. This great shift to mass production by machine was immediately reflected in shorter hours. In the next decade our manpower input increased by only one million man-years, and after 1920 it leveled off and remained almost constant until the early 1940's. Even at the peak of the recent war effort our total labor input, with an enormously larger population, was only 10 per cent greater than in 1910. Automatization will accelerate the operation of forces which have already shaped the development of this country for nearly half a century.

The new technology will probably have a much more revolutionary effect on the so-called underdeveloped countries than on the U.S. or other old industrial nations. Shortage of capital and lack of a properly conditioned and educated labor force have been the two major obstacles to rapid industrialization of such backward areas. Now automatic production, with its relatively low capital and labor requirements per unit of output, radically changes their prospects. Instead of trying to lift the whole economy by the slow, painful methods of the past, an industrially backward country may take the dramatic shortcut of building a few large, up-to-date automatic plants. Towering up in the primitive economy like copses of tall trees on a grassy plain, they would propagate a new economic order. The oil refineries of the Near East, the integrated steel plant built after the war in Brazil, the gigantic fertilizer plant recently put into operation in India — these are examples of the new trend in underdeveloped regions of the world. How formidable the application of modern technology in a backward country may become is demonstrated by the U.S.S.R.'s recent great strides in industrialization.

At the outbreak of the First World War the U.S. suddenly lost its source of many indispensable chemicals in Germany. Domestic production had to be organized practically overnight. The newly created U.S. chemical industry had no force of experienced chemical craftsmen such as Germany had. The problem was solved, however, by the introduction of mechanization and automatization to a degree theretofore unknown. The American plants were run with amazingly small staffs of skilled workers. The same thing is now happening, and possibly will continue on a much larger scale, in backward countries. Advanced design, imported mostly from the U.S., will compensate at least in part for their scarcity of high-quality labor.

Naturally automatization, while solving some problems, will everywhere create new and possibly more difficult ones. In Western civilization the liberation from the burdens of making a living has been going on for some time, and we have been able to adjust to the new situation gradually. In the rising new countries economic efficiency may at least temporarily run far ahead of progress toward social maturity and stability. Much of the stimulus for the educational advancement of the Western nations came from economic necessity. Automatization may weaken that powerful connection. It remains to be seen whether the backward countries will find a driving force to help them develop the social, cultural, and political advances necessary to help them cope with the new economic emancipation.

7 Consumer sovereignty

Kathleen O'Donnell

What things will be produced is determined by the dollar votes of consumers – not every 2 or 4 years at the polls, but everyday in their decision to purchase this item and not that.[1]

Introduction

The concept of consumer sovereignty is of central importance to neoclassical economic theory; it is the cornerstone around which the whole edifice of consumer and production theory is constructed. It embodies the main principles of neoclassical economics, namely, that the satisfaction of consumers' wants directs the purpose of all economic activity. Production is the means, consumption the end. In the light of this the erosion of this concept will have the effect of weakening neoclassical theory. Not surprisingly, then, both critics and defenders of the market economy have focused their attention on the concept.

These critics can be very broadly divided into two schools: those who believe that the absence of consumer sovereignty in the real world is attributable to imperfections in the market system – a view closely identified with Galbraith – and those who locate the problem in the actual structure and development of capitalism where production is organised not for consumption but for profit.

Section 1 discusses the importance of the concept to neoclassical economics. In Section 2 the Galbraithian criticisms and the response by market economists is considered. Finally we examine the arguments put forward by writers in the Marxist tradition.

The importance of consumer sovereignty to neoclassical economics

The sovereignty of the consumer has long been held sacred in neoclassical

Source: Article commissioned for this Reader. Kathleen O'Donnell is a PhD student at Birkbeck College, University of London.

economic theory.[2] The reason it is held in such high esteem is because it describes a highly desirable aspect of an economic system. To be sovereign means to have sole power, and the view associated with consumer sovereignty sees the consumer as having sole power in the economy to decide what is produced, how much is produced and how the produced goods are allocated. Only those things are produced that consumers want, and the quantity produced is determined by how much consumers want them.

In this way the satisfaction of consumers' wants directs all economic activity such that the production and distribution of commodities is designed towards the purpose of maximising consumers' welfare. This view begs the questions: where does consumer power come from and how is it exercised? The relevance of these questions is obvious from just a cursory glance at the real world where decisions about production are made by managers of firms. How do they know what consumers want? How can consumers be sovereign in a world where they do not appear to make any of the decisions about what is produced?

Prior to looking at the question of who decides what is actually produced it is useful to pursue the more fundamental question of why there is a problem in the first place. Posing the question of who decides what is produced implies that a choice has to be made over the production of commodities. This in turn implies that there must exist some form of constraint on the production of commodities — not all that consumers want can be produced. According to neoclassical theory the constraint is imposed by the limited resources available in the world. When this finite amount of raw materials is combined with the number of people able to work and the level of technology available, then the total number of commodities which can be produced is determined. However, a problem arises if this total bundle of commodities is insufficient to meet the demands of consumers. As neoclassical economists assume that individuals have an infinite number of wants, then the problem of scarcity arises. Decisions, then, have to be made about what to produce, how much and for whom. This is often referred to as the basic economic problem.[3]

The main objective of neoclassical economics is to solve this problem. As with most problems there are many solutions. Thus, given the level of finite resources, there are many different bundles of commodities which could be produced. How can we decide which bundle is best? The criterion used by neoclassical economics is that resources should be allocated to produce that bundle of commodities which brings most benefit to the largest number of people. This optimum situation is said to have been achieved when it is possible to make someone better off only by making someone else worse off.[4] The problem then becomes how to allocate resources to achieve this aim.

According to neoclassical economics this ideal allocation of resources will occur if consumers are allowed to make the decisions about what is produced. This view is predicated on the idea that the consumer knows best what he likes. He is able to decide which goods he prefers and how much of each good he wishes to purchase. However, in the same way that the economy as a whole faces a constraint in the form of the finite number of resources, the consumer is also constrained. The constraint in this case is determined by the individual's income, which in turn is determined by the quantity of resources he owns and the prices at which he is able to sell the services of these resources. In most cases individuals own only their ability to work, and thus their income depends on the wage offered for their particular skill and the number of hours which they are prepared to work. The consumer's problem is how to spend his income so that he receives the most benefit. Obviously there are certain basic necessities which have to be purchased by everyone (for example, housing, food and clothing), but within this broad range of goods the consumer has a choice. Does she wish to live in a two-bedroom flat or a semi-detached house? Does he wish to pay rent or maintain a mortgage? Would she rather spend less money on housing and more on food and clothing? Clearly the bundle of commodities chosen will vary from consumer to consumer depending on such factors as the size of income, size of family and, ultimately, tastes.

At the aggregate level of the economy, then, the basic economic problem is that there are a large number of consumers each with an infinite number of wants, but there is only a limited supply of resources. The problem is deciding what to produce. Each individual constrained by the level of income received, albeit variable within certain limits, is able to purchase only a certain number of commodities from an enormous array of goods. The consumer has to decide what to consume. This dual problem — what to produce for society as a whole and what to consume at the individual level — is resolved in neoclassical theory by consumers deciding what to consume and transmitting that information to firms in order that they know what to produce.

We still have to explain how this complex system of allocating scarce resources to consumers' chosen wants is achieved. How are consumers able to transmit their wishes to producers? The neoclassical answer is that consumers exert their influence through the price system.[5] The economy is viewed as a collection of numerous market places. Each commodity has its own market where buyers and sellers congregate. If consumers wish to purchase a particular commodity they will indicate their willingness to do so by placing a bid in the form of money. The good with the most votes is produced in the greatest quantity. In order for consumers' power to be effective in the market place it must be supported by money. If a consumer wants a commodity but is unable to pay for it, the demand will be ignored. An individual's ability to consume crucially depends on ability to pay and hence on the level of income received.

The sovereignty of the consumer is illustrated by the following example. Suppose, because of a change in the tastes of consumers (for the moment we will leave aside the difficult question of whether tastes are innate or socially conditioned), the demand for a particular commodity increases. In the period immediately following this change, the quantity produced by firms is fixed at a certain level because it takes time for a firm to arrange to employ more labour and buy new machines. Consequently consumers are rationed in the sense that they cannot buy all that they wish. In other words, the present level of production is insufficient to meet the demands of consumers. At that point, to overcome this problem of scarcity, some system of rationing has to be introduced. In a market system this rationing process occurs as individuals, against one another in the market, bid up the price of the quantity supplied. As prices rise some consumers will reconsider and decide whether they still wish to purchase the commodity at the new higher price or whether they would prefer to spend that amount of money on some other good. In addition to functioning as a rationing mechanism, prices also provide information to producers. An increase in price indicates to firms that there is an inadequate supply, and if they produce more they will be able to sell more. Since firms are concerned only about making as much profit as possible, and given a higher price means that they will collect more revenue and hence generate higher profits, firms are given an incentive to produce more. Once provided with information and the incentive to act, firms will set about increasing the quantity they produce by employing more labour and machines. Moreover the increased profitability of the industry will also be noticed by firms operating in other industries. If the rate of profit is higher than that they earn at present, they will start to produce the more profitable commodity. In this way resources are re-allocated from one area of the economy to another depending upon the wishes of consumers. Labour and capital move from industries where demand is declining to new, profitable, expanding industries. The quantity of output will be increased, both by existing firms expanding their level of output and by new firms entering the industry, up to the point at which consumers are able to buy as much as they wish. However, suppose for the moment that firms continue to increase the quantity produced. Steadily the quantity supplied will outstrip the level of demand. Stocks will accumulate and firms will realise they are producing too much. Firms' immediate response to accumulated stocks is to reduce the price in order to eliminate the surplus. As prices fall, revenues fall and hence profits. In response they will make plans to reduce the capacity of their factories by redundancies and plant closures. Over time the quantity produced will be equalised with the quantity wanted by consumers.

We have seen then that the basic economic problem of what to produce, how much and how to allocate the produced commodities is resolved, according to neoclassical economists, by the price mechanism. Prices coordinate the activities of consumers and firms by performing two roles. First they transmit information. For example, a rising price indicates a lack of supply and, conversely, a falling price reflects a lack of demand. The transmission of information alone, however, is not sufficient to ensure the working of the price mechanism. People must act on the information received in order to achieve the aim of satisfying consumers' wants. Second, prices must also act as incentives. Changing prices encourage consumers to decide whether they still wish to consume that particular good and at the same time, through their effect on revenues and profits, they stimulate firms to produce either more or less. Thus prices, by transmitting consumers' wants to firms, determine what is produced and by acting as incentive they regulate the quantity produced.

Prices in their dual role of transmitting information and providing incentives solve the problems, respectively, of what to produce and how much. We still have to explain how the produced goods are allocated according to the market mechanism. We have, however, mentioned that individuals' ability to consume depends on their ability to pay and hence to earn. Thus the distribution of commodities is determined in the market mechanism by the distribution of income. The more you earn or the more money you possess, the greater is your market power in determining which goods are produced. Although each individual vote in the market system is equal, the number of votes which each individual possesses may vary enormously.

If the price system works in the manner described, the chain of command is quite clearly from consumers to producers. Firms respond to the signals consumers send out, and thus the market mechanism allows consumers to be sovereign. However, this is not to argue that consumers can be sovereign only in a market system. It is possible to imagine a system achieving the same end of satisfying consumers' wants but using a different mechanism. For example, a centrally planned economy could use non-market devices such as questionnaires to discover consumers' preferences and then allocate resources in response to the filed answers. This poses the question: what are the advantages of the market mechanism? Is it better than allocating resources by other methods such as by favouritism, bribery or choice?

Advocates of the market mechanism believe it promotes freedom of choice in the market place. Moreover they view economic freedom as being an essential requisite for political freedom.[6] The price mechanism, then, coordinates individuals' activities without infringing on their privacy. To understand how the price system achieves these results we have to explain why people react to changes in price. This involves tracing the origins of the concept of consumer sovereignty.

Although the term was not explicitly used until 1936, much of the substance of consumer sovereignty can be found in the writings of Adam Smith.[7] Smith's belief in the efficiency of the market system was based on the view that if each individual pursued his own interest, then the interests of all would be served. He argued that no voluntary exchange between two individuals would occur unless both believed they would benefit from it. 'It is not from the benevolence of the butcher, the brewer or the baker that we expect our dinner, but from their regard to their own self-interest. We address ourselves not to their humanity but to their self love, and never talk to them of our own necessities but of their advantages.'[8] Producers respond to the wishes of consumers not because they are altruistic but because they are acting in their own self-interest. Since producers' interest is to make as much profit as possible, the most direct method of achieving this aim is to produce goods that consumers want to buy.

The sovereignty of the consumer prevails in the market mechanism by the pursuit of self-interest. Consumers pursue their self-interest directly by choosing which goods they wish to consume. Producers follow this course by making goods that consumers want in order to make a profit. Thus the price mechanism enables people to cooperate to promote their separate interests.

Are consumers sovereign in the real world?

Undoubtedly within neoclassical theory consumers are sovereign. However, for many economists the crucial question is whether the concept sheds any light on how the economy operates in the real world. Galbraith, for instance, would argue that real conditions have altered so significantly since the original conception of consumer sovereignty that it is now a redundant concept.[9] A more fundamental approach to the problem is taken by some writers who question the basic tenet that consumers are free to choose.[10] This involves a critical examination of the structure and development of capitalism.

First we shall examine the views of those who subscribe to the idea that market failures have eroded the power of the consumer. As we have seen, prices occupy a central role in the decentralised market economy coordinating the activities of consumers and producers. To accomplish this task they provide information and also act as incentives to transactors to follow the information received. Although it is generally agreed that people do respond to changes in price, there is some doubt as to whether they provide all the information necessary for consumers and producers to make a decision. To examine this view we have to understand how prices are determined in the market.

A stable market price is reached when the amount consumers want to buy is equal to the amount producers want to sell. Consumers' demand for a commodity, as we have seen, depends upon many factors, but finally it hinges upon individual preferences. We have not, however, pursued the question of what determines the quantity producers want to sell. If we accept that firms are acting in their own self-interest to make as much profit as possible, then, at any given level of output, they have to compare the costs of production incurred with the revenue received from the sale of the produced goods. Clearly firms will produce only when revenue is in excess of costs. Revenue depends upon consumers' demand for the commodity, but what determines the costs of production? An individual firm takes account of all the raw materials used in the production process, the number of workers it has employed, the costs of machines and the factory itself. These are known as the private costs of production because they relate specifically to the firm. However, a glance at most industrial estates suggests that there are other costs associated with the production of some commodities. For example, smoky, dense atmospheres, polluted rivers and waterways, noise and congested roads are all characteristics of industrialised areas. The burden of these social costs of production falls most heavily on those people living in the immediate area surrounding a factory and thus have become known as neighbourhood or external effects. Undoubtedly, if individuals have to suffer these undesirable side-effects of a production process, their views on the desirability of that particular commodity will be coloured by them. However, if a consumer lives outside the affected area, he will be ignorant of the adverse social costs because the market price takes account only of the private costs of production. If we define the correct total costs of producing a commodity as the sum of private costs and the costs to society as a whole, then the market price will be wrong if a divergence exists between private and social costs. If neighbourhood effects occur, it is possible to imagine a situation where a consumer would purchase a different commodity if he knew the correct cost of production.

When social costs exist it is clear that the market mechanism does not provide sufficient information. Consequently the market price may lead consumers into making wrong decisions and ultimately result in scarce resources being allocated inefficiently, in the sense that they do not bring the maximum satisfaction to consumers. This is referred to as a market failure because the market mechanism fails, through the transmission of inadequate information, to allocate resources in an optimum fashion.

Apart from the problem of prices not providing sufficient information, there is also the question of whether consumers have access to all information on the wide range of goods and services available. Although a great deal of resources are devoted by firms to advertising, market research and sales promotion, doubt is expressed over the purpose of this expenditure. Clearly a narrow line exists between providing information and using persuasive measures to promote the sales of a good. If consumers are unaware of all the available choices, how can they choose what they prefer? This is particularly relevant to the emergence of new products. Before a product is invented, do consumers have an innate desire for that good which is simply lying dormant? For example, before the invention of television sets, did consumers have a latent desire for such a commodity? The important question is whether consumers actually want a commodity or are they being persuaded to purchase it.

J. K. Galbraith, one of the main sceptics of the sovereignty of the consumer in the modern economy, has developed this theme and sought to explain why firms are unhappy about relying on the wishes of consumers. He terms the unidirectional flow of information from consumer to market to producer the 'accepted sequence', and much of his work is devoted to explaining the breakdown of this sequence in terms of changes in the structure of the economy. The changes he refers to are the concentration of industry and the growth of producer power. Indeed there has been a dramatic shift from the many small firms characterising the nineteenth-century laissez-faire market economy to present-day capitalism where large corporations dominate the scene. Some of the large firms extend their operations over national boundaries to form multinational companies with factories located all over the world. The scale of the operation of these companies implies that firms have to take enormous risks when deciding which goods to produce. The risk involved is high because firms have to buy large and expensive machinery in order to produce, and consequently they want to be sure that they will be able to sell their product for years ahead. The crucial question is whether they can rely on the vagaries of consumers' wishes. If for some reason consumers' tastes change and the demand for a product suddenly plummets, the firm previously producing the good will be left with a factory of redundant machines and workers. To avoid this risk firms take the problem of consumers' demands into their own hands. Instead of relying on consumers' wants they try to manage the level of demand for their product. It follows that the 'accepted sequence' is no longer a description of reality. Producers control the market and on beyond to manage consumer behaviour, thus shaping the social attitudes of those, ostensibly, that it serves. The sovereignty of the individual is surrendered to the producer in this revised sequence of events.

The erosion of the power of the consumer has occurred, according to Galbraith, because of the growth of multinational corporations. He identifies a link between the size of firms and their market power. Thus he accepts that the degree of producer *v.* consumer sovereignty varies in intensity across the economy. Markets characterised by many small firms, such as those for agricultural products, are sensitive to changes in consumers' tastes; whereas producers such as those in the car industry, which is dominated by a few large firms, exert a greater influence over the demands of consumers.

In response to Galbraith's criticisms, advocates of the free market system tend to assert that he exaggerates the degree of producer sovereignty and the manipulation of consumers' tastes. Friedman, for example, argues that consumers cannot be led by the nose by advertising. It is much more sensible for producers to try to appeal to the real wants of consumers than to try to manufacture artificial wants.[11] However, these comments are little more than assertion with very little empirical support.

Friedman and other free-marketeers, such as Lerner,[12] have conceded that the monopoly power of firms can be detrimental to consumers, in so far as it limits choice. Lerner argues that, to restore the sovereignty of the consumer, government legislation has to be introduced. The government must actively encourage the dissemination of information and remove market imperfections that hinder the operation of a free market economy. Consequently, though this may appear contradictory, the government has to intervene to maintain a laissez-faire economy. Thus a government committed to the power of the consumer will pursue such policies as ensuring freedom of entry into markets, abolishing incomes and price controls, relaxing exchange controls and generally encouraging competitive forces to be established. As Friedman argues, 'the consumer is protected from being exploited by one seller by the existence of another seller from whom he can buy and who is eager to sell to him.'

Neoclassical economics concedes that there is a role for government in the running of a market economy. However, in the real world, it is obvious that the government does not simply perform the role of policing the economy to protect the consumer. There are some sectors of the economy where because of the lack of provision by private firms the government has had to intervene to serve the needs of consumers. Why do private firms not provide defence, policing services, street lighting and other such public amenities? There is a demand for these goods, yet firms do not react to consumers' wishes in these cases. Why do private markets not exist for these? The answer is to be found in the free-rider problem. If, for example, street lighting is provided for one consumer, it is difficult to prevent other consumers also from benefiting. Thus no individual consumer will be prepared to pay for the good since it is possible to benefit without paying. Given that we accept that firms act in their own self-interest and not out of love for consumers, clearly firms will not be prepared to provide such goods.

The public provision of certain goods suggests that the desire of consumers alone is insufficient to ensure production. Firms must be able to make a profit as well. This implies that consumers are sovereign in a market economy only when the criterion of profitability is satisfied.

The aim of production is profit, not consumption: a Marxist view

The appearance of the criterion of profitability raises the question of whether, in determining what is produced, profits are more important than the wishes of consumers. Why else is it that some consumers' basic needs such as housing, clothing and food go unheeded while at the same time scarce resources are devoted to the manufacture of nuclear weapons, the number of which far exceeds the demand (if one exists at all)? As we have seen, neoclassical economists believe that the monetary votes of consumers determine what is produced and how much and for whom. Each consumer receives goods according to the level of his income, and thus the market mechanism does not ensure an equitable distribution of commodities. However, writers in the Marxist tradition argue that the neoclassical view of how the economy works is incorrect since it ignores the actual organisation and social relations of capitalist methods of production. The basic division in capitalist society is not between consumers and firms but between those who own and control the means of producing commodities and those who own only their labour power, that is to say, capitalists and workers respectively. Although marxist writers would agree that production is controlled by one section of society, they would argue that the sovereign group is not consumers but capitalists. Consequently the ultimate purpose of production is not consumption but rather to reflect the interests of capitalists, namely profit.

To illustrate this argument we shall follow neoclassical theory and start our analysis with the individual. According to neoclassical theory, individual consumers are constrained in their choice of commodities only by their income, the level of which is at their discretion. This argument presupposes that individuals are free to choose between work and leisure. However, this abstracts from the real world where a relatively small group of society own the means of production. Workers who own only their ability to labour have in reality very little choice and freedom. In order to survive, they have to sell their ability to work to the owners of the means of production. Their only choice is which individual firms to work for. Once workers have agreed to work for a firm, that is, sold their ability to produce goods, then they become, during the working day, the property of the firm. The firm specifies the nature and length of time of the working day.

The all-important question is what principle governs the behaviour of the capitalist. The capitalist sets up the production process with a sum of money with which he purchases the means of production and raw materials, labour and machines. He organises the production process and produces commodities which he then sells in exchange for money. Thus the whole process begins and ends with money. If, following neoclassical economics, we do not expect the capitalist to be altruistic, then presumably the purpose of the exercise is to make a profit.

The purpose of production in capitalist society according to the marxist viewpoint is the creation of profit. Consumers do play a role in this theory, since it is clear that commodities have to be wanted by consumers, and hence sold, before a profit can be realised. However, although consumption is a necessary condition for production to be carried out under capitalism, it is not a sufficient condition. Production and consumption are simply means to achieving the ultimate aim of creating profits.

I should like to thank Ben Fine, Laurence Harris, Susan Himmelweit and Peter Nolan for helpful comments on an earlier draft.

Notes

1 Samuelson (1976), p. 44.
2 Although the actual term 'consumer sovereignty' was not introduced until 1936 by W. H. Hutt in *Economists and the Public*, it had been discussed implicitly by earlier writers.
3 For example, see Samuelson (1976), p. 23; Lipsey (1975), p. 51 and Friedman (1962), p. 6.

4 This definition of optimality is associated with Pareto and is often referred to as 'Pareto-optimality'.
5 The price of allocating resources is also known as the 'free-market mechanism' or 'laissez-faire market economy'.
6 See Friedman and Friedman (1980) for an account of the relationship between economic freedom and political freedom.
7 Smith (1974).
8 Ibid., p. 119.
9 Galbraith (1965, 1967).
10 S. Mohun (1977), essay reprinted in F. Green and P. Nore (1977).
11 Friedman and Friedman (1980), pp. 266–7.
12 Lerner (1972).

References

Friedman, M. (1962) *Price Theory*, Chicago, Aldine.
Friedman, M. and Friedman, R. (1980) *Free to Choose*, Penguin.
Galbraith, J. K. (1965) *The Affluent Society*, Penguin.
Galbraith, J. K. (1967) *The New Industrial State*, Penguin.
Green, F. and Nore, P. (1977), *Economics: an Antitext*, Macmillan.
Lerner, A. P. (1972) 'The economies and politics of consumer sovereignty', *American Economic Review*, Papers and Proceedings.
Lipsey, R. G. (1975) *An Introduction to Positive Economics*, 4th ed., Weidenfeld and Nicolson.
Rothenberg, J (1968) 'Consumer sovereignty', in *International Encyclopaedia of the Social Sciences*, Macmillan and the Free Press.
Samuelson, P. (1976) *Economics*, 10th ed., McGraw-Hill.
Smith, A. (1974) *The Wealth of Nations*, Penguin.

SECTION 3

The Production of Social Divisions

Introduction

John Clarke

Over twenty years ago, C. Wright Mills wrote of the 'Sociological Imagination', and argued that it 'enables us to grasp history and biography, and the relations between the two within society'.[1] That brief statement still sets the aims and tasks of sociology. To say that it *still* sets those aims is not to identify some failure on the part of sociologists to fulfil that promise, but to take account of the scope of the challenge which that brief statement makes.

Mills was asking that sociologists should analyse the patterns of behaviour and thought, the institutions, and the relationships between groups that went to make up the social structure of a society. He was asking that they should be studied historically — that sociology should offer us an understanding of how societies change and develop. But he also insisted that sociology should trace the connections between these social patterns and processes and the lives of the members of society. It should help us to grasp how individual biographies are shaped and fashioned by the sorts of social arrangements within which they are lived. Finally, his programme for the sociologist required that he or she should study how the actions of individual men and women, of groups and of classes, influence and change the way in which society develops, and affect the direction in which it moves.

We do not expect the brief extracts in this section of the Reader to be able to fulfil all of those promises, but they do offer examples of how sociological work can illuminate some of those connections around one particular issue. The issue is one which has always been a central feature of sociology — that of analysing and explaining the social divisions that exist within a society.

A society is not a homogeneous mass made up of completely identical individuals. The members of a society are divided into social groupings, and the existence of these divisions affect and constrain the biographies of particular individuals in different ways. These divisions are not just matters of sociological attention: in everyday conversation, for example, we use terms about the groupings people belong to as ways of passing information about what sort of people they are – how they are likely to behave and think. We refer to their occupations, their religion, their educational background and their class background as ways of 'placing' them for other people.

For sociology, the first task is to identify what the main lines of division in a society are – is the society divided into different groups along the lines of religion, is it divided by racial differences, is it divided into classes? Sociology also questions the consequences of these divisions for the members of the groups – in what ways do they shape their access to resources – jobs, wealth, health, power, and so on.

But as well as dealing with differentiation and division, sociologists have to ask questions about social integration – how do these groups fit together to form a whole society? What sorts of relationships exist between the different groups? Where, before, we were asking questions about the consequences for the members of the groups, we must now ask questions about the consequences of these divisions for the pattern and direction of society as a whole. Are the divisions integrated into a stable pattern, do the different groups acquiesce in their relative positions in the social structure? Or are the relationships between them antagonistic, are they in conflict over their situation?

In Section 3, we have tried to show how these questions shape sociological research and to demonstrate some of the answers that relate to modern British society. The pieces selected refer to three main areas of social division which are visible in Britain, and are of major significance for the character and direction of our society. But they are divisions which have a broader significance than just their appearance in British society. They can be found, in slightly different forms, in all the societies which make up the 'western world', those industrialized capitalist societies of Western Europe and North America.

The lines of division exemplified by the extracts are those of class, of race and of gender. Class divisions and the relationships between classes have been a central concern of sociology since its beginnings in the industrializing societies of nineteenth-century Europe. They have remained a major theme – although one which has been hotly disputed and contested within sociology. The arguments have raged around whether class divisions have receded from western societies, and around just what sorts of divisions are at stake when we talk about class – are they based on the ownership of capital, are they related to occupational divisions, do they rest on the control of power and authority? These different criteria for identifying classes have led to the construction of a variety of class 'maps' ranging from hierarchies of up to seven different classes to the basic marxist identification of two major classes, those of capital and labour.

The extract relating to class divisions is taken from Huw Beynon's *Working for Ford*, a study of the problems, experiences and conflicts of workers on the production line at a car factory. This extract dramatically highlights the antagonistic relationships created between management and workers by the way in which production for private profit is organized. It deals with the localized forms which class conflict takes in a society shaped by the division between capital and labour, and focuses on the roles played by the representatives of those groups — managers on the one hand, and shop stewards on the other.

Our second field of divisions — those around racial and ethnic differences — have also been studied within sociology for some time. However, rather than being a central concern, they have, through sociology's professional division of labour, tended to be relegated to a small outpost of the sociological empire — the field of 'race relations'. More recently, events and developments outside sociology have tended to thrust questions of racial divisions and racism into a more significant position. Among these developments, it is worth noting the struggles for national independence in one-time colonial states in the Third World; and the struggles for civil liberties, equality, and the reassertion of their own cultural heritages by blacks and other ethnic minorities in the United States. Finally, the British experience of discrimination among black minorities, the increasing refusal of the 'Black British' to accept the status of second-class citizens, coupled with the rise of extreme racist political organizations such as the National Front and the British Movement, have brought 'race relations' increasingly into public view, and into the foreground of sociology.

Our article here is taken from a book by Ken Pryce which investigates the situation of black youths who have been born British. It examines the ways in which, although nominally members of British society, they have been systematically treated as 'outsiders', subject to well-documented discrimination and persecution — a situation of what the book's title calls 'Endless Pressure'. The extract deals with some of the ways in which this group have begun to respond to these pressures, developing new attitudes and new identities as ways of surviving and responding to their position in British society.

The final extract deals with one aspect of sexual divisions. Unlike our other two fields of interest, sexual division has not had a long-standing place in the world of sociological investigation and analysis. Sociologists, like many others, had been willing to note the existence of different roles and positions for men and women in our society, but left the explanation in the realm of the 'natural'. Even in the face of striking comparative material from other societies that indicated the incorrectness of assuming that the division of roles between men and women was natural and inevitable, any investigation of these problems was strikingly absent from the agenda of sociological inquiry. This failure of the sociological imagination has begun to be remedied only under pressure from other events. The revival of feminism since the late 1960s, in a variety of forms, has subjected the assumptions of the 'natural role' of women to increasing scrutiny and criticism. Its revival has also inspired a great deal of investigation both in history and sociology that aims to uncover the social sources of women's position, and to demonstrate some of the beliefs and ideologies which have supported the inequalities which women have experienced.

One of the main areas of investigation has been that of 'women's work', and within this a number of major findings have been advanced. Far from the assumption that women were naturally domestic — family-centred homemakers — much research has demonstrated that they have long played a major role in paid employment. But within this, they have been used as both a supply of cheap labour, with wage rates persistently lower than men's, and a highly mobile supply of labour that can be used and then rejected as economic interests require. The piece we have chosen deals with the creation of one particular field of 'women's work' — clerical work. It uncovers some of the circumstances under which women were first allowed into office work, and the ideologies that were used to control women's work in offices. Although it is based on American material, Margery Davies's article, 'Women's Place is at the Typewriter', illuminates social processes and patterns of belief similar to those which have shaped clerical work, and women's place in it, in this country. It presents a clear and well-informed study of how one particular change in women's so-called 'natural position' took place.

As we said earlier, these articles by no means represent the scope and range of sociology as a whole, but they do show something of the inquiry, insight and illumination that can be produced when the 'sociological imagination' is set to work.

Note

1 *The Sociological Imagination*, New York, Oxford University Press, 1959, p. 6.

8 Eldorado

Huw Beynon

The business of manufacture

Industry is organized to make profit. Most people accept this as fact, and recognize that the more profit their company makes the better chance it has of providing a good standard of living and security for its employees and their families. This is not only because everybody's future earnings depend on the Company continuing to make a profit, but because a good profit encourages more investment — a good safeguard for the future.

A look at profits in our own business shows that they are closely linked to how much use we make of plant and equipment. This is because it takes a lot of expensive space and plant to make our products and the more we make with the same resources the more profit we get. In fact, unless we are building at a good rate we are not even paying our way — on a two shift system without overtime our plants are standing idle for a third of the day.

From *Two Heads are Better than One*: Ford Motor Company Department of Labour Relations.

The people

Plant is only one of the factors, however. In Britain today, people are, by and large, enjoying a good standard of living and compared with many countries wages are high (although, of course, not as high as most people would like). Human resources, however, are scarce and expensive and therefore it makes sense to see that they are fully used and not misused. Just as it does not make sense to build more plants before we fully use the ones we have, neither does it make sense to keep on hiring men when some of those we have cannot make a full contribution because of bad organization or working habits.

There are two ways, therefore, in which a company can increase its efficiency:

Source: *Working for Ford*, Penguin Books, 1973, extracts from ch. 4, pp. 88–91, 94–107.

1   By better use of plant.
2   By better use of people.
One way to achieve these aims is to work plant and equipment more hours either by adding hours on to existing shifts, i.e. overtime or by working different shifts, or by a combination of both. Not everybody understands the reasons behind this.

From *Two Heads are Better than One*: Ford Motor Company Department of Labour Relations.

The only time the Ford Motor Company helps a worker is when he's dead.

Operator: Cortina Engine Dress, Halewood 1967.

Ford began operating in Liverpool toward the end of 1962. 'This place was a bit of an Eldorado at the time,' said one of the stewards. 'Everybody wanted to come here. They were coming here from all over Lancashire. Y'know expecting the pavements in the Press Shop to be lined with gold.' Entry into Eldorado however was limited. Merseyside and Lancashire was a depressed area. Traditional industries were in decline. Unemployment figures were high and wages were low. Everybody wanted to go to Ford's but not everybody was allowed in. Ford's had the pick of the labour market, and the Company followed a recruitment policy which was consistent with its aim of obtaining a trouble-free plant on Merseyside. It aimed to recruit from 'the cream of the labour market' and although the rate of pay it offered was lower than at Dagenham and significantly lower than the rates operating in the Midlands, the state of the labour market on Merseyside made it high enough to serve the Company's purpose. Family men with commitments came first. Stable men who were tied down with debt and responsibility were given priority. Men under twenty were formally barred and there was little welcome in Halewood for men off the dock or the buildings. Seamen weren't very high up the list either. Neither were the unemployed. Two of the personnel officers on the plant at the time have recounted their experiences of recruitment. They explain that they were on the lookout for adaptable men from whom years of 'service' could be expected. Eighty-nine per cent of the earliest recruits were aged between twenty and forty. Only 14 per cent of these early Halewood workers came to the factory off the dole and 'it could reasonably be supposed' that the recruiting officers 'regarded the unemployed with some element of suspicion'.

The Ford Motor Company was after 'green labour'. Something over 60 per cent of its first recruits were entirely new to factory work. They never knew what hit them. A steward recollects that 'they were a really green bunch of lads. Not a typical Merseyside labour force at all. Y'know, they weren't objecting or complaining. They were trying to do the job. I'm not decrying those lads. They came here from all over – Wigan, Widnes, everywhere. They tried to do the job but the job just couldn't be done. Not the way Ford's wanted it.' The recruitment policy ran into difficulties because the recruited labour wasn't staying at Halewood. The stable men were moving on. They weren't used to factories, let alone the Ford assembly line, and the pay wasn't that good. By 1965 enough of them had left for the age requirement to be dropped to eighteen. Turnover rates were high and continued to be so throughout the 1960s. The story that management and workers told most often recounts how men arrive at the plant for their first shift, see the job and ask for their cards. In 1966 the PTA[1] plant lost 1140 manual employees out of a total labour force of 3200. The number declined to about 800 in 1967 but in 1968 it was 1160 and in 1969 1800. As a result of men voting with their feet the Company recruitment policy foundered. All they were left with was a watchful eye for the militant and the intelligent. As one personnel officer put it: 'Anyone who puts an intelligent man on the sort of job that we've got here is asking for trouble. We've had it as well. Whoever recruited intelligent blokes like Roberts and Flaherty want their arses kicking. Intelligent blokes are bound to get militant if you stick them on the trim line.' Apart from this they'd take all comers. One of this personnel man's colleagues argued that 'there's only one way to recruit men in this industry. You don't want to bother with aptitude tests and interviews. If you want 200 men just send down the labour for 400. Get them to come to the gates for 9.00 and let them in at 10.00. That's how to recruit men in this industry.'

Over 80 per cent of the manual jobs in an assembly plant contribute to the productive monotony of the assembly line. In 1967 the men who performed these jobs were called operatives, classified as semi-skilled and paid an average of 8/9d. per hour. For a forty hour week, on days, they earned £17.10.0. They worked a night shift fortnightly about, and were paid time and a third for doing so. All the men in the sample of members were assembly line workers. They, like men in the PTA generally, came to Ford's with a diverse work experience. They had found their previous employment across a wide range of semi- and unskilled jobs in the area. Many of them had 'moved around a bit', always looking for somewhere better. Seventeen of the stewards and eighteen of the members had had three or more jobs in the ten years that preceded their employment at the car plant. They had been lorry drivers, hod carriers, seamen, dockers, telephone engineers and butchers. In the main they were young – all had been under forty when recruited

— and were married with young children. They came in search of
Eldorado and in 1967 at least they were still helping to make motor
cars in the PTA plant at Halewood.

Often it is quite inappropriate to talk of 'car workers' in the same
way as one would talk of 'miners', for many of them do not consider
themselves to be 'car workers' in that sense. They see themselves more
as workers who *happen* to be working in a car plant. They've done
other jobs in the past and they expect to do others in the future. They
don't want to grow old on the line. They work in a car plant because of
the money: 'Money and a five day week' was the stock response to the
question 'Why Ford's?' Occasionally the size of the plant was mentioned,
together with the general idea that work in a car plant would be a bit
different, a bit interesting and afforded the chance to get on. In the
main, though, it was the money — thirty-two of the stewards and forty
of the members mentioned this as one of their main reasons for coming
to the plant. They came to Ford's because they needed to make a living
and there were limited opportunites for doing that on Merseyside. For
many people Ford's move to Halewood seemed like the big chance. [. . .]

For many workers the Ford Motor Company was, in 1967, the nearest
thing to an 'ideal firm' that they had come across on Merseyside. A
worker on the trim line made this explicit when he said 'if I tell you
that this is the most ideal firm I've worked for, you can picture the
others. Compared with the alternatives this *is* ideal.' Many of the
stewards would have agreed with this, nevertheless they were highly
critical of the Company and the wage rates paid to Ford workers.
While the majority of the sample of members based their evaluation
of the firm upon their own immediate experience of the labour market
on Merseyside, the stewards consistently tended to take a wider view.
Frequently they based their evaluation of wage rates upon what they
felt the company could *afford* to pay, supporting their arguments by
reference to profits and the rates paid by other motor manufacturers
in the Midlands. This wider awareness, combined with their experiences
of low rates and a rampant management during the start-up period at
Halewood, crystallized in a sophisticated understanding of how wage
rates were established and changed.

The stewards considered that all the good things offered to workers
at the Ford Motor Company had had to be fought for. They were seen
as the fruits of trade union organization and struggle rather than grace
and favour of an ideal employer. Many of the stewards made some
reference to the early days of the plant and made it clear that certain
lessons had to be learned from this experience. Eric put it like this:

What we've got we've fought for, and fought hard at that. When I came here first we were worked really hard and if you had a complaint you couldn't get a steward. Now a man can get a steward pretty quickly. It took a lot of hard work. The rate was bad and the job was bad . . . People have got short memories, though, and new ones come. They see the job now and they think 'this isn't so bad'. They forget that it wasn't always like this. We *earned* it like it is and if we don't watch out with this Company we'll be back where we started.

Involvement in the shop stewards committee and identification with its aims clearly affected the thinking of the shop stewards at Halewood. In particular it affected their understanding of trade unionism and the function of management within the factory, and this in its turn affected their relationship with their members and fellow workmates. While the past can be seen to have structured the present in the way that it provided the steward with a 'pragmatic charter' for his everyday activities in the plant, such charters are invariably questioned and need defending in a complex society. Part of the process of being a steward at Halewood involved argument with the members over the *correct* interpretation of the present. There is no easy, straightforward way of dealing with the fact that shopfloor union activism differentiates the steward from the mass of the membership. The nature of the differentiation will vary from situation to situation. What is clear, however, is that at Halewood involvement in the early struggles in the plant, together with day to day contact with events throughout the plant, created within the shop steward committee a more radical critique of the Ford Motor Company than existed generally within the factory. This is revealed most clearly by the way the stewards and their members understand the Ford management.

The motor industry is a highly competitive industry. Large companies with excess capacity in their plants compete with each other across a wide range of models. Computerization, technological sophistication, increased productivity, and regular changes of models have been acute features of the British motor industry since World War Two. A visit to the office of a production manager in a car plant vividly highlights the consequences of these changes. The walls are covered with charts — output, labour costs, projections — everywhere you look. They dominate the consciousness of the manager and his aides. They point them out to you as one would a particular piece of countryside. At one point during my stay in the plant I went into the Trim Assembly Department with a Personnel Officer in the hope of obtaining the release of some workers off the job for a talk. 'Could we possibly have about ten operatives for a short while?' — 'Fuck off' — 'But be reasonable.

I'd only want them for about half an hour' — 'Half an hour, ten men, that's five hours, do you know how many cars that is . . . How much that will cost me? Get me a note for five hours from the Works Manager and you can have them. Otherwise fuck off.' Time is money and money is everything in a car plant. The cars take shape along an assembly line. Over the length of the line some 16,000 components are screwed, stuck or spotwelded together. Each of these components has to be delivered to the assembly plant, stored and allocated to the various assembling points along the line. Spatial and budgeting constraints prevent large stores being kept. Time and space is money. Unexpected interference with supplies will cause havoc in no time. Model changes don't help much either, for this means a complete retooling of the plant and a redefinition and redistribution of work tasks. Also it means 'teething problems'.

If a car plant is about money a plant manager's job is about pressure. In him complicated administrative and technical tasks coexist with market pressures, deadline dates and the like. It's not surprising that Turner should suggest that these managers often welcome, if not provoke, strikes which can get them off the hook of a missed output target. There is frequent evidence in a car plant of the pressure that production management works under. At Halewood, for example, the three plants formed an integrated technological unit. This integration was not reflected in accountancy practices. The manager of the Trim Assembly department bought painted body shells from the manager of the Paint Shop who had previously bought the shell from the manager of the Body Plant. Wrangles and stand up rows were not uncommon along the frontiers of the departments. 'Take the fucking things back. I'm not having crap like that. Look at that fucking finish. I'm not having that.' The lads watched, waited for their foreman to get a bollocking and kept their eye on their steward.

The production managers are the hard heads. For them money is success, the difference between failure and success lying in the extra car or two that they can squeeze out of the lads. They're not daft. They know this. They are the hard heads, the supporters of the 'firm line'. Often they come into conflict with 'Personnel'. The history of the Halewood Estate in fact is one in which power ebbs and flows between these two managerial power groups. The 'firm line' doesn't always work. While the Personnel Manager's job is less easily appraised in terms of money he too is out to make his name. While I was at the PTA I bumped into a man I'd met in the Regional Headquarters of the Electricity Generating Board. He was a Personnel Officer in the MSB[1] plant. He'd come there 'for the experience because there's no place like a car plant for negotiating experience. You get as much experience in this place in a year as you'd get in a lifetime in the Electricity Board.' A successful negotiation is a feather in the cap and a failure can be put down to experience.

All plant managers have something in common. Unless they're on the scrap-heap they're looking upward. In the car industry to look up is to look out. To be on the move from plant to plant. A success here, a killing there, and you're near the top of the tree. The Company's management training scheme is on the lookout for extroverts and individualists — polite parlance for 'big heads'. They take them on, build them up and not infrequently cut them down, for with competition and technical change comes organizational change. You may be left and overlooked, but that may be preferable to finding that your job no longer exists. British Leyland is still in the throes of such rationalization. Ford went through it all in the late 1960s. In 1967 brick walls started appearing across offices in the administration block at Halewood. Everything was to be changed. A new administrative structure left several middle managers with a salary but no 'function'. 'They should give you longer than two years' one said. He had tears in his eyes. 'If you've got a family they should give you more than two years. I thought I'd be settled for a bit here. It's not right. It's . . .'. The young, ambitious graduate smiled in reply and said: 'You've got to keep moving. It's no good standing still.' He'd move all right. What else could he do?

Sixty per cent of the graduates recruited by the Ford Motor Company in 1966 had left the Company by 1971
While these figures appear to be high, by comparison with British Industry as a whole we know that we have a lower than average termination rate for graduates within the first years of their employment.

There are various reasons why people leave the Company. Some decide that Industry is not for them and return to the academic life, either to pursue post-graduate studies or to go into lecturing or teaching. Others leave to take jobs of increased responsibility in a smaller company or to move into a consultancy, both of which we would regard as a reflection of the excellent experience they have obtained within the Company.

From *Graduates in Ford*.

Pressure and strain is structured into the very heart of a car plant. Structured into a game in which there are no real winners. In this world negotiations were often a battle, occasionally a subtle psychological war.

Out of this the stewards came to an understanding of the role of management in the plant and the way to relate to managers as individuals. It will be remembered that neither the stewards nor the sample of members thought that the Ford Motor Company rates highly as a 'considerate employer'. Only three of the stewards considered that the Company was even 'average' in this respect, while thirty of the sample of members considered the firm to be no better than average. Even its strongest supporter considered the Company to be a hard employer who was obsessed with production. The stewards, however, were vehement in their criticisms of the way the Company's management treated the workers. An indication of the strength of this feeling is shown by the fact that twenty-eight of the stewards considered that it was the attitude of the management that was most in need of change in the company. Some of their comments illustrate this:

They treat the labour as machinery here. The Personnel Department just don't exist. In many cases they are just *cruel*. All they're concerned with is production problems. It's production, production all the time with them.

They go on about getting people to cooperate. To spend their lives here and make a go of things and all that bullshit. But they don't even assist in making it bearable.

You're just counted as a number here. Treated like a lot of robots. You could be in desperate trouble and they wouldn't help you.

Several of the stewards made explicit the fact that their criticism of management derived from their experiences as stewards:

The supervisors here are just not trained in the right attitudes. That's why we're young. We've got to be to take it. We're young and we're militant. Not militant in that we take the blokes outside the gate — but in sticking up for them against the foreman. Standing up for their rights.

As a shop steward I see the main problem to be the centralization of power on both the management and trade union side. This is bad for the operator as well because both the steward and the operator get frustrated when things get taken above their heads. You need to have much more autonomy for shop-floor unionism.

I've found that with management it's always the case of passing the buck. They're all *afraid* to make a decision in case they drop a goolie. If anything goes wrong they don't want to know. They don't want to find out what or why they just want a scapegoat. Always find someone to blame.

In their discussion of plant management the stewards continually made reference to the fact that an unpleasant job was often made intolerable by management's self-interested concern for production and their own careers. A concern which rode over any consideration for or obligation towards the workers. Management, as far as the stewards could see, were out for themselves. Tied in with this is the idea that management aren't their own masters anyway, that all the important decisions are taken at Warley, or Detroit, and that plant management simply wants to keep its nose clean and get a good name. These two themes crop up continually, and can be seen as elements within what might be called a working-class *factory consciousness*.

The history of British trade unionism is built on various levels of factory class consciousness. Trade unionism and workshop organization is, and always has been, a direct response to economic forces. A response to a world where goods are exchanged as commodities on an open market. Where workers have nothing to sell but their labour power and where this too is bought and sold on the market. A factory class consciousness grew out of this; it understands class relationships in terms of their direct manifestation in conflict between the bosses and the workers within the factory. It is rooted in the workplace where struggles are fought over the control of the job and the 'rights' of managers and workers. In as much as it concerns itself with exploitation and power it contains definite political elements. But it is a politics of the factory. Implicitly tied up with the day-to-day battle with the boss. Factory class consciousness finds its historical antecedent in syndicalism — the idea of workers' control of the factories, adhered to most strongly by skilled workers which was most developed in Britain in the shop steward movement that occurred during and after World War One. While this was the high water mark of this tradition, strong elements of it still permeate the British working class. In its least developed form it is revealed in sporadic bloody-mindedness and 'malingering' — the 'fuck 'em' attitude that most managers are familiar with and find distasteful. The underlying structure of this view is not radically different from that which underpinned the consciousness of the stewards at Halewood. Their class consciousness can be seen as a higher development in as much as they had worked out a sophisticated understanding of how they were exploited in the factory and how they could best combat management there. Not infrequently this involved them in bloody-mindedness.

Particular features of the PTA plant at Halewood during the 1960s contributed to a heightened development of class awareness in this plant. All of the stewards and each of the forty-three members felt that if management were given the chance they would 'put one over on the workers'. This view was either supported by the simple statement: 'They've *done* it' or by the claim that all managers were the same in this respect. One Paint-Shop worker put it this way:

> Well it's the same everywhere really isn't it? That's what management is for really isn't it? . . . to get as much off you as they can. To get away with things like. This lot here is probably a bit worse than most, mind. The pressures are greater here.

In the interview I asked the stewards and members whether or not they agreed with a series of statements about management. The information is collated in Table 8.1 from which it can be clearly seen that the stewards possessed a consistently critical attitude toward management. A clear majority of the stewards felt that management was paid too much; that although they understood the problems faced by the workers, they were not prepared to do anything about them; that they were mainly concerned with efficiency, and that they wouldn't be prepared to assist the workers even if they had a clear opportunity to do so. It is important that not only did each of these responses have a clear majority amongst the stewards, but that twenty-two stewards gave all four responses. Within the steward organization, therefore, there had been developed a very clear, consistent understanding of the role of management within the factory. In comparison with this the responses of the membership are markedly uncertain and confused. Certainly they are much less consistently critical − only two of the member sample giving all four responses. To a large extent this difference can be explained by the different experiences of the stewards: i.e. as a *consequence* of trade union activity. For example, over half the members felt unable to comment on whether or not the Ford management were paid too much because they didn't know how much managers earned. In contrast the stewards were in a position to have a better idea not only of how much managers earned but also to know what they did in return. Only three stewards replied that they couldn't comment because of lack of information. Similarly the stewards frequently justified their responses to other questions by referring to specific incidents which they had been involved in as stewards and which for them typified the nature of managerial activity within the PTA plant. It was through these incidents that the stories of the past were lived out and developed within the committee. To take another example:

Table 8.1 Assessment of management

	Shop stewards	Members	Totals
1 Are the management paid too much?			
Too much	26	11	37
Too little			
About right	5	9	14
Don't know	5	23	28
Totals	36	43	79
2 Do management understand the problems faced by the workers?			
Understand	26	26	52
Ignorant	9	1	10
50/50		11	11
Don't know	1	5	6
Totals	36	43	79
3 Is management mainly concerned with efficiency or the personal welfare of the workers?			
Efficiency	35	24	59
Welfare			
50/50		19	19
Don't know	1		1
Totals	36	43	79
4 If given opportunity would management try to assist the workers?			
Yes	1	11	12
No	24	4	28
50/50	1	22	23
Don't know	10	6	16
Totals	36	43	79

when the members were asked whether they thought management would assist the workers if they were given the opportunity to do so, three-quarters of them were at least prepared to give them the benefit of the doubt. Twenty-four of the stewards were adamant in the judgement that they would never do it. Eighteen of these justified their scepticism by detailed reference to incidents where they felt that management had had an opportunity to assist the workers at little or no cost to themselves but had failed to make use of it. One said:

They've had golden opportunities here to help the lads and they've done nothing. Just take that Blue Book. That Blue Book is just a licence to rob. Whoever signed that for us ought to be shot. This

Company thinks it's so powerful that it can change the clock. On a Bank Holiday the lads have to come in for the night shift — that's for a start like — but then they don't get paid the time and a half for the morning that they're working during the Bank Holiday. No. The Ford Motor Company says that the Bank Holiday starts at seven o'clock in the fucking morning. It's OK for them. We spend half the weekend in bed.

And another

They've *always* got opportunities but they never help the lads. Even when the opportunity isn't obvious they could make the opportunity if they wanted to. You should see them move and manipulate when they want something for themselves. They forget there's rules then . . . when production is threatened.

What would be a good example? Well just take an easy one — holidays. We get a problem with this every year. What we try to do before the holidays is to arrange so that the lads on nights work a 'lieu shift' instead of the Friday shift. You want to get off perhaps on the Saturday and you're knackered after a night in this place. This year they said 'all right work a "lieu shift"' — they want to arrange it as much as us, you see, because they know half the lads won't turn in on the Friday anyway — that's the only reason they consider it at all — 'but you'll have to work the Sunday previous'. Well, we said 'what's wrong with Saturday?' — they wanted the lads to work for *single time* on the Sunday you see. And they replied 'you'll work when we say you work'. They had ample opportunity to show some goodwill to the lads there. The lads told them to stick it and no one came in on the Saturday, Sunday or Friday.

You get a lot of things, a lot of little things, when everything would be so much easier if they'd bend a bit. But they won't. I don't know what it is. I think they just don't trust the lads. But the lads are OK if you treat them all right.

These two quotations are interesting in the light of recent arguments over the 'instrumentality' of the new 'affluent' sector of the British working class. Some sociologists have maintained, for example, that this sector of the working class has, during the 1960s, been increasingly concerned about money to the neglect of 'traditional' brotherhood with their workmates. While these responses appear superficially to be indicative of some form of 'pure' instrumentalism, a concern for money and nothing else, it should be noted that, for the stewards, the question of premium payments was a moral question. One of them said: 'I think it's morally wrong to ask a man to work overtime, nights and weekends, it's even more wrong to ask him to work it without a premium payment and it's a crime if that man accepts. Because it's wrong, morally wrong . . .' If you are going to sell yourself you should at least attempt to have *some* say in the terms. Others took this further.

> Well, let's get this straight. I don't want nothing from this Company. I don't ask for no favours. If they want to be nasty that suits me. You know where you are then. They're just a bunch of crooks and we're going to stop them doing too much thieving. So I don't want any handouts. It's just that I think they're stupid that's all. I don't think they ought to be nice to us, I don't even want them to be nice to us, but you can't help thinking how fucking stupid they are. We have a great time with them. But seriously you get it all the time. The job could be run twice as good, with everybody having a better time and *more* work getting done if it were more flexible. All the supervisors here, see, are shit-scared. They've got a big book in their office and if it isn't in there it can't be done. If it isn't in Mr Ford's book they've never heard of it, it can't happen and they don't want to know. Now as I say that suits me. It's not my job to run the section.

The men who came to Halewood to work for Ford came from diverse employment backgrounds yet brought broadly similar expectations to the plant. In this respect the stewards were in no way different from the sample of members. Their direct involvement in the early struggles with management in the plant produced within the committee a critical understanding of the function of management at Ford, and this understanding was reinforced by their day-to-day contact with management and with each other. The collective involvement of the stewards in building an organization and struggling with management produced a committee with a coherent ideology — a highly developed awareness of the class structure in the factory. It is in its coherence that this ideology differs from the understanding arrived at by stewards in many other plants and by the membership as a whole in the Halewood plant. And their critique of management can be seen to demonstrate this awareness. It is a central pivot within the ideology of the stewards committee.

Since the war sociologists have taken it into their heads to interview workers and ask them whether or not they consider the factory to be like 'a football team'. Affirmative answers have been taken as an indication of a lack of class consciousness. This, however, misses the fundamental point about capitalist production. It isn't an either–or question of being like a football team *or* being like two opposing camps. Factory production involves *both*. Because production has a social basis the factory can obviously be seen, at some level, as a collectivity with management operating in a coordinating role. The contradiction of factory production, and the source of contradictory elements within class consciousness, is rooted in the fact that the exploitation of workers is achieved through collective, coordinated activities within both the factory and society generally. Frequently the PTA stewards attempted to resolve this contradiction in moral terms.

The stewards' critique of management can be presented in terms of two dimensions. The one structural, which places the action of management within the structure of the large capitalist corporation; the other moral, which involves a criticism of the action management take in the plant and a moral judgement of the managers as men. The last quotation (on p. 119) illustrates the tension between these two aspects of the critique. Management is there to make profit, therefore you expect them to be concerned about efficiency and the like; you don't expect them to be considerate to the lads, in fact, it might make things more complicated if they were. Nevertheless they *should* treat the lads better — if only because the lads would be that bit more cooperative if treated decently.

Revised nightshift hours
As you all know, the most recent attempt to improve the conditions of the nightshift workers has been our application to Management that for the period that overtime is not being worked on nights you should only have to work nine nightshifts instead of the ten each fortnight; production time to be made up by one hour of overtime being attached to eight of the shifts worked. This request seemed to be met by local Management with a not unreasonable response, and it was clear to your JWC Members that some Managers were openly in favour of what is a perfectly legitimate and logical submission by us. However, at the time of writing, our request has been turned down after having been referred to 'Central Staff'. Again our Managers here at Halewood have demonstrated their ineffectiveness and their inability to truly negotiate with us. The reasons given to us for the rejection have not been accepted by us as valid, and have the usual lame ring of feeble excuses about them. We now await a meeting with higher Management in the hope that commonsense will prevail, and for once Ford Management can demonstrate that they do have the wisdom to manage and respond to the reasonable wishes of their employees . . . We are sceptical.

From *PTA Voice*, 1970.

Car plants are about profit and pressure and so is plant management. A perpetual struggle to reduce costs by increasing the rate of output. Keep the line going continuously! There is an inevitable conflict on the shop floor of a car plant. This is one of the facts of life, something the shop steward has to live with. It can push him along the road to militancy or stifle his spirit — because this is the guts of it; the inevitability of struggle, day in, day out. To see this, accept it and carry on is to expose fundamental questions about the structure of relations within the plant and within society generally. This can lead to an understanding of management as mere pawns in the game, victims of forces that they cannot adequately control or understand. Bill McGuire put it like this:

> Well it's a bit difficult to work it out actually. I've thought about it a lot. With some of them it's easy because they're bastards; they're not all like that though. Some of them are quite nice blokes who believe in the Ford Motor Company. They do you know. Some of them believe all the shit that's given them.
>
> I don't see myself being any better than them *as a man*. It's just the situation that they're in. They've just got to make a profit or they get the sack. It's as easy as that. They've got to screw the blokes or they get screwed. That's the way it is . . .

But trade unionism cannot resolve this problem for trade union activity in itself is manifestly incapable of altering the entire *raison d'être* of the capitalist enterprise. The activity of the steward stems from a much less complex concern — from the need to obtain at least some control over the decisions that management make. To obtain at least some slight reform of the system of control that operates within the factory. The structural criticism is given strength by a moral criticism. It may be inevitable that the blokes get screwed but this doesn't make it right. Screwing people is wrong and it must be challenged. Management may be pawns, they may be just doing their job, they may be nice blokes, but by challenging the moral rights of workers they make themselves morally culpable. It is by this means that the stewards come to activism. It is this which gives force to the ideology of trade unionism and the idea of trade union principles. Johnny Jones said:

> Well it's like this you see Huw, a lot of things that management do I consider to be morally wrong. I fight Ford's because of this. Take dismissals — we'll *always* fight a dismissal. I believe that when a man is about to be sacked — his livelihood taken off him; a man with kids say — then everything ought to be brought into account. I had a number of dismissal cases last week, blokes who'd been late over the

last month — they'd already had their final warnings like. Now as far as Ford's go — you know the disciplinary procedure they've got? — well as far as they're concerned when a bloke's had a final warning he's had it if he sets a foot wrong. That was it you see, I was called in and they just assume six dismissals as if there was nothing to be said. I think that's wrong. I think it's wrong to just sack a man no matter what he's done. We've had terrible weather this past month — ice, fog and everything. I said to Obbart — 'You look at the records of some of the best timekeepers in this plant over the past month — look at mine, look at Eddie Roberts's — and they'll be as bad as these lads.' Oh it had been really bad. It took me three hours to get to the plant one morning. It had been murder getting in. Anyway I only got one lad off, the other five got the sack. It makes me sick that not being able to get a lad off. You see what I mean. Those lads shouldn't have been sacked but it didn't matter much to Ford's. It just goes on their turnover rate.

Maybe the Company had to make a profit. Maybe that was the way things were in the world, and management had its own problems but it was, nevertheless, bloody hard for the lads on the line. The working class. The idea that workers and managers belong to different classes and as a result have different loyalties and understandings is central here. Unlike managers, workers have to get up at half past five in the morning, catch buses or wait on the corner for their lift. Getting to work is, for them, often a struggle and the stewards understand these struggles because they experience them themselves.

The plant then can be seen, and is seen by most of the stewards, as an arena of limited class conflict. A shop stewards committee which had developed out of the conflicts within the PTA plant was held together by a sophisticated factory class consciousness. A consciousness which told them that management was on the other side and had to be opposed by the lads. This understanding also revealed management as pawns in the profit game, and here was the difficulty. To know that you are involved in an inevitable economic conflict, a perpetual day to day struggle with the boss can take you so far. There comes a point when it brutalizes you. Many stewards balked long before this, weighed down by the contradiction that management may be on the other side but they are human 'like us'. These stewards just didn't have the stomach for confrontation after confrontation, slanging match after slanging match. They were too nice, too soft, they lacked, as one of them put it, 'the killer instinct'. At certain times in a car plant, however, a steward who lacks such instincts gets into severe difficulties. A humanitarian act in the office can have adverse consequences for the steward's membership.

Management may be pawns, but in a car plant they're paid to be lethal pawns. One of the stewards said: 'If you've got one of them down, he's bleeding and everything, there's just no point in going over to help him up because as soon as he's back on his feet he's going to start hitting you.'

To take an extreme case. One of the middle managers at Halewood had been worn down by his career with the Ford Motor Company and was receiving regular psychiatric treatment. The stewards knew this, 'he was a nerve case, Ted. He used to go off every month to get his shock treatment. He'd be right as rain when he came back, but in a couple of weeks he'd be shaking again.' This man occupied an important position within the negotiating procedure. If the stewards failed to obtain an agreement in their negotiation with him the problem would formally have to be referred to the national committee, which would take time without a guarantee of success. Ted Bates (a pseudonym) then was a key man in the negotiations set-up at Halewood. Management often use procedures as stalling devices. At Halewood the stalling devices were quite complex. Fall guys would be set up to block demands for a period of time. Supervisors were regularly used as fall guys, so was Ted Bates. The shop stewards' convenor and the District Officer had developed an understanding with Ted Bates' superior – Goodman (another pseudonym). Although not formally in the procedure, Goodman wanted to act as a backstop. If all else failed his door would always be open to the convenor. The convenor had as a right something which few middle managers were confident of. He could see Goodman whenever he wanted to. Goodman had specifically asked him to see him if a problem cropped up which seemed likely to stop the plant. Both the convenor and the District Officer knew that they had immediate recourse to a senior manager, outside the formal procedure, and they also knew that Goodman used Bates as a fall guy.

It didn't happen once you know it happened very often. It was a regular occurrence. Ted was all right. If it was something within his domain you'd get a decent decision out of him. Regularly though we bloody well knew that he had no power in the situation and that he'd been sent in by Goodman to sort us out. 'I can assure you', he used to say, 'I can assure you that I have complete management backing on this item and the answer is no.' It was all pretty despicable really in human terms because he had been used so blatantly. We'd say all right we'll go and see Goodman. 'I'm not sure if Mr Goodman will see you.' 'He'll see us, Ted, tell him we're coming.' It was really sick because we'd go out of this office along the corridor into Goodman's luxurious suite and we'd get what we wanted. Ted would be there eyes standing out of his head, almost crying.

How did Goodman justify all this to Bates?

> I don't know. He'd probably say something like, 'What's the matter, Ted? We're paying you a good salary, aren't we? We're making motors aren't we? Quality's all right isn't it? We've got to placate these bastards. Go on back to your cage.' And off he'd go for his shock treatment. Strapped to the battery again.

Some stewards wouldn't be able to cope with this, they wouldn't have the stomach. But what should a steward do under such circumstances? Humanitarian considerations might lead him to go easy, take Ted's word for it, let the issue pass over or refer it to the NJNC.[2] But where does this leave the lads on the line, the subjects of the dispute? This is the crucial point. Managers negotiate with stewards and union officials about the lives of other people, people not directly involved in the face to face negotiation. Men who regularly negotiate with each other get to know each other and develop a certain amount of give and take with each other. They come to some day to day accommodation and in this situation both the manager and the union negotiator will be inclined to go easy if their opponent is on the ropes. That such give and take is an important feature of management–union relations throughout industry is undeniable. What is also undeniable, however, is that this institutionalized leniency often breaks down. While the negotiating situation has an important degree of autonomy from the work situation, ultimately the pattern of negotiations will always be coloured by the balance of forces in that situation. Under certain circumstances any humanitarian concern that the steward may feel for his opponent across the table will openly conflict with his duty as the representative of his workmates. It cuts even deeper the other way. A manager in a car plant may let a steward off the hook, but if he does it often enough, on issues important enough, he'll find his journey to the top halted. Car plants are about profit and pressure. They very quickly sort the men out from the boys. You've got to be a very hard man to get to the top in the industry. You've got to be equally hard if you want to be a useful steward and union organizer.

As I have hinted, shop stewards occupy an ambiguous position within a factory. The steward is frequently involved in the process of translating experiences – of explaining to one group of people the significance that a particular occurrence has for another group of people. Quite often this ambiguity, derived from regular contact with 'the office', can turn the steward against his workmates and encourage him to take the job as supervisor. Shop stewards are regularly, and have always been, bought off in factories up and down the country. The same ambiguity, however, can, when allied with other factors, serve as an important radicalizing agent. This proved to be the case at Halewood. A severe period of struggle during the early years of the plant provided the experience which moulded the ideology of the stewards committee. Struggle over the line speeds, lay-offs, victimization and the like fostered the articulation of a highly developed form of factory class consciousness. This class consciousness has been termed a *factory* consciousness because as an ideology its cutting edge is essentially limited to the confines of the arena of production. [. . .]

Editors' notes

1 PTA (Paint, Trim and Assembly plant) and MSB (Metal Stamping and Body plant) are two of the major plants at Ford's Halewood Estate.
2 The NJNC (National Joint Negotiating Committee) is an inter-union committee that negotiates between the unions and the Ford Management.

9 Black identity and the role of reggae

Ken Pryce

Reggae is an urbanized form of West Indian pop music, which comes direct from the slums of Kingston, Jamaica, and must be seen as an offshoot of calypso (called 'mento' in Jamaica), which was rural in origin. Reggae is a music of protest and owes its existence to the abject condition of the poor in Jamaica and to the changing moods of the people in the immediate post-independence period, when the music quickly established itself as a popular form of artistic-expression among the masses. Culturally, reggae erupted out of the syncretic Afro-Christian subsoil, which has been the traditional basis of Negro culture in Jamaica. This subsoil consists of such elements as Bedwardism, revivalism, Pentecostalism and Garveyism. However, the most direct contributions to the development of reggae music have been made by the Rastafarians (and their allies, the rudies), who are a radical Afro-oriented cult group hostile to the official establishment in Jamaica. But to understand the nature and significance of the Rastas' contribution to the growth of reggae and the influence of the music in linking teenyboppers with their opposite numbers in Jamaica — rudies and Rastas — we must first know more about the Rastas themselves, and their relation to rudies and teenyboppers.

Rastafarianism is a millenarian cult movement, based on the ideas of exile and Zionism. It flourishes because of the extreme poverty in Jamaica, the low social status and the extreme deprivation and racial humiliation of the black majority. Marcus Garvey, the high priest of black nationalism all over the Western world, is the acknowledged forerunner of the Rastafarian movement, though very little is known about the precise connection between him and the early Rastas. It does not, however, require an expert to trace the influence of Garvey in the fantastic creed of the Rasta man. The Garvey Back-to-Africa theme has been taken over whole, developed and systematized. In a society as Negrophobic as Jamaica, a black backlash in the form of an ideological counter-racism was inevitable. The Rastas have supplied this. [. . .]

Source: 'The quest for solution: black identity and the role of reggae', ch. 14 in *Endless Pressure: a Study of West Indian Life-styles*, Penguin Books, 1979, extracts from pp. 144–61.

How did the Rasta movement actually begin? It is said that Garvey had predicted that the deliverance of the black race would occur when a black king was crowned in Africa. In 1930 Ras Tafari (the name of Selassie before his coronation) was crowned Haile Selassie, Emperor of Ethiopia, a formerly obscure African kingdom. With this, Garvey's words began to take on significance for many Negroes in the New World, who came to realize that there was in fact an independent African state with its own monarchy and cultural heritage.

The Ethiopian government responded to outside interest by forming in 1937 the Ethiopian World Federation, Inc., to foster racial solidarity. This was exactly what the people later to become Rastafarians were waiting for. They reciprocated in Jamaica by forming organizations such as the United Ethiopian Body, the United Afro-West Indian Brotherhood, the Ethiopian Youth Faith, the Men of Nyabingi, etc.

Rastafarianism is not a coherent movement with a clearly defined system of leadership. It is estimated to have between 10 and 15,000 supporters, but they are split up into sects. The only thing that unites them is a common belief system based on black solidarity and black dignity. Their cohesion, such as it is, lies in the fact that they all look outward to Africa for redemption – a fact which is due directly to their spiritual and psychological alienation from the imitation-British Jamaican society. [. . .]

During the fifties Rasta believers had visions of leaving Jamaica for Africa and various attempts were made by them to board ships docked in Kingston harbour, because they believed these ships had come to take them back to Africa.

The typical Rastafarian is non-conformist, utterly rejects the bourgeois life-style of the wider society and carries himself in such a way as to shock the uninitiated. The more respectable you are the more likely you are to be shocked. The Rasta is usually a lower-class black man. In appearance, his most distinguishing feature is his hair. He grows it long, never washes it, and allows it to become thick and matted so that it hangs down in numerous spiky strands, his 'locks' or 'dread-locks'. A Rasta-man is a 'locksman'. In the initial stages, when he first starts to grow his hair long, he is 'dreading'. A Rasta might even eschew conventional clothes for rough rags. He may carry a staff, so that he looks like an East African shepherd or a primitive tribesman. The idea is to look as dreadful as possible, as black as possible, as primitive as possible – the extreme and complete antithesis of the European-dominated Jamaican conception of beauty. As far as the Rastafarian is concerned, 'the blacker the better'.

In their religious creed ganja or marijuana has a special significance. The 'herb' is described in the Book of Genesis as a sacred 'weed', and the Rastas justify their use of it by arguing that it gives them health and strength and unites them spiritually with God through the 'wisdom' they derive from it. Ganja is the 'wisdom weed'.

The Rastas are commonly regarded by all and sundry as experts on the Bible. They are particularly addicted to the apocalyptic concepts of the Old Testament and their parable-like speeches and enunciations generally reverberate with Old Testament images such as: 'Valleys of Death', 'false prophets', 'Lakes of Fire', 'brimstone', 'fire 'pon dem', 'burn dem up', 'beasts', 'thunder', 'lightning', 'falling heads', etc.

Like the Pentecostalists they can usually justify and account for every occurrence in terms of their own peculiar interpretation of the Bible. For example, it was their study of the Book of Revelation that persuaded them Haile Selassie was divine. To them this had to be so, because the Emperor's titles include 'King of kings, Lord of lords and the conquering Lion of Judah'.[1]

> The strict Rastafarian [says Katrin Norris] is proud, erect with a stern Mosaic morality, outraged at the treatment of the Negro in Jamaica . . . He keeps his independence from society by refusing to beg or to work for wages and takes pride in a craft or an enterprise such as fishing or farming where he can be self-employed. Some have even set up communal workshops where the week's profits are shared out equally among all hands. They stick together with their own people among whom there is no need for them to show respect for the white man. They are deeply religious, call themselves brethren and profess to live according to a creed of 'Peace and love'. They have developed their own crude art, their own songs and rhythms and keep alive their history of slavery which is officially forgotten.

The Rasta creed is probably the best example of the functional reinterpretation of African and Christian concepts in the black Jamaican lower-class search for recognition and a positive identity. But though they have evolved out of the cultic messianism of revivialism, the Rastas are only superficially religious. Their religious dogmas are solidly buttressed by a conscious and clearly enunciated ideological racism. The Rastas' rejection of the white man's God goes hand in hand with their rejection of his other values. By their bold assertion of the concept of 'Africa', they seek to reverse the disproportionate significance of the 'white bias' in Creole culture in favour of the African component represented by the majority. In this way they also attempt to cope with the inadequately explained areas of their existence, in order that, in the words of a Rasta man, they may be 'liberated from the obscurity of themselves'.[2]

The rude-boys in Jamaica

Over the past fifteen years, successive governments in Jamaica have engaged in attempts to placate the Rastafarians and stem the appeal of their doctrine for the masses. About fifteen years ago a delegation consisting of officials and Rastafarians was sent to Africa to explore the possibilities of Rastafarians' immigrating there. What is more, immediately after independence, Marcus Garvey was declared the principal hero of Jamaica. But it was too late. By this time the persistence of the intolerable conditions of the country had already alienated a considerable proportion of the young deprived blacks. These younger dissidents argued that their deprivation was a result of the society's rigid colour/class stratification and responded by engaging in crime, violence and terrorism. Out of this unrest, which surfaced in the sixties and is gathering momentum today, has emerged the rude-boy phenomenon. 'Rude-boy' (rude-bwoy) is Jamaican for the delinquent, black, lower-class youth. It is the phenomenal unemployment situation which has thrown up the rude-boys. But the rude-boy is more than a delinquent: he is a revolutionary and, as a way of manifesting his resentment and articulating his grievances, he identifies with the Rastafarians and adopts their life-style. A degree of legitimacy was given to their activities when middle-class youths and intellectuals of leftish persuasion began to identify with the movement.

Rex Nettleford was told by a rude-boy:[3]

'There are thousands of them [i.e. rude-boys] out there with ambition, seeking jobs, looking work and get none. Some of the places they go, they really turn them away. They feel as if they are not part of the society and nobody wants them around.' The frustration frequently resulted in a turn of anger. 'A hungry man becomes an angry man,' explained a rude-boy, 'and . . . these boys can't get no way of obtaining shelter nor having food nor clothes and when you look at them their ages just 15 to 20 . . .' Garth White, a young commentator on the rude-boys, says that the majority of youth coming from the lower 60 per cent of the population that shares approximately 19 per cent of the National Income is angry — angry to the point of violence. In fact, violence was a feature of the rude-boy phenomenon in the wake of the mid sixties. At first directed against members of their own deprived class, the angry young men were soon to acquire a 'high consciousness', according to one member, and to realize that 'it's not the suffering brethren you should really stick up [with German-made ratchet knives and guns, according to White], it is these big merchants that have all these twelve places and living in apartments – all fifteen – with the whole heap of different luxurious facilities'. The speaker continued: 'We no longer going to hold up our brothers and sisters because they haven't got what we want. What we really want is this equal rights and justice. Every man have a good living condition, good schooling, and then I feel things will be much better as long as we get this right of equality.'

Here is a shift of emphasis from classic Rastafari doctrine. There is no question of deliverance in Ethiopia ruled by a Divine Haile Selassie. Deliverance must be in Jamaica. Change must come not by escape from the system but by the shaking up of the system – even if by violence. The Robin Hood morality of robbing the rich to give to the poor is also evident here, where it is absent from Rastafarianism. Nor did the rude-boys establish a religious base for their position. Theirs is a secular social and political 'philosophy' that invokes the right to work, stresses the obligation that society has to the individuals born in it, demands equitable distribution of wealth with special considerations for the deprived black majority and calls for universal justice . . . Although Garth White correctly thinks that the rude-boy is less ambivalent in his attitudes to the wider society than, say, the Rastafarian, the ambivalence is there nonetheless. The rejection of 'middle-class standards and values' is never complete for their group – the acquisition of middle-class education, motor cars, homes with swimming pools, salaries of four figures and regular secure employment (whether self-employed or otherwise) are still objectives which determine the protest.

Reggae

Reggae erupted among the youth of shanty-town areas of Kingston simply from the need of rude-boys, Rastafarians and others to earn a living through music and dance (and other forms of artistic expression). But in the process the music was used for the conscious investigation and expression of the grim realities of society, and for the diffusion of 'Upper Nigger consciousness'[4] and the Rastafarian doctrines of negritude and African redemption. The Rasta and rude-boy musicians did this by concentrating on the composition of what are known as 'dread tunes'. To understand the core of the rudie-Rasta influence in reggae and its hold on the teenybopper, we must understand more clearly the meaning of 'dread' which is rooted in the cultural predicament in Jamaica (and in the West Indies in general).

Jamaica is caught in the grip of two gigantic, seemingly insoluble social problems, which were identified as poverty (due to imperialism) and lack of an authentic sense of national identity. The rudies and the Rastafarians believe that the lack of a sense of identity in Jamaica is due to deep-seated psychological feelings of inferiority embedded in the psyche of a population that looks to Europe for validation, as well as to the emasculation of the majority, which is ashamed of its past. They believe that a nation that is ashamed of itself can create nothing, and that a nation that creates nothing can achieve nothing, least of all its own liberation. A valid sense of identity can only come from a deeply felt national consciousness and from pride in its own values and achievements. Jamaicans will only be free when they cease to live on a borrowed and hypocritical culture and begin to see themselves as a potential rival to the white man in creativity and achievement. The music of the Rastafarians is devoted to these beliefs. In it they do two things: they continually hark back to Africa as the original spiritual home of the black man, and they plumb the depths of their own submerged local roots to revive and glorify black lower-class themes and motifs that were hitherto disparaged and despised. The dread element in the music celebrates the quest for and the realization of their spiritual discoveries. The music is meant to be an excavation in the very grounds of being – i.e. 'black' being – with a view to implode society with a consciousness of itself as essentially black and African – 'the Upper Nigger consciousness'. This comes out clearly in the dread content of the music, which is no more than the distillation of visceral images of sex, violence and protest, accompanied by aggressively menacing and uncompromising drum beats, and lyrics which articulate the mood and grievances of the people. Dreading in reggae is meant to elaborate musically what is already manifested in the black lower-class life-style. To deepen the 'dread' in their music the Rastafarians have reintroduced the traditional African form of drumming, rhythmic syncopation and collective improvisation. The heavy drumming is what gives the music its rooted cool and menace. The African call and response (lead singer/ accompaniment-chorus) relationships, as well as the African form of folk-reportage, have also been adapted. In all this the Rastafarians have evolved a local expressional code which is unmistakably black, indigenous and non-European.

But there are other ingredients in the music: blues, rock and roll, rhythm and blues, and jazz from near-by America. These have blended with the other black elements to produce a rich blend of musical data. The original Calypso couldn't carry the weight, and the burden, of the folk-urban rebellion taking place in Jamaica. Blues was a heavier in-gredient and was injected by the rude-boys the better to express the suffering of the people, thereby giving the music its social reference and replacing the popular-appeasing element in calypso, which had become tourist-oriented. Jazz has influenced the instrumental expression of the black ideas and emotions. But the basic calypso-mento element was retained, and this is what gives the music its specifically West Indian flavour. But in all this — especially in 'dread tunes' ('raw reggae', 'ethnic reggae', 'underground reggae', 'real reggae') — the rastafarianized drumming and rhetoric of Ethiopia, Babylon and Apocalypse breaks through to saturate the consciousness of the listener.

With the help of the sound system and the high-powered, self-constructed speakers used by West Indian DJs in Jamaica (and in England), reggae burst out forcefully from the slums and became a popular and common mode of expression for a wide cross-section of the Jamaican youth. Its appeal, first and foremost, was the appeal of pop music anywhere. At first the response from the middle class was one of sneer and snobbery, but soon the music penetrated their own privileged ranks and they had to give way to the sheer force of reggae as a pop form that was acceptable to both poor and middle-class youths alike. A British commentator, researching in Jamaica, describes the retreat of the Jamaican bourgeoisie in the face of the mass enthusiasm unleashed by the reggae craze. The occasion was the premier showing of the rude-boy/reggae film *The Harder They Come.*[5]

All the top reggae singers, Jimmy Cliff and Desmond Dekker and Bob Marley and the Wailers and the Maytals, all of them, they all came out of West Kingston. And now there's a movie out, *The Harder They Come*, the first rude-boy movie.

They turned out for that. When it opened in Kingston to a celebrity audience that included the new Prime Minister and most of the Cabinet and ranking Kingston society, the rudies turned out in such jubilant force that the doors gave in. They packed the Carib theater till the P.M. was sitting three to a seat, and everybody stripped down and got high and it was a hell of a hot night. *The Harder They Come* does for the rude-boys what *Rebel Without a Cause* did for juvenile delinquents and *Easy Rider* did for acid-eating paranoids and *Shaft* did for Harlem. It's the story of a boy from the hills who hits town, gets stung, can't get a break, stalks the ghettoes till he flukes a chance to cut a record and ends up with 20 bucks for his trouble — that's the way the music business works in Kingston.

Eventually, with promotion by radio stations and the spread of the use of sound systems, reggae became more commercialized, and was appropriated by the wider society. The politicians, fully comprehending the implications of the mass appeal of reggae, capitalized on the Rasta symbols and motifs of the life-style surrounding the music and made regular pilgrimages to the ghettoes in order to exploit the vote-catching potential of the movement.[6]

Last year, when Michael Manley was running for prime minister against the incumbent Labour government, he took to the hills in his shirt-sleeves carrying a long staff — the Rod of Correction he called it, with which he swore to drive out the demons — and the five-acre farmers and dirt poor and downtrodden turned out in throngs wherever he went, chanting Joshua! Joshua! and Manley held out the Rod and cried, 'When I look at my people, my heart bleeds!' and the people strained to touch the Rod, to feel the almighty power, and Manley wept and cried, 'It is love!' He also made a record, a reggae thing called Better Must Come, pitching power for the people, with a chorus singing in the background and the bass thumping. It made the charts, Number One. He was elected with the biggest majority in Jamaican parliamentary history.

And Clancy Eccles, who produced 'Better Must Come', said:
'We knew we were more powerful than the politicians. The people hear us on the radio everyday. If Manley gets lazy, don't believe that we won't start hitting him.'

Reggae was, therefore, fused with politics in the slums of Kingston at the same time as it was being identified with politically over here in England.

In the fifties and sixties especially, the record industry in Jamaica boomed, and with the latter stages of this development went the increasing popularization and commercialization of reggae. The singers and performers were now mainly rude-boys out to make 'bread' rather than doctrinaire Rastafarians. The producers (all light-skinned middle-class individuals sharing a different background from the boys), sensitive to commercial demands for danceable pop music, as opposed to political slogans, insisted on the cleaning up of the music and, as a result, reggae became bowdlerized, diluted and watered down. In this process the dread element became temporarily suppressed and the overall shape and form of the music became stylized to make the music more digestible and acceptable to a wider market of consumers. But the basic beat, the most important part of the music, remained — deep, dark and pulsating — as well as the rudie social commentary on the general state of poverty and distress in Jamaica. At this time the influence of rock was uppermost, and quite suddenly and unexpectedly the lyrics of reggae began to betray a rather strong, almost lurid, supersexual preoccupation. Corresponding to the variations in the quality and sound of presentations were constant changes in the name of the labels used to refer to the music. At first it was 'blue beat', then the name changed to 'ska', then to 'rock steady' and finally to 'reggae', the current label, which many believe is here to stay. However, by the time the reggae sound broke out in England, mainly in its watered-down commercialized form, the songs were already returning to Rastafarian themes, and the original rudie preoccupation with the misery and hardships in their general situation was becoming pronounced again. There were, by this time, two distinct types of reggae tunes: 'raw' reggae and 'sweet' or commercialized reggae. It was the 'sweet', bowdlerized, cleaned up reggae, palatable to English ears, that surfaced in the charts in England; 'real' reggae, because of its incomprehensibility to outsiders and its uncompromisingly ethnic character, stayed underground in the black community, where its message could be understood and appreciated. [...]

In Bristol (and elsewhere in Britain), reggae took hold and helped to inject a much needed sense of ideological and cultural solidarity into the life-style and thinking of the disaffected and anti-social teenybopper, not only because it was an easy kind of dance music, but also because its messages and self-conscious critical and political commentaries on society were relevant to his particular needs and desires. The eruption of the music in the late sixties — when the Rastafarian dread element of Babylon and eschatology returned to reggae — coincided with the worsening of race relations in Britain, the introduction of race into local politics, West Indians' externally induced self-awareness of themselves as a separate ethnic entity, the increasing ghetto-ization of their communities due to hard-line racialist attitudes, the unearthing of a hitherto submerged racism and hostility by Enoch Powell, the successive betrayals of the Labour government, which was thought to have the interest of the black worker at heart, and the vacillations and feet-dragging of the race-relations bureaucracy and its failure to make 'integration' a reality. All this happened at a time when young West Indians, materially and culturally deprived, were becoming more and more enraged with their inferior position in society. For these reasons, reggae satisfied deep cultural and political needs. Not only did it (with the aid of 'soul') help to revolutionize the attitudes of teeny-boppers and fuse in their minds the relevance of the universal liberation struggle to their own situation, but, through a kind of transcultural process, it transplanted the particularities of the Rasta-rudie black-oriented counter-culture, thus making the entire identity of the teenybopper youth revolve around the ethnic style and symbolism of the music.

The 'message' in reggae

Reggae, quite apart from its danceability, is information-oriented and contains a high degree of reportage. In tunes like '007 Shanty Town' and 'Judge Dread' by Prince Buster, which tell of the injustices committed against 'rude-boys' and of their delinquent activities on the streets of Jamaica, teenyboppers experienced a kind of vicarious participation and could not resist making a connection between themselves and the rude-boys in the home country.

Judge Dread

Judge: Order! for my court is in session. Will you please stand. First let me introduce myself. My name is 'Judge 100 years'. Some people call me 'Judge Dread'. Now I'm from Ethiopia to try all you rude-boys for shooting black people. In my court only me talk because I am vexed, for I'm the rude-boy today. [*Judge shouts out*] Rude-boy!

Rude-boy: Yes, sir.

Judge: Rude-boy Adolphus James?

Rude-boy 1: Yes, sir.

Judge: Hmmm . . . Rude-boy Emmanuel Zakepalin!

Rude-boy 2: Yes, sir.

Judge: George Grab and Flee.

Rude-boy 3: Present.

Judge: Hmmm . . . Adolphus James, I see where you've been charged with shooting with intent, five murder charge, six grab and flee charge.

Adolphus James: But your honour . . .

Judge: Shut up! Guilty or not guilty.

Adolphus James: Not guilty, sir.

Judge: I don't care what you say, take 400 years. Stand down!

Judge: Emmanuel Zakepalin!

Emmanuel Zakepalin: Yes, sir.

Judge: You are charged with fifteen charge of shooting with intent, fifteen murder charge and I heard that you were the one round there in Sutton Street* who told the judge: 'Rude-boy don't care'. Well, this is King Street* and my name is Judge Dread and I don't care. Now take 400 years!

Emmanuel Zakepalin: Now, hear what I have to say, your honour . . .

Judge: Hush up, whe' you trying to do, shoot me too?

Emmanuel Zakepalin: No, your honour . . .

* Some of the main court-houses in Jamaica are situated on Sutton Street and King Street in Kingston.

Judge: Quiet! 400 more years for you!

Judge: George Grab and Flee.

George Grab and Flee: Yes, sir.

Judge: Stop your crying! Rude-boy don't cry. That's what I hear.

George Grab and Flee [*crying and sobbing*]: But I didn't do it, you know, sir. Dem frame me and I am not guilty.

Judge: I don't care. This is my court. Hush up. You are charged with robbing schoolchildren. Robbery with aggravation.

George Grab and Flee [*complaining*]: Old man, I not taking any sentence from you. You hear me, sir. 'Is somebody else do it, and look how him mek this judge coming to try me now.

Judge: George Grab and Flee!

George Grab and Flee: Yes, sir.

Judge: You rob schoolchildren, you bomb the people's houses, you shoot black people.

George Grab and Flee: But your honour, I didn't do it, sir . . .

Judge: Hush up! Just for talking, I now charge you for contempt, and that is a separate hundred years. I hereby sentence you to 400 years!

George Grab and Flee: Mumble . . .

Judge: I said hush up! Hush up! You are sentenced to 400 years and 500 lashes. I've got to set example. Rude-boy don't cry, rude-boy don't cry. When I was in Africa, I hear you are tough.

George Grab and Flee: Mumble . . .

Judge: Court adjourn! Take him away!

007 Shanty Town

> 007
> 007
> At Ocean 11
> And now rude-boys have a wail
> Cause them out a jail
> Rude-boys cannot fail
> Cause them must get bail
> Dem a-loot, dem a-shoot, dem a-wail
> A' shanty town.

The identification with the behaviour and experiences of the trouble-makers typified in songs like these was instant, and teenyboppers began to discover and work out their relationship to society. They renamed St Paul's 'Shanty Town' (calling it 'the Jungle' and 'the Village' as well) and began to call themselves 'rudies'. And today, not only in Bristol's Shanty Town but in West Indian communities all over Britain, a teeny-bopper is known as a 'rudie'.

In very broad terms, successive songs spoke to them of their heritage and lack of identity, suggesting strongly that they have been wronged.

African People

> They took the whole African nation
> Changed our laws and valuation
> Took away our whole way of life
> And spilt our gold and all our wine
> Took away our native tongue
> Taught their English to our young
> And the things we never had
> Are nowadays made in Japan.
> African People! African Tribes!
>> So proud we live
>> So proud we die.
>
> They took our whole African nation
> Taught us so-called civilization
> Although they changed our ways of old
> They'll never change our hearts and souls.
> African People! African Tribes!
>> So proud we live
>> So proud we die.
>
> But there'll be someday when they'll learn
> African people will return
> They've got to return!
> Listen, the African people, they've got to
>> return!

In the midst of total despair and disorientation, the messages plead affirmation and self-acceptance as in the following tune, 'Young, Gifted and Black'.

Young, Gifted and Black

> Young, gifted and black
> Oh, what a lovely precious dream

> To be young, gifted and black
> Open your heart to what I mean
> There's a whole wide world to know
> There's some little boys and girls
> Who are young, gifted and black
> And that's a fact
> Young, gifted and black
> You mustn't fear because you are young
> There's a world waiting for you
> It is a thing that's just begun
> When you feel really low
>   Yeah
> There's a virtue you should know
> To be young, gifted and black
> You are so intact
> Oh, young, gifted and black
> Yes, oh I long to know the truth
> Though at times when I was black
> Then I was haunted by my youth
> But what matters today is that
> We can all cry out and say
> To be young, gifted and black
> Is where it's at
> Young, gifted and black.

The goal of 'Freedom' is also continually emphasized by reggae singers, who reassure their listeners that revolution is on their side and that there is a glorious future to come. But underlying this quest for freedom is the philosophy of 'peace and love' which is fundamental to the creed of Rastafari, despite its sonorous and racialist overtones.

> Man and woman, girl and boy
> Let us try and give a helping hand
> This I know and I am sure
> With love, we could all understand . . .

There is, of course, another side to teenyboppers' involvement with reggae. Not every teenybopper consciously relates to the political messages in the music. Those with talent see in it the means whereby they can earn a living through a show-business career. Others are attracted by the glamorous life-style of stars who have achieved fame, and the music for them holds out the possibility that they themselves can achieve similar success. Indeed, the reggae music business is seen by many teenyboppers as one of the few avenues of achievement open to them in which they do not have to bother too much about the snobbery and exclusive attitudes of white society. The things about him that white society defines as a disadvantage — his broken English, his blackness, his lower-class attitudes, his extraversion, his spontaneity and 'excitability', his supersexuality and his emotionalism — are the very things that are idealized in the black music business and will take him to the top. The world of reggae is a world of escape and refuge from white society. In that world the black West Indian is a king. He can relax and be himself without fear of being considered inferior. In this world his disadvantages become virtues. What is more, the black music business offers the possibility of escape from obscurity and inferiority into a world of *hauteur*, ostentatiousness and recognition. These are reasons why even the non-ideological teenybopper sooner or later comes spiritually to 'identify' with the 'blackness' in reggae. [. . .]

Notes

1 Katrin Norris, *Jamaica — The Search for an Identity*, IRR-OUP, 1962, p. 46.
2 G. Llewellyn Watson, 'Social Structure and Social Movements: The Black Muslims in the United States and the Rastafarians in Jamaica', unpublished, 1972.
3 Rex Nettleford, *Mirror, Mirror: Identity, Race and Protest in Jamaica*, Collins Sangster (Jamaica), 1974, pp. 95–7.
4 See article in *Rolling Stone*, 19 January 1973.
5 Ibid., 19 July 1973, p. 35.
6 Ibid.

10 Woman's place is at the typewriter: the feminization of the clerical labor force

Margery Davies

A large proportion of the recent historical research about women in the labor force has focused on industrial workers, using their specific factory experiences as a model for viewing the class as a whole. On the other hand, relatively little attention has been given to clerical workers. This is surprising: in 1968 for example, over 40 percent of women in the U.S. labor force were employed as clerical and sales workers, while only 16.5 percent were employed in the industrial work force.[1] This essay is a contribution to a discussion aimed first at clarifying the role of a 'secretarial proletariat,' and second at broadening the definition of the working class to include other than those in industrial production. In particular, there are millions of low-level clerical workers, most of them women, who form an important segment of the working class.

The essay is historical in scope and focuses on the feminization of the clerical labor force. Women now form the majority of the clerical work force, but this was not always the case. How did women enter and come to dominate clerical work? How did the ideology with respect to women office workers change? What are the connections between a sexual segmentation of the clerical labor force and hierarchical relations in the office? The first step in answering these questions is to look at the nineteenth-century office.[2]

Two of the basic characteristics of nineteenth-century offices in the United States are that they were small and staffed almost exclusively by men.[3] Census data for 1870, for example, show that out of 76,639 office workers in the United States, women numbered only 1,869; men were 97.5 percent of the clerical labor force.[4] With the exception of a few banks, insurance companies, and governmental branches, most offices in the United States prior to the Civil War usually contained about two or three clerks. This is not surprising, since most capitalist firms were also relatively small until the last decades of the nineteenth century. For example, in 'Bartleby' Herman Melville described a Wall

Source: Z. R. Eisenstein (ed.), *Capitalist Patriarchy and the Case of Socialist Feminism*, New York, Monthly Review Press, 1979, pp. 248–66.

Street lawyer's office of the 1850s which consisted of the lawyer, three copyists, and an errand boy.[5]

The small size of offices at this time meant that the relationship between employer and employee tended to be very personalized. The clerks worked under the direct supervision, and often the direct eyesight, of their employers. Although the tasks of a clerk were generally well defined – the job of the copyists in 'Bartleby' was to transcribe legal documents – they were often asked to do numerous other tasks. It was clearly the employer who set the limits of the clerk's job – there was no question of the clerk being ruled by the inexorable pace of a machine.

The personal benevolence of an employer could go a long way toward making the hierarchical relations within an office more tolerable. An employer who spoke nicely to his clerks, let them leave early if they were feeling sick, or gave them a Christmas goose helped to create working conditions against which the clerks were not likely to rebel. By treating his clerks with kindness or politeness, a paternalistic employer was also likely to be able to get them to work harder.

This personalization of the work relationship in the nineteenth-century offices lies at the root of the phenomenon of employees being 'devoted to the firm.' A clerk who spent forty or fifty years working for the same small office of an insurance company did not necessarily work so long and so hard out of a belief in the importance of promoting that particular company's kind of insurance. The source of his devotion was much more likely the network of personal relations he had built up in the office over the years. It was probably more important to the employee to 'produce' a good working relationship with his boss, with whom he was in constant contact, than to produce, for example, improvements in the insurance company's filing system. Needless to say, that good working relationship no doubt depended in part on the employee producing improvements in the filing system. But whether the employee cared more about the selling of insurance or his personal relationship with his employer, the end result tended to be the same: the clerk became a 'devoted employee of the firm' who was not likely to rebel or go out on strike.

Not all clerks in the nineteenth-century office spent all their working days in clerical positions. A clerkship also served as an apprenticeship for a young man who was 'learning the business' before he moved on to a managerial position. These were often nephews, sons, or grandsons of the firm's managers and owners. Most clerks, however, ended up with gold watches, instead of managerial posts, in return for their years of devoted service. Thus, the clerks in an office at any particular time came from different class backgrounds and were likely to have very different occupational futures.

Political-economic changes

In the last few decades of the nineteenth century, American corporations underwent a period of rapid growth and consolidation. These changes, which marked the rise of modern industrial capitalism, had been signalled by development in banks, insurance companies, and public utilities; they had spread to manufacturing enterprises by the turn of the century.[6] As business operations became more complex, there was a large increase in correspondence, record-keeping, and office work in general. This expansion created a demand for an expanded clerical labor force. In 1880 there were 504,454 office workers who constituted 3 percent of the labor force; by 1890 there were 750,150 office workers.[7] The number of office workers has been increasing ever since (see Table 10.2). In order to fill the need for clerical workers, employers turned to the large pool of educated female labor.

As early as the 1820s women had been receiving public high school educations. Worcester, Massachusetts opened a public high school for girls in 1824; Boston and New York City did so in 1826.[8] In 1880, 13,029 women graduated from high school in the United States, as compared to only 10,605 men. The figures for 1900 show an even greater disparity: 56,808 female high school graduates and 38,075 male.[9]

Until the end of the nineteenth century, schools were the main place of employment for these educated women. The feminization of elementary and secondary teaching had taken place with the introduction of compulsory public education and consequent increase in teaching jobs. In 1840 men were 60 percent of all teachers and in 1860 they made up only 14 percent.[10] Women were hired in education because they were a cheap replacement for the dwindling supply of male teachers. 'As Charles William Eliot observed some years after the feminization of primary school teaching was largely completed: "It is true that sentimental reasons are often given for the almost exclusive employment of women in the common schools: but the effective reason is economy . . . If women had not been cheaper than men, they would not have replaced nine tenths of the men in American public schools." '[11]

But teaching was about the only job that drew on the pool of educated female labor in substantial numbers. The 'professions' – law, medicine, business, college teaching – both excluded women and did not employ large numbers of people. The 1890 census, for instance, counted only 200 women lawyers.[12] Social work was still the preserve of moral reformers like Jane Addams; the growth of social work as an occupation with government funding did not come until the twentieth century. Nursing was beginning to employ some women by the end of the nineteenth century: in 1900 there were 108,691 nurses and midwives, although only 11,000 of them had become graduate nurses and achieved professional status.[13]

In the last decades of the nineteenth century, the situation was, then, the following. There were more women than men graduating from high school every year. These women constituted a pool of educated female labor which was being drawn upon only by elementary and secondary schools. Consequently, there were literally thousands of women with training that qualified them for jobs that demanded literacy, but who could not find such jobs. Excluded from most of the professions, these women were readily available for the clerical jobs that started to proliferate at the end of the nineteenth century. The expansion and consolidation of enterprises in the 1880s and 1890s created a large demand for clerical labor; the large pool of educated female labor constituted the supply.

Women enter the office

Prior to the Civil War there were no women employed in substantial numbers in any offices, although there were a few women scattered here and there who worked as bookkeepers or as copyists in lawyers' offices.[14] During the Civil War, however, the reduction of the male labor force due to the draft moved General Francis Elias Spinner, the U.S. treasurer, to introduce female clerical workers into government offices. At first women were given the job of trimming paper money in the Treasury Department, but they gradually moved into other areas of clerical work. The experiment proved successful and was continued after the war. Commenting upon this innovation in 1869, Spinner declared 'upon his word' that it had been a complete success: 'Some of the females [are] doing more and better work for $900 per annum than many male clerks who were paid double that amount.'[15] At the time, men clerks were being paid from $1200 to $1800 per year.[16]

Despite this start, it was not until the 1880s that they began to pour into the clerical work force. In 1880, the proportion of women in the clerical labor force was 4 percent; in 1890 it had jumped to 21 percent. By 1920, women made up half of the clerical workers: 50 percent of all low-level office workers (including stenographers, typists, secretaries, shipping and receiving clerks, office machine operators, and clerical and kindred workers not elsewhere classified) were women. In 1960, 72 percent of them were (see Table 10.2). This tremendous increase in the number of women office workers has changed the composition of the female labor force. In 1870, less than 0.05 percent of the women in the labor force were office workers; by 1890 1.1 percent were. In 1960,

29.1 percent of all women in the labor force were office workers.

The Treasury's precedent facilitated the entrance of women into the clerical labor force; the prejudices against women working in offices had already started to deteriorate by 1880. A second factor that eased women into the office was the invention of the typewriter. By the 1890s the typewriter had gained widespread acceptance as a practical office machine.[17]

Various American inventors had been working on 'writing machines' since the 1830s. They had generally been thought of as crackpots by capitalists and the general public alike. But by the early 1870s, an inventor named Christopher Latham Sholes had managed to produce a fairly workable machine. The Remington family, which had manufactured guns, sewing machines, and farm machinery, bought the rights to start making typewriters. They did not sell well at first. People bought them out of curiosity for their own private use, but it was not until the last two decades of the nineteenth century that businesses began to buy the machines in large quantities.

It seems fairly clear that it was not until businesses began to expand very rapidly that employers saw the usefulness of a mechanical writing machine. Changes in the structure of capitalist enterprises brought about changes in technology: no one was interested in making the typewriter a workable or manufacturable machine until its utility became clear. But the typewriter also gave rise to changes in office procedure. Writing was faster; the increase in correspondence and record-keeping was caused in part by the existence of the machine. For example, Robert Lincoln O'Brien made the following comment in the *Atlantic Monthly* in 1904:[18]

> The invention of the typewriter has given a tremendous impetus to the dictating habit . . . This means not only greater diffuseness, inevitable with any lessening of the tax on words which the labor of writing imposes, but it also brings forward the point of view of the one who speaks.

The typewriter also facilitated the entrance of women into the clerical labor force. Typing was 'sex-neutral' because it was a new occupation. Since it had not been identified as a masculine job, women who were employed as typists did not encounter the criticism that they were taking over 'men's work.' In fact, typing soon became 'women's work'; in 1890, 63.8 percent of the 33,418 clerical workers classified as stenographers and typists were women; by 1900, that proportion had risen to 76.7 percent. The feminization of low-level clerical work proceeded extremely rapidly.

It is important to determine why women wanted to become office workers. Most women at the end of the nineteenth century probably worked out of economic necessity. This holds true for the unmarried single woman of middle-income origins as well as for the immigrant working-class woman, single or married, who worked to keep her family from starving.

Clerical work attracted women because it paid better than did most other jobs women could get. In northeastern American cities clerical wages were relatively high: domestic servants were paid $2 to $5 a week, factory operatives, $1.50 to $8, and department store salesgirls, $1.50 to $8, whereas typists and stenographers could get $6 to $15.[19]

Clerical work also enjoyed a relatively high status. A woman from a middle-income home with a high school education was much more likely to look for clerical work than for work as a house servant or as a factory girl making paper boxes, pickles, or shoes. Clerical positions were coveted by working-class women who usually could find work only in sweatshops, factories, or department stores.

Despite the fact that women were pouring into offices at the end of the nineteenth century, they still met with disapproval. An engraving of 1875 shows a shocked male government official opening the door on an office that has been 'taken over by the ladies.'[20] The women are preening themselves before a mirror, fixing each other's hair, reading *Harper's Bazaar*, spilling ink on the floor — in short, doing everything but working. The engraving makes women working in an office seem ludicrous: women are seen as frivolous creatures incapable of doing an honest day's work.

Table 10.1 Stenographers and typists by sex, 1870-1930

	Total	Male	Female	% Female
1870	154	147	7	4.5
1880	5,000	3,000	2,000	40.0
1890	33,400	12,100	21,300	63.8
1900	112,600	26,200	86,400	76.7
1910	326,700	53,400	263,300	80.6
1920	615,100	50,400	564,700	91.8
1930	811,200	36,100	775,100	95.6

Source: Alba M. Edwards, *Comparative Occupational Statistics for the United States, 1870-1940*. Published as part of Volume IV of the *Report on Population of the 16th Census of the United States*, Washington, D.C., 1943. Tables 9 and 10. Figures for 1880 on are to the nearest hundred.

Outright contempt was not the only negative reaction. Bliven cites
the following passage from *The Typewriter Girl*, a novel by Olive Pratt
Rayner whose heroine is an American typist fallen on hard financial
times in London:[21]

> Three clerks (male), in seedy black coats, the eldest with hair the
> color of a fox's, went on chaffing one another for two minutes after
> I closed the door, with ostentatious unconsciousness of my insignifi-
> cant presence . . . The youngest, after a while, wheeled around on his
> high stool and broke out with the chivalry of his class and age, 'Well,
> what's your business?'
>   My voice trembled a little, but I mustered up courage and spoke.
> 'I have called about your advertisement . . .'
>   He eyed me up and down. I am slender, and, I will venture to say,
> if not pretty, at least interesting looking.
>   'How many words a minute?' he asked after a long pause. I
> stretched the truth as far as its elasticity would permit. 'Ninety-
> seven,' I answered . . .
>   The eldest clerk, with the foxy head, wheeled around, and took
> his turn to stare. He had hairy hands and large goggle-eyes . . . I
> detected an undercurrent of double meaning . . . I felt disagreeably
> like Esther in the presence of Ahasuerus — a fat and oily Ahasuerus
> of fifty . . . He perused me up and down with his small pig's eyes, as
> if he were buying a horse, scrutinizing my face, my figure, my hands,
> my feet. I felt like a Circassian in an Arab slavemarket . . .

The overtones of sexuality are hard to miss. The implication seems to
be that a decent girl is risking her morality if she tries to invade the
male preserve of the office. Whether or not such sensationalism was
backed up by many instances of seduction or corruption, the message
seems clear: the office was a dangerous place for a woman of virtue.

Even in 1900, some people counseled women to leave the office and
return to their homes, where they rightfully belonged. The editor of the
Ladies' Home Journal, Edward Bok, gave just such advice in the pages
of his magazine in 1900:[22]

> A business house cannot prosper unless each position has in it the
> most competent incumbent which it is possible to obtain for that
> particular position. And, although the statement may seem a hard
> one, and will unquestionably be controverted, it nevertheless is a
> plain, simple fact that women have shown themselves naturally
> incompetent to fill a great many of the business positions which
> they have sought to occupy . . . The fact is that not one woman in a

hundred can stand the physical strain of the keen pace which competition has forced upon every line of business today.

The shift in ideology

Sixteen years after Bok used the pages of the *Ladies' Home Journal* to admonish women to return home, another writer in the same magazine not only took for granted the fact that women worked in offices but also found that certain 'feminine' qualities were particularly suited to clerical work. 'The stenographer plus' was described by Harry C. Spillman:[23]

> I should describe the equipment of the ideal stenographer as follows: Twenty percent represents technical ability — that is, the ability to write and read shorthand and to typewrite rapidly and accurately; thirty percent equals general information — that is, education other than that in shorthand and typewriting; and the last and most important fifty percent I should ascribe to personality . . .
> There are two kinds of personality — concrete and abstract: the one you can see, the other you can feel. The concrete side is that which the stenographer sees when she looks in the mirror. The stenographer who wins must look good — not in the sense that she must be beautiful, for dividends are never declared on pink cheeks and classic features; but she should make the very most of her personal equipment . . .
> That other kind of personality — the abstract kind — is the more important element in the stenographer's equipment, for it involves her temperament. Thousands of stenographers stay in mediocre positions because they lack the ability to adapt their conduct to those fixed principles of harmony and optimism which must prevail in all big undertakings.

Fortune magazine, in a series of unsigned articles on 'Women in Business,' carried the argument a step further and equated secretaries with wives:[24]

> The whole point of the whole problem, in other words, is that women occupy the office because the male employer wants them there. Why he wants them there is another question which cannot be answered merely by saying that once there they take to the work very nicely. It is doubtless true that women take to the work nicely. Their conscious or subconscious intention some day to marry, and their conscious or subconscious willingness to be directed

by men, render them amenable and obedient and relieve them of the ambition which makes it difficult for men to put their devotion into secretarial work. But that fact only partially explains the male employer's preference. It indicates that women and by virtue of some of their most womanly traits are capable of making the offices a more pleasant, peaceful, and homelike place. But it does not indicate why the employer desires that kind of office rather than an office full of ambitious and pushing young men intent upon hammering their typewriters into presidential desks. To get at that problem pure speculation is the only tool.

One might well speculate somewhat as follows: the effect of the industrial revolution was the dedomestication of women . . . In the process the upper-class home, as the upper-class home was known to the Victorians, disappeared. The male was no longer master in his own dining room and dreadful in his own den nor did a small herd of wives, daughters, and sisters hear his voice and tremble. He was, on the contrary, the more or less equal mate of a more or less unpredictable woman. And he resented it.

He resented the loss of his position. He regretted the old docility, the old obedience, the old devotion to his personal interests. And finding himself unable to re-create the late, lost paradise in his home he set about re-creating it in his office. What he wanted in the office was not the office mistress described at least fifty-two times a year by American short-story writers. His very pretty and very clever and very expensive wife was already mistress enough and to spare. What he wanted in the office was something as much like the vanished wife of his father's generation as could be arranged – someone to balance his checkbook, buy his railroad tickets, check his baggage, get him seats in the fourth row, take his daughter to the dentist, listen to his side of the story, give him a courageous look when things were blackest, and generally know all, understand all . . .

Whether or not any such speculative explanation of the male desire for a female office is sound there can be no doubt that the desire exists and that it is the male employer who is chiefly responsible for the female secretary.

In 1900, the *Ladies' Home Journal* warned women that they could not stand the physical strain of working in a fast-paced business office. But by 1916 the *Journal* was comparing the faithful female secretary to some heavenly body who 'radiated the office with sunshine and sympathetic interest.' It had not taken very long for the ideology to shift and for people to accept the presence of women in offices. Bok had argued in 1900 that women, by virtue of their 'nature,' were unsuited to the office. But only a few years later, the *Journal* came close to arguing that the 'natural' temperament of women made them good stenographers. And by 1935, *Fortune* had concocted a full-fledged historical justification for the assertion that 'woman's place was at the typewriter.'

Women, so the argument went, are by nature adaptable, courteous, and sympathetic — in a word, passive. This natural passivity makes them ideally suited to the job of carrying out an endless number of routine tasks without a complaint. Furthermore, their docility makes it unlikely that they will aspire to rise very far above their station. Thus their male boss is spared the unpleasant possibility that his secretary will one day be competing with him for his job.

The image of the secretary as the competent mother-wife who sees to her employer's every need and desire was a description which most fitted a personal secretary. Here certain 'feminine' characteristics ascribed to the job of personal secretary — sympathy, adaptability, courtesy — made women seem the natural candidates for the job. Not all clerical workers were personal secretaries. For the large proportion of clerical workers who were stenographers, typists, file clerks, and the like, another ideological strain developed, emphasizing the supposed greater dexterity of women. These workers were seldom assigned to one particular boss, but instead constituted a pool from which any executive could draw as he wished. In the case of these low-level clerical workers, personal characteristics such as sympathy and courtesy seemed less important. Dexterity — the ability to do work quickly and accurately — was much more important. Not long after the typewriter began to be used as a matter of course in business offices, people started to argue that women, endowed with dextrous fingers, were the most fitting operators of these machines. Elizabeth Baker states that 'women seemed to be especially suited as typists and switchboard operators because they were tolerant of routine, careful, and manually dextrous.'[25]

Women's place in the office hierarchy

Whether it was for the warmth of their personalities or the dexterity of their fingers, women came to be viewed as 'natural' office workers. Why did this ideology develop?

The ideology is obviously connected to the feminization of the clerical labor force. If women were employed in large numbers in offices, then it was not surprising that an ideology justifying their presence there developed. Women were originally employed in offices

Table 10.2 Feminization of the clerical labor force

		Bookkeepers, accountants, and cashiers	Messengers, errand and office boys and girls[a]	Stenographers, typists, and secretaries	Shipping and receiving clerks	Clerical and kindred workers[c]	Office machine operators
1870	total	39,164[d]	7,820[f]			29,655[g]	
	female	893[e]	46			930[h]	
	% female	2%	6%			3%	
1880	total	75,688[i]	12,447			64,151[j]	
	female	4,295[i]	228			2,315[j]	
	% female	6%	2%			4%	
1890	total	160,968	45,706			219,173[g]	
	female	28,050	1,658			45,553[g]	
	% female	17%	4%			21%	
1900[b]	total	257,400	63,700			357,100	
	female	74,900	3,800			104,400	
	% female	29%	6%			29%	
1910	total	491,600	95,100			1,034,200	
	female	189,000	6,400			386,800	
	% female	38%	7%			37%	
1920	total	742,000	99,500			2,092,000	
	female	362,700	8,100			1,038,400	
	% female	49%	8%			50%	
1930	total	940,000	79,500		2,754,000		36,200
	female	487,500	5,100		1,450,900		32,100
	% female	52%	6%		53%		89%

1940	total	931,300	60,700	1,174,900	229,700	1,973,600	64,200
	female	475,700	3,000	1,096,400	9,100	702,500	55,100
	% female	51%	5%	93%	4%	36%	86%
1950	total	—	59,000	1,629,300	297,400	2,354,200	146,200
	female	—	10,600	1,538,000	20,700	1,252,900	120,300
	% female	—	18%	94%	7%	53%	82%
1960	total	—	63,200	2,312,800	294,600	3,016,400	318,100
	female	—	11,200	2,232,600	25,000	1,788,700	236,400
	% female	—	18%	96%	8%	59%	74%

Sources: For 1870–1940: Janet M. Hooks, *Women's Occupations through Seven Decades*, U.S. Department of Labor, Women's Bureau, Bulletin 218 (Washington, D.C.: GPO, 1947), Table IIA: Occupations of Women Workers, 1870–1940; Table IIB: Occupations of all Workers, 1870–1940.
For 1950–1960: Bureau of the Census, *Census of Population, United States Summary* (Washington, D.C.: GPO, 1960), Table 201: Detailed Occupation of the Experienced Civilian Labor Force, by Sex, for the United States: 1960 and 1950.

a Messengers, errand and office boys and girls includes 'telegraph messengers' through 1900.
b Figures from 1900 on are rounded off to the nearest hundred.
c Not elsewhere classified.
d Census figures estimated and 374 added because of undercount in 13 southern states.
e Census figures estimated and 2 added because of undercount in 13 southern states.
f 70 added because of undercount in 13 southern states.
g Partly estimated and 494 added because of undercount in 13 southern states. Figures do not include 'Abstractors, notaries, and justices of peace,' classified in 1940 in the group 'clerical workers.'
h Partly estimated and 6 added because of undercount in 13 southern states. Figures do not include 'Abstractors, notaries, and justices of peace,' classified in 1940 in the group 'clerical workers.'
i Estimated.
j 1890 and 1900 data partly estimated and 1880 data entirely estimated. Figures do not include 'Abstractors, notaries, and justices of peace,' classified in 1940 in the group 'clerical workers.'

because they were cheaper than the available male labor force. As corporations expanded at the end of the nineteenth century, they were forced to draw on the pool of educated females to meet their rapidly increasing demand for clerical workers. But the expansion of capitalist firms did not entail a simple proliferation of small, 'nineteenth-century' offices. Instead, it meant a greatly expanded office structure, with large numbers of people working in a single office. No longer were some of the clerks, in effect, apprenticing managers. The expanded structure, on the contrary, brought with it a rapid growth of low-level, deadend jobs.

By 1920 over 90 percent of the typists and stenographers in the United States (see Table 10.1) were women − whose 'natural' docility and dexterity made them the ideal workers for these jobs. By harping upon the docility of the female character, writers like Spillman in the *Ladies' Home Journal* provided a convenient rationalization for women's position on the bottom of the office hierarchy.

It is important to point out that differentiating office workers by sex is not the same as dividing them into groups distinguished, say, by eye color. The sexual division of labor in the office − where men hold the majority of managerial positions and women fill the majority of low-level, clerical jobs − is strengthened by the positions men and women hold outside the office.

When the ideology of passive female labor first manifested itself in the early twentieth century, the United States was, by and large, a patriarchal society. Patriarchal relations, in which men made decisions and women followed them, were carried over into the office. These patriarchal social relations meshed very conveniently with office bureaucracies, where the means by which workers were told what to do was often an extremely personalized one. For although the number of clerical workers was large, they were often divided into small groups of five or six typists, stenographers, or file clerks directly accountable to one supervisor. And since that supervisor was usually a man and those clerical workers women, it is easy to see how patriarchal patterns would reinforce the office hierarchy.

The segmentation of the office work force by sex thus promoted a situation where a docile mass of clerical workers would follow without rebellion the directives of a relatively small group of managers. The ideology that women were naturally suited to those jobs can be seen as an important buttress of the hierarchical office structure.

Notes

1 U.S. Department of Labor, Women's Bureau, *1969 Handbook of*

Women Workers, Women's Bureau Bulletin 294 (Washington: Government Printing Office, 1969), p. 90.

2 Concrete information about female office workers is not easy to find. In a comprehensive bibliographical *Guide to Business History* (1948), Henrietta Larson points out that 'it is significant that the works dealing with the subject [office management] are concerned largely with "systems" and machines — the office worker has been left in neglected obscurity' (pp. 771–2).

There are a few analytical studies of office workers, the most notable of which are David Lockwood's *The Blackcoated Worker* and C. Wright Mills's *White Collar: The American Middle Classes* (New York: Oxford University Press, 1956). Grace D. Coyle focuses on women in offices and the kind of work they do in 'Women in the clerical occupations,' *Annals of the American Academy of Political and Social Science*, 143 (May 1929); *Fortune* published a series of articles on 'Women in Business' in 1935; the Women's Bureau of the U.S. Department of Labor has issued a number of bulletins on office workers. In addition, there is quite a long list of books addressed to women which tell them how to be better secretaries: the main point of these manuals seems to be that women should be certain to please their (male) bosses and that they should be neat and accurate about any number of office tasks. And dotted throughout the prominent women's magazines are articles about the 'business woman.'

Finally, there are some fictional works which provide a certain amount of insight into office work. 'Bartleby' (1856) by Herman Melville is set in a Wall Street lawyer's office of the 1850s and describes the men who work there as copyists; *Alice Adams* (1921) by Booth Tarkington is about the daughter of a white-collar employee who is forced to give up her hopes of joining the upper-class social clique in town, accept her own middle-class status, and finally climb the 'begrimed stairway' of the local business college in preparation for becoming a 'working girl.'

But all in all there is very little information about the history of female clerical workers. However, there are bits and pieces of evidence, upon which this essay is based.

3 For the purposes of this discussion the term 'nineteenth-century office' will be used to describe those office structures which existed prior to the widespread monopolization and bureaucratization of capitalist corporations, a process which was well underway in the United States by the end of the nineteenth century. 'The modern office' will be used to describe the structures which developed after that bureaucratization. The description of the nineteenth-century office which follows is based primarily on Lockwood's *The Blackcoated Worker* and on Mills's *White Collar*.

4 Janet M. Hooks, *Women's Occupations through Seven Decades*, Women's Bureau Bulletin 218 (Washington: Government Printing Office, 1947), Tables IIA and IIB.

5 Herman Melville, 'Bartleby,' in *The Piazza Tales* (1856; Garden City: Doubleday, 1961).

6 See Alfred Chandler, *Strategy and Structure* (M.I.T. Press, 1962). See also Stephen Hymer, 'The multinational corporation and the law of uneven development' in *Economics and the World Order*, ed. Jagdish Bhagwati (Collier-Macmillan, 1972).

7 Bureau of the Census, Department of Commerce and Labor, Special Report of the 12th Census. *Occupations at the 12th Census* (Washington, D.C., 1904). Data is for 'number of persons engaged in specified occupations.' 'Office workers' includes bookkeepers and accountants; clerks and copyists; and stenographers and typewriters (typists).

8 Elizabeth Faulkner Baker, *Technology and Women's Work* (Columbia University Press, 1964), p. 57. Baker argues that girls were given high school educations because the number of women teachers was increasing: 'Men were being attracted by business opportunities and skilled trades, and the phenomenal growth of public schools created an alarming shortage of teachers . . . But relief from the scarcity of male teachers of course required that girls as well as boys be taught' (p. 57). However, the fact that so many girls got high school educations in the nineteenth century still seems rather surprising; unfortunately, recent analysts of the rise of mass education in the United States do not remark upon it. See Michael Katz, *The Irony of Early School Reform* (Harvard University Press, 1968) or Samuel Bowles, 'Unequal education and the reproduction of the social division of labor,' *Review of Radical Political Economics* (winter 1971). For more information about the history of women's education see also Thomas Woody, *A History of Women's Education in the United States* (New York, 1929).

9 Data for high school graduates from Federal Security Agency, Office of Education, *Biennial Survey of Education*. Cited in the *Statistical Abstract of the United States* (1952), p. 121. One possible explanation for the fact that more women than men were graduating from high school is the following: in the case of working-class men and women, the boys left school to work. The money they could earn was badly needed by their families. But if girls entered the factory labor force, their wages would be considerably lower than those of their brothers. This fact, coupled with attitudes that men were the more important bread winners and that woman's place was in the home, may have resulted in working-class girls staying in school longer than their brothers. At any rate, it is clear that figures on high school graduates must be broken down by class, and probably also by ethnic group, before the disparity between male and female high school graduates can be adequately explained.

10 Katz, *Irony of Early School Reform*, p. 58.

11 Ibid., p. 58.

12 Robert W. Smuts, *Women and Work in America* (Columbia University Press, 1959).

13 Baker, *Technology and Women's Work*, pp. 62–3.

14 Helen L. Sumner, *History of Women in Industry in the United States* (61st Congress, 2nd session, U.S. Senate Document 645; Bureau of Labor, 1911), p. 239.

15 'Women in Business: I,' *Fortune*, 12 (July 1935), p. 53.

16 Ibid., p. 53.

17 The following account of the development of the typewriter is based on Bruce Bliven, Jr, *The Wonderful Writing Machine* (New York: Random House, 1954).

18 Ibid., p. 134.

19 Smuts, *Women and Work*, p. 90. It is very difficult to find statistics about clerical wages at the end of the nineteenth century broken down by sex; Bliven and Smuts do not cite sources for their wage statistics.

20 The engraving is reproduced in Bliven, *Wonderful Writing Machine*, p. 73.

21 Ibid., pp. 75–6. Bliven gives no date for *The Typewriter Girl*, but the context of his argument leads to the conclusion that the novel was a late nineteenth-century potboiler.

22 Edward Bok, 'The Return of the Business Woman,' *Ladies' Home Journal* (March 1900), p. 16. I am indebted to Elaine Wethington of the University of Michigan at Ann Arbor and her unpublished manuscript, 'The Women's Magazines and the "Business Woman," 1890–1919' for this reference. Wethington notes that Bok did not shrink from also pointing out that office work was the 'best paid and most respectable employment for young women'; he was quite happy to have his magazine reflect opposing opinions in order not to alienate any of its one million subscribers. Wethington's paper is extremely useful as a source for articles about office workers in the prominent American women's magazines.

23 Harry C. Spillman, 'The Stenographer Plus,' *Ladies' Home Journal* (February 1916), p. 33.

24 'Women in Business: II,' *Fortune*, 12 (August 1935), p. 55. It is interesting to speculate why *Fortune* published its defense of women in the office in 1935. It is possible that during the Depression there was some criticism of the employment of women as clerical workers when unemployment rates for men, the traditional breadwinners, were so high.

25 Baker, *Technology and Women's Work*, p. 74.

SECTION 4

Politics, Legitimacy and the State

Introduction

David Potter

Societies are divided. Individuals, groups and classes have many real differences of interest and outlook. How, then, do societies hold together through time? This fundamental question poses particularly interesting problems when examining societies with capitalist economies and democratic politics. The issue involves questions of social control and social order, and provides the main focus for both this section of the Reader and the next one on conformity, consensus and conflict.

At first glance, the question of how a society holds together might seem to be that certain agencies of government administering the law keep society in order. That is indeed part of the answer, but there is much more to it than that. In addition to what government agencies do, the whole area of politics, legitimacy and the state can be considered in this connection. Politics and government, however, are not only relevant to explaining how societies hold together. It is through acting together politically that men and women through history have worked together to achieve collective goals, to change or even transform the societies in which they live. Politics and government, in short, are also at the centre of social change. Students of the subject have therefore paid particular attention to how it is that collective goals are formulated in democracies through the political process and how public policies, once agreed on, are implemented. In exploring the ways in which politics and government relate to both social control and social change, one encounters questions like these: What does the government or the state do that helps to hold society together? Why do people accept what it does (or perceive the government as legitimate)? To what extent do the people voting in an election influence what the government does? To what extent are interest groups in society able to influence what the state does? Can democratic governments in the western world cope with the increasing demands made upon them?

157

Is Britain becoming harder to govern, perhaps heading towards some sort of political crisis in the 1980s?

The thing about these sorts of questions (which are explored in Block 4 of D102) is that there are no straightforward answers to them. This is hardly surprising, given the multi-theoretical nature of the social sciences referred to in the general introduction to this book. As soon as one tries to deal with such questions, one gets involved in the central dispute in political science. It is an exciting, important debate, and it has been going on for a long time. The nature of the debate keeps changing as the societies in which the debate takes place change. At the end of the 1960s, for example, each side of the debate looked like holding an agreed position; there was 'the pluralist perspective' and 'the marxist perspective'. By the 1980s, the picture had become more complex, with important debates taking place between rival positions within pluralism and within marxism. The readings in this section bring out the principal features of the two main positions, the changing nature of the debate between them, and the ways in which different theories can produce different answers to questions about government and politics in society.

Two such questions related to British politics are examined. The first is: To what extent are interest groups in society able to influence what the state does? This is Hewitt's concern, and his analysis provides an example of how the pluralist-marxist debate in the early 1970s could affect the work of a political scientist. Hewitt's interest was to describe the distribution of political power in the United Kingdom during the fairly straightforward exercise, he had to summarize the theoretical debate in which the question was lodged, the debate between those who argued that power was held by a ruling group and those who argued that it was widely dispersed in a plurality of groups. Hewitt then adopted the issue approach to studying how policy was made in the UK. As the name suggests, the issue approach consists of studying issues. His method of approach (which he describes carefully) identified twenty-four important issues during the period 1944-64. He then proceeded to examine the influence of organized groups in society on decisions taken on those issues. The results of his analysis led him to the conclusion that a pluralist picture of the national power structure in the UK was the more accurate, since his evidence indicated that 'a diversity of conflicting interests are involved in many issues, without any one interest being consistently successful in realizing its goal.'

Morriss wrote a critique of Hewitt's analysis, to which Hewitt replied in a spirited defence.* Morriss's critique focused particularly

---

* Peter Morriss, 'The pluralist case not proven: Hewitt on Britain', *British Journal of Political Science*, vol. 5 (1975), pp. 383–9; Christopher Hewitt, 'Pluralism in British policy-making: a reply to Morriss', *British Journal of Political Science*, vol. 6 (1976), pp. 351–6.

on Hewitt's method of selecting 'important' issues, arguing that Hewitt's method led him to exclude other issues which, if built into the analysis, might have led Hewitt to an elitist or marxist conclusion. Morriss suggested that

> issues which never come to a head because of anticipated reactions, issues which rarely hit the headlines but are important because they are always there, issues which involve selective non-enforcement of the laws, and routines which determine which issues are considered by the elites, are all important facets of political life; a study of power is highly selective, if not definitely biased, if it systematically ignores all of them (p. 386).

The exchange between Hewitt and Morriss illustrates how a seemingly straightforward question like that can be highly contentious because important theoretical disputes are involved.

The other question examined in this section is: Why is Britain becoming harder to govern? This was a particularly prominent question in the latter part of the 1970s. Again, one finds that different answers to the question are advanced depending on the theoretical position of the author. The papers by King and by Coates illustrate this nicely. King's answer is broadly within the pluralist tradition; he argues in part that Britain is becoming harder to govern because excessive demands are made upon government by interest groups in society. Coates analyses the question from an avowedly marxist position; government is locked into the structure of the economy, and the principal reason why governing Britain is becoming more difficult is because it takes place within a growing crisis of capitalism.

It is important to appreciate, however, that by the 1980s there was no longer a debate between just two positions. King's analysis represents only one of several variants within pluralism, Coates's only one variant within marxism. This increased complexity is evident in Dunleavy's paper. We asked him to write for this volume a short summary of the nature and direction of the pluralist-marxist debate in the 1980s. This was an exceedingly demanding assignment, and his summary is necessarily condensed and challenging to read. But the main point comes through very clearly. Conventional pluralism is still important, but has split into several distinct variants. Two of these are neo-pluralist theory and liberal anti-pluralism (sometimes called the New Right). Conventional marxist views of liberal democratic politics are still important, but again, variants have come to the fore. The two that Dunleavy identifies and discusses are structural marxism and theories of legitimation crisis. In short, the analysis of politics and government does not appear to be heading toward some grand synthesis or one true position. The debates go on, and the friction that is produced lights the way forward. A flickering light it may be, but we would be lost without it.

11 Elites and the distribution of power

Christopher Hewitt

This paper is concerned in a general sense with elite relationships and the distribution of power in modern society. Its specific focus, however, is upon elites and their role in the national power structure of a single country during a particular historical period. It is offered as a case study of the distribution of political power in the United Kingdom during the 1944-64 period.

The term 'national power' structure is here understood as the pattern of relationships that exists between the State and various social groups.[1]

> The power structure of modern societies is usually conceived as the interplay between the institutions of government and the multitude of politically active intermediary groups. It is often stressed that the role of intermediary groups determine the power structure even more than the formal governmental institutions.

More precisely it consists of the relationships within and between three kinds of groups, political elites, social elites and non-elites. The term elite is used to describe those who occupy the leading positions in organizations or institutions. Political elites are those who occupy such positions in the State, that is the elected political representatives and the top civil servants. Social elites are those who control the non-political organizations that either embody sectional interests like 'business', 'labour', 'the professions' or represent attitudes and opinions. The non-elites are made up of subordinates and rank and file members in organizations as well as unorganized publics.

It should be stressed that the definition of the power structure that is being used here is restricted to a consideration of the distribution of power in the political system and hence to the influence which groups have over the activity of the State. The power relationships that groups have outside of this political sphere are not considered, so that such

Source: P. Stanworth and A. Giddens (eds), *Elites and Power in British Society*, Cambridge University Press, 1974, pp. 45-6, 48-64, 227-30.

matters as the power of an elite over its organizational subordinates (of owners or managers over workers in a factory, for example) are outside the scope of the paper.[2] It is certainly true that the exercise of political power is affected by the exercise of non-political power and *vice versa*. Thus on the one hand the investment policies of private corporations must be taken into account by those responsible for Government regional policy-planning and such regional policies will on the other hand provide the context for corporate investment decisions. The term 'political power' will be used, however, only when it is exercised deliberately and directly to affect State action.

The elitist–pluralist debate

There is a long-standing controversy as to the form that the national power structure takes in contemporary western industrial societies, that is societies characterized by the existence of political democracy, a high level of industrialization, and the predominance of 'capitalist' enterprise in the economic system.[3] Lenski introduces his discussion of national power in modern society by distinguishing two viewpoints.

> With the rise and spread of political democracy, students of power have become increasingly divided over the applicability of the concept of a governing or ruling class in industrial societies. Some claim to see no great change from the past, and write persuasively of the Power Elite and The Establishment; others deny their existence, and write no less persuasively of Political Pluralism, Countervailing Power and Strategic Elites.

The first of these theories will be labelled the 'elitist' view, since its proponents argue that a single group is dominant over other groups. The second theory will be referred to as the 'pluralist-democratic' view. [. . .]
Pluralists, say Dahl,[4]

> suggest that there are a number òf loci for arriving at political decisions; that business men, trade unions, politicians, consumers, farmers, voters and many other aggregates all have an impact on policy outcomes; that none of these aggregates is homogeneous for all purposes; that each of them is highly influential over some scopes but weak over many others.

[. . .] Although there are important differences within each school, there is manifestly a significant dispute between the two.

Furthermore the points of disagreement are quite specific, and appear to be recognized on both sides. Before discussing the kind of evidence that could be used in support or refutation of either view, it will be useful therefore to formulate the controversy somewhat more precisely.

1   All the writers agree at least implicitly that the controversy concerns the way that the state acts, that policy is made and decisions taken.

2   Elitists consider that it is possible to identify a unified and cohesive 'ruling group'. This ruling group is sometimes seen as a social class or as an economic class or interest or as an organizational elite. Although there are certain disagreements between elitists concerning the correct conceptualization of the ruling group and its composition, in practice the different terms are used almost interchangeably. In general the ruling group is considered to include the business elite plus other elites drawn from the same social class, and with common interests or values. Pluralists conceive of the elites as lacking in cohesion and frequently in conflict with one another.

3   Elitists see the ruling group as active in more than one policy area. Pluralists consider elite involvement as specialized either in terms of issue-areas or even in terms of particular issues within a given policy area.

4   Because of the opposition of other elites who are not part of the ruling group, or because of the activity of the public as a whole, pluralists would claim that the power of any particular elite to obtain what it wants from the political elites is greatly reduced. In contrast the elitists anticipate that public opinion will either be controllable by the ruling group, or that it and the demands of other elites will be ignored by the political elite who will function as the agent of the ruling group.

5   Both elitists and pluralists are making general statements about the power structure. The elitists do not see the ruling elite as totally cohesive, active in every policy issue, nor completely successful in getting their way, and the pluralists are not unaware of the existence of powerful interest groups. It seems, however, that the elitists are making the stronger statement if one accepts the way that Miliband formulates the matter: 'The question is not whether this class has a *substantial* measure of political power and influence . . . The question is a different one altogether, namely whether this dominant class also exercises a much greater degree of power and influence than any other class; whether it exercises a *decisive* degree of political power.'[5]

Methodological issues in studying power structures

To determine which theory is the more accurate, that is what type of power structure exists either in a local community or the national society, three kinds of methods have been proposed, the 'reputational', the 'issue', and the 'positional' or 'sociology of leadership'.[6] The first method has been used frequently in studies of community power but only once to discover the national power structure.[7] The second method, which involves the analysis of a sample of policy issues, has been utilized occasionally for the study of community power but never for national power. The third method supplemented by various kinds of indirect evidence has been utilized by almost all the major studies of national power.

The absence of studies using the issue-method is somewhat surprising given that many if not most writers in the elitist-pluralist controversy have couched their hypotheses in terms of the ability of groups to influence the policy-making process. The reasons why no studies of national power using this method have been made are due it seems to the practical problems involved. The more serious difficulties in its application involve the selection of a 'fair sample', gathering material on the policy issues, and the problem of how to analyse this material.[8]

Despite these methodological problems it is my contention that the study of national issues is in fact more practicable than critics have assumed. Furthermore there are grounds for considering that the results of the sociology of leadership method are capable of being misinterpreted, and that in fact most elitists have made some rather dubious assumptions about the significance of such data. Therefore the value of examining national power by an alternative and previously untried method seemed to justify studying national policy-making in a systematic fashion.

In order to select a sample of important national policy issues the following procedure was used. First, a list of policy issues was collected for the 1944-64 period from a survey of several history texts. Policy issues were considered to consist of (1) crises and the response to them, (2) authoritative decisions or actions taken by the political elites and the events leading up to them, or (3) controversies which were discussed by the political elites even if no decision was taken on the matter, that is if the *status quo* remained unchanged. The issues on the list were then divided in an *a priori* fashion into four different policy areas: foreign affairs and defence, economic affairs, welfare policy, and a residual 'social' policy area. A panel of five 'judges' then individually selected the ten 'most important' issues in each category. Finally, for each category, the three most frequently selected issues in the 1944-51 period and the three most frequently selected issues in the 1951-64 period were chosen for analysis. The twenty-four issues selected in this fashion were therefore drawn equally from two political regimes, Labour and Conservative, as well as being spread over four different policy-areas. Although there is an obviously subjective element in the selection process, this procedure does reduce the danger of the researcher deliberately selecting only those issues which validate a particular viewpoint and also selects out the less important issues. Published secondary sources were used as data and evidence was gathered for each issue on the following matters: the policy-preferences and activities of formal organizations, the state of public opinion, the attitudes of various political groups (Members of Parliament, party activists, civil servants) and the history and final 'outcome' of the issue.[9] The issues chosen were:

Foreign policy

1   Indian independence 1947.
2   The shift in Anglo-Russian relations from war-time coalition to the setting up of NATO and British re-armament.
3   The Abadan crisis of 1951 over the nationalization of the British oil industry in Persia.
4   The Suez crisis of 1956.
5   The attempt at creating an independent nuclear deterrent in the mid nineteen-fifties.
6   The creation of the Central African Federation.

Economic policy

1   The United States loan of 1946.
2   The nationalization of road haulage.
3   The nationalization of the steel industry by the 1945 Labour Government.
4   The abolition of resale price maintenance 1960-4.
5   Britain's bid to enter the Common Market under Macmillan up to the French veto in 1963.
6   The reorganization and 'rationalization' of British Railways under Dr Beeching.

Welfare policy

1   The Education Act of 1944 and its implementation.

2   The National Health Service Act of 1946.
3   The National Insurance Act of 1946.
4   The Rent Act of 1957.
5   The comprehensive schools issue throughout the nineteen-fifties and early nineteen-sixties.
6   The motorways issue throughout the nineteen-fifties and early nineteen-sixties.

Social policy

1   The Town and Country Planning Act of 1946.
2   The attempt to liberalize the divorce laws in the early nineteen-fifties.
3   The temporary abolition of capital punishment in 1957.
4   The introduction of commercial television in 1954.
5   The Commonwealth Immigration Act of 1962.
6   The Clean Air Act of 1956.

Organized groups

To a great extent the 'pluralism' of the power structure depends upon the unit of analysis that one chooses to adopt. Riesman's pluralist position, for example, is largely contingent upon his defining 'interests' in a microscopic fashion as specific organizations. If one follows such a strategy it is much more likely that one will discover that a particular interest is only involved in a very narrow range of issues than if one defines interests more broadly. The same point could be made in interpreting the results of the New Haven study in which Dahl found that very few individuals were involved in more than one issue area. Given that similar kinds of individuals with similar values were active in most issues the pattern would appear far less pluralist.

As a first stage in the analysis it is instructive to focus, however, upon individual organizations to see if they are involved in several issues or just in one. To answer this question every organization that was involved in each issue was noted even if the involvement comprised no more than the taking of a position. The lists of organizations were then compared to see how much continuity there was between issues. The results are presented in Table 11.1 below, the organizations being classified into seven types.

The classification of organizations is generally self-explanatory. The Business organizations (representing 'capitalist' ownership interests) include firms (such as Shell, ICI, etc.) and trade associations (e.g. the

British Iron and Steel Federation). Two types of occupational associations were distinguished according to the class status of their members;
the 'higher professions' (i.e. the self-employed, those in top administrative
positions, and occupations requiring a university degree or its equivalent), and intermediate white-collar occupations made up one category,
while blue-collar unions formed the other. 'Promotional' groups were
defined as organizations devoted to the advancement of a particular
cause rather than to representing the sectional interests of their members.
The category includes both permanent multi-purpose groups, such as
the Fabian Society and *ad hoc* groups (created during the issue, or with
very limited goals) such as the National Council for the Abolition of the
Death Penalty, as well as some residual miscellaneous organizations.

Table 11.1 Continuity of individual organizations between issues by
type of organization

Type of organization	Total no. of organizations	No. involved in only one issue	No. involved in two issues	No. involved in three issues	No. involved in four or more issues
Business organizations	173	145	16	6	6
White-collar occupations	85	77	3	3	2
Blue-collar unions	36	26	4	2	4
Religious organizations	11	4	1	1	5
Local government bodies	53	44	7	0	2
Research organizations	33	32	0	0	1
Promotional organizations	190	172	9	6	3
Total all organizations	581	500	40	18	23

The degree of continuity of individual organizations is clearly
extremely low. Overall 86 per cent of the organizations were involved
in only one issue and almost half of the overlapping organizations were
involved in only two issues. Only twenty-three organizations (less than
4 per cent) were involved in four or more issues.[10]

Some caution must be exercised in the interpretation of these results.
First it is clear that the activity of certain organizations may be ignored
by the data sources used and furthermore that the sources are themselves of varying reliability. It seems probable, however, that it is the
less important groups which will be most commonly ignored.

A second methodological problem lies in the fact that the sources
sometimes make general references to the 'Building Trade', the 'Steel
Companies', etc., or to individuals rather than to particular organizations.
In such cases these were assumed, in the absence of any contradictory

evidence, to be references to organizations and coded as such. Various objections could be raised to the conclusion that the low degree of continuity is significant. It might be argued that the most active organizations in any issue are more likely to be involved in several issues. Thus an analysis of the 'significantly involved' organizations alone would produce a different picture. To check this the continuity of such organizations was examined. Significant involvement by an organization was considered to include any of the following activities.

1   The initiation of some policy proposal that was accepted, or at least seriously considered in Parliament or by the Government.
2   Extensive lobbying of or consultation with ministers, civil servants, or some bloc of MPs.
3   Threatening some action against, or offering some inducement in support of a given policy, that was not obviously ignored by the politicians.
4   Propaganda activity aimed at changing or mobilizing public opinion.
5   Organizing concerted action by like-minded groups, providing support for active pressure groups (e.g. financial aid or other facilities) or serving as a 'transmission belt' for the opinions of important groups to reach the political decision-makers.

Very few organizations were involved 'significantly' in more than one issue, and the proportion of overlapping organizations was in fact slightly lower than for all the organizations.

The organizations that were involved in several issues could themselves be considered as the nucleus of a power elite. In fact, however, such organizations make up a rather disparate collection of interests, as well as including some organizations that were involved in only rather trivial ways. The organizations involved in four or more issues include the Federation of British Industries, National Union of Manufacturers, Associated British Chambers of Commerce, British Iron and Steel Federation, National Farmers Union, British Medical Association, National Union of Teachers, British Council of Churches, Catholic Church, Methodist Church, Church of Scotland, National Council of Women, Co-operative Movement, the London County Council, Association of Municipal Corporations, PEP and three of the six largest trade unions (TGWU, NUR, USDAW). The three most 'involved' organizations were the Fabian Society (11 issues), the Church of England (12 issues), and the TUC (17 issues).

Given that individual organizations are involved in a very limited range of issues the question then becomes whether or not organizations can be aggregated into larger groupings which do attempt to influence policy in all or most issues. Is it possible to consider the different business organizations, for example, as a cohesive entity? In measuring the cohesion of an interest bloc it seems reasonable to concentrate upon the *general* position of organizations since there are always likely to be minor differences over points of detail even within groups united by an overall consensus. The four main sectional interests, business, white collar occupations, unions, and religious groups, were therefore examined to discover how cohesive they each were.

Table 11.2 Consistency of alignments within categories of organizations

Type of organization	Total no. of organizational involvements	Total no. of organizational stands known	Total no. of consistent stands	Percentage of consistent stands to all known stands
Business organizations	225	172	160	93
White-collar occupations	100	54	42	78
Blue-collar unions	73	64	61	97
Religious organizations	41	39	36	92

The cohesion of each category was measured in the following way. For every issue in which an interest group category was involved a judgement was made as to the position of the category *as a whole* (i.e. the position of most groups in that category). Then an aggregate measure for all the issues was calculated, and the degree of cohesion of a category expressed as the percentage of times in which the organizations were aligned with the majority of the groups in that category.

In some issues the position of an organization changed over time. In these cases the organization was classified in terms of the position which it held for the longest period of time.

These results suggest that each of the interests is highly cohesive since even the most heterogeneous category, the white collar occupational group, is generally aligned as a bloc. The business group was seriously divided on only two issues and the unions on one. Although business interests provided substantial backing for the National Smoke Abatement Society, the Clean Air Act was opposed by the Cotton and Chemical industries and the Federation of British Industries wanted a much less stringent policy towards pollution. On the issue of Commercial Television, groups like the Newspaper Proprietors Association, and the Cinematograph Exhibitors Association were opposed to the introduction of Commercial Television, which was supported by advertising groups and the manufacturers and retailers of television equipment. Professional groups were split over the same issue, and also over Divorce Reform and Comprehensive Education. The Religious group was divided over one aspect of the Education Act, the role of the Church schools and state aid for them, but united in support of the Act in general. Over the Nuclear Deterrent, individual Churches as well as the Religious bloc as a whole were divided. One category of organizations, the promotional type, is clearly heterogeneous and lacking in cohesion. This general category can be subdivided, however, into somewhat more homogeneous blocs. The most numerous type of promotional organization includes those left-of-centre groups which advocate 'progressive' causes such as the Fabian Society and other offshoots of the Labour movement, Pacifist, anti-colonialist organizations etc. [. . .] Their right-wing counterparts are much less numerous. Various pro-business organizations such as Aims of Industry [. . .] constitute another small category of right-wing groups. The only other numerous types of promotional organization are charitable and welfare groups, tenants' and residential associations, women's organizations and groups which serve as fronts for several sectional interests. Overall the diversity of opinions embodied by promotional organizations and the large number of left-of-centre organizations appear to make the political process more rather than less pluralist.[11]

Given that the interest group categories are generally internally cohesive it seems legitimate to consider which of them are involved in each issue. Before doing this, however, it seems useful to examine the state of public opinion on each of the issues so that it can be compared to the positions of the various organized interests.

Public opinion

Some theorists have suggested that a precondition for democratic influence is the existence of competition between elite groups.[12] Other writers have seen the influence of mass public opinion as a limitation upon elite power. Given that the role of public opinion is a matter of concern to many writers, an attempt will be made here to characterize the state of public opinion on the different issues.

Both from the point of view of the politician in assessing what the public wants, and the observer who is trying to estimate the degree of democracy that the policy-making process reveals, public opinion situations can be classified into three categories.

1   Issues in which a clear majority of the public desires a given general outcome, such a majority being stable over time in aggregate terms.
2   Issues in which public opinion is fairly evenly divided and stable over time with no large net shifts.

3   Issues marked by an unstable and/or confused public opinion situation. These would be indicated by a high proportion of 'don't knows' in the polls, large net shifts in opinion or internally contradictory responses.

On certain issues it is possible to make a valid dichotomy of opinion; people can be distinguished into those who are 'for' or 'against' a given policy. Relevant opinion polling data exist for eleven such issues,[13] and are presented in Table 11.3. When more than one poll exists, the average has been calculated.

Table 11.3 Division of public opinion on selected issues

Issue	No. of polls	Division of public opinion (%)	Don't know (%)	Majority opinion
Suez	6	44:40	16	Against intervention
Steel	2	52:26	22	Against nationalization
Railways	4	39:39	22	Beeching doing a good job
Resale price maintenance	4	52:28	20	For abolition of RPM
Common Market	8	43:29	28	For joining the Market
National Health	1	55:32	13	Approve NHS proposals
Rent Act	1	35:33	32	Against decontrol
Capital punishment	8	61:27	12	For retention of death penalty
Television	5	44:40	16	Against commercial TV
Divorce reform	1	43:31	23	Make divorce more difficult
Immigration	3	68:17	15	For restricting immigration

On the basis of these statistics it is suggested that five issues (steel nationalization, resale price maintenance, National Health, capital punishment and immigration) fit into the first category. Based upon less direct evidence, six other issues are also included as cases in which a clear majority supported a given policy.

As regards the Education Act of 1944, the public appears to have been in support, and in fact to have been somewhat more 'radical' or advanced than the government, since 44 per cent thought that the 'best' school leaving age was sixteen, while only 20 per cent favoured fifteen (the government proposal in the Act). Furthermore, as regards the other controversy of the Education Act, the role of the Church Schools, a large majority (61 per cent) thought that they should be taken over by the state.[14]

Over India there seems to have been little opposition to the principle of ultimate independence and the controversy revolved around the question of when self-government should be given. Twice during the war the public was asked whether India should be given self-government 'immediately, or after the war'. Fifty-one and 41 per cent were in favour of granting independence after the war, although between the two polls the proportion of those favouring immediate independence increased from 26 to 31 per cent.[15]

On two other issues, National Insurance, and Town and Country Planning, there are no directly relevant poll results, but such evidence as we have suggests that the public supported the basic direction of policy and might even have favoured more radical change. A 1945 poll[16] found that over half would approve of the 'nationalization' of land with less than a third disapproving. We can therefore reasonably assume that the 1947 Act which merely controlled land use and profits was acceptable to the general public. Similarly with National Insurance, most contemporary commentators[17] assert that the Beveridge plan was hugely popular, and criticism seems to have focused on the government's slowness in implementing the plan or on restrictions in its scope.[18] After the 'Great Smog' of 1952, public feeling was strongly in favour of some anti-pollution law.[19] In the late nineteen-fifties poll data show that a large majority of the population favoured 'more and better designed roads' and supported increased expenditure on motorway construction.[20]

In three issues, as Table 11.3 above indicates, public opinion was evenly divided. These are the Suez, railway and commercial television issues. The other issues seem to be marked by a low level of public concern, or a high degree of instability and ambivalence.[21]

Group involvements, alignments and the policy outcome

In Table 11.4, the major involvements and positions of the main interest groups have been listed for all the issues as well as the positions of the general public. The table presents the data in a summary fashion and ignores minor involvements by certain organizations and slight differences between groups in their attitudes towards the issues. Setting out the data in this fashion allows one to make comparisons between groups regarding the number of issues in which they were involved, and also to see if any patterns of conflict or coalition are revealed between different groups.

The business group was involved in more issues than any other interest, but the union group was involved in almost as many. White collar occupations and the Churches were active in a substantial minority of the issues. In very few issues does one find that any particular group is the only one involved, and often several groups are concerned with an issue.

Table 11.4 Alignments by interest on different issues

Issue	Successful policy outcome	Business	White collar	Unions	Religious	Public opinion
India	Independence for India	–	–	–	–	Pro
Russia	Hard-line policy to Russia	–	–	Pro	–	–
Abadan	Sanctions against Iran	Pro	–	–	–	–
Suez	Military intervention	–	–	Anti	Anti	Divided
Nuclear deterrent	Independent deterrent policy	Anti	–	Divided	Divided	–
Central Africa	Federation	–	–	–	Anti	–
U.S. loan	Loan negotiated	–	–	–	–	–
Road haulage	Nationalization	Anti	–	Pro	–	Pro
Steel	No effective nationalization	Pro	–	Anti	–	Pro
Resale price maintenance	Abolition of RPM	Anti	–	–	–	–
Common market	No entry	Anti	–	Pro	–	Divided
Railways	Beeching's rationalization policy	Pro	Pro	Anti	–	Pro
Education Act	Education Act	Pro	Pro	Pro	Pro	Pro
National Health	National Health Service	–	–	–	Pro	Pro
National Insurance	National Insurance Act	Anti	–	Pro	Pro	Pro
Rent Act	Rent decontrol	Pro	Pro	Anti	–	–
Comprehensives	No support for comprehensives	–	Divided	–	–	–
Motorways	Motorway programme	Pro	Pro	Pro	–	Pro
Town and country	Town and Country Planning Act	Anti	Pro	Pro	–	Pro
Divorce	No change in divorce laws	–	Divided	–	Pro	–
Capital punishment	Abolition of capital punishment	–	Anti	–	Pro	Anti
Television	Commercial Television	Divided	Divided	Anti	Anti	Divided
Immigration	Immigration control	–	–	–	Anti	Pro
Clean air	Clean Air Act	Divided	Pro	–	–	Pro

Usually the business group and the unions are found on opposite sides if they are involved in the same issue, but apart from this the alignments between different groups do not appear to be very consistent. This seems to correspond generally to the hypothesis suggested by Rose of multi-lateral conflict in which the sides change from issue to issue.

The final question concerns the policy outcome, and leads to a consideration of which groups were favoured by government action. In some issues the overall policy pursued by the government or the final legislative outcome was clearly compatible with the preferences of certain interests and incompatible with those of other interests. The groups in favour of a 'hard line' policy on Russia, Indian independence, the National Health Service, National Insurance, the nationalization of road haulage, the control of Commonwealth immigration, the Central African Federation, the decontrol of rents, the abolition of resale price maintenance, the control of air pollution, Beeching's railway policy, a motorway construction programme, and no substantial change in the divorce laws were in this sense 'successful'.

In other issues, the final outcome generally favoured certain groups but substantial concessions were made to the opposing interests. Thus the Town and Country Planning Bill became law but considerable concessions were made as regards compensation prices. Over the capital punishment issue, the abolitionists got what they wanted but only for an experimental five year period. Similarly, substantial concessions were made to the opponents of commercial television as regards programming controls etc. The teachers' unions made considerable concessions to the Churches in the Education Act.

In other cases it is harder to define what the successful policy was because the government policy itself either appears ambiguous or changed over time. In some of these issues the uncertainty is increased by the fact that the ability of the government to achieve policy goals is limited by the activity of other national governments (as in foreign policy issues) or by the need to achieve co-operation from local government bodies (e.g. in the comprehensive schools issue).

The Steel Nationalization issue could be considered resolved finally in a way that was compatible with the wishes of the pro-nationalization groups, but the apparent unwillingness of the Labour government to act on the matter until just before the return of a Conservative government (which denationalized the industry) makes it more reasonable to consider the outcome of this issue as one which favoured the anti-nationalization groups. The Common Market issue can be seen as a victory for the 'marketeers' because negotiations were opened, or alternatively for the 'anti-marketeers' because the negotiations failed. It is assumed[22] that the negotiations failed because the anti-marketeers were able to impose such conditions on the concessions that the British negotiators could make, that a French veto was virtually inevitable. Over the Suez question one could argue that because the intervention failed, those opposed to the use of force were successful. On the other hand it is more plausible to argue that the intervention failed because of pressures from the United States, and to see the fact of intervention as a defeat for those opposed to the use of military force. The collapse of Sandys's independent deterrent policy was a result of the inherent impracticality of such a scheme for a Power with Britain's resources, although assisted to a degree by domestic criticism. Since the policy was maintained for so long, however, it is considered a defeat for those groups opposed to an independent British deterrent. The Government responded somewhat ambiguously to the nationalization of the British oil industry by Iran, since they resisted the call to use military force but instead tried to prevent the Persians from selling the oil. Although the resistance of many local education authorities was the primary factor, the lack of Government support also contributed to the slow development of the comprehensive schools system.

If these policy outcomes are compared to the preferences of the different groups it seems that no one group was generally successful in getting what it wanted. Neither the business group nor any other appears to be especially favoured by the government.

Discussion

From the evidence presented, it is clear that policy-making does not appear to be 'elitist' in the sense that any single elite or interest is dominant. Instead the picture of national power that is revealed suggests a 'pluralist' interpretation since a diversity of conflicting interests are involved in many issues, without any one interest being consistently successful in realizing its goals. Furthermore, each interest appears to be limited in the range of its involvement. These findings appear to be so divergent from the expectations of the elitist or ruling class theorists that some attention must be given to the question of why this difference exists, assuming that the picture of the policy-making process given in the previous section is generally correct.

First it could be argued that the ruling class or elitist theorists are not in fact concerned with the policy-making influence of the business elite or the upper class, but with their general control over society. In other words their power over economic institutions may be sufficient for them to be referred to as a ruling class. However, as the quotations from the elitist writers cited in the first section of the paper reveal, most do in fact refer to the *political* influence and policy-making role of the ruling groups.

Another position which is increasingly popular is to conceive of policy influence in a negative fashion. This objection is more basic and argues that to interpret the results of decision-making studies as confirmation of the pluralist position is invalid since elite power may be exercised in restricting, through a variety of means, the issues that arise to those that do not threaten their position.[23] This 'non-decision making' aspect of power operating through the 'mobilization of bias' certainly does exist, but whether it is exercised as the elitists claim is highly problematical, and not much evidence has been offered to support their contention.[24] The fact that gross inequalities in the distribution of income and wealth exist and that no real attempt has been made to modify this situation does not in itself constitute evidence for non-decision making power.[25] An alternative and more likely explanation is that very few people know about or consider such inequality unjust or important.

Regardless of whether the political dominance of the socially advantaged groups in society is conceived of in a positive or a negative fashion it is still incumbent upon those who support such a view to explain why the political authorities should respond primarily to such groups. A variety of explanations can be found in the literature.

Many of the reasons given to explain why Government should be dominated by upper class or business interests represent, however, as Finer argues in his classic articles, 'abstract possibilities . . . not effective capacity' and almost all the examples of such activities (e.g. the seduction of the police and armed forces, bribery, the maintenance of private armies, etc.) are drawn from non-British history.[26] Some plausible reasons remain; business as a source of party funds to the Conservative Party and the ability of business and certain professional groups to obstruct the government by not co-operating with its policies and 'refusing the Government the expert, scientific and technical advice on which it relies'. Both of these factors seem to be exaggerated. As Sampson[27] points out, the disclosures forced by the 1967 Companies Act revealed that the majority of the largest 100 Companies did not give donations to the Conservative Party, and none of the fourteen largest did. Finer argues that Big Business even in the 1945–51 period did not deny the government its co-operation 'not only out of fear of reprisals, but from a strong sense of law-abidingness'.[28] The power of the business groups is also to a certain extent balanced by the 'countervailing power' of the unions with their powers of obstruction and non-co-operation, and political levy in favour of the Labour Party.

The evidence most commonly used in support of a ruling elite model is derived from the sociology of leadership method. This involves defining the key decision-making groups in the political process and then examining the socio-economic characteristics and career patterns of the individuals in such positions. An extensive literature exists on the background of MPs (and other political elites such as Administrative class civil servants, the Judiciary, members of Royal Commissions, etc.) and the results are fairly consistent. The political elites are 'firmly rooted in the general social elite', the higher socio-economic groups such as old Etonians, businessmen and professionals being over-represented and the working class drastically under-represented.[29] The problem then becomes one of deciding what can be concluded about the power-structure and the relationships between the political elite and other social groups from this evidence. Some analyses simply stop at this stage and *define* a governing or ruling class in terms of the social origin of the decision-makers.[30]

Frequently, however, the plausible assumption is made that such evidence can be used as an indicator of the attitudes and role of the political elite. The more sophisticated writers are careful to avoid any crude formulation of this argument, or are aware of the problems involved. Domhoff, for example, says that a 'drawback' of social background studies is that they 'do not demonstrate consequences from upper class control. Do upper class leaders have "special interests"?' Neither does social background analysis, he admits, answer the argument that 'real power' is in the masses. He is very evasive about this, and the related point, that the social background of the decision-makers may not affect significantly the outcome of the decisions.[31] However, this objection appears to be crucial, since if social background does *not* serve as a substantial predictor of the way that decision-makers *act* then why study it — apart from the intrinsic interest of studying social mobility in any area? [...]

A final criticism of the sociology of leadership method, however, is that it often fails to predict the behaviour (i.e. the political stands and actions) of politicians even if it is accurate in inferring their personal preferences. If one considers the eleven issues for which there was a clear public opinion majority, in four either the MPs of both parties or the MPs of the majority party were in accord with the public opinion majority, and the outcome was compatible with this Parliamentary and Public consensus. These were the National Health, National Insurance, Education Act, and Town and Country Planning issues. On these issues the alleged unrepresentativeness of the politicians' opinions is not supported, but it is the remaining issues which are most interesting. For the sociology of leadership method to have utility, politicians' opinions must affect significantly what politicians *do* as well as what they would *like* to do. Yet the personal preference of most MPs of both parties against restricting immigration and in favour of divorce reform, and of MPs of the majority party in favour of Steel Nationalization, and retaining resale price maintenance were a poor guide to the eventual outcome of these issues, and the public opinion majority was in fact closer to the outcome. Only over the capital punishment issue did the effect of politicians' personal sympathies lead to an undemocratic' outcome; that is one opposed to the wishes of the majority of the electorate.

While this general compatibility between public opinion and issue outcomes is not taken as validating any simplistic model of democracy it does seem to suggest that the policy process is not explicable in terms of the nature of the political elite. If as Bertrand Russell suggests 'Power is the production of intended effects' then we should look directly at how policy – the production of intended effects – is created through the interplay of public opinion, and organized pressure groups operating on the political system. The present essay is offered as a preliminary attempt to discover the power structure of Britain by using such a strategy.

Notes

1 Hans Evers: *Case Studies in Social Power*, Brill, Leiden, 1969, p. 129.
2 Also excluded from consideration in this paper is the effect of the exercise of organizational power upon *non-members*, such as the effect of business upon consumers or community residents involved in marketing policies or plant relocation policies. The 'cultural hegemony' argument in which elites are seen as creating or reinforcing social values is also ignored.
3 Gerhard Lenski: *Power and Privilege*, McGraw-Hill, New York, 1966, p. 325.
4 Robert Dahl: *Social Science Research on Business*, Columbia University Press, 1959, p. 36.
5 Ralph Miliband: *The State in Capitalist Society*, Weidenfeld & Nicolson, London, 1969, p. 48.
6 For a full discussion of these methodologies, see Arnold Rose: *The Power Structure*, Oxford University Press, New York, 1967, pp. 255-80.
7 The reputational method involves asking a panel of 'knowledgeables' to list the powerful individuals. The only national study using this method was Floyd Hunter: *Top Leadership USA*, University of North Carolina Press, 1959.
8 On the problems and disadvantages of the issue method see Rose: op. cit., pp. 277-8.

9 For a fuller description of the panel method, data sources and other methodological questions see the author's 'Policymaking in postwar Britain', *British Journal of Political Science*, April 1974. The distribution of issues between Labour and Conservative regimes is somewhat arbitrary given that issues overlapped sometimes between regimes, particularly in social policy. These were some of the main sources: James Christoph: *Capital Punishment and British Politics*, Allen & Unwin, London, 1962. H. H. Wilson: *Pressure Group*, Secker & Warburg, London, 1961. David Steel: *No Entry*, Gollancz, London, 1969. Harry Eckstein: *The English Health Service*, Harvard University Press, 1958. Janet Beveridge: *Beveridge and his Plan*, Hodder & Stoughton, London, 1954. H. C. Dent: *The Education Act*, Routledge & Kegan Paul, 1944. Michael Parkinson: *The Labour Party and the Organization of Secondary Education*, Routledge & Kegan Paul, 1970. Andreas Kazamias: *Politics, Society and Secondary Education in England*, University of Pennsylvania Press, 1966. Malcolm Barnett: *The Politics of Legislation*, Weidenfeld & Nicolson, London, 1969. George Ross: *The Nationalization of Steel*, MacGibbon & Kee, London, 1965. Lord Windlesham: *Communication and Political Power*, Cape, London, 1966. Keith Waltz: *Foreign Policy and Democratic Politics*, Little, Brown, Boston, 1967. Ronald Butt: *The Power of Parliament*, Constable, London, 1967. Leon Epstein: *British Politics in the Suez Crisis*, Pall Mall, London, 1964. Laurence Martin: 'The market for strategic ideas in Britain: the Sandys era', *American Political Science Review*, 1962, pp. 23–41. William Snyder: *The Politics of British Defense Policy, 1945–62*, Ohio State University Press, 1964. Robert Lieber: *British Politics and European Unity*, University of California Press, 1970. A. W. Ford: *The Anglo-Iranian Oil Dispute*, University of California Press, 1954. David Goldsworthy: *Colonial Issues in British Politics*, Clarendon Press, 1971.

10 The low degree of continuity overall does not mean that particular pairs of issues may not have a large number of organizations in common. Eleven common organizations were involved in the Motorways and Road Haulage issues, and there were significant overlaps between the two educational policy issues, and the two issues concerned with housing and property development.

11 Slightly less than a third of the involvements by promotional organizations were by left-of-centre groups.

12 William Kornhauser: *The Politics of Mass Society*, Free Press, Glencoe, 1959.

13 In order the sources are: Epstein: op. cit., pp. 141–5. Richard Rose: *Influencing Voters*, Faber, London, 1967, p. 184. *Gallup Political Index* (October 1962, April 1963, July 1964, August 1964). *Gallup Political Index* (January 1964, February 1964, March 1964, June 1964). Windlesham: op. cit., p. 158. Eckstein:

op. cit., p. 144. Barnett: op. cit., p. 116. Christoph: op. cit., p. 117. Burton Paulu: *British Broadcasting*, University of Minnesota Press, 1956, pp. 375–80. Charles Hanser: *Guide to Decision*, Bedminster Press, Totowa, 1965, p. 103. *Gallup Political Index* (November 1961, December 1961).

14   Hadley Cantril: *Public Opinion 1935–46*, Princeton University Press, p. 187.

15   Ibid., p. 327.

16   Ibid., p. 399.

17   Beveridge: op. cit.

18   Cantril: op. cit., p. 362.

19   John Sanderson: 'The National Smoke Abatement Society and the Clean Air Act', *Political Studies*, July 1961.

20   *Gallup Political Index* (January 1960, February 1960, June 1960).

21   See Parkinson: op. cit., p. 81. Snyder: op. cit., pp. 52–62. Cantril: op. cit., p. 276. Tom Harrisson: 'British opinion moves toward a new synthesis', *Public Opinion Quarterly*, 1947–8, pp. 327–41. No data could be found on the Central African Federation, Road Haulage, American Loan or Abadan Issues.

22   Cf. Nora Beloff: *The General Says No*, Penguin Books, 1963.

23   Peter Bachrach and Morton Baratz: 'Two faces of power', *American Political Review*, 1962, pp. 947–52.

24   See Mathew Crenson: *The Unpolitics of Pollution*, Johns Hopkins University Press, 1971, for one attempt to study non-decision making.

25   William Domhoff: *Who Rules America?*, Prentice-Hall, 1967, p. 144.

26   Samuel Finer: 'The political power of private capital', *Sociological Review*, 1955, pp. 279–94, 1956, 5–30.

27   Anthony Sampson: *The New Anatomy of Britain*, Hodder & Stoughton, London, 1971, pp. 117–18.

28   Finer: op. cit., p. 15.

29   W. Guttsman: *The British Political Elite*, MacGibbon & Kee, London, 1963. See also Domhoff: op. cit., and Andrew Roth: *The M.P.s Chart*, Parliamentary Profile Services Ltd, 1965.

30   'A Governing class is a social upper class which . . . contributes a disproportionate number of its members to the controlling institutions and key decision-making groups of the country'; Domhoff: op. cit., p. 5.

'There exists today in Britain a ruling class if we mean by it a group which provides the majority of those who occupy positions of power and who, in their turn, can materially assist their sons to reach similar positions', Guttsman: op. cit., p. 356. Guttsman is talking about political and non-political elites.

31   Domhoff: op. cit., pp. 143–4. Guttsman specifically denies that 'a socially broadly based representation is either a symptom or a precondition of an effective democratic system', op. cit., p. 373, but seems to believe that in practice upper class occupants of

political positions cannot or will not adequately represent the interests and desires of other groups. 'This distance (i.e. the social gap between MPs and electors) will in turn affect the quality of the dialogue between the ordinary men and their elected representatives and act as a barrier to democracy'. He thinks that the membership of advisory bodies 'should be much more broadly based and that those who sit around the polished horseshoe tables should be *genuinely* representative of thought and feelings of wide sections of the population'.

12   The problem of overloaded government

Anthony King

Why has Britain become so much harder to govern over the past twenty years or so? It was once thought that Governments would be extremely difficult to remove from office, given their ability to manage the economy. Now we are inclined to assume the opposite: that the tenure of Governments is precarious and that for the foreseeable future it will be a lucky Government that survives for more than a term. It was once thought that Britain was an unusually easy country to govern, its politicians wise, its parties responsible, its administration efficient, its people docile. Now we wonder whether Britain is not perhaps an unusually difficult country to govern, its problems intractable, its people bloody-minded. What has happened? What has gone wrong? [. . .]

Let us begin by reminding ourselves of some of the indications that the business of government in Britain has become more difficult. The number of such indications is vast. A sampling of them can be listed, in no particular order.

In the 1960s the conventional wisdom had it that the country's local government system was badly in need of reform. There were too many local government units, they were of the wrong size, their functions were wrongly distributed among them, they were based on an out-of-date distinction between town and country. All sorts of benefits would accrue if the system were 'streamlined'. The system has now been streamlined, but somehow things are not working out quite as expected. The benefits from the new system are scarcely discernible; the costs have proved enormous. Quite apart from the costs of the changeover as such, the new system is proving more expensive administratively than the old. Almost everyone who worked in the old system has had to be found a new job. Since virtually the same number of jobs is organised in fewer hierarchies, the number of jobs within each hierarchical structure is larger and the men at the top of each structure have to be paid more. It has proved a game of musical chairs. With the

Source: Anthony King (ed.), *Why is Britain Becoming Harder to Govern?*, London, BBC Publications, 1976, extracts from pp. 8–25, 28–9.

music stopped, only the ratepayers are left standing. [. . .]

Our experience of incomes policy offers a different sort of example. In this case, everyone is clear what the purposes of such a policy would be, but no one knows how to go about producing a successful policy that will last. As successive Governments have discovered, all incomes policies, whether labelled 'voluntary' or 'compulsory', are in fact voluntary. As successive Governments have also discovered, everybody's interest is nobody's interest. It is wholly rational for any single group of workers to use its bargaining power to increase the level of its money wages even though the cumulative effect of all groups of workers using their power in this way may be to reduce the level of real wages of every one of them. In retrospect, the remarkable thing is not that incomes policy has failed to work in the 1960s and 1970s but that it worked at all in 1948–49.

The failure of incomes policy is obviously related to the failure of economic policy generally. It labours the obvious to point out that, whatever their aims – a high rate of growth, stable prices, a surplus on the balance of payments, a reduction in industrial unrest – post-war Governments have failed to achieve them, at least for any sustained period. [. . .]

One further indication that the business of government has become more difficult is worth remarking on. It is the increasing difficulty that both major political parties seem to have in carrying out their election manifestos. The fit between what the Labour party said it would do in 1945 and what the Labour Government actually achieved between 1945 and 1951 is astonishingly close. Most of *Let us Face the Future*, Labour's manifesto in 1945, reads like a prospective history of the immediate post-war period. Since about 1959, however, the fit has become less close. Not only do parties in office increasingly fail to do the things they said they were going to do: they increasingly do things that they pledged themselves specifically not to do. [. . .] Since there is no reason to believe that the political parties are any less serious now than they were after the war about what they say in their manifestos, there is every reason to suppose that somehow, in some way, the business of government has become harder to carry on in the intervening period.

Examples like the above could be multiplied indefinitely. One thinks of the growth of crime despite the best efforts of government, of the failure of economic planning, of the intractability of the Northern Irish problem, of the misguidedness, as it has turned out, of much recent energy policy – and so on, and on. Americans used to write of 'Big Government' as though the state, in becoming all-embracing, would become all-powerful. Today our image of government is more that of the sorcerer's apprentice. The waters rise. The apprentice rushes about with his bucket. The waters rise even faster. And none of us knows when, or whether, the magician will come home.

Great expectations

The argument of this article is that a large part of the explanation for this state of affairs can be stated in two propositions. Each of them is reasonably familiar in itself, though the first, as it happens, is more familiar than the second. What is not generally appreciated is what happens when both propositions turn out to be true at the same time.

The first, more familiar proposition is that the range of matters for which British Governments hold themselves responsible − and for which they believe that the electorate may hold them responsible − has increased greatly over the past ten or twenty years, as well as over the past fifty, and is still increasing at a rapid rate. [. . .]
[King goes on to describe the extension of government activity and discusses as one example how the successful running of the nationalised industries has become a political issue.]

In circumstances of intense electoral competition, when Governments hold themselves responsible (and are held responsible) for the management of the economy as a whole, they cannot not intervene in the affairs of nationalised industries. On the one hand, the affairs of the nationalised industries impinge directly on the lives of voters; and for what happens in these industries voters hold the Government of the day responsible, not the chairmen of the various boards. On the other hand, even if Governments were not held responsible for the nationalised industries, they would be held responsible for managing the economy as a whole and, on political grounds alone, no Government could afford to deny itself one of its main means of controlling − or at least trying to control − the whole economy. The enlargement of the public sector has led to increased burdens being placed on government; the increased burdens placed on government have contributed to the enlarging of the public sector. In an era of incomes policy, investment policy, prices policy and regional policy, no Government, even if it wanted to, could in practice permit the management of the nationalised industries 'to get on with its work'. [. . .]

This line of thought might once have been taken as anti-socialist − as an argument against taking industries into public ownership. Perhaps it is. But that is beside the point, which is that there is now hardly anything in which Governments can avoid taking an interest. The distinction between 'private' and 'public' has, as is well known, become hopelessly blurred. The border between the private and public domains resembles the border between New York and Connecticut far more than that between France and Germany (much less than between China and Russia). To be held responsible for everything is to feel compelled to intervene in everything. A Conservative Government rescues Upper Clyde Shipbuilders and nationalises part of Rolls-Royce, a Labour Government nationalises British Leyland and even picks up the pieces after the collapse of Court Line, a privately owned airline and holiday company that was not particularly important to the national economy. Public is still public; private in 1976 is also public. [...]

Once upon a time, then, man looked to God to order the world. Then he looked to the market. Now he looks to government. The differences are important. God was irremoveable, immutable. The market could be removed or mutated but only, it was thought, at a very high price. Government, by contrast, is removeable, mutable — and corporeal. One blames not 'Him' or 'it' but 'them'. The Mass has given way to the general election, which is (to coin a phrase) a whole new ball game. How difficult a time Governments are having in trying to play God we shall see in the next section.

The problem of intractability

Our first proposition was that Governments today are held responsible for far more than they ever were before. This in itself might not matter much if they were able to carry out their new responsibilities. It does not matter how many debts a man has if he has enough money in the bank or a good enough line of credit. But our second proposition is that, just as the range of responsibilities of Governments has increased, so, to a large extent independently, their capacity to exercise their responsibilities has declined. The reach of British government exceeds its grasp; and its grasp, according to our second proposition, is being enfeebled just at the moment when its reach is being extended.

It is easy to prove that this second proposition is true, it is more difficult to explain why it is true. The proofs lie all around us (some were mentioned earlier): the failure to achieve a higher rate of economic growth, the failure to bring inflation under control, the failure to put right the balance of payments, the failure to build enough houses, the failure to reduce the level of violent crime, the failure to reform the trade unions, the failure to make a commercial success of Concorde. Almost the only unqualified success of British legislation in the past twenty years has been the Clean Air Act of 1956. Britain's buildings are indubitably cleaner. [...]

Let us consider four reasons why men and women might fail to achieve what they set out to achieve — four possible reasons for failure, all of them beyond the control of the individual would-be achiever.

1 One reason a man might fail is because what he set out to achieve was physically impossible to achieve, given current technology. Examples can be found, though with some difficulty, even in the 1970s. Rolls-Royce collapsed because the RB–211 aeroengine proved colossally expensive to develop — and was anyway clearly never going to function quite as intended because the engine's carbon-fibre propellor blades, despite their enormous pretensile strength, tended to break up on impact, even with objects as light as raindrops. There was nothing, in the short term, that Rolls-Royce's technicians could do about it. The company, given its fixed-price contract with Lockheed and promised delivery dates, went broke.

But such examples, although they can be found, are not common. Companies and governments do not normally set out to achieve the impossible or even what they have reasons for supposing may be impossible. [...]

2 Another reason why a man or government might fail is simply because he or it lacked the necessary resources, or had to contend with too many claims on them. One reason why there are not enough houses in Britain (or in most other countries) is simply that available resources have been diverted elsewhere: construction workers to the building of motorways, bricks and cement to the building of office blocks and new universities. The problem of scarce resources is likely to be serious in most Western countries for the foreseeable future. In almost all non-Western countries it always has been. Given our low rate of economic growth, conflicts over resource allocation can be expected to be especially acute in Britain.

But, again, there is nothing new about the problem of scarcity, and it does not seem to offer an adequate, even plausible, explanation for the failure of local government reform, for the failure of incomes policy, for the failure of economic policy generally. It certainly cannot explain the almost universal feeling that the country has become harder to govern. Resources, after all, were far scarcer forty years ago when Britain seemed almost the only country that was relatively easy to govern. We must look further.

3 Another reason why someone might fail to achieve something is because he was dependent on someone else for the achieving of it and that other person failed, for some reason, to do whatever was required [...]

And here we come to the heart of the matter. If Britain has become harder to govern, it is almost certainly partly because the number of dependency relationships in which government is involved has increased substantially, and because the incidence of acts of non-compliance by the other participants in these relationships has also increased substantially. Most of us are dependent not only on the plumber but also on the electrician, the carpenter, the heating engineer, our garage mechanic and the man who delivers the Sunday papers. If any one of them failed to turn up when we needed him, we could be in trouble. These two points are related empirically, very closely; but they are separate logically and we will deal with them separately.

First, the sheer number of dependency relationships – and the degree of dependence inherent in them. Though it is by now a cliché that our world has become increasingly interdependent, no one has attempted to estimate the number of relationships of dependence that exist. It must be enormous, running into thousands of thousands. The number has increased with the division of labour, the increases in standards of living, the increases in the scale and complexity of international trade. Governments are involved in a large proportion of these relationships. Sometimes they are directly involved, as purveyors of electricity supplies, medical services and (ideally) a stable currency. Sometimes they are indirectly involved, as when they are forced to respond to, without being able to control, the consequences of (say) foreign-exchange transactions between foreign nations. [...]

But for our purposes the details do not matter. The big picture does; so do its consequences. Some idea of the scale of change within living memory can be grasped if we compare – as seems reasonable to do – the miners' strike of February–March 1974 with the miners' strike of 1926. [...]

The 1974 strike lasted for rather less than a month, though it had been preceded by an overtime ban lasting several weeks. Its effects were felt immediately. The country's industry was put on a three-day week; there was a sharp fall in industrial production. Had the strike gone on much longer, power cuts would have been necessary despite the three-day week; the country's balance-of-trade deficit would have worsened greatly. Politically, the effects of the strike were even more spectacular. It destroyed an essential element in the Heath Government's economic policy, its Stage III incomes policy. It led directly (though perhaps not inevitably) to the holding of a general election and to the Heath Government's downfall. Not only did the miners win, but their victory had far-reaching consequences for the conduct of economic policy by any future Government. By making it plain that, in the field of incomes policy, government had ceased to be the 'authoritative allocator of values for the society' and had become merely one participant, albeit a powerful one, in a complex process of bargaining, the miners' success effectively restricted the range of choices open to government. It greatly increased the probability, for example, that future incomes policies, if they were conducted at all, would be conducted by fiscal rather than direct-interventionist means.

The 1974 miners' strike was thus a major political, even constitutional event. Everyone knew it; no one was surprised by it. Contrast 1974 with 1926. In 1926 the miners were out not for one month but for six; for eight days in May most of the other workers in the country were out too. The 1926 strike did have economic consequences. Half a million men were thrown out of work for a time and valuable coal exports were lost. It also had political consequences. The miners' strike, and in particular the General Strike, led to the passage of the Trade Union and Trade Disputes Act of 1927 and may have contributed to the Conservatives' loss of the 1929 general election. Nevertheless, if the 1926 miners' strike had not been accompanied, somewhat fortuitously, by the General Strike, it would today almost certainly be largely forgotten (except by the miners); its place in history would be small. The Baldwin Government did not fall; on the contrary, its authority, and the authority of government generally, was strengthened. The strike itself 'did not so much end as crumble away'. The miners were forced to accept a reduction in wages.

A full account of the 1926-74 contrast would have to allow for a wide variety of factors. For example, the average miner was undoubtedly richer in 1974 than in 1926; this alone strengthened his and his union's bargaining position. But it seems reasonable to argue that the main difference between 1926 and 1974 lay in the increased range of responsibilities placed upon government coupled with the vastly increased number of dependency relationships in which government found itself involved — not only involved but involved in such a way that it was dependent on others, not others on it. On the one hand, the Heath Government's handling of the 1973-4 dispute can be understood only in terms of its determination to maintain Stage III of its incomes policy; but the Baldwin Government did not have an incomes policy and could hardly have conceived of itself as having one. On the other, Britain and British industry by the winter of 1973-4 were dependent on coal in a way that would have been unthinkable fifty years before. Worker and householder alike depended on electricity; electricity depended on coal. Its, and their, dependence on coal might have been reduced by an increase in oil consumption; but Britain was dependent for oil on foreigners whom she could not control and who had just put up their prices. This would have been serious enough in any case but was made even more serious by the fact that, if Britain were to be able to meet the increased cost of oil, she would have to sell more to foreigners or borrow more from them. Either way Britain as a country was dependent on foreigners, and so was British government. Each dependence — on miners, on oil exporters, on foreign importers of British goods, on foreign lenders — reinforced the others. Their cumulative effect was to make the enterprise of government far more difficult to carry on. [...]

We have been discussing what happens when the sheer number of dependency relations in the world increases. Given some probability of the occurrence of acts of non-performance or non-compliance, the probability of a government, or anyone else, getting its way is reduced. But, second, what happens when not only is the absolute number of dependency relations increased but so is the probability of an act of non-compliance in any one of them? The answer is obvious: the chances of non-achievement, of failure are increased even further. [...] Again, it seems clear that the chances of acts of non-compliance occurring in the real world have in fact increased enormously in the past few years. Miners were no more likely not to comply in 1974 than in 1926, but doctors, nurses, dustmen, students, teachers, local government officials, criminals, farmers, sugar producers, oil exporters were much more likely not to. Dependence is thus in the 1970s compounded by non-feasance. [...]

4 Physical impossibility, lack of resources and dependence/non-compliance are three reasons why men and women may fail to achieve what they set out to achieve. A fourth possible source of failure is intellectual. [...]

Lack of understanding, whether acknowledged or not, has of course been a problem for governments since government began. The Aztecs thought, wrongly, that they could keep their enemies at bay by means of human sacrifice; Ramsay MacDonald thought, wrongly, that a balanced budget was a necessary condition of full employment and would have wanted to balance the budget in 1931 even if foreign bankers had not required him to. Nonetheless, it does appear to be the case that men understand less, and realise that they understand less, now than twenty years ago. There are now few policy areas in which politicians and civil servants are prepared to say confidently, 'Yes, we understand. We know that, if this happens, we must do that.' The world, which twenty years ago seemed, if not always hospitable, at least familiar, no longer seems familiar. Politicians used to decide, or at least believe that they were deciding. In the 1970s they merely grope. [...]

Britain, then, has become harder to govern. The reason it has become harder to govern is that, at one and the same time, the range of problems that government is expected to deal with has vastly increased, and its capacity to deal with problems, even many of the ones it had before, has decreased. It is not the increase in the number of problems alone that matters, or the reduction in capacity. It is the two coming together. [...]

Consequences

If overload is a bad thing, what, if anything, can be done about it?

In principle, one could tackle the problem on the demands/expectations/responsibilities side or on the failure/intractability side. One could try either to decrease government's reach or to increase its grasp. In practice, there does not seem to be much to be looked for on the failure/intractability side. Dependency relations are not likely to become less frequent in the future; rather the reverse. Acts of non-compliance are likewise unlikely to become less frequent. Our understanding of social complexity will undoubtedly increase, but not necessarily faster than the growth of complexity itself. We shall probably have to run very hard, intellectually, to stay in the same place.

We have, therefore, to look to the demands/expectations side. 'Government,' said Burke, 'is a contrivance of human wisdom to provide for human wants.' Wisdom and the ability to provide for wants being in short supply, it seems prudent to try to reduce the incidence of wants, or at least of wants-of-government. How? It is disconcerting that the suggestions that come to mind are almost boy-scoutish in their banality — and in their dependence on good will and on long-term rather than immediate self-interest. One possibility might be to try [...] to remove some of the functions of government from the purview of the politically-elected Government and to persuade politicians, in their own long-term self-interest, to agree that such functions, once removed, should not be un-removed. But this seems a forlorn hope. [...]

Even a change of style — in which politicians ceased to claim that they alone knew how to solve the country's problems, and ceased to blame other politicians quite so enthusiastically for failing to solve them — would be very hard to achieve in circumstances of electoral competition, though it must be said that the leaders of all of the major parties have already adopted a tone somewhat more humble than in the past. The most that can be hoped for is probably a marginal reduction in the work load of ministers by devolving onto other authorities some of the more routine elements of public administration and by abandoning formally the doctrine that the minister is personally responsible for everything that happens in his or her department. This sort of unrealism anyway only encourages unrealism about government in general.

It is hard not to be a little pessimistic about the future. Governments have tried to play God. They have failed. But they go on trying. How can they be made to stop? Academic political scientists have traditionally been concerned to improve the performance of government. Perhaps over the next few years they should be more concerned with how the number of tasks that government has come to be expected to perform can be reduced.

13   Politicians and the sorcerer: the problems of governing with capitalism in crisis

David Coates

I want to argue that the only way in which the present political situation can be fully understood is in terms of a crisis generated by capitalism. [...] To persuade you of this it will be necessary to explain what I mean by 'capitalism' and to try and show the force of a Marxist explanation of our situation. [...]

Inequality in a class society

Perhaps the first thing to say of our society is that it is divided by class. However often we are told that a certain job is more important than another, or is more skilled, or carries more responsibility and the like, we should never forget that the production of the goods and services on which our way of life (indeed our very existence) depends involves each and every one of us playing a part. Production is a collective act to which, directly or indirectly, now or in the future, all of us are essential. And yet the goods and services that we produce collectively, and the social power and prestige that we generate, are not divided equally among us. Rather our access to goods, services, power and prestige differs with the position in the class structure into which we were born, or into which (for a surprisingly small number of us) we move. [...]

Behind this lies a dimension of social power. We are not a totalitarian state, nor a dictatorship, and democratic liberties count for much. But the recognition of our democratic freedoms should not be allowed to obscure from view the heavy concentration of power that lies behind them. The right to initiate the majority of the rules under which we live, the predominant influence over the ideas and opinions to which we are regularly exposed, and the ultimate control of the forms of coercion to which we are subject, are all in the hands of a relatively small group of men. These men either own or control (or share similar

Source: Anthony King (ed.), *Why is Britain Becoming Harder to Govern?*, London, BBC Publications, 1976, extracts from pp. 34–43, 46, 48–52, 54–5.

social backgrounds and identifications with those who own and control) the means of production, distribution and exchange in a complex capitalist economy. Although as a class they are often divided internally on many issues, they are nonetheless capable of showing a truly remarkable degree of unanimity and resolve in crisis or under challenge. They are the group of men which Governments find it particularly difficult to control, and whom in only a limited sense can Governments be said to 'govern' at all.*

Of course it is true that the precise impact of these inequalities of industrial experience, material reward and social prestige are moderated by the degree of organisation and militancy displayed by institutions created or sustained by the working class (into which social grouping must now increasingly be included the growing body of routine white-collar workers). But the allocation of social rewards and power against which trade unions struggle is neither random nor accidental, nor is it one governed by principles of human need or by the genetically-transmitted distribution of aptitudes and skills between individuals or groups. Rather trade unions and workers find that some men, and only some men, are in a position to monopolise a disproportionately large share of the social product, and to transmit the advantages of their class position more or less easily to their children. They can do this because they successfully lay claim to the ownership of the machinery and the products of the collective acts of labour, and because they occupy positions of command within the central owning institutions of contemporary capitalism (that is, in the multi-national corporations, the joint-stock companies, the finance houses and the public corporations that dominate production in our society). Similarly it is because the majority of men and women do not own either the tools with which they work, or the products of their collective act of labour, and because they occupy subordinate positions in the bureaucracies of capitalism, that they experience a different and more limited set of life chances. And it is because the working class occupy the lowest position in these bureaucracies that their experience of the instabilities and inequalities of such a social order are so extreme. It is this tenacious and class-based inequality that Governments face – with the radically different life styles and interests that it necessarily produces – that is the first key to any fully adequate explanation of why Britain is becoming so difficult to govern.

* For a discussion of the character of the power structure in Britain, see R. Miliband, *The State in Capitalist Society* (London: Weidenfeld & Nicolson, 1969); also P. Stanworth and A. Giddens, eds, *Elites and Power in British Society* (Cambridge University Press, 1974); and J. Urry and J. Wakeford, eds, *Power in Britain* (London: Heinemann, 1973).

But of itself this is not enough. Such a stable and persistent pattern of class inequalities can offer a clue to why Government appeals for national unity tend to fail, and it certainly suggests that Governments are being either stupid or disingenuous when they deny the actual bias of their policies against some groups in favour of others. What it cannot do is explain why, in the 1970s, governing has suddenly become so much more difficult. To handle that problem we need to look too at the processes at work on this structure of class-based inequalities. We need to look, that is, at what is specifically 'capitalist' about it. [. . .]

The instability of capitalism

For Marxists [. . .] capitalism is to be understood as a society whose system of production is characterised by two main features. First, the production of wealth is carried out by wage labourers − men and women who sell their labour power to others in return for money wages. These wage labourers do not own the goods and services that they produce. Nor do they own the tools or machinery with which they work. All that they own is their labour power, and to survive they have to sell that to other men, who own the machinery of production and distribution and who successfully lay claim to the ownership of all that is produced by the labourers they employ. This latter class of men − the capitalist bourgeoisie − create and maintain their social position in two ways: first by requiring their employees to perform surplus labour (that is, to go on working for longer than is necessary merely to meet their own needs); and then by realising, as their profit, the additional value created in those extra hours through the sale in the world market of the total goods and services that their labour force has produced. Capitalism, that is, is not simply based on wage labour. Its second main feature is that it is also a system of production in which goods are produced, not for immediate consumption by the producers, but for exchange; as a result, it is a system in which the criteria that govern production are not those of immediate human needs but are rather those of profit-making and capital accumulation through exchange and trade. In both of these respects, capitalism differs from the feudal society that preceded it, where production was predominantly based on a subsistence agriculture, with only a limited exchange of surpluses between the countryside and the small guild manufacturers of the emerging urban centres.

The main point to be grasped if we are fully to understand why Britain is becoming so difficult to govern is that the capitalist system under which we live is a relatively recent form of social organisation and production. [...] The World has not always been capitalist, and governing it is difficult to a very large extent only because it is.

For from the outset this capitalist system of production has been uniquely unstable and prone to crisis. True, there have been periods lately in which that instability has been damped down, and in which Governments have come to believe that they control, and even remove, the propensity of the economic system to periodically overproduce, resulting in workers laid off and plants left idle. But we are discovering again now that the optimism of Keynesian economics was misplaced, and that there is still an inherent long term tendency in capitalist production for the rate of profit to fall. The explanation of this tendency, as Marx explained in Volume III of *Capital*, lies in capitalism's propensity to replace men (the source of value, and hence profit in the system) by machines and it is this that gives to the kind of social and economic order under which we live a central instability which no Government can totally eradicate, however hard it tries. Its major immediate consequence is the perpetual re-creation of the tension between capitalist and worker, as workers unite to resist their employer's repeated attempts to intensify and/or extend the period of their work, so as to increase the productivity of their labour, which is the main strategy available to him in his attempt to offset this erosion of his rate of profit. The falling profit rate also inspires (and is then intensified by) competition between capitalists, and extends that competition onto a world scale, as new markets are sought and still more productive machinery is introduced, to compensate for the falling rate of return on previous investment in existing markets. A new market, or a new technology, provides for the individual capitalist some temporary respite from the pressure on profits, but one that is only temporary, as the new markets are invaded by competitors and as successful technological innovations are first copied and then superseded. In the periodic crises of overproduction that accompany these competitive struggles, small companies are inevitably destroyed, leaving the fight against the erosion of profit rates in the next period in the hands of fewer and larger companies. It is in this way that under capitalism we are left with a system of production in which frenetic competition and a desperate search for corporate profits goes on at a steadily higher level of investment, dependent on an ever higher level of demand, but with in the end a declining rate of profits for the capitalist class as a whole. [...]

Of course Marx seriously underestimated capitalism's capacity to sustain itself, to survive its crises, and we would be foolish to do the same. At certain moments, when the self-destructive tendencies of capitalist production have been masked, by increased labour productivity or by the development of new markets for example, Western Europe has known periods of relatively steady economic growth and prosperity. We have just lived through one such period. Britain is becoming more difficult to govern now because that period of steady growth appears to be over. [...]

[Coates goes on to summarise recent trends in both the British economy and the international economy. He suggests, for example, that mergers and take-overs, particularly involving multi-national companies, are not only reducing the numbers of major firms but also making those that remain more difficult to control by the British Government. At the same time, both investment and productivity in British industry as a whole remain chronically low. Inflation in Britain, coupled with the development of a worldwide recession in the 1970s, added the final touches to this depressing picture for British capitalism. This economic crisis has inevitably come to dominate British politics.]

The weakness of British capitalism

Throughout the 1960s and 1970s requests came from firms in particularly acute commercial difficulties for government credits to save jobs and to prevent any loss of national production. Increasingly, as international competition grew and intensified, Governments also came under heavy pressure to control wages, to increase the productivity of labour, and to take the pressure of organised groups of workers off already heavily-squeezed profit margins. In this last respect at least, the weakness of British capitalism in our period led Governments to make a sharp break with their traditional peacetime practice of leaving industrial relations and collective bargaining in the private sector well and truly alone.

This demand for government action against organised labour connects with one last aspect of why Britain is becoming more difficult to govern: namely the strength and growing militancy of the trade-union movement. It is clearly dangerous to generalise on the industrial experience of over 24,000,000 working people, though possibly generalisations are more valid now than in the early 1950s because of the growing impact on all of us of recent government policies on income restraint, productivity bargaining and industrial relations reform. Yet there are discernible patterns in British industrial relations since the 1950s, patterns that indicate the impact of the growing weakness of British capitalism on the workers who produce its wealth, and the increasing involvement of Governments in their attempts to replace that weakness with a high rate of economic growth, a strong pound sterling, a favourable balance of payments and a high level of investment in manufacturing plant. [...]

The crisis in competitiveness and profits that hit British capitalism in the 1960s brought Governments into increasing conflict with well-organised sections of the labour movement, even when those Governments were Labour Governments, dependent on working-class votes. In a very real sense no Government had much choice. It did not make the world it was trying to control, and the continuity of that world was more than enough to ensure a marked similarity in policy between Governments of supposedly different political persuasions. Any Government was under heavy pressure from business leaders for assistance in controlling wage costs and increasing productivity, in order to strengthen the competitive position and the profit levels of industry. Henry Ford even arrived in person, you may remember, to tell Edward Heath this, and to persuade the Government to mend its ways if it wanted to see any more of his company's investments. Governments were even more tightly constrained by the balance of payment deficits created by the lack of competitiveness, for foreign loans were available only on terms that insisted on increasingly strong Government action against wage drift, industrial militancy and so-called restrictive practices. And Governments were pulled in the same direction by their own interventionist propensities, and by their need for higher productivity if their policies of social reform were to be funded without creating inflation. Even before spiralling prices added their own imperative, both Labour and Conservative Cabinets found themselves drawn into a more regular involvement in the problems of industrial and labour management, with all the pitfalls this could involve when that management clashed with the interests of well-placed groups of workers and their union officials. [...]

It is the repeated failure of public policy to generate sustained growth and competitiveness, that lies behind so much of the current disquiet about the ability of Governments to govern.

But that inability should no longer be surprising. The tasks that Governments set themselves involve nothing less than correcting the weaknesses of investment, competition and profits that are endemic to capitalist production. This would be hard enough without trade union militancy, but militancy is not likely to go away. The very crisis that necessitates strong Government action also generates the conditions for militancy against it. Workers experience falling competitiveness, and the low profits and inflation that this brings, as threats to their living standards, their work routines and their jobs. When capitalism is in crisis, they face speed-ups and redundancy. When Governments try to 'solve' the crisis, they add to these dangers of speed-ups, declining living standards and unemployment by the policies they introduce. It is no wonder that trade unionists object. What is

amazing is that their opposition is so muted and so sporadic. Governments will not be able to legislate away either falling rates of profit or
competition. Nor will they easily ban worker alienation and militancy.
Politics in the future will continue to be dominated by the struggle
between a weak capitalism and a militant labour force, and that is
going to make the job of a practising politician particularly difficult
and unrewarding. [. . .]

Political alternatives

Governments are overloaded not mainly because of electoral demands,
but because of the pressures created by the crises in the productive
system that surrounds them. No strong political or industrial leadership
can talk the crisis away and 'responsibility' in trade-union leadership
would be less a solution than a stage in driving militancy into unofficial
hands. An attack on 'idleness' and 'restrictive practices' will ease the
pressure for as long as it can be maintained, but only at the price of
intensifying the work routines of an already intensely-worked and
alienated labour force. Nor will conspiracy theories help us to a true
understanding of our situation. The Communist party has not had the
impact on industrial relations that its supporters, and the right-wing
press, would have us think it has had. Industrial militancy now involves
too many people, and too serious a set of issues, to be dismissed as the
work of a handful of 'misguided and mischievous' people. Nor are most
foreign holders of sterling balances merely idle speculators gambling
for quick returns at the nation's expense. Among the major holders of
foreign currency are multinational corporations and finance houses
driven by the weakness of British capitalism to move their money out
of sterling in order to maintain their profit levels in a world of uncertain
exchange rates. The job of governing Britain is difficult because Governments find themselves constrained, as they have always been, by the
concentrations of power in business, finance and labour. It is becoming
more difficult now because, amid those concentrations of power, the
need to accumulate capital and to maintain profits is setting up ever
sharper tensions between capitalist and capitalist, and between capitalist
and worker. [. . .]

It should [also] be remembered that ideas play a crucial role in
stabilising an unequal society. If, and only if, governments can persuade
people on a large scale that what we are living through is not a crisis of
'capitalism' but one of 'democracy' will they be able to gain widespread
support for their assertion that it is no longer legitimate to struggle against
any Government policy which maintains or increases present inequalities.

And in their attempt to win popular support, ministers have much going for them, including their generalised legitimacy, their access to the mass media, and the way in which the trade-unions' defensive actions are more visible than are the processes of capitalist exploitation which have really caused the crisis. All these will combine to persuade many people that a solution to inflation and uncompetitiveness is within our grasp at very little cost. Indeed it is for this reason that the spread of explanations of our current difficulties that fail to link them to the wider instabilities of capitalism are significant. For they help to persuade people that certain events and certain policies are inevitable, when in reality those events and policies are necessary only to maintain a particular, highly unequal system of private ownership and control. In the battle for public support, such arguments – and the parallel call by politicians for national restraint and trade-union moderation – gather force too, because they are related to that belief, so strong in British popular culture, that 'problems' necessarily have 'solutions' within the existing framework of government and property if only 'men of good faith' can act together 'responsibly'. It is therefore to be expected that Governments, industrialists, editors and even some trade-union leaders will continue to present our present difficulties in such terms and will bewail the absence of a national consensus without admitting how the consensus that they seek can only benefit privileged groups and injure the dispossessed so long as capitalist inequalities remain. For the task of governing Britain [...] will be more or less easy for practising politicians precisely to the degree to which their view of things becomes generally shared, and trade unions and their members can be persuaded to accept cuts in their living standards and power. Politicians will strive endlessly to persuade people to accept cut-backs and unemployment without disturbing the existing distribution of wealth, income and power. But they will find that the pressures generated by capitalist instability and inequality will always militate against any permanent creation of such a general consensus against trade union action. Although Governments will call repeatedly for unity and co-operation, they will find that there is no easy solution to the tension between capital and labour in a world of international capitalism. The problems will not go away. On the contrary, as the crisis deepens, the problems of governing Britain will grow ever larger.

14 Alternative theories of liberal democratic politics: the pluralist-marxist debate in the 1980s

Patrick Dunleavy

This paper discusses what has happened to the pluralist-marxist debate about liberal democracy since the late 1960s, and tries to make some assessment of the current state of this central dispute in political science as we enter the 1980s.[1] This is a much more difficult task than it once was, for the earlier debate between fairly rough-and-ready positions has been succeeded by a much more complex picture. Both sides of the argument have been elaborated into a number of different variants, and clearly I cannot hope to describe here more than one or two of these. Thus I have had to choose a small number of contemporary positions which have been either important elements of the debate in the recent past, or which I guess may be seen as significant in the future.

On the pluralist side of the argument I briefly recapitulate the *classical or conventional pluralism* set out by the mid-1960s, but which is still an important pattern of argument today. The two variants of this position analysed here diverge sharply in emphasis. *Neo-pluralist theory* seeks to defend the established emphases of pluralism by refurbishing the position to accommodate elite theory critiques and changes in the organization of advanced industrial societies in the 1970s. But *liberal anti-pluralists* interpret the same changes (primarily the growth of the state) as signs that pluralism itself needs to be questioned: in their view liberal and democratic values are best served by reducing pluralist elements in the political system to more manageable proportions.

On the other side of the argument I first summarize the conventional or orthodox marxist view of liberal democratic politics, which remains vigorously supported by some writers. The two neo-marxist variants analysed again diverge in terms of their direction of development. *Structuralist marxism* seeks to develop a highly formalized and sophisticated model of the way in which economic processes fundamentally structure all other aspects of social development, whereas *theories of legitimation crisis* offer an account of how political and ideological

Source: Article commissioned for this Reader. Patrick Dunleavy is Lecturer in Government, London School of Economics and Political Science.

conflicts have assumed progressively greater importance as influences on the development of advanced capitalist societies.

Developments in pluralist approaches

(a) *Classical pluralism* at the end of the 1960s defined the liberal 'consensus' in western political science.[2] It presented liberal democratic politics in terms of four main components: an emphasis on the role of party competition; a view of interest groups as expressing differential preference intensities; and the twin claims that economic and political power bases are highly separated, while policy outputs demonstrate the state's broad neutrality in dealing with different social groups.

Before pluralist theory developed, the dominant paradigm for describing political input processes was the theory of representative government. This focused on citizens electing individual representatives to constitute a legislature, which in turn would debate issues, choosing policies in the public interest and producing a governmental team to carry them through.[3] Pluralism displaced this anachronistic conception by a view of elections as primarily competitions between two or more organized political parties, each capable of forming the government. Leaders and citizens, on this view, are widely separated in terms of political knowledge or social status. But because parties must compete for mass endorsement, the government in power is constrained to anticipate the voters' reactions to its policies for fear of losing office to its rivals, leading it to adopt policies which will command popular support.

Elections count preferences and emphasize majority rule. But in addition citizens in liberal democracies can form voluntary associations to promote specific aspects of their interests to government. Resources to make such organizational tactics effective (such as organizational know-how and media coverage) are widely distributed, and the interest-group process which results is seen by pluralists as a relatively equitable one in which most sizeable groups and many minorities can secure a public hearing for their views. The depth of citizens' feelings on an issue is the key factor in determining whether and where interest groups spring up — and how active they are in pressing their case through the media, lobbying, protests, information-gathering and (occasionally) civil disobedience. By allowing people with particularly intense preferences at least the potential to secure more influence over policy, the interest-group process provides additional information to government, allowing decision-makers to *weight* preferences, not just count them. So strong opposition from a minority may modify those government proposals which command only fairly apathetic approval from a majority of voters. The result is to shift the polity away from a simple majority-rule basis (in which any proposal with 51 per cent support is implemented), some way towards a unanimity-rule basis (in which only proposals with which everyone agrees can be implemented). Since pure unanimity-rule decisions (of 100 per cent agreement) would be unworkable, the practical effect is to increase the level of support needed for decisions to one of a large majority or 'consensus' of people, perhaps lying somewhere between 60 and 80 per cent agreement.

Of course, if money or economic power are translated directly into interest-group effectiveness, the result would be a 'consensus' biased towards the economically powerful groups in society. But pluralists claim that no such translation occurs. The government system operates largely separate from private business, with separate personnel recruited into a politically neutral civil service, responding to political controls and influences and not to economic power. Politicians are specialist personnel, with little overlap with business or other elite groups. And economically powerful interest groups generally are balanced by equally well organized 'countervailing powers' (e.g. business influence is balanced by the trade unions), in a way which effectively diffuses and offsets the political impact of concentrations of economic power.

Finally pluralists argue that the development of state policies provides ample evidence that liberal democratic governments are responsive to ordinary citizens' wishes. The introduction of the 'welfare state', the transformation of life chances for the least well-off sections of western societies, and the subordination of private economic power to an increasingly regulated and mixed economy — all these demonstrate in their view that government retains and has used the power to transform society in response to mass political demands. Thus the character of political outputs is seen as firm evidence of the overall neutrality of the state in its dealing with different interests, and hence of its effective autonomy from control by any one grouping in liberal democratic societies. The political process remains one in which there are multiple (plural) centres of power, and one in which the ordinary citizen can intervene relatively easily and effectively.

(b) *Neo-pluralism* emerged primarily as the result of problems in the classical pluralist view highlighted by the social trends of the late 1960s and 1970s in most advanced industrial countries.[4] Economic growth slackened off and a series of latent social tensions in liberal democratic states erupted into violence. The city riots of the late 1960s in the USA and the anti-Vietnam war protests; the swift growth of sectarian conflict in Northern Ireland and the re-emergence of overt class conflict into British party politics in the 1970s; the 1968 demonstrations and strikes in France — all these unpredicted crises and changes seemed to fit badly with conventional pluralist optimism and stress on 'consensus'.

Perhaps as influential were the criticisms of pluralism mounted by elite theorists arguing for a view of liberal democracies as dominated by a small and cohesive ruling minority. In the past these writers concentrated on attempts to show that political control was tied into or subordinate to other forms of social power. In the 1950s C. Wright Mills claimed that a three-way 'power elite' of top businessmen, military leaders and political influentials (mostly recruited from business) dominated US policy-making on major issues, 'the history-making decisions'.[5] Mills did not dispute the existence of the input political processes on which pluralists concentrated. But he relegated party-political, interest-group or Congressional influences to 'the middle levels of power', to relatively small scale or peripheral issues. In the late 1960s this pattern of argument was taken up and expressed in a more general and influential form, focusing on the dwindling proportion of state activity which could be controlled by representative political input processes. Pluralists by and large assumed that the state could be pictured as a pyramid with democratically elected institutions placed unequivocally at its apex, controlling all of the key decisions (Figure 14.1a). They took it as read that Parliament, the Cabinet, political parties and interest groups shape the basic decisions, leaving only their routine implementation to other elements in the state apparatus. The new elitist critique argues in contrast that the rapid growth of the state apparatus in the mixed economy has produced a major reduction in the proportion of its activities which can be scrutinized or shaped by representative institutions.[6] The extended 'welfare state' is no longer a stratified pyramid controllable by a basically nineteenth-century legislature and simple executive institutions. Rather it is an increasingly amorphous structure in which only a small and not clearly decisive set of issues is subject to representative political controls (Figure 14.1b). Nor is it so important to this brand of elite theory to show the subordination of the public sector to outside interests. With effective democratic influences removed, they are free simply to conclude that over large areas of state activity technocrats and bureaucrats pursue the logic of their organizational interests, in more or less close collaboration with sectional private interests, but largely immune to the views of citizens as a whole. Thus they do not deny that pluralists have identified some prominent feature of liberal democratic politics; instead they argue that such factors make little difference to the direction or pace of social development.

Neo-pluralist writers have responded to this elite theory critique by trying to absorb it into a revitalized and redrawn pluralist model

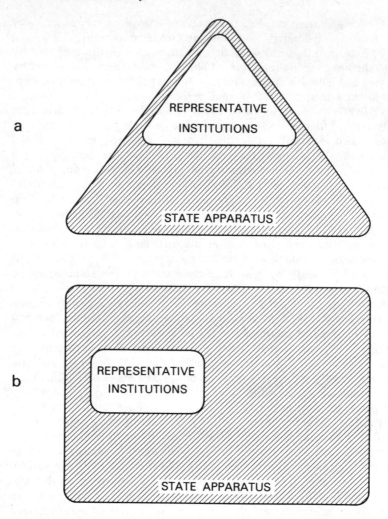

04   *Patrick Dunleavy*

Figure 14.1 Representative institutions and the state apparatus: (a) pluralist view; (b) elite theory view

emphasizing some significantly different features from classical models. In particular they stress the professionalization of decision-making in the advanced industrial state, the high level of fragmentation of state organizational structures and the growth of a 'liberal corporatist' system of centralized economic management.

The professionalization of decision-making in the advanced industrial state is seen by neo-pluralists as part and parcel of an overall societal trend towards more complex forms of social organization. The growth of the state has broadened the sphere of activities being carried out in the public sector qualitatively as well as quantitatively. Government is now involved in large-scale investment and production decisions, in planning the development of the economy and directly controlling some of its key sectors, and in delivering a complex web of welfare state services to citizens. None of these tasks fits very easily into the conventional mode of civil service or bureaucratic operations. Increasingly, skilled and expert personnel are needed to develop knowledge and technologies in highly specialized areas, or to control decisions which have the most fundamental significance for individual citizens or families (such as decisions over publicly supplied schooling, medical or welfare services). These personnel are now overwhelmingly drawn from *professional* occupational groups. These groups are normally distinguished by their operation of strict internal controls requiring high standards to be observed either in the impartial development of knowledge and techniques, or in respect for the interests of the profession's 'clients'. A profession is a form of self-regulating 'closed shop' which is underwritten by the state in return for these internal controls being developed in professional education and policed in practice by professional institutions.[7] Neo-pluralists stress that professionalized decision-making provides a substitute for external political controls in many areas of state activity where the conventional pluralist emphasis on party politics and interest groups would be inappropriate. For example, they suggest few citizens would want nuclear power programmes and the complex technological decisions associated with them to be determined by highly 'political' coalition-forming or lobbying. Equally, most people would not be happy about 'political interference' with doctors' clinical freedom in the NHS to prescribe treatment as they think best for patients. Thus where decisions' technical rationality is important, or where deeply personal decisions are being made, professionals can be trusted to make decisions in the public interest where the conventional pluralist solution of representative input politics controlling an otherwise self-interested bureaucracy would be inappropriate.

The fragmentation and decentralization of government organization in the extended state provides the context for this neo-pluralist argument to retain plausibility. They point out that the growth of state intervention in most liberal democracies has not been concentrated either in organizational or financial terms in the key central departments linked to representative institutions, directly controlled by ministers and directly answerable to Parliament. Rather the central state has become more of a strategic, 'money-moving', administration. Direct delivery of services, or the organization of production, have been concentrated in two kinds of other agencies. The first are multi-issue local governments. Here control of decisions is fragmented on a spatial basis with direct local electoral and political inputs compensating for these authorities' broad coverage of many 'welfare state' services. Local authorities have accounted for much of the post-war public sector manpower growth in many countries. The second type of agency where growth has been concentrated are single-issue 'quasi-government agencies' (or QGAs). These include a whole range of administrative and executive bodies run by politically appointed boards, but at one stage removed from day-to-day control by representative political mechanisms. Examples of such bodies are the nationalized industries; a wide range of other public corporations; notionally private firms with total or majority state shareholdings; semi-independent agencies (such as tourist boards, development agencies, research institutes, universities); regional or local executive arms of state services (such as the health authorities in the NHS); an enormous range of tribunals, inspectorates and quasi-judicial bodies; and numerous advisory committees. Frequently the most professionalized areas of government are organized as QGAs, such as the health service, or the nuclear power programme (run in Britain by the UK Atomic Energy Authority and a clutch of other QGAs). Almost all of these agencies have 'non-political' channels of 'public participation' or public consultation committees of varying levels of effectiveness built into them; many also operate public inquiry systems. Both these innovations may be seen as methods of uncovering citizens' preferences while avoiding potentially distorting or 'irrational' political processes of the kind stressed in conventional pluralism. The primary effect of this decentralized network of state agency growth has been that neo-pluralists can rebut the elite theory claim of concentrations of power outside citizen control. On their view there is no single elite: rather there are many separate elites with few significant lines of contact between them. Thus the growth of a fragmented, professionalized state apparatus is compatible with the neo-pluralist claim that there are still many centres of power in liberal democratic society, while the professionalization of decision-making supports the idea that the operations of power remain directed to the public interest.

Finally these micro-level arguments are supplemented by the neo-pluralists' stress on a macro-level means of strengthening 'consensus', the emergence of liberal corporatism.[8] This is a more or less formalized system of national economic management and planning, centring on bargaining between the government and the 'peak associations' representing business and the trades unions. Unlike ordinary interest groups, peak associations (such as the CBI or TUC) are interest groups for representing the views of other interest groups; they are only indirectly elected or responsive to their ultimate membership (e.g. a trades union member in Britain cannot vote directly about who's to run the Trades Union Congress). Their purpose is to allow similar interest groups to present a 'common front'. The key area of growth for liberal corporatist strategies has been in securing compliance. Thus governments may need to convince the peak associations to persuade their members to accept unusual constraints such as the temporary limitation of union collective bargaining over wages, or of firms' independent price-setting practices. In return for co-operation on prices or incomes limits, the peak associations may negotiate concession on other areas of policy, such as the tax cuts result from the 1975-8 'social contract' between the trades unions and the Labour government in Britain. Occasionally backed up by direct legislative controls for short periods, systems of liberal corporatism also tend to oscillate between periods of greater and lesser co-ordination and negotiation. Neo-pluralists see this as indicative of the necessarily voluntary and co-operative character of this form of social integration. In their view it is a more formalized and rational mechanism for defining a 'consensus' on central economic issues, supplementing the conventional political process. It serves to identify the common interests of capital, labour and government, and can more easily achieve workable compromises in the attainment of 'national interest' objectives. This stress on overall welfare maximization in state policy remains the second distinctively *pluralist* feature of neo-pluralism, even when it downgrades many of the democratic input processes valued so highly in classical pluralism. Sartori expresses this orientation, thus:[9]

> What can still be mightily improved [in large western democracies] is not the power end of the problem — more power to the people — but its end result — more equal benefits or less unequal privations to the people . . . It can hardly be denied that for the public at large popular rule means the fulfillment of popular wants and needs.

(c) *Liberal anti-pluralism* has emerged since the late 1970s as a second key response to the problems of classical or conventional pluralism.[10] While the neo-pluralists have tried to up-date and refurbish some of the endangered pluralist axioms, other liberal writers have seen in the modern industrial state signs that pluralism itself needs to be limited or constrained. The existence of many centres of political power, and their ability to influence government within a political space bounded only by countervailing powers, are seen as underlying some of the critical contemporary problems of liberal democracies.

This view is a fairly novel one within liberal political theory — by which I understand approaches placing the individual citizen at the centre of their view of the world, and construing the essential purpose of social organization in terms of the maximization of citizens' welfare. Of course, there has been a long and continuous tradition of *conservative* anti-pluralism produced by writers with quite different assumptions valuing tradition and continuity more than welfare maximization. But conservative theories have been relatively uninfluential, since their position often lapses into an overtly anti-democratic defence of any 'established' system of privilege or authority. (For example Scruton in 1980 concluded: 'No conservative, then, is likely to think that democracy is an essential axiom of his politics', while describing democracy elsewhere as a 'disease' and a 'contagion'.[11]) Liberal anti-pluralists in contrast draw a clear line between their support of democracy and 'human rights', and their view of pluralism as impugning the maximization of social welfare.

The key methodological innovation of the liberal anti-pluralists has been to import into political analysis the theories and techniques of 'mainstream' economics — i.e. 'neo-classical' as distinct from marxist economics. They take as given many of the conclusions of mainstream economics about the welfare optimality of private market processes of economic organization. Thus the liberal anti-pluralists acquire in one simple move a whole theory of what is an appropriate form of social organization for a democracy. This theory also specifies the limits within which the political process itself must operate in a market society (something to which classical pluralism pays little attention since it is a purely political theory). This theory of the limits to politics then suggests an additional criterion for assessing what can go wrong in a liberal democracy, namely the distortion of state policy outputs away from an outcome judged to be utility maximizing by welfare economics methodologies. In practice, most anti-pluralist work concentrates on one particular form of such distortion — the growth of the state beyond the level necessary to satisfy citizens' demands for publicly supplied 'goods'.

Excessive state growth on this view can be caused by three aspects of pluralism. First, the competition between political parties for office in situations short of citizens' having perfect information about what is feasible is seen as a source of 'economic contradictions of democracy'.[12] In order to win elections, parties promise far more than they can deliver in any given state of the economic situation, continuously rivalling each other in bidding up voters' expectations of what government can and should do. The 'unrealistic' expectations thus generated fatally constrain party behaviour in government. While they may tackle the problems of the 'real economy' at the start of their term of office, as the next election approaches they will depart from 'rational' economic policies in order to create a more advantageous climate for their re-election.

Second, the interest-group process encourages the over-production of government outputs. It creates situations where politicians can build coalitions of many different groups, each with its own minority special interest policy. A successful coalition may produce majority support for a package of policies each of which has a negative effect on the overall social welfare and would be rejected by voters if considered on its own, rather than as one bit of an aggregate manifesto.

Third, the liberal anti-pluralists develop and extend the original pluralist view of the bureaucracy as a set of self-interested actors needing external political control. On their view, state bureaucracies exercise a monopoly of information over their own activities.[13] Thus taxpayers (or representatives acting for taxpayers) cannot know with any accuracy how the money they vote for bureau budgets is being spent. Bureaucrats therefore have considerable discretion to pursue objectives other than policy goals voted by citizens (or the government acting for citizens). These other objectives will be identified by bureaucrats' own self-interest. In a market society, bureaucrats' interests are best served by trying to maximize their bureau's budget and staff allocation. Expanding the scope of a bureau's activities will most effectively facilitate promotion chances, salary increases and gains in social status and political power by its senior policy-making managers.

For liberal anti-pluralists, then, the continuous growth of the state in all western democracies since 1945 emerges as the cumulative result of pathologies intrinsic to the pluralists' key decision-making processes — party competition, interest-group influence and an independent bureaucracy. But they argue that curtailing the scope of pluralist procedures and returning again to a more formalized notion of representative government could help to eliminate the bias to state growth in liberal democracy. Thus they argue for the enactment of constitutional amendments limiting the growth of state budgets; for laws or programmes with built-in time limits to their application (known as 'sunset legislation'); for a strengthening of the influence of legislatures; and for changes in voting rules and electoral systems designed to require high levels of support for interventionist policies before they can be implemented. In all this they rely crucially on the assumption that citizens' preferences are qualitatively capable of being reconciled within the *status quo* by mainly legal and procedural devices.

Developments in marxist approaches

(a) *Conventional marxism* offers a radically different view of liberal democratic politics from that suggested by pluralist writers.[14] Marxist accounts start by pointing out that all liberal democracies are capitalist societies, and hence essentially dependent on a system of private property and capital accumulation via profits. (Of course the inverse of this statement does not apply: most capitalist societies are *not* liberal democracies.)

For Marx the capitalist mode of production could be understood primarily in terms of the interactions between owners of capital (i.e. tools, buildings, land, machines; or money capable of buying such essential means of production), and non-owners of capital, who must sell their labour to survive. These different groups of people are fundamentally opposed social classes, since the process of capital accumulation via profit-making relies on capitalists being able to extract more from their workers in terms of production than they actually pay them in terms of wages. This extra element, the level of 'surplus value', is shaped by a continuous process of social struggle between the two classes. Where the level of surplus value falls, as it will gradually tend to, profit opportunities disappear, capital owners cease hiring workers, and the economy enters a slump. It will recover from recession only if some out-of-date capital stocks are written off and if wage rates are driven down far enough for profit levels on the remaining capital to rise. As (and if) these periodic economic crises worsen, so marxists argue that workers will increasingly reject the continued existence of the whole economic and social system, seeking to transform it radically rather than merely to protect or enhance their situation within it.

In a liberal democratic regime such a course might be seen as realizable via the political process. But marxists stress that the economic power of owners of capital (the 'bourgeoisie') is invariably paralleled by their effective control of the political and ideological aspects of social life. Liberal democracies have all emerged (mostly in the last century) from a period of restricted property franchises into an era of formal political equality. But the initial dominance of political life by established bourgeois parties and organizations at the time of this transition has been perpetuated into the modern period. To a great extent marxists see this as reflecting the penetration of most areas of social life by a 'dominant ideology' and system of values which is both shaped by and advances the interest of the owners of capital: its essential features are the attempt to mask or disguise the class struggle endemic to capitalism by presenting society as a co-operative mechanism working in the interest of all social groups. Three particular features of liberal democratic politics are singled out by conventional marxist accounts as indicative of this political dominance of capital.

First, they argue that the state apparatus is largely staffed by personnel who are either directly owners of capital (e.g. businessmen or landowners who have entered politics), or by people who are drawn from this kind of social background even if they are now full-time politicians or administrators; or are drawn from other social groupings closely allying themselves with owners of capital. As direct business involvement in political life has tended to decline in most western democracies in this century, the last two claims have assumed more importance. In particular, marxists have developed a more sophisticated view of the class structure of advanced industrial societies. Self-employed owners of small businesses (the 'petite bourgeoisie'), and wage-earners whose jobs centrally involve controlling other people's labour (such as managers, supervisors and perhaps foremen) are both identified as classes distinct from the bourgeoisie who will none the less normally support capitalist interests. In a more general way, employers have encouraged wage-earners with non-manual jobs to distance themselves socially from manual workers by a variety of detailed employment practices. The partial business withdrawal from personal involvement in the political process has thus opened up positions in political life or the state administration primarily for such middle-class groups. Meanwhile the vast bulk of people are effectively excluded by educational, cultural or social barriers from attaining decision-making positions.

Second, the staffing of the state apparatus by personnel committed to the maintenance of the existing social order is greatly strengthened by the possibilities which exist for transforming economic power into political influence. While the corrupt purchase of political influence has tended to decline, owners of capital are still in a favourable position to acquire political or ideological power. They can, for example, acquire control of commercial news and entertainment media. They can sustain the best organized interest groups and subsidize favourably inclined political parties. They can finance opinion-forming campaigns and opinion polls. They can buy off potential opposition personalities or groups to a limited extent. And control of wealth can in many ways smooth the path to favourable treatment by a variety of institutional 'gatekeepers' involved in the production of 'issues' and political debate. In addition, of course, owners of capital collectively shape market processes in ways which may effectively bring massive pressure to bear on reforming or radical parties and governments. Policies regarded unfavourably by business will automatically generate pessimistic 'expectations' about future profit levels of production and possibly even endanger the external value of the currency. This shaping of the 'economic facts of life' by capital-owners has been increased by the concentration of capital into giant corporations. By spanning national boundaries and being able to deploy resources flexibly across numerous capitalist economies in a detailed way, these firms can maintain 'market disciplines' on all the governments involved. This overweening business influence is not capable of being matched or significantly redressed by a reformist trades union movement; at best, trades union militancy can worsen the crisis tendencies of advanced capitalism in growth periods without providing any defence against recession and unemployment.

Finally marxists argue that the political dominance of capital can be directly charted in the class-specific character of state policy outputs. Four specific arguments are advanced here. (i) Much state intervention in social life is directly 'instrumental' for owners of capital, supporting private property ownership, aiding employers in their attempts to extract 'surplus value' from their workers, and coercively maintaining a restricted pattern of political activity and social life. Examples cited here usually involve legislation limiting the right to strike, protecting private property, enforcing tight 'public order' rules and allowing the state extensive scope to collect information about or to harass 'subversive' or 'suspect' political groups. (ii) The growth of the mixed economy on the marxist view has primarily involved the state in underwriting private capital accumulation by nationalizing unprofitable but economically essential industries, by financing risky technologies, by subsidizing out-of-date capital and by creating areas of 'waste' (such as defence spending) where capital stocks can be continuously written off at state expense. (iii) In a similar way, marxists argue that much 'welfare state' legislation can be understood not as genuine concessions to the interests of workers, but as the state taking on costs of production which would otherwise have to be borne by employers. State education, for example, transfers the costs of training the workforce to general taxation levied on wages as well as profits. Overall, they suggest that the 'welfare state' maintains existing levels of social inequality in a sanitized form. Income is redistributed *within* classes, from those in employment to the sick, the old and the unemployed, while leaving fundamental class inequalities untouched. (iv) Marxists interpret instances where genuine concessions to working-class interests are made, or where major shifts in the social structure threatening to owners of capital do occur, as almost entirely the product of disruptive shocks to the social system mounted by workers' parties or movements. Thus any major reforms are interpreted as coerced ameliorations of class inequalities, implemented by the state only under threat of serious social unrest.

(b) *Structuralist marxism* is one of a number of well-developed neo-marxist variants which have developed since the late 1960s, largely in an attempt to come to terms with the same phenomena which posed problems for contemporary pluralism.[15] But these phenomena take on a new perspective from within a marxist tradition, creating some distinctive explanatory inadequacies. In the first place, all marxist accounts of politics under capitalism rest extensively on counter-factual claims, on statements about what would have happened under conditions other than those which in fact applied. For example, the claim that workers' fundamental class interests would be best served by a radical transformation of the socio-economic system, and that they would define and perceive these interests in the absence of a 'dominant ideology' which induces a 'false consciousness' about their interests, rests on a whole series of counter-factuals. Second, conventional marxism's emphasis on processes of class struggle sits uncomfortably with the general political stability of liberal democracies. Equally it does not obviously explain the growth of disruptive forms of political protest or social tensions on issues which cannot easily be reduced to conflicts between social classes, such as racial antagonisms. Nor does marxism offer much of an account of those issues which have displaced overt class conflict; instead rather vague references are made to the 'immediate interests', which absorb the practical energies of working-class parties or unions. Third, conventional marxists seem to reduce political processes to economic ones, reading off developments in the political 'superstructure' in a simple and deterministic way from changes in the economic 'base'. These tendencies become serious limitations in applying marxist approaches in an empirical way, or in developing them with much intellectual coherence to apply to the complex political phenomena of modern industrial societies.

Structuralist marxism emerged from France, quite largely after the May 1968 'events' — a series of linked strikes and demonstrations, mainly in Paris. The theory is severely critical of much earlier marxist argumentation about liberal democratic politics. In particular, writers in this perspective reject any attempt to infer the direction of state policies from the social biases involved in recruiting personnel to man the state apparatus. Even if such contingent recruitment biases could be removed, they argue, the fundamental character of the state in capitalist society would not change simply because different individuals occupied decision-making positions.

From a structuralist perspective, the interpretation of liberal democratic politics cannot be undertaken in terms of individual actors or their values, backgrounds and decisions. Rather an attempt must be made to understand the complex, systemic processes by which different levels of social wholes (or social units) interact, develop and change.

Structuralists seek to derive an understanding of political phenomena from the fundamental economic relations involved in the capitalist mode of production. But they achieve this via a much more complex set of categories and concepts than conventional marxism, and claim in doing so to be following strictly logical principles.

Structuralists see state policies as being determined by impersonal changes in the economic and political/ideological systems. These systems or structures develop fairly independently of each other, although economic developments will ultimately always constrain the scope of political changes. A society may move into crisis in one of these systems but not the other, e.g. experiencing an economic slump without political instability (as in Britain in the 1930s) or a politico-ideological crisis without an economic one (as in May 1968 in France). The development of these structures influences the state apparatus in a number of ways, without these changes necessarily being the conscious goals of any individuals involved in producing them.

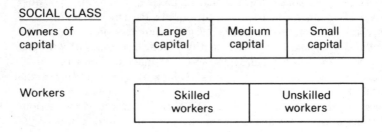

SOCIAL CLASS

| Owners of capital | Large capital | Medium capital | Small capital |

| Workers | Skilled workers | Unskilled workers |

Figure 14.2 Examples of within-class differences

In addition to this reconceptualization of how state policies are shaped, structuralists have tried to rethink the categories of social classes suggested by conventional marxism. They emphasize the contemporary growth and importance of a number of 'intermediate categories' between the bourgeoisie and the working class proper, who are broadly seen as manual workers in productive industry. (On a strict definition of this kind, only about a quarter of the modern US workforce might qualify as 'working class', however.) The intermediate groups – such as self-employed people, non-managerial 'middle-class' groups, the intelligentsia and state workers – are seen as potentially crucial allies of a radical movement or party, allies whose support may need to be won for any fundamental programme of change. And structuralists distinguish within-class differences in interests, between 'fractions' or 'strata' of the main social classes (Figure 14.2). For example, the bourgeoisie are often divided into a finance fraction and an industrial fraction, itself split between a monopoly fraction and a small/medium capital 'fraction'; all of these are organized politically and are engaged in a competitive struggle to advance their particular interests over those of other fractions. The working class is seen as divided more by 'strata', i.e. non-organized groupings of workers with partially perceived distinct sets of interests: conflicts between skilled and unskilled manual workers are seen in these terms.

Both the structuralists' view of the systematic determinants of societal change, and their more complex model of divisions between and within social classes, work through into a view of the state which is significantly different from that of conventional marxism. Because governments are seen as responding more to the logic of their situation under capitalism; and because there is no homogeneous 'dominant class' united on a detailed political programme, the broad trend of state policy is seen as unlinked to any direct response to pressure from capital or from individual actors favouring the bourgeoisie. Such factors, structuralists argue, may influence the details or timing of policy changes, or fairly small-scale choices among policy options. But the essential direction of policy change will be set in a filtered and structured way by the development of the mode of production and by the level of class conflict. The state apparatus will act with a measure of 'relative autonomy' from owners of capital. And the direction of state policy may be more towards the preservation of an entire social order within which processes of private capital accumulation are dominant than towards a totally consistent support of short-run interests of the bourgeoisie. As well as fostering increased capital accumulation, state policies will be directed towards legitimating the social order as one which is rationally and equitably organized. This legitimation imperative is seen as a crucial influence on the post-war growth of the welfare state, and it also figures importantly in the second neo-marxist variant I shall review here.

(c) *Theories of legitimation crisis* differ from both conventional and structuralist Marxism primarily in their downgrading of economic factors from a position of key explanatory importance.[16] Writers in this perspective have renounced any attempt to reduce all social conflicts to class conflicts or to try and show that economic changes are 'determinant in the last instance' of other kinds of social development. In particular they argue that political and ideological/cultural changes need to be analysed in their own right and in their full complexity.

One starting point which additionally differentiates theorists of legitimation crisis is their more articulated model of social conflicts under capitalism. They identify some limited but important areas of 'cross-class interests' (Figure 14.3), which provide a basis for common action by people of different classes working in the same *sector* of the economy. For example, they argue that large, oligopolistic corporations have been able to reach a 'class compromise' with their workforce. Under this, parts of the rapid productivity gain from high investment is 'bottled up' in the sector by high wage rises, rather than being passed on to consumers in lower prices. In contrast, workers in small firms are weakly organized, and their firms are in no position to 'manage' their prices in the face of stiff market competition; workers in the market sector thus fall behind those in the corporate sector in terms of wage levels. Meanwhile well-organized unions in the state sector may enable workers there to keep pace with corporate sector wage rises, but with state sector productivity rising only very slowly, if at all. Over time, this process is expected to lead to a progressive increase in the real costs of providing a given level of state services. This increase may help to divert significant unplanned resources from profit-making industry into the public sector; or rising state budgets may trigger a backlash against rising level of personal taxation. Carried to an extreme this process may engender a 'fiscal crisis of the state' in which state service growth runs up against acute financial constraints, necessitating drastic and politically dangerous cuts in public services.

SOCIAL CLASS

Owners of capital	Large capital	Small capital	Public 'quasi' capital
	Monopoly sector	Competitive or market sector	State sector
Workers	Monopoly sector workers	Market sector workers	State workers

Figure 14.3 Examples of cross-class differences

But the core arguments of theories of legitimation crisis centre on a theory of how class conflicts in capitalist societies may be displaced by state intervention from the economic system into a number of apparently far-removed areas of social life. They argue that overall liberal democratic regimes have successfully tackled and partially neutralized the threat of economic crises — by politicizing processes of price and wage determination, by increasing interference in investment practices, and by skilful demand-management techniques. The 'class compromise' in the corporate sector subverts industrial militancy, while 'welfare state' policies compensate unorganized workers. Economic problems may now be internalized within the structure of state policies, emerging as acute 'rationality deficits' in the administrative process only from time to time.

But the more far-reaching implications of this strategy for managing advanced capitalism will show up in the field of ideological relations. In particular, problems will increasingly arise with the motivational system tying a majority of people into operating a basically capitalist society. Resolving economic crises by moving production decisions into the state apparatus may politicize the society beyond levels where market outcomes are seen as 'natural' or inevitable. Instead social inequalities may be highlighted as politically determined decisions; the impersonal discipline of market forces may be replaced as the perceived cause of social problems by administrative or political actions; and the moral authority of the social system may be eroded as progressively fewer social activities are seen as immune from state intervention or amelioration. In a society where the state appears omnipresent, almost all social problems may take on the character of political problems. The cost of resolving economic crises may be to precipitate a 'legitimation crisis' in which more people perceive the social system as irrationally or unjustly organized.

Equally fundamentally the nature of welfare state interventions will tend to remove more and more sections of society from direct involvement in market processes, so that the key importance ascribed to participation in productive labour in the 'dominant ideology' of capitalism is eroded. People may drop out of the race for material incentives or out of the labour-force altogether; pressures on workers and even capital to reskill, retrain or move between areas may ease; and trades unions may acquire considerable power to cushion their members by restrictive practices from employers' demands for higher outputs or work rates. Above all, the rival moral values of the 'welfare state' may increasingly undermine the 'work ethic' and the 'payment for consumption' ethic essential to capitalist commodity production. These long-run motivational problems for capitalism — many of them encapsulated in the notion of the 'British disease' — may provoke so severe a legitimation crisis, on this view, that the state apparatus attempts to create a state-managed, 'artificial' economic crisis in order to reassert under controlled conditions the social primacy of capitalist production. Arguably Mrs Thatcher's Conservative Government of 1979 embarked on just such a strategy, using monetarist policies and exchange-rate manipulations to trigger favourable background conditions for a policy of industrial confrontation with the trades union movement and state workers.

Conclusions

Where then does the pluralist-marxist debate stand at the start of the 1980s? One over-simple answer is that it has disintegrated into two camps feuding more among themselves than bothering to fight each other. For example, the debates between liberals who still support a version of pluralism and those who do not have reached previously unparalleled levels of dissension. Marxist writers, of course, have always had a more developed reputation for sectarian hostilities.

But oddly enough, behind this appearance of fragmentation, some quite startling shifts and realignments have occurred between parts of the two sides of the debate on particular issues. For example, in 1977 the leading classical pluralist Charles Lindblom published a major work, *Politics and Markets*, in which he largely conceded elite theory and marxist claims for the privileged position of business in pluralist societies — while denying, however, that socialist forms of economic organization offered any effective alternative solutions.[17] Similarly, the liberal anti-pluralist analysis of the 'economic contradictions of democracy' is strikingly similar in many of its propositions to the theories of 'legitimation crisis' developed by some neo-marxists.[18] Perhaps, more fundamental still, the 1970s have shown signs of a far-reaching reassessment by marxist theoreticians of the utility of liberal democratic (and even pluralist) politics as a guarantee of working-class interests and as a framework for effecting far-reaching societal transformations.[19] It would overstate the case to view any of these as signs of a general convergence of pluralist and marxist views, for no such convergence has taken place or is in prospect. But it does not seem utopian to detect substantial signs of empirically supported common ground underlying the fundamental theoretical disputes which separate the two halves of the debate. At the very least, the bases of theoretical controversy in political science have moved on from the first-approximation positions of the 1960s to a new level of theoretical sophistication and a new realism about the importance of empirical disputes in the debate.

Notes

1   A good way into the 1960s debate is R. Miliband, *The State in*

Capitalist Society (London, Quartet, 1973), a critique of pluralism from a mixed elite theory/marxist perspective.

2 Pluralist works used in this section include R. Dahl, *A Preface to Democratic Theory* (Chicago University Press, 1958), *Polyarchy* (Yale University Press, 1971) and *Who Governs* (Yale University Press, 1961); A. M. Birch, *Representative and Responsible Government* (London, Allen & Unwin, 1964); C. Lindblom, *The Policy Making Process* (Prentice-Hall, 1968). For summary accounts of variations in pluralist theory, see D. Nicholls, *Three Varieties of Pluralism* (London, Macmillan, 1975) and A. S. MacFarland, *Power and Leadership in Pluralist Systems* (Stanford University Press, 1969).

3 A classic statement of this theory is J. S. Mill, *Representative Government* (London, Dent, 1910).

4 Neo-pluralist works used in this section include A. Etzioni, *The Active Society* (New York, Free Press, 1968); J. K. Galbraith, *The New Industrial State* (Penguin Books, 1969); D. Bell, *The End of Ideology* (New York, Crowell Collier, 1961) and *The Coming of Post-Industrial Society* (New York, Basic Books, 1973). For a critical account of neo-pluralism, see B. J. Kleinberg, *American Society in the Postindustrial Age* (Columbus, Ohio, Merrill, 1973).

5 C. Wright Mills, *The Power Elite* (New York, Oxford University Press, 1956).

6 Newer elite theory criticisms are raised in W. E. Connolly (ed.), *The Bias of Pluralism* (Chicago, Atherton, 1969) and P. Bachrach, *The Theory of Democratic Elitism* (University of London Press, 1969).

7 T. J. Johnson, *Professions and Power* (London, Macmillan, 1972), provides a good account of the professions.

8 The central account of contemporary liberal corporatism is given by P. Schmitter, 'Still the century of corporatism', *Review of Politics*, 34 (1976).

9 G Sartori, 'Will democracy kill democracy?', *Government and Opposition*, 10 (1975), 131–58, p. 150.

10 Liberal anti-pluralist works are sometimes misleadingly labelled neo-conservative: in fact they are not related to traditional conservatism at all. The description 'new Right' is admissible, however, since many variants of liberalism are closely linked to right-wing political parties and movements. Key sources used here are J. M. Buchanan and G. Tullock, *The Calculus of Consent* (University of Michigan Press, 1962); A. Breton, *The Economic Theory of Representative Government* (Chicago, Aldine, 1974); and D. C. Mueller, *Public Choice* (Cambridge University Press, 1979), especially chapters 6, 8 and 13.

11 R. Scruton, *The Meaning of Conservatism* (London, Macmillan, 1980), pp. 56 and 53.

12 See, for example, S. Brittan, 'The economic contradictions of

220   *Patrick Dunleavy*

democracy', *British Journal of Political Science*, 5 (1975).
13 W. A. Niskanen, *Bureaucracy and Representative Government* (Chicago, Aldine-Atherton, 1971).
14 Conventional marxist sources used in this section include R. Miliband, *The State in Capitalist Society* and *Marxism and Politics* (Oxford University Press, 1977); P. Anderson, *Considerations on Western Marxism* (London, New Left Books, 1976); J. Westergaard and H. Resler, *Class in a Capitalist Society* (Penguin Books, 1977).
15 Structuralist marxist sources used in this section include N. Poulantzas, *Political Power and Social Classes* (London, New Left Books, 1975) and *State, Power, Socialism* (London, New Left Books, 1979); M. Castells, *The Urban Question* (London, Arnold, 1977).
16 Sources used in this section include: J. Habermas, *Legitimation Crisis* (London, Heinemann, 1976); J. O'Connor, *The Fiscal Crisis of the State* (New York, St Martin's Press, 1973); C. Offe and V. Ronge, 'Theses on the theory of the state', *New German Critique*, no. 6 (1975), pp. 137–45.
17 C. Lindblom, *Politics and Markets* (New York, Basic Books, 1977).
18 Compare for example the accounts given by Brittan, 'The economic contradictions of democracy' and Habermas, *Legitimation Crisis*, part II.
19 See Miliband, *Marxism and Politics*, ch. 6. In part this movement reflected the shift to 'Eurocommunist' approaches in some countries.

SECTION 5

Conformity, Consensus and Conflict

Introduction

Stuart Hall

The readings in this section continue to explore the problem of 'social order'. What makes Britain in the 1980s — despite its many differences, conflicts and tensions — sufficient of a unity to allow us to speak of it in the singular: British society? We know that the economic system coordinates many different decisions and activities — and thus helps to integrate society. There are different social classes, ethnic groups and genders — but they all cohere within a pattern of relationships and positions which we describe as 'the social structure' of our society. Power is unevenly distributed: yet the very function of the political system is to *link* government, power and policies to the citizen. The state represents the 'unity' of all citizens within the nation, their association under one government, one law. Social organization, by definition, involves linking, connecting, coordinating, integrating different groups, institutions and functions into some kind of unity. Of course, the *type* and *degree* of integration varies. Some societies are tightly bound — people and institutions must conform within very narrow limits; wide deviations from the norm are not tolerated. Other societies — like ours — are more 'open', pluralistic, diverse. The differences (between employers and workers, rich and poor, men and women, black and white, 'the people' and the power-bloc, citizens and nation) remain; they generate different social interests, often leading to conflict, and sometimes to radical change. But wherever there is 'society' there is a measure of social integration. The readings which follow explore some *wider* aspects of this question.

It can, of course, be examined at many different *levels* and from different vantage-points. We may want to ask, 'How (and how far) do *individuals* come to conform to the standards and patterns of behaviour which others expect of them?' This would be to look at social order from the viewpoint of conformity between the individual and the social group — and very much reflects the perspective of the social psychologist. This is the perspective adopted by Haney, Banks and Zimbardo in reading no. 15.

In fact, it is still an open question in social science whether people behave as they do because they act in accordance with their own deeply-held values, or whether their behaviour owes much, if not everything, to the social situations in which they find themselves, or to some more general process of 'socialization' into the values of society at large. Most people, after all, associate with others with whom they have something in common, and often choose the situations in which they find themselves. So their behaviour may be *both* in accordance with their personalities *and* appropriate to their situation. Using a method typical of the social psychological approach, the authors set up an experimental situation — a simulated prison — allocating *at random* normal people to the contrasting roles of 'prisoner' and 'guard'. The demands of the situation led to startlingly different behaviour between the two groups. Almost at once the 'prisoners' became passive, apathetic and stressed: the guards became aggressive, strongly committed to their role.

This study suggests, then, that the context of the immediate situation is of greater significance to how people act and react than their personalities. Remember, though, that both 'prisoners' and 'guards' were stripped of what Goffman, in his study of patients entering a mental hospital, called 'props to their identity' (*Asylums*, Penguin Books, 1968). This affects how the subjects reacted to the situation they were put in. The study was designed to yield insights into the inter-personal dynamics between *real* prisoners and guards. However, the study was also relevant to wider questions, prominent at the time, particularly the anxieties aroused in the public and the military over attempts at mass indoctrination of Allied prisoners of war during the Korean conflict in the 1950s. The present study shows the effects on prisoners of isolation and disorientation, and points to how soldiers might be prepared through training to resist psychological pressures. (It is because of this interest that the study was financed by the US Office of Naval Research.) But we have used the study here to throw light, from an experimental situation, on the wider question of how far we 'invent' roles, and how far roles define us.

The question of social integration can also be examined from a society-wide or 'macro-social' perspective. This is the position adopted by Edward Shils (no. 16) and by those sociologists who analyse social order in terms not of individuals, but of *institutions*. Typical questions here would be: 'How (and how well) do the economy, work, the family and the education system "fit together"? What function does each serve in maintaining social integration? What binds the different parts of society into a viable unity?' Shils argues that society 'holds together' because it has a 'centre'. The centre consists of the dominant major institutions in society. These institutions maintain a pattern of roles and activities into which people are bound. More significantly, for Shils, they sustain between them a set of common values, beliefs and symbols. 'The centre' defines roles and values for the rest of society. Drawing the whole of society into these patterns makes 'the centre' a source of social order. But because it also carries 'authority' (Shils says it is associated with what we think of as 'sacred'), the 'centre' places a stamp of legitimacy on the values and beliefs which it maintains. In societies like ours, he argues, the distance between 'centre' and 'periphery' has greatly diminished. People are more in contact with the centre: the values of the centre are more widely diffused across society. Therefore though the central value. system will become weaker, more attenuated, as we move towards the periphery, there are very few peripheral groups which are outside the reach of the consensus, and there are fewer sharp breaks or divergences between the values of 'centre' and 'periphery' than in earlier societies.

Shils writes with the authority of a learned, senior sociologist, and a leading collaborator of Talcott Parsons, whose 'structural-functional' approach to the question of social integration was the dominant socio-logical theoretical perspective in the 1950s and 1960s, and remains a major sociological paradigm today. It was, however, sometimes criticized for over-emphasizing the integrative, consensual character of modern societies, and for playing down the question of conflict and cleavage — though, as we have seen, Shils did not argue for a simple 'consensus' model of society, and acknowledged that questions of the 'order' and 'legitimacy' of the centre were linked to its position of power and authority.

Two questions might, however, be asked about 'consensus' or 'common value system' theories of social order. Empirically, how wide and all-inclusive *is* the 'consensus' in different societies? And is Shils correct to argue that integration is best explained in terms of the consensus on values and norms — on a *normative* type of integration? These issues are addressed in Michael Mann's classic paper (no. 17), which was published in 1970 at the height of the dominance of 'consensus theories', and which reviews a massive number of American and British empirical studies which throw light on the questions: 'To what extent do the different classes in society internalize norms, values and beliefs which legitimate the social order?' and 'How can we best explain the degree of legitimation and integration which we find?'

Mann's extensive review of the literature makes him conclude (for a number of different reasons) that 'value-consensus' of the wide-ranging, integrative type does *not* on the whole exist, even in well-integrated, pluralistic societies like Britain and the US. But since it is also true that these societies remain stable and cohesive, and do not constantly break down into openly warring elements, the basis on which social order is maintained still has to be explained. Mann offers some interesting and important suggestions as to how this question can be more fully explored. These include the 'manipulative socializing' role of the education and mass media systems; the pragmatic acceptance of lower status by those who have become habituated to it and can see no practical alternative way of arranging society; and what he calls the 'mobilization of bias'. But he issues a clear warning against taking too simplistic a view of indoctrination, and the dangers of arguing that the mass of people are simply duped into a state of 'false consciousness', falsely perceiving the interests of the 'centre' and the 'periphery' as the same.

Reading no. 18, a revised version of a paper by Stuart Hall, takes up some of these questions in relation to the ways in which the mass media shape values, beliefs and ideologies by offering a limited number of ways of 'defining social reality'. Hall contests both the benign view − that there *is* 'consensus' and all the media do is to 'reflect' it − and the simple alternative − that the media and broadcasters are simply 'biased' in favour of the *status quo* and circulate only what Marx called 'ruling ideas'. Hall analyses the dominant practices by means of which the media are said to operate in a 'balanced, objective, neutral and independent' manner; and argues, instead, that these are related to the determinate conditions in which the media function. He tries to show that, though the media are formally independent of the political system, they are nevertheless part of the 'system of power', and tend to take what the state defines as 'reality' and 'in the national interest' as their base-line. This gives them an objective tendency to favour the existing arrangements of society, though they never reproduce the views of the powerful in a monolithic fashion. The argument translates what is usually discussed in terms of 'value consensus' into the alternative concept of ideology. It makes a case for considering the mass media as among the most important ideological institutions in modern society.

The readings in this section all turn on the question of social order − whether this is considered from the perspective of social conformity (Reading 15), social integration (Reading 16), social consensus (Reading 17) or social ideology (Reading 18). Explaining social order is a − some people would argue *the* − fundamental problem in social science. It is addressed directly in this and the preceding section; but all the social processes and structures discussed in these readings throw light, directly or indirectly, on it. Here we have chosen readings which treat the problem on a wide canvas, drawing on different disciplines and using different, often competing, theoretical perspectives. None returns a definitive answer to the problem. Each illuminates an aspect of the problem. They cannot all be equally useful — or, indeed, correct. But even the errors and weaknesses of approach, analysis and argument may help us, in the future, to construct our questions about social order in a better, more productive, way.

15   A study of prisoners and guards in a simulated prison

Craig Haney, Curtis Banks and Philip Zimbardo

Method

Overview

The effects of playing the role of 'guard' or 'prisoner' were studied in the context of an experimental simulation of a prison environment. The research design was a relatively simple one, involving as it did only a single treatment variable, the random assignment to either a 'guard' or 'prisoner' condition. These roles were enacted over an extended period of time (nearly one week) within an environment that was physically constructed to resemble a prison. Central to the methodology of creating and maintaining a psychological state of imprisonment was the functional simulation of significant properties of 'real prison life' (established through information from former inmates, correctional personnel and texts).

The 'guards' were free within certain limits to implement the procedures of induction into the prison setting and maintenance of custodial retention of the 'prisoners.' These inmates, having voluntarily submitted to the conditions of this total institution in which they now lived, coped in various ways with its stresses and its challenges. The behavior of both groups of subjects was observed, recorded, and analyzed. The dependent measures were of two general types: (1) transactions between and within each group of subjects, recorded on video and audio tape as well as directly observed; (2) individual reactions on questionnaires, mood inventories, personality tests, daily guard shift reports, and post experimental interviews.

Subjects

The 24 subjects who participated in the experiment were selected from an initial pool of 75 respondents, who answered a newspaper ad asking for male volunteers to participate in a psychological study of 'prison life' in return for payment of $15 per day. Each respondent completed

Source: *Naval Research Reviews*, vol. 30, part 9, 1973, pp. 4-17.

an extensive questionnaire concerning his family background, physical and mental health history, prior experience and attitudinal propensities with respect to sources of psychopathology (including their involvements in crime). Each respondent also was interviewed by one of two experimenters. Finally, the 24 subjects who were judged to be most stable (physically and mentally), most mature, and least involved in anti-social behaviors were selected to participate in the study. On a random basis, half of the subjects were assigned the role of 'guard,' half were assigned to the role of 'prisoner.'

The subjects were normal, healthy, male college students who were in the Stanford area during the summer. They were largely of middle class socio-economic status and Caucasians (with the exception of one Oriental subject). Initially they were strangers to each other, a selection precaution taken to avoid the disruption of any pre-existing friendship patterns and to mitigate against any transfer into the experimental situation of previously established relationships or patterns of behavior.

This final sample of subjects was administered a battery of psychological tests on the day prior to the start of the simulation, but to avoid any selective bias on the part of the experimenter-observers, scores were not tabulated until the study was completed.

Two subjects who were assigned to be a 'stand-by' in case an additional 'prisoner' was needed were not called, and one assigned to be a 'stand-by' guard decided against participating just before the simulation phase began — thus, our data analysis is based upon ten prisoners and eleven guards in our experimental conditions.

Procedure

Physical aspects of the prison
The prison was built in a 35-foot section of a basement corridor in the psychology building at Stanford University. It was partitioned by two fabricated walls: one was fitted with the only entrance door to the cell block and the other contained a small observation screen. Three small cells (6 X 9 ft) were made from converted laboratory rooms by replacing the usual doors with steel barred, black painted ones, and removing all furniture.

A cot (with mattress, sheet and pillow) for each prisoner was the only furniture in the cells. A small closet across from the cells served as a solitary confinement facility; its dimensions were extremely small (2 X 2 X 7 ft), and it was unlighted.

In addition, several rooms in an adjacent wing of the building were used as guards' quarters (to change in and out of uniform or for rest and relaxation), a bedroom for the 'warden' and 'superintendent,' and an interview-testing room. Behind the observation screen at one end of the 'Yard' (small enclosed room representing the fenced prison grounds) was video recording equipment and sufficient space for several observers.

Operational details

The 'prisoner' subjects remained in the mock-prison 24 hours per day for the duration of the study. Three were arbitrarily assigned to each of the three cells; the others were on stand-by call at their homes. The 'guard' subjects worked on three-man, eight-hour shifts; remaining in the prison environment only during their work shift and going about their usual lives at other times.

Role instructions

All subjects had been told that they would be assigned either the guard or the prisoner role on a completely random basis and all had voluntarily agreed to play either role for $15 per day for up to two weeks. They signed a contract guaranteeing a minimally adequate diet, clothing, housing and medical care as well as the financial remuneration in return for their stated 'intention' of serving in the assigned role for the duration of the study.

It was made explicit in the contract that those assigned to be prisoners should expect to be under surveillance (have little or no privacy) and to have some of their basic civil rights suspended during their imprisonment, excluding physical abuse. They were given no other information about what to expect nor instructions about behavior appropriate for a prisoner role. Those actually assigned to this treatment were informed by phone to be available at their place of residence on a given Sunday when we would start the experiment.

The subjects assigned to be guards attended an orientation meeting on the day prior to the induction of the prisoners. At this time they were introduced to the principal investigators, the 'Superintendent' of the prison (the author) and an undergraduate research assistant who assumed the administrative role of 'Warden.' They were told that we wanted to try to simulate a prison environment within the limits imposed by pragmatic and ethical considerations. Their assigned task was to 'maintain the reasonable degree of order within the prison necessary for its effective functioning,' although the specifics of how this duty might be implemented were not explicitly detailed. They were made aware of the fact that, while many of the contingencies with which they might be confronted were essentially unpredictable (e.g., prisoner escape attempts), part of their task was to be prepared for such eventualities and to be able to deal appropriately with the variety of situations that might arise. The 'Warden' instructed the guards in the administrative details, including: the work-shifts, the mandatory daily completion of shift reports concerning the activity of guards and prisoners, the completion of 'critical incident' reports which detailed unusual occurrences, and the administration of meals, work and recreation programs for the prisoners. In order to begin to involve these subjects in their roles even before the first prisoner was incarcerated, the guards assisted in the final phases of completing the prison complex — putting the cots in the cells, signs on the walls, setting up the guards' quarters, moving furniture, water coolers, refrigerators, etc.

The guards generally believed that we were primarily interested in studying the behavior of the prisoners. Of course, we were as interested in the effects which enacting the role of guard in this environment would have on their behavior and subjective states.

To optimize the extent to which their behavior would reflect their genuine reactions to the experimental prison situation and not simply their ability to follow instructions, they were intentionally given only minimal guidelines for what it meant to be a guard. An explicit and categorical prohibition against the use of physical punishment or physical aggression was, however, emphasized by the experimenters. Thus, with this single notable exception, their roles were relatively unstructured initially, requiring each 'guard' to carry out activities necessary for interacting with a group of 'prisoners' as well as with other 'guards' and the 'correctional staff.'

Uniforms
In order to promote feelings of anonymity in the subjects each group was issued identical uniforms. For the guards, the uniform consisted of: plain khaki shirts and trousers, a whistle, a police night-stick (wooden batons), and reflecting sunglasses which made eye contact impossible. The prisoners' uniform consisted of a loose fitting muslin smock with an identification number on front and back, no underclothes, a light chain and lock around one ankle, rubber sandals and a cap made from a nylon stocking. Each prisoner also was issued a toothbrush, soap, soapdish, towel and bed linen. No personal belongings were allowed in the cells.

The outfitting of both prisoners and guards in this manner served to enhance group identity and reduce individual uniqueness within the two groups. The khaki uniforms were intended to convey a military attitude, while the whistle and night-stick were carried as symbols of control and power. The prisoners' uniforms were designed not only to deindividuate the prisoners but to be humiliating and serve as symbols of their dependence and subservience. The ankle chain was a constant reminder (even during their sleep when it hit the other ankle) of the oppressiveness of the environment. The stocking cap removed any distinctiveness associated with hair length, color or style (as does shaving of heads in some 'real' prisons and the military). The ill-fitting uniforms made the prisoners feel awkward in their movements; since these 'dresses' were worn without undergarments, the uniforms forced them to assume unfamiliar postures, more like those of a woman than a man — another part of the emasculating process of becoming a prisoner.

Induction procedure
With the cooperation of the Palo Alto City Police Department all of the subjects assigned to the prisoner treatment were unexpectedly 'arrested' at their residences. A police officer charged them with suspicion of burglary or armed robbery, advised them of their legal rights, handcuffed them, thoroughly searched them (often as curious neighbors looked on) and carried them off to the police station in the rear of the police car. At the station they went through the standard routines of being fingerprinted, having an identification file prepared and then being placed in a detention cell. Each prisoner was blindfolded and subsequently driven by one of the experimenters and a subject-guard to our mock prison. Throughout the entire arrest procedure, the police officers involved maintained a formal, serious attitude, avoiding answering any questions of clarification as to the relation of this 'arrest' to the mock prison study.

Upon arrival at our experimental prison, each prisoner was stripped, sprayed with a delousing preparation (a deodorant spray) and made to stand alone naked for a while in the cell yard. After being given the uniform described previously and having an I.D. picture taken ('mug shot'), the prisoner was put in his cell and ordered to remain silent.

Administrative routine
When all the cells were occupied, the warden greeted the prisoners and read them the rules of the institution (developed by the guards and the warden). They were to be memorized and to be followed. Prisoners were to be referred to only by the number on their uniforms, also in an effort to depersonalize them.

The prisoners were to be served three bland meals per day, were allowed three supervised toilet visits, and given two hours daily for the privilege of reading or letterwriting. Work assignments were issued for which the prisoners were to receive an hourly wage to constitute their $15 daily payment. Two visiting periods per week were scheduled, as were movie rights and exercise periods. Three times a day all prisoners were lined up for a 'count' (one on each guard work-shift). The initial purpose of the 'count' was to ascertain that all prisoners were present, and to test them on their knowledge of the rules and their I.D. numbers. The first perfunctory counts lasted only about ten minutes, but on each successive day (or night) they were spontaneously increased in duration until some lasted several hours. Many of the pre-established features of administrative routine were modified or abandoned by the guards, and some privileges were forgotten by the staff over the course of study.

Results

Overview

Although it is difficult to anticipate exactly what the influence of incarceration will be upon the individuals who are subjected to it and those charged with its maintenance, especially in a simulated reproduction, the results of the present experiment support many commonly held conceptions of prison life and validate anecdotal evidence supplied by articulate ex-convicts. The environment of arbitrary custody had great impact upon the affective states of both guards and prisoners as well as upon the interpersonal processes taking place between and within those role-groups.

In general, guards and prisoners showed a marked tendency toward increased negativity of effect, and their overall outlook became increasingly negative. As the experiment progressed, prisoners expressed intentions to do harm to others more frequently. For both prisoners and guards, self-evaluations were more deprecating as the experience of the prison environment became internalized.

Overt behavior was generally consistent with the subjective self-reports and affective expressions of the subjects. Despite the fact that guards and prisoners were essentially free to engage in any form of interaction (positive or negative, supportive or affrontive, etc.), the characteristic nature of their encounters tended to be negative, hostile, affrontive and dehumanizing. Prisoners immediately adopted a generally passive response mode while guards assumed a very active initiative role in all interactions. Throughout the experiment, commands were the most frequent form of verbal behavior and, generally, verbal exchanges were strikingly impersonal, with few references to individual identity. Although it was clear to all subjects that the experimenters would not permit physical violence to take place, varieties of less direct aggressive behavior were observed frequently (especially on the part of guards). In lieu of physical violence, verbal affronts were used as one of the most frequent forms of interpersonal contact between guards and prisoners.

The most dramatic evidence of the impact of this situation upon the participants was seen in the gross reactions of five prisoners who had to be released because of extreme emotional depression, crying, rage and acute anxiety. The pattern of symptoms was quite similar in four of the subjects and began as early as the second day of imprisonment. The fifth subject was released after being treated for a psychosomatic rash which covered portions of his body. Of the remaining prisoners, only two said they were not willing to forfeit the money they had earned in return for being 'paroled.' When the experiment was terminated prematurely after only six days, all the remaining prisoners were delighted by their unexpected good fortune. In contrast, most of the guards seemed to be distressed by the decision to stop the experiment and it appeared to us that they had become sufficiently involved in their roles that they now enjoyed the extreme control and power which they exercised and were reluctant to give it up. One guard did report being personally upset at the suffering of the prisoners, and claimed to have considered asking to change his role to become one of them — but never did so. None of the guards ever failed to come to work on time for their shift, and indeed, on several occasions guards remained on duty voluntarily and uncomplaining for extra hours —without additional pay.

The extremely pathological reactions which emerged in both groups of subjects testify to the power of the social forces operating, but still there were individual differences seen in styles of coping with this novel experience and in degrees of successful adaptation to it. Half the prisoners did endure the oppressive atmosphere, and not all the guards resorted to hostility. Some guards were tough but fair ('played by the rules'), some went far beyond their roles to engage in creative cruelty and harassment, while a few were passive and rarely instigated any coercive control over the prisoners.

Reality of the simulation

At this point it seems necessary to confront the critical question of 'reality' in the simulated prison environment: were the behaviors observed more than the mere acting out of assigned roles convincingly? To be sure, ethical, legal and practical considerations set limits upon the degree to which this situation could approach the conditions existing in actual prisons and penitentiaries. Necessarily absent were some of the most salient aspects of prison life reported by criminologists and documented in the writing of prisoners. There was no involuntary homosexuality, no racism, no physical beatings, no threat to life by prisoners against each other or the guards. Moreover, the maximum anticipated 'sentence' was only two weeks and, unlike some prison systems, could not be extended indefinitely for infractions of the internal operating rules of the prison.

In one sense, the profound psychological effects we observed under the relatively minimal prison-like conditions which existed in our mock prison made the results even more significant, and force us to wonder about the devastating impact of chronic incarceration in real prisons. Nevertheless, we must contend with the criticism that our conditions were too minimal to provide a meaningful analogue to existing prisons. It is necessary to demonstrate that the participants in this experiment transcended the conscious limits of their preconceived stereotyped roles and their awareness of the artificiality and limited duration of imprisonment. We feel there is abundant evidence that virtually all of the subjects at one time or another experienced reactions which went well beyond the surface demands of role-playing and penetrated the deep structure of the psychology of imprisonment.

Although instructions about how to behave in the roles of guard or prisoner were not explicitly defined, demand characteristics in the experiment obviously exerted some directing influence. Therefore, it is enlightening to look to circumstances where role demands were minimal, where the subjects believed they were not being observed, or where they should not have been behaving under the constraints imposed by their roles (as in 'private' situations), in order to assess whether the role behaviors reflected anything more than public conformity or good acting.

When the private conversations of the prisoners were monitored, we learned that almost all (a full 90 per cent) of what they talked about was directly related to immediate prison conditions, that is, food, privileges, punishment, guard harassment, etc. Only one-tenth of the time did their conversations deal with their life outside the prison. Consequently, although they had lived together under such intense conditions, the prisoners knew surprisingly little about each other's past history or future plans. This excessive concentration on the vicissitudes of their current situation helped to make the prison experience more oppressive for the prisoners because, instead of escaping from it when they had a chance to do so in the privacy of their cells, the prisoners continued to allow it to dominate their thoughts and social relations. The guards too, rarely exchanged personal information during their relaxation breaks. They either talked about 'problem prisoners,' other prison topics, or did not talk at all. There were few instances of any personal communication across the two role groups. Moreover, when prisoners referred to other prisoners during interviews, they typically deprecated each other, seemingly adopting the guards' negative attitude.

From post experimental data, we discovered that when individual guards were alone with solitary prisoners and out of range of any recording equipment, as on the way to or in the toilet, harassment often was greater than it was on the 'Yard.' Similarly, video-taped analyses of total guard aggression showed a daily escalation even after most prisoners had ceased resisting and prisoner deterioration had become visibly obvious to them. Thus, guard aggression was no longer elicited as it was initially in response to perceived threats, but was emitted simply as a 'natural' consequence of being in the uniform of a 'guard' and asserting the power inherent in that role. In specific instances we noted cases of a guard (who did not know he was being observed) in the early morning hours pacing the Yard as the prisoners slept — vigorously pounding his night stick into his hand while he 'kept watch' over his captives. Or another guard who detained an 'incorrigible' prisoner in solitary confinement beyond the duration set by the guards' own rules, and then he conspired to keep him in the hole all night while attempting to conceal this information from the experimenters who were thought to be too soft on the prisoners.

In passing we may note an additional point about the nature of role-playing and the extent to which actual behavior is 'explained away' by reference to it. It will be recalled that many guards continued to intensify their harassment and aggressive behavior even after the second day of the study, when prisoner deterioration became marked and visible and emotional breakdowns began to occur (in the presence of the guards). When questioned after the study about their persistent affrontive and harassing behavior in the face of prisoner emotional trauma, most guards replied that they were 'just playing the role' of a tough guard, although none ever doubted the magnitude or validity of the prisoners' emotional response. The reader may wish to consider to what extremes an individual may go, how great must be the consequences of his behaviour for others, before he can no longer rightfully attribute his actions to 'playing a role' and thereby abdicate responsibility.

When introduced to a Catholic priest, many of the role-playing prisoners referred to themselves by their prison number rather than their Christian names. Some even asked him to get a lawyer to help them get out. When a public defender was summoned to interview those prisoners who had not yet been released, almost all of them strenuously demanded that he 'bail' them out immediately.

One of the most remarkable incidents of the study occurred during a parole board hearing when each of five prisoners eligible for parole was asked by the senior author whether he would be willing to forfeit all the money earned as a prisoner if he were to be paroled (released from the study). Three of the five prisoners said, 'yes,' they would be willing to do this. Notice that the original incentive for participating in the study had been the promise of money, and they were, after only four days, prepared to give this up completely. And, more surprisingly, when told that this possibility would have to be discussed with the members of the staff before a decision could be made, each prisoner got up quietly and was escorted by a guard back to his cell. If they regarded themselves simply as 'subjects' participating in an experiment for money, there was no longer any incentive to remain in the study and they could have easily escaped this situation which had so clearly become aversive for them by quitting. Yet, so powerful was the control which the situation had come to have over them, so much a reality had this simulated environment become, that they were unable to see that their original and singular motive for remaining no longer obtained, and they returned to their cells to await a 'parole' decision by their captors.

The reality of the prison was also attested to by our prison consultant who had spent over 16 years in prison, as well as the priest who had been a prison chaplain and the public defender, all of whom were brought into direct contact with our simulated prison environment. Further, the depressed affect of the prisoners, the guards' willingness to work overtime for no additional pay, the spontaneous use of prison titles and I.D. numbers in non role-related situations all point to a level of reality as real as any other in the lives of all those who shared this experience.

To understand how an illusion of imprisonment could have become so real, we need now to consider the uses of power by the guards as well as the effects of such power in shaping the prisoner mentality.

Pathology of power

Being a guard carried with it social status within the prison, a group identity (when wearing the uniform), and above all, the freedom to exercise an unprecedented degree of control over the lives of other human beings. This control was invariably expressed in terms of sanctions, punishment, demands, and with the threat of manifest physical power. There was no need for the guards to rationally justify a request as they did their ordinary life, and merely to make a demand was sufficient to have it carried out. Many of the guards showed in their behavior and revealed in post-experimental statements that this sense of power was exhilarating.

The use of power was self-aggrandizing and self-perpetuating. The guard power, derived initially from an arbitrary and randomly assigned label, was intensified whenever there was any perceived threat by the prisoners and this new level subsequently became the baseline from which further hostility and harassment would begin. The most hostile guards on each shift moved spontaneously into the leadership roles of giving orders and deciding on punishments. They became role models whose behavior was emulated by other members of the shift. Despite minimal contact between the three separate guard shifts and nearly 16 hours a day spent away from the prison, the absolute level of aggression, as well as more subtle and 'creative' forms of aggression manifested, increased in a spiralling function. Not to be tough and arrogant was to be seen as a sign of weakness by the guards, and even those 'good' guards who did not get as drawn into the power syndrome as the others respected the implicit norm of *never* contradicting or even interfering with an action of a more hostile guard on their shift.

After the first day of the study, practically all prisoner rights (even such things as the time and conditions of sleeping and eating) came to be redefined by the guards as 'privileges' which were to be earned by obedient behavior. Constructive activities such as watching movies or reading (previously planned and suggested by the experimenters) were arbitrarily cancelled until further notice by the guards — and were subsequently never allowed. 'Reward,' then, became granting approval for prisoners to eat, sleep, go to the toilet, talk, smoke a cigarette, wear eyeglasses, or the temporary diminution of harrassment. One wonders about the conceptual nature of 'positive' reinforcement when subjects are in such conditions of deprivation, and the extent to which even minimally acceptable conditions become rewarding when experienced in the context of such an impoverished environment.

We might also question whether there are meaningful non-violent alternatives as models for behavior modification in real prisons. In a world where men are either powerful or powerless, everyone learns to despise the lack of power in others and in oneself. It seems to us, that prisoners learn to admire power for its own sake — power becoming the ultimate reward. Real prisoners soon learn the means to gain power whether through ingratiation, informing, sexual control of other prisoners or development of powerful cliques. When they are released from prison, it is likely they will never want to feel so powerless again and will take action to establish and assert a sense of power.

The pathological prisoner syndrome

Various coping strategies were employed by our prisoners as they began to react to their perceived loss of personal identity and the arbitrary control of their lives. At first they exhibited disbelief at the total invasion of their privacy, constant surveillance, and atmosphere of oppression in which they were living. Their next response was rebellion, first by the use of direct force, and later with subtle divisive tactics designed to foster distrust among the prisoners. They then tried to work within the system by setting up an elected grievance committee. When that collective action failed to produce meaningful changes in their existence, individual self-interests emerged. The breakdown in prisoner cohesion was the start of social disintegration which gave rise not only to feelings of isolation, but deprecation of other prisoners as well. As noted before, half the prisoners coped with the prison situation by becoming 'sick' − extremely disturbed emotionally − as a passive way of demanding attention and help. Others became excessively obedient in trying to be 'good' prisoners. They sided with the guards against a solitary fellow prisoner who coped with his situation by refusing to eat. Instead of supporting this final and major act of rebellion, the prisoners treated him as a trouble-maker who deserved to be punished for his disobedience. It is likely that the negative self-regard among the prisoners noted by the end of the study was the product of their coming to believe that the continued hostility toward all of them was justified because they 'deserved it' (following Walster, 1966). As the days wore on, the model prisoner reaction was one of passivity, dependence, and flattened affect.

Let us briefly consider some of the relevant processes involved in bringing about these reactions.

Loss of personal identity. For most people identity is conferred by social recognition of one's uniqueness, and established through one's name, dress, appearance, behavior style and history. Living among strangers who do not know your name or history (who refer to you only by number), dressed in a uniform exactly like all other prisoners, not wanting to call attention to one's self because of the unpredictable consequences it might provoke − all led to a weakening of self identity among the prisoners. As they began to lose initiative and emotional responsivity, while acting ever more compliantly, indeed, the prisoners became deindividuated not only to the guards and the observers, but also to themselves.

Arbitrary control. On post-experimental questionnaires, the most frequently mentioned aversive aspect of the prison experience was that of being subjugated to the patently arbitrary, capricious decisions and rules of the guards. A question by a prisoner as often elicited derogation and aggression as it did a rational answer. Smiling at a joke could be punished in the same way that failing to smile might be. An individual acting in defiance of the rules could bring punishment to innocent cell partners (who became, in effect, 'mutually yoked controls'), to himself, or to all.

As the environment became more unpredictable, and previously learned assumptions about a just and orderly world were no longer functional, prisoners ceased to initiate any action. They moved about on orders and when in their cells rarely engaged in any purposeful activity. Their zombie-like reaction was the functional equivalent of the learned helplessness phenomenon reported by Seligman & Groves (1970). Since their behavior did not seem to have any contingent relationship to environmental consequences, the prisoners essentially gave up and stopped behaving. Thus the subjective magnitude of aversiveness was manipulated by the guards not in terms of physical punishment but rather by controlling the psychological dimension of environmental predictability (Glass & Singer, 1972).

Dependency and emasculation. The network of dependency relations established by the guards not only promoted helplessness in the prisoners but served to emasculate them as well. The arbitrary control by the guards put the prisoners at their mercy for even the daily, commonplace functions like going to the toilet. To do so, required publicly obtained permission (not always granted) and then a personal escort to the toilet while blindfolded and handcuffed. The same was true for many other activities ordinarily practiced spontaneously without thought, such as lighting a cigarette, reading a novel, writing a letter, drinking a glass of water, or brushing one's teeth. These were all privileged activities requiring permission and necessitating a prior show of good behavior. These low level dependencies engendered a regressive orientation in the prisoners. Their dependency was defined in terms of the extent of the domain of control over all aspects of their lives which they allowed other individuals (the guards and prison staff) to exercise.

As in real prisons, the assertive, independent, aggressive nature of male prisoners posed a threat which was overcome by a variety of tactics. The prisoner uniforms resembled smocks or dresses, which made them look silly and enabled the guards to refer to them as 'sissies' or 'girls.' Wearing these uniforms without any underclothes forced the prisoners to move and sit in unfamiliar, feminine postures. Any sign of individual rebellion was labelled as indicative of 'incorrigibility' and resulted in loss of privileges, solitary confinement, humiliation or punishment of cell mates. Physically smaller guards were able to induce stronger prisoners to act foolishly and obediently. Prisoners were encouraged to belittle each other publicly during the counts. These and other tactics all served to engender in the prisoners a lessened sense of their masculinity (as defined by their external culture). It followed then, that although the prisoners usually outnumbered the guards during line-ups and counts (nine *v.* three) there never was an attempt to directly overpower them. (Interestingly, after the study was terminated, the prisoners expressed the belief that the basis for assignment to guard and prisoner groups was physical size. They perceived the guards were 'bigger,' when, in fact, there was no difference in average height or weight between these randomly determined groups.)

In conclusion, we believe this demonstration reveals new dimensions in the social psychology of imprisonment worth pursuing in future research. In addition, this research provides a paradigm and information base for studying alternatives to existing guard training, as well as for questioning the basic operating principles on which penal institutions rest. If our mock prison could generate the extent of pathology it did in such a short time, then the punishment of being imprisoned in a real prison does not 'fit the crime' for most prisoners — indeed, it far exceeds it! Moreover, since both prisoners and guards are locked into a dynamic, symbiotic relationship which is destructive to their human nature, guards are also society's prisoners.

References

Glass, D. C. and Singer, J. E., 'Behavioral after-effects of unpredictable and uncontrollable aversive events,' *American Scientist*, 6 (4), 457–65, 1972.

Seligman, M. E. and Groves, D. P., 'Nontransient learned helplessness,' *Psychonomic Science*, 19 (3), 191–2, 1970.

Walster, E., 'Assignment of responsibility for an accident,' *Journal of Personality and Social Psychology*, 3 (1), 73–9, 1966.

16   Center and periphery

Edward Shils

I

Society has a center. There is a central zone in the structure of society. This central zone impinges in various ways on those who live within the ecological domain in which the society exists. Membership in the society, in more than the ecological sense of being located in a bounded territory and of adapting to an environment affected or made up by other persons located in the same territory, is constituted by relationship to this central zone.

The central zone is not, as such, a spatially located phenomenon. It almost always has a more or less definite location within the bounded territory in which the society lives. Its centrality has, however, nothing to do with geometry and little with geography.

The center, or the central zone, is a phenomenon of the realm of values and beliefs. It is the center of the order of symbols, of values and beliefs, which govern the society. It is the center because it is the ultimate and irreducible; and it is felt to be such by many who cannot give explicit articulation to its irreducibility. The central zone partakes of the nature of the sacred. In this sense, every society has an 'official' religion, even when that society or its exponents and interpreters conceive of it, more or less correctly, as a secular, pluralistic, and tolerant society. The principle of the Counterreformation − *Cuius regio, eius religio* − although its rigor has been loosened and its harshness mollified, retains a core of permanent truth.

The center is also a phenomenon of the realm of action. It is a structure of activities, of roles and persons, within the network of institutions. It is in these roles that the values and beliefs which are central are embodied and propounded.

Source: *Center and Periphery: Essays in Macro-Sociology*, University of Chicago Press, 1975, pp. 3–16.

II

The larger society appears, on a cursory inspection and by the methods of inquiry in current use, to consist of a number of interdependent subsystems — the economy, the status system, the polity, the kinship system, and the institutions which have in their special custody the cultivation of cultural values, e.g. the university system, the ecclesiastical system, etc. (I use 'ecclesiastical' to include the religious institutions of societies which do not have a church in the Western sense of the term.) Each of these subsystems itself comprises a network of organizations which are connected, with varying degrees of affirmation, through a common authority, overlapping personnel, personal relationships, contracts, perceived identities of interest, a sense of affinity within a transcendent whole, and a territorial location possessing symbolic value. (These subsystems and their constituent bodies are not equally affirmative vis-à-vis each other. Moreover the degree of affirmation varies through time, and is quite compatible with a certain measure of alienation within each elite and among the elites.)

Each of these organizations has an authority, an elite, which might be either a single individual or a group of individuals, loosely or closely organized. Each of these elites makes decisions, sometimes in consultation with other elites and sometimes, largely on its own initiative, with the intention of maintaining the organization, controlling the conduct of its members and fulfilling its goals. (These decisions are by no means always successful in the achievement of these ends, and the goals are seldom equally or fully shared by the elite and those whose actions are ordained by its decisions.)

The decisions made by the elites contain as major elements certain general standards of judgment and action, and certain concrete values, of which the system as a whole, the society, is one of the most preeminent. The values which are inherent in these standards, and which are espoused and more or less observed by those in authority, we shall call the *central value system* of the society. This central value system is the central zone of the society. It is central because of its intimate connection with what the society holds to be sacred; it is central because it is espoused by the ruling authorities of the society. These two kinds of centrality are vitally related. Each defines and supports the other.

The central value system is not the whole of the order of values and beliefs espoused and observed in the society. The value systems obtaining in any diversified society may be regarded as being distributed along a range. There are variants of the central value system running from hyperaffirmation of some of the components of the major, central value system to an extreme denial of some of these major elements in the central value system; the latter tends to, but is not inevitably associated with, an affirmation of certain elements denied or subordinated in the central value system. There are also elements of the order of values and beliefs which are as random with respect to the central value system as the values and beliefs of human beings can be. There is always a considerable amount of unintegratedness of values and beliefs, both within the realm of value of representative individuals and among individuals and sections of a society.

The central value system is constituted by the values which are pursued and affirmed by the elites of the constituent subsystems and of the organizations which are comprised in the subsystems. By their very possession of authority, they attribute to themselves an essential affinity with the sacred elements of their society, of which they regard themselves as the custodians. By the same token, many members of their society attribute to them that same kind of affinity. The elites of the economy affirm and usually observe certain values which should govern economic activity. The elites of the polity affirm and usually observe certain values which should govern political activity. The elites of the university system and the ecclesiastical system affirm and usually practice certain values which should govern intellectual and religious activities (including beliefs). On the whole, these values are the values embedded in current activity. The ideals which they affirm do not far transcend the reality which is ruled by those who espouse them.* The values of the different elites are clustered into an approximately consensual pattern.†

---

* This set of values corresponds to what Karl Mannheim called 'ideologies,' i.e., values and beliefs, which are congruent with or embodied in current reality (*seinskongruent*). I do not wish to use the term 'ideology' to describe these value orientations. One of the most important reasons is that in the past few decades the term 'ideology' has been used to refer to intensely espoused value orientations which are extremely *seinstranszendent*, which transcend current reality by a wide margin, which are explicit, articulated, and hostile to the existing order. (For example, Bolshevist doctrine, National Socialist doctrine, Fascist doctrine, etc.) Mannheim called these 'utopias.' Mannheim's distinction was fundamental, and I accept it, our divergent nomenclature notwithstanding.

† The degree of consensuality differs among societies and times. There are societies in which the predominant elite demands a complete consensus with its own more specific values and beliefs. Such is the case in modern totalitarian societies. Absolutist regimes in past epochs, which were rather indifferent about whether the mass of the population was party to a consensus, were quite insistent on consensus among the elites of their society.

One of the major elements in any central value system is an affirmative attitude toward established authority. This is present in the central value systems of all societies, however much these might differ from each other in their appreciation of authority. There is something like a 'floor,' a minimum of appreciation of authority in every society, however liberal that society might be. Even the most libertarian and equalitarian societies which have ever existed possess at least this minimum appreciation of authority. Authority enjoys appreciation because it arouses sentiments of sacredness. Sacredness by its nature is authoritative. Those persons, offices, or symbols endowed with it, however indirectly and remotely, are therewith endowed with some measure of authoritativeness.

The appreciation of authority entails the appreciation of the institutions through which authority works and the rules which it enunciates. The central value system in all societies asserts and recommends the appreciation of these authoritative institutions.

Implicitly, the central value system rotates on a center more fundamental even than its espousal by and embodiment in authority. Authority is the agent of *order*, an order which may be largely embodied in authority or which might transcend authority and regulate it, or at least provide a standard by which existing authority itself is judged and even claims to judge itself. This order, which is implicit in the central value system, and in the light of which the central value system legitimates itself, is endowed with dynamic potentialities. It contains, above all, the potentiality of critical judgment on the central value system and the central institutional system. To use Mannheim's terminology, while going beyond Mannheim, every 'ideology' has within it a 'utopian' potentiality. To use my own terminology, every central value system contains within itself an ideological potentiality. The dynamic potentiality derives from the inevitable tendency of every concrete society to fall short of the order which is implicit in its central value system.

Closely connected with the appreciation of authority and the institutions in which it is exercised, is an appreciation of the *qualities* which qualify persons for the exercise of authority or which are characteristic of those who exercise authority. These qualities, which we shall call secondary values, can be ethnic, educational, familial, economic, professional; they may be ascribed to individuals by virtue of their relationships or they may be acquired through study and experience. But whatever they are, they enjoy the appreciation of the central value system simply because of their connection with the exercise of authority. (Despite their ultimately derivative nature, each of them is capable of possessing an autonomous status in the central zone, in the realm of the sacred; consequently, severe conflicts can be engendered.)

The central value system thus comprises secondary as well as primary values. It legitimates the existing distribution of roles and rewards to persons possessing the appropriate qualities which in various ways symbolize degrees of proximity to authority. It legitimates these distributions by praising the properties of those who occupy authoritative roles in the society, by stressing the legitimacy of their incumbency of those roles and the appropriateness of the rewards they receive. By implication, and explicitly as well, it legitimates the smaller rewards received by those who live at various distances from the circles in which authority is exercised.

The central institutional system may thus be described as the set of institutions which is legitimated by the central value system. Less circularly, however, it may be described as those institutions which, through the radiation of their authority, give some form to the life of a considerable section of the population of the society. The economic, political, ecclesiastical, and cultural institutions impinge compellingly at many points on the conduct of much of the population in any society through the actual exercise of authority and the potential exercise of coercion, through the provision of persuasive models of action, and through a partial control of the allocation of rewards. The kinship and family systems, although they have much smaller radii, are microcosms of the central institutional system and do much to buttress its efficiency.

III

The existence of a central value system rests, in a fundamental way, on the need which human beings have for incorporation into something which transcends and transfigures their concrete individual existence. They have a need to be in contact with symbols of an order which is larger in its dimensions than their own bodies and more central in the 'ultimate' structure of reality than is their routine everyday life. Just as friendship exists because human beings must transcend their own self-limiting individuality in personal communion with another personality, so membership in a political society is a necessity of man's nature. This by no means implies that the satisfaction of the intermittently intense need to be a member of a transcendent body, be it a tribe or a nation or a political community, exhausts the functions of political community. A political community performs many functions and satisfies many needs which have little to do with the need for membership in a political community. There is a need to belong to a polity just as there is a need for conviviality. Just as a person shrivels, contracts, and corrupts when separated from all other persons or from those persons who have entered into a formed and vital communion with him, so the man with political needs is crippled and numbed by his isolation from a polity or by his membership in a political order which cannot claim his loyalty.

The need for personal communion is a common quality among human beings who have reached a certain level of individuation. Those who lack the need and the capacity impress us by their incompleteness. The political need is not so widely spread or so highly developed in the mass of the population of any society as are the need and capacity for conviviality. Those who lack it impress by their 'idiocy.' Those who possess it add the possibility of civility to the capacity for conviviality which we think a fully developed human being must possess.

The political need is of course nurtured by tradition, but it cannot be accounted for by the adduction of tradition. The political need is a capacity like certain kinds of imagination, reasoning, perceptiveness, or sensitivity. It is neither instinctual nor learned. It is not simply the product of the displacement of personal affects onto public objects, although much political activity is impelled by such displacement. It is not learned by teaching or traditional transmission, though much political activity is guided by the reception of tradition. The pursuit of a political career and the performance of civil obligations gains much from the impulsion of tradition. None the less, tradition is not the seed of this inclination to attach oneself to a political order.

The political need, which may be formed into a propensity towards civility, entails sensitivity to an order of being where 'creative power' has its seat. This creative center which attracts the minds of those who are sensitive to it is manifested in authority operating over territory. Both authority and territory convey the idea of potency, of 'authorship,' of the capacity to do vital things, of a connection with events which are intrinsically important. Authority is thought, by those with the political or civil need, to possess this vital relationship to the center from which a right order emanates. Those who are closely and positively connected with authority, through its exercise or through personal ties, are thought, in consequence of this connection, to possess a vital relationship to the center, the locus of the sacred, the order which confers legitimacy. Land, which is a constituent of 'territoriality,' has similar properties, and those who exercise authority through control of land have always been felt to enjoy a special status in relation to the core of the central value system. Those who live within given territorial boundaries come to share in these properties and thus become the objects of political sentiments. Residence within certain territorial boundaries and rule by common authority are the properties which define membership in society and establish its obligations and claims. It is not entirely an accident that nationalism is connected with land reform. Land reform is part of a policy which seeks to disperse the special relationship to a higher order of being from a few persons, that is, the great landlords in whom it was previously thought to be concentrated, to the large mass of those who live upon the territory.

It must be stressed that the political need is not by any means equally distributed in any society, even the most democratic. There are human beings whose sensitivity to the ultimate is meager, although there is perhaps no human being from whom it is entirely absent. Nor does sensitivity to remote events which are expressive of the center always focus on their manifestations in the polity.

Apolitical scientists who seek the laws of nature but are indifferent, except on grounds of prudence, to the laws of society are one instance of this uneven development of sensitivity to ultimate things. Religious persons who are attached to transcendent symbols which are not embodied in civil polity or in ecclesiastical organization represent another variant. In addition to these, there are very many persons whose sensitivity is exhausted long before it reaches so far into the core of the central value system. Some have a need for such contact only in crises and on special, periodic occasions, at the moment of birth or marriage or death, or on holidays. Like the intermittent, occasional, and unintense religious sensibility, the political sensibility, too, can be intermittent and unintense. It might come into operation only on particular occasions, for example, at election time, or in periods of severe economic deprivation or during a war or after a military defeat. Beyond this there are some persons who are never stirred, who have practically no sensibility as far as events of the political order are concerned.

Finally, there are persons, not many in any society but often of great importance, who have a very intense and active connection with the center, with the symbols of the central value system, but whose connection is passionately negative. Equally important are those who have a positive but no less intense and active connection with the symbols of the center, a connection so acute, so pure, and so vital that it cannot tolerate any falling short in daily observance such as characterizes the elites of the central institutional system. These are often the persons around whom a sharp opposition to the central value system and even more to the central institutional system is organized. From the ranks of these come prophets, revolutionaries, doctrinaire ideologists for whom nothing less than perfection is tolerable.

IV

The need for established and created order, the respect for creativity, and the need to be connected with the center do not exhaust the forces which engender central value systems. To fill out the list, we must consider the nature of authority itself. Authority has an expansive tendency. It has a tendency to expand the order which it represents toward the saturation of territorial space. The acceptance of the validity of that order entails a tendency toward its universalization within the society over which authority rules. Ruling indeed consists in the universalization — within the boundaries of society — of the rules inherent in the order. Rulers, just because of their possession of authority and the impulses which it generates, wish to be obeyed and to obtain assent to the order which they symbolically embody. The symbolization of order in offices of authority has a compelling effect on those who occupy those offices.

In consequence of this, rulers seek to establish a universal diffusion of the acceptance and observance of the values and beliefs of which they are the custodians through incumbency in those offices. They use their powers to punish those who deviate and to reward with their favor those who conform. Thus, the mere existence of authority in society imposes a central value system on that society. I would regret an easy misunderstanding to which the foregoing sentences might give rise. There is much empirical truth in the common observations that rulers 'look after their own,' that they are only interested in remaining in authority, in reinforcing their possession of authority and in enhancing their security of tenure through the establishment of a consensus built around their own values and beliefs. None the less these observations seem to me to be too superficial. They fail to discern the dynamic property of authority as such, and particularly of authority over society.

Not all persons who come into positions of authority possess the same responsiveness to the inherently dynamic and expansive tendency in authority. Some are more attuned to it; others are more capable of resisting it. Tradition, furthermore, acts as a powerful brake upon expansiveness, as does the degree of differentiation of the structure of elites and of the society as a whole.

V

The central institutional system of modern societies, probably even in revolutionary crises, is the object of a substantial amount of consensus.

The central value system which legitimates the central institutional system is widely shared, but the consensus is never perfect. There are differences within even the most consensual society about the appreciability of authority, the institutions within which it resides, the elites which exercise it, and the justice of its allocation of rewards.

Even those who share in the consensus do so with different degrees of intensity, whole-heartedness, and devotion. As we move from the center of society, the center in which authority is possessed, to the hinterland or the periphery, over which authority is exercised, attachment to the central value system becomes attenuated. The central institutional system is neither unitary nor homogeneous, and some levels have more majesty than others. The lower one goes in the hierarchy, or the further one moves territorially from the locus of authority, the less one appreciates authority. Likewise, the further one moves from those possessing the secondary traits associated with the exercise of authority into sectors of the population which do not equally possess those qualities, the less affirmative is the attitude towards the reigning authority, and the less intense is that affirmation which does exist.

Active rejection of the central value system is, of course, not the sole alternative to its affirmation. Much more widespread, in the course of history and in any particular society, is an intermittent, partial, and attenuated affirmation of the central value system.

For the most part, the mass of the population in premodern societies have been far removed from the immediate impact of the central value system. They have possessed their own value systems, which were occasionally and fragmentarily articulated with the central value system. These pockets of approximate independence have not, however, been completely incompatible with isolated occasions of articulation and of intermittent affirmation. Nor have these intermittent occasions of participation been incompatible with occasions of active rejection and antagonism to the central institutional system, to the elite which sits at its center, and to the central value system which that elite puts forward for its own legitimation.

The more territorially dispersed the institutional system, the less the likelihood of an intense affirmation of the central value system. The more inegalitarian the society, the less the likelihood of an intense affirmation of the central value system, especially where, as in most steeply hierarchical societies, there are large and discontinuous gaps between those at the top and those below them. Indeed, it might be said that the degree of affirmation inevitably shades off from the center of the exercise of authority and of the promulgation of values.

As long as societies were loosely coordinated, as long as authority lacked the means of intensive control, and as long as much of the economic life of the society was carried on outside any market or almost exclusively in local markets, the central value system invariably became attenuated in the outlying reaches. With the growth of the market, and the administrative and technological strengthening of authority, contact with the central value system increased.

When, as in modern society, a more unified economic system, political democracy, urbanization, and education have brought the different sections of the population into more frequent contact with each other and created even greater mutual awareness, the central value system has found a wider acceptance than in other periods of the history of society. At the same time these changes have also increased the extent, if not the intensity, of active 'dissensus' or rejection of the central value system.

The same objects which previously engaged the attention and aroused the sentiments of a very restricted minority of the population have in modern societies become concerns of much broader strata of the population. At the same time that increased contact with authority has led to a generally deferential attitude, it has also run up against the tenacity of prior attachments and a reluctance to accept strange gods. Class conflict in the most advanced modern societies is probably more open and more continuous than in premodern societies, but it is also more domesticated and restricted by attachments to the central value system. Violent revolutions and bloody civil wars are much less characteristic of modern societies than of premodern societies. Revolutionary parties are feeble in modern societies which have moved toward widespread popular education, a greater equality of status, etc. The size of nominally revolutionary parties in France and Italy is a measure of the extent to which French and Italian societies have not become modernized in this sense. The inertness, from a revolutionary point of view, of the rank and file of these parties is partially indicative of the extent to which, despite their revolutionary doctrines, the working classes in these countries have become assimilated into the central value system of their respective societies.

The old gods have fallen, religious faith has become much more attenuated in the educated classes, and suspicion of authority is much more overt than it has ever been. Nonetheless in the modern societies of the West, the central value system has gone much more deeply into the heart of their members than it has ever succeeded in doing in any earlier society. The 'masses' have responded to their contact with a striking measure of acceptance.

VI

The power of the ruling class derives from its incumbency of certain key positions in the central institutional system. Societies vary in the extent to which the ruling class is unitary or relatively segmental. Even where the ruling class is relatively segmental, there is, because of centralized control of appointment to the most crucial of the key positions or because of personal ties or because of overlapping personnel, some sense of affinity which, more or less, unites the different sectors of the elite.

This sense of affinity rests ultimately on the high degree of proximity to the center which is shared by all these different sectors of the ruling class. They have, it is true, a common vested interest in their position. It is not, however, simply the product of a perception of a coalescent interest; it contains a substantial component of mutual regard arising from a feeling of a common relationship to the central value system.

The different sectors of the elite are never equal. One or two usually predominate, to varying degrees, over the others, even in situations where there is much mutual respect and a genuine sense of affinity. Regardless, however, of whether they are equal or unequal, unitary or segmental, there is usually a fairly large amount of consensus among the elites of the central institutional system. This consensus has its ultimate root in their common feeling for the transcendent order which they believe they embody or for which they think themselves responsible. This does not obtain equally for all elites. Some are much more concerned in an almost entirely 'secular' or manipulative way with remaining in power. Nonetheless, even in a situation of great heterogeneity and much mutual antipathy, the different sectors of the elite tend to experience the 'transforming' transcendental overtones which are generated by incumbency in authoritative roles, or by proximity to 'fundamentally important things.'

VII

The mass of the population in all large societies stands at some distance from authority. This is true with respect both to the distribution of authority and to the distribution of the secondary qualities associated with the exercise of authority.

The functional and symbolic necessities of authority require some degree of concentration. Even the most genuinely democratic society, above a certain very small size, requires some concentration of authority for the performance of elaborate tasks. It goes without saying that non-democratic societies have a high concentration of authority. Furthermore, whether the society is democratic or oligarchical, access to the key positions in the central institutional system tends to be confined to persons possessing a distinctive constellation of properties, such as age, education, and ethnic, regional, and class provenance, etc.

The section of the population which does not share in the exercise of authority and which is differentiated in secondary properties from the exercises of authority is usually more intermittent in its 'possession' by the central value system. For one thing, the distribution of sensitivity to remote, central symbols is unequal, and there is a greater concentration of such sensitivity in the elites of the central institutional system. Furthermore, where there is a more marginal participation in the central institutional system, attachment to the central value system is more attenuated. Where the central institutional system becomes more comprehensive and inclusive so that a larger proportion of the life of the population comes within its scope, the tension between the center and the periphery, as well as the consensus, tends to increase.

The mass of the population in most premodern and non-Western societies have in a sense lived *outside* society and have not felt their remoteness from the center to be a perpetual injury to themselves. Their low position in the hierarchy of authority has been injurious to them, and the consequent alienation has been accentuated by their remoteness from the central value system. The alienation has not, however, been active or intense, because, for the most part, their convivial, spiritual, and moral center of gravity has lain closer to their own round of life. They have been far from full-fledged members of their societies and they have very seldom been citizens.

Among the most intensely sensitive or the more alertly intelligent, their distance from the center accompanied by their greater concern with the center, has led to an acute sense of being on 'the outside,' to a painful feeling of being excluded from the vital zone which surrounds the center of society (which is the vehicle of 'the centre of the universe'). Alternatively these more sensitive and more intelligent persons have, as a result of their distinctiveness, often gained access to some layer of the center by becoming schoolteachers, priests, administrators. Thus they have entered into a more intimate and more affirmative relationship with the center. They have not in such instances, however, always overcome the grievance of exclusion from the most central zones of the central institutional and value systems. They have often continued to perceive themselves as outsiders, while continuing to be intensely attracted and influenced by the outlook and style of life of the center.

VIII

Modern large-scale society utilizes a technology which has raised the standard of living and which has integrated the population into a more unified economy. In correspondence with these changes, it has witnessed a more widespread participation in the central value system through education, and in the central institutional system through the franchise and mass communication. On this account, it is in a different position from all premodern societies.

In modern society, in consequence of its far greater involvement with the central institutional system, especially with the economy and the polity, the mass of the population is no longer largely without contact with the central value system. It has, to an unprecedented extent, come to feel the central value system to be its own value system. Its generally heightened sensitivity has responded to the greater visibility and accessibility of the central value system by partial incorporation. Indeed, although, compared with that of the elite, its contact is still relatively intermittent and unintense, the enhanced frequency and intensity of that contact are great universal historical novelties. They are nothing less than the incorporation of the mass of the population into society. The 'process of civilization' has become a reality in the modern world.

To a greater extent than ever before in history the mass of the population in modern Western societies feel themselves to be part of their society in a way in which their ancestors never did. Just as they have become 'alive' and hedonistic, more demanding of respect and pleasure, so, too, they have become more 'civilized.' They have come to be parts of the civil society with a feeling of attachment to that society and a feeling of moral responsibility for observing its rules and sharing in its authority. They have ceased to be primarily objects of authoritative decisions by others; they have become, to a much greater extent, acting and feeling subjects with wills of their own which they assert with self-confidence. Political apathy, frivolity, vulgarity, irrationality, and responsiveness to political demagogy are all concomitants of this phenomenon. Men have become citizens in larger proportions than ever before in the large states of history, and probably more, too, than in the Greek city states at the height of the glory of their aristocratic democracies.

The emergence of nationalism, not just the fanatical nationalism of politicians, intellectuals, and zealots, but a sense of nationality and an affirmative feeling for one's own country, is a very important aspect of this process of the incorporation of the mass of the population into the central institutional and value systems. The more passionate type of nationalism is an unpleasant and heroic manifestation of this deeper growth of civility.

IX

None the less, this greater incorporation carries with it also an inherent tension. Those who participate in the central institutional and value systems — who feel sufficiently closer to the center now than their forebears ever did — also feel their position as outsiders, their remoteness from the center, in a way in which their forebears probably did not feel it. The modern trade union movement, which has disappointed those whose revolutionary hopes were to be supported by the organized working classes, illustrates this development. The leaders of the trade unions have come to be part of the central institutional system and accordingly, at least in part, they fulfill the obligations which are inherent in the action within that system. At the same time, the unions' rank and file members also have come to share more widely and intensely in the central value system and to affirm more deeply and continuously than in the past the central institutional system. Nonetheless, the leaders, deriving from sections of the society which have felt themselves to be outside the prevailing society, still and necessarily carry traces of that position in their outlook; the rank and file, less involved in the central institutional system than the leadership, experience even more acutely their position as outsiders vis-à-vis the central value system. The more sensitive among them are the most difficult for the leaders of the unions to hold in check.

Parallel with this incorporation of the mass of the population into society — halting, spotty, and imperfect as this incorporation is — has gone a change in the attitudes of the ruling classes of the modern states of the West. (In Asia and Africa, the process is even more fragmentary, corresponding to the greater fragmentariness of the incorporation of the masses into those societies.) In the modern Western states, the ruling classes have come increasingly to acknowledge the dispersion, into the wider reaches of the society, of the charisma which informs the center. The qualities which account for the expansiveness of authority have come to be shared more widely by the population, far from the center in which the incumbents of the positions of authority reside. In the eyes of the elites of the modern states of the West, the mass of the population have somehow come to share in the vital connection with the 'order' which inheres in the central value system and which was once thought to be in the special custody of the ruling classes.

The elites are, of course, more responsive to sectors of society which have voting powers and, therewith, legislative power, and which possess agitational and purchasing powers as well. These would make them simulate respect for the populace even where they did not feel it. Mixed with this simulated respect, however, is a genuine respect for the mass of the population as bearers of a true individuality, and a genuine, even if still limited, appreciation of their intrinsic worth as fellow members of the civil society and, in the deepest sense, as vessels of the charisma which lives at the center of society.

X

There is a limit to consensus. However comprehensive the spread of consensus, it can never be all-embracing. A differentiated large-scale society will always be compelled by professional specialization, tradition, the normal distribution of human capacities, and an inevitable anti-nomianism to submit to inequalities in participation in the central value system. Some persons will always be a bit closer to the center; some will always be more distant from the center.

Nonetheless, the expansion of individuality attendant on the growth of individual freedom and opportunity, and the greater density of communications, have contributed greatly to narrowing the range of inequality. The peak at the center is no longer so high; the periphery is no longer so distant.

The individuality which has underlain the entry into the consensus around the central value system might in the end also be endangered by it. Liberty and privacy live on islands in a consensual sea. When the tide rises they may be engulfed. This is another instance of the dialectical relationships among consensus, indifference, and alienation, but further consideration must be left for another occasion.

17   The social cohesion of liberal democracy

Michael Mann

[...] The theoretical orthodoxy of those I loosely term 'consensus theorists' is to be found in this quotation from an editorial introduction to an American symposium on political socialization:

> Political socialization refers to the learning process by which the political norms and behaviors acceptable to an ongoing political system are transmitted from generation to generation ... A well-functioning citizen is one who accepts (internalizes) society's political norms ... Without a body politic so in harmony with the ongoing political values, a political system would have trouble functioning smoothly ... (Sigel, 1965:1; for a similar statement see Rose, 1965:29).

Using such an approach, several well-known studies have argued that the stability and 'success' of democratic societies depend on the sharing of general political and propolitical values. [...] Thus, Dahl (1967: 329–30), reviewing previous studies, concludes that 'Americans ordinarily agree on a great many questions that in some countries have polarized the citizenry into antagonistic camps. One consequence of this massive convergence of attitudes is that political contests do not usually involve serious threats to the way of life of significant strata in the community,' while Rose has stated: 'enduring consensus is one of the most distinctive features of politics in England' (1969:3; see also his 1965 work).

We now might ask 'what is this consensus about?' And here different writers would produce different answers. First, there are those who stress the commitment of social members to *ultimate values*, of which examples might be generalized beliefs in equality and achievement (Lipset, 1964). Others, however, stress commitment to social *norms*, of which well-known examples are an adherence to the 'rules of the democratic game' and opposition to those who introduce strong conflictual elements (such as class ideology) into politics (Dahl, 1967;

Source: *American Sociological Review*, vol. 35, no. 3, June 1970, extracts from pp. 423–32, 435–9.

McKenzie and Silver, 1968). Finally, there are writers who stress commitment to *beliefs* about how society is actually organized. [. . .]

Just as no consensus theorist would posit the existence of complete harmony, no Marxist would claim that complete disharmony character- ized society. He would admit, firstly, that some form of social co- operation is necessary in the pursuit of scarcity, and, secondly, that subordinate classes within society always appear to 'accept' their position at least to some extent (Giddens, 1968: 269). Yet the precise meaning of this word 'accept' has greatly troubled Marxists. We must distinguish two types of acceptance: *pragmatic* acceptance, where the individual complies because he perceives no realistic alternative, and *normative* acceptance, where the individual internalizes the moral expectations of the ruling class and views his own inferior position as legitimate. Though pragmatic acceptance is easy to accommodate to Marxism, normative acceptance is not, and the unfortunate popularity of the latter concept has contributed to the inadequacies of much modern Marxist theory. [. . .]

We are now in a position to derive testable propositions from each of the broad theoretical positions described above. The crucial questions are empirical: *to what extent do the various classes in society internalize norms, values and beliefs which legitimate the social order? And, do such norms, values and beliefs constitute true or false consciousness*, as defined above? Present sociological writings offer no coherent answer to these questions. [. . .]

The data

The data consist of a variety of findings from other writers' empirical investigations into value-commitment in Britain and the United States. The values, norms, and beliefs analyzed here are all ones supporting, or destructive of, the present social structure of those countries. Most concentrate on issues regarding the legitimacy of the social stratification system. Following Parkin (1967), I have labeled supporting values *dominant*, and destructive values *deviant*. Dominant values are generally promulgated by ruling groups to legitimate their rule; deviant values, by groups contesting that legitimacy.

Nearly all the results used here consist of responses to agree-disagree questions. They are presented in Tables 1 to 4. [Only Tables 17.1 and 17.2 are reproduced in this extract.] The first column of these tables contains the investigator's name and reference, together with references to other studies which produced similar findings. The second column gives brief details of the sample used, and the third column gives the gist of the question asked. The fourth column gives details of sub-samples where available. This paper gives only the subsamples corresponding to the broad occupational stratification hierarchy in liberal democracies, with the groups presented in descending order. The term 'class' will be loosely used in the text to describe the main groups, though the authors of the studies themselves use a variety of terms. The fifth column shows the percentage agreement among the sample to the question. The final column presents a classification system designed to show briefly which, if any, theory the finding tends to support. If 75% or more of respondents agree with a dominant value, the final column contains 'Dominant Consensus.' If 75% agree with a deviant value, this is labeled 'Deviant Consensus.' Obviously, 75% is an arbitrary cutoff point between consensus and dissensus, but its general level seems not unreasonable. [...]

Results

In this section we analyze respondents' views on the legitimacy of social structure, and particularly class structure, in Britain and the United States. As the principal function of a social stratification system is to regulate the distribution of scarce resources, we will start by observing how much people, particularly working-class people, want those scarce resources.

Sociological studies of 'achievement motivation' are our first pieces of evidence. Several have shown that almost all persons, of whatever class, will agree with statements like 'It is important to get ahead' (Scanzoni, 1967:456; Mizruchi, 1964:95; Veness, 1962:153), and some useful pointers to what respondents mean by this are now emerging. Most important, working-class people are more likely than middle-class people to think of success as achieved solely in the occupational sphere, and are more likely to conceive of it as materialistic, economic success (Mizruchi, 1964:77-90). The crucial question then is 'Can their economic aspirations be met, given the constraints of the stratified occupational system?' There is evidence that the answer to this is 'No.' In a comparative analysis of British and American schoolboys, Stephenson demonstrated that the lower the social class of the boy, the more his occupational aspirations outran his occupational expectations. Thus, later on it is the working-class pupils 'who lower most their aspirations when it comes to considering plans or expectations' in the occupational sphere (Stephenson, 1958:49, for supporting evidence see Caro and Pihlblad, 1965). This process seems to continue in the world of work itself. It has been a frequent research finding in industrial sociology that,

Table 17.1 The legitimacy of the opportunity structure

Author	Sample	Statement	Subsample	% Agreement	Classification
Mizruchi (1964:82) (cf. Berelson et al., 1954:58; Lenski, 1963:165)	U.S. small town adults	Ability determines who gets ahead	(a) Social classes I–III (b) Social classes IV, V	97 92	Dominant Consensus
Veness (1962:144)	(a) English boys and girls aged 13–17, representative national sample	Hard work (and not luck or influence) is how to get on	(a) Grammar school (b) Technical school (c) Modern school	88 93 88	Dominant Consensus
	(b) Boys only	Status achieved by effort in children's essays	(a) Grammar school (b) Technical school (c) Modern school	79 63 30	Dissensus between classes
Kornhauser (1965: 210)	U.S. male workers	Luck and 'pull' determine who gets ahead	(a) White collar workers (b) Nonfactory workers (c) All factory workers (including d and e)	13 26 36	Dissensus between classes
			(d) Small town factory workers	32	Dominant consensus in middle class
			(e) Routine production workers	50	
Blauner (1964:206)	U.S. factory workers, national sample	'Cynical' factors determine promotion in own organization	Ditto	39	Dominant Dissensus
Mercer & Weir (1969: 122)	English male clerical and technical workers, large town	Ditto	Ditto	28	Dominant Dissensus
McKenzie & Silver (1968:140)	English urban working class. Labour and Conservative voters only	Too hard for a man with ambition to get ahead	Ditto	51	Dissensus

in identical jobs, older workers are more satisfied than younger ones. The most probable explanation of this is Kornhauser's, applied to his own findings: 'men in the routine types of work come over the years to accept and make the most of their situation' (1965:77). From a very early age the lower class person begins to realize that he is at the bottom of a stratification hierarchy (Bettelheim and Sylvester, 1950; Himmelweit et al., 1952). Probably starting with universalistic achievement values, he gradually redefines his aspirations in a more and more role-specific way, so that his lot can become acceptable.

The nature of this 'acceptance' is, of course, crucial as I argued earlier. Does this redefinition of goals lead to normative or to pragmatic acceptance? One test of this is the extent to which lower classes regard as legitimate the opportunity structure which has disadvantaged them. In this respect, dominant values are clear: success comes to those whose energies and abilities deserve it, failures have only themselves to blame. Is this argument accepted by lower class persons? Table 17.1 provides an answer.

We can see that, by and large, the sample hold dominant beliefs about the opportunity structure. Though these results show clearly the biasing effects of leading questions, almost all respondents endorse the key cues of 'ability' and 'hard work' while much smaller numbers endorse 'luck,' 'pull' and 'too hard for a man.' Yet there are slight indications here that these beliefs might not be of great significance for the respondents. Thus the Blauner and the Mercer and Weir studies show that respondents are more likely to be cynical about the opportunity structure that confronts them in their actual working lives. This kind of interpretation is strengthened by the Veness (1962) findings. These are based on schoolchildren's essays describing imaginary 'successes' in future life. Very large class differences emerge in the essays. In the essays of the grammar and technical schoolboys (destined for the most part for occupational success), success and status are seen as coming from steady achievements in the occupational sphere. In those of the secondary modern boys (the future manual workers), however, the idea of cumulative status is usually absent, and, instead, success comes from either a quiet, happy life or sudden fame in sport and entertainment. From this, it seems probable that, though lower class children may endorse general platitudes about the importance of ambition, these have little actual relevance for their own life-projects. Turner (1964), in his study of American high-school seniors, also comes to this conclusion, stressing that we can only assess the importance of values in society by considering their *relevance* to people's lives.

For further tests of our theories we can turn to respondents' images of the entire social structure to see whether *they* hold to theories of

Table 17.2 Harmonistic and conflictual images of society

Author	Sample	Statement	Subsample	% Agreement	Classification
Form & Rytina (1969:23)	U.S. adults, medium town (the 'analytic sample')	Holding pluralist models of society rather than class or power elite models	(a) Rich (b) Middle (c) Poor	65 59 57	Borderline Dissensus Class differences not significant
Lewis (1964-5:176)	U.S. white males, medium town	Rating U.S. citizenship more important than class membership	Ditto	'Almost' 90	Dominant Consensus
Manis & Meltzer (1954:33–5)	U.S. male textile workers, medium town with history of labor disputes	(a) Social classes are inevitable and desirable	Ditto	56	Dissensus
		(b) Social classes are *either* enemies or in conflict, *or* partners or in paternalistic relationship	Ditto	33 ⎤ 46 ⎦	Dissensus
Leggett (1964:230)	U.S. male manual workers, metropolis	The rich get the profits	(a) Employed (b) Unemployed	62 76	Deviant Dissensus
McClosky (1964:370)	U.S. national ('general electorate') sample	(a) The laws are rich man's laws	Ditto	33	Dominant
		(b) Poor man doesn't have a chance in the law courts		43	Dissensus

Source	Sample	Statement	Group	%	Classification
Kornhauser (1965: 220) (cf. Haer, 1956–7:140; Lipsitz, 1964:957)	U.S. male workers	Big business has too much power	(a) White collar workers	54	Dissensus between classes
			(b) All factory workers	79	Deviant consensus within lower class
Nordlinger (1967:178)	English male urban manual workers*	Class conflict is important in England	Ditto	55	Dissensus
McKenzie & Silver (1968:135) (cf. Cannon, 1967:168)	English urban workers, Labour and Conservative voters only	Upper class has always tried to exploit working class	Ditto	51	Dissensus
Goldthorpe et al. (1968b:26)	English affluent workers, medium town	The laws favor the rich	(a) White collar	59	Virtual deviant
			(b) Manual workers	72	Dissensus
Mercer & Weir (1969:121)	English male clerical and technical workers, large town	Management and workers are a team, and not on opposite sides	Ditto	54	Dissensus
Goldthorpe et al. (1968a:73, 85)	As above	(a) Ditto	(a) White collar	76	Dominant
			(b) Manual workers	67	Dissensus
		(b) Work study engineers are antiworker	Manual workers only	55	Dissensus
Goldthorpe et al. (1968b:26) (cf. Cannon, 1967: 168; McKenzie & Silver, 1968:127)	As above	(a) Big business has too much power	(a) White collar	63	Deviant
			(b) Manual workers	60	Dissensus
		(b) Trade unions have too much power	(a) White collar	72	Dissensus between classes
			(b) Manual workers	43	

* As only one-third of manual workers vote Conservative, the Conservative bias of this sample has been removed by weighting double the % of Labour voters in all cases.

harmony or conflict. Table 17.2 presents the relevant findings.

This mass of conflicting results permits no easy generalizations. It is true that significant class differences in the direction predicted by Marxist theory emerge in several parts of this table. But not even the statement 'Big business has too much power' evokes deviant consensus among the working class of both countries. In only two other cases is there even a clear majority for a deviant value among the working class: for 'The rich get all the profits' and (probably) for 'The laws favour the rich.' And when we examine these most favoured statements we see that none mentions 'class' and all are couched in what might be termed simplistic 'common man' language. By contrast in Table 17.2, all the more abstract and sophisticated models of society evoke less support, whether they be basically dominant or deviant in content. We may note, for example, in the studies of Form and Rytina (1969) and of Manis and Meltzer (1954) that dissensus results from presenting alternative abstract theories of society to working-class respondents. Moreover, the single word 'class' produces dissensus among them whenever it occurs, except significantly when in the Lewis study it is decisively rejected in favor of nationality. This, then, is another problem to be faced later: why is the working class able and willing to produce deviant simplistic views of society but not deviant abstract ones? [...]

There seems to be a disjunction between general abstract values and concrete experience. Such a disjunction is the main theme of Free and Cantril's (1967) study of American political attitudes, and their evidence can advance our argument considerably. They asked respondents two series of questions to test their liberalism/conservatism, the first on specific issues of government intervention in favor of redistribution (which they term the 'operational' spectrum), the second on general issues of individualist versus interventionist philosophies (the 'ideological' spectrum). [...]

As the authors comment, the results are positively schizophrenic, with a large proportion of the electorate operationally liberal but ideologically conservative. Significantly, while manual workers are among the most schizoid groups (though Negroes are consistently liberal). Similar findings have also been reported by Selznick and Steinberg (1969:220). [...]

From all these findings four trends, which are in need of explanation, clearly emerge:

1   value consensus does not exist to any significant extent;
2   there is a greater degree of consensus among the middle class than among the working class;

3   the working class is more likely to support deviant values if those values relate either to concrete everyday life or to vague populist concepts than if they relate to an abstract political philosophy;
4   working-class individuals also exhibit less internal *consistency* in their values than middle-class people.

We can now return to our general theories with these trends in mind.

Discussion

If there is not value consensus, what remains of value consensus theory? Obviously the more extreme and generally stated versions of the theory are untenable, but many others have been rather more cautious, asserting merely that some 'minimum' level of consensus about certain 'critical' values is necessary to social cohesion. As this level is never precisely specified, we cannot very easily come to grips with the argument. Let us approach the problem by asking *why* some measure of consensus is considered necessary for social cohesion. The answer lies in one of sociology's most sacred tenets: that values are by definition beliefs governing action. As action itself must be considered nonrandom, and as men do actually cooperate with one another, then it would seem to follow that there is some degree of congruence between their values. This seems plausible, for if men cooperate they must come to some form of agreement, explicit or implicit, to share power. There is, of course, no such social contract which does not rest on shared normative understandings (Durkheim, 1964:206–19).

But when we consider whole complex societies, it is not clear that all social members can be considered as parties to the social contract. The ordinary participant's social relations are usually confined to a fairly narrow segment of society, and his relations with society as a whole are mostly indirect, through a series of overlapping primary and secondary groups. We may characterize his meaningful life as being largely on an everyday level. Thus his normative connections with the vast majority of fellow citizens may be extremely tenuous, and his commitment to general dominant and deviant values may be irrelevant to his compliance with the expectations of others. As long as he conforms to the very specific role behavior expected of him, the political authorities may not trouble themselves with his system of beliefs.

If this is so, we might develop the following hypothesis: *only those actually sharing in societal power need develop consistent societal values.* [...]

We have seen that two types of deviant values are widely endorsed by working-class people: first, values which are expressed in concrete terms corresponding to everyday reality, and, second, vague simplistic divisions of the social world into 'rich' and 'poor.' Everyday social conflict is experienced, and to some extent is referred to what Ossowski has described as the eternal struggle between 'rich' and 'poor,' 'rulers' and 'ruled,' 'idle drones' and 'worker bees' (Ossowski, 1963:19–30). But the one is concrete and the other is vague; there is no real political philosophy uniting the two in the working-class consciousness. Instead, at the political level are rather confused values with surprisingly conservative biases. How these political values come to be is of crucial theoretical importance, for it is their presence which keeps the working class from non-compliance in the political order. It is not value-consensus which keeps the working class compliant, but rather a *lack* of consensus in the crucial area where concrete experiences and vague populism might be translated into radical politics. Whether a harmonistic or a conflictual theory can best account for their compliance now turns on whether this lack of consensus is 'free' or 'manipulated,' on how it is produced. Though we need more studies of the operation of socialization processes, at least one of them, the school system, has been extensively studied.

Studies of the school systems of Britain and the United States have generally concluded that the school is a transmitter of political conservatism, particularly to the working class. Hess and Torney (1967) find that the school is the most important political socialization agency for the young child, and that its efforts are directed toward the cultivation of nationalism and a benevolent image of established political authority. [...] As Litt puts it, politics is presented as a 'formal mechanistic set of government institutions with the emphasis on its harmonious legitimate nature rather than as a vehicle for group struggle and change' (1963:73). Abrams (1963) comes to a similar conclusion from his review of textbooks used in British schools: he notes that they often try to avoid mentioning non-benevolent occurrences such as economic slumps or industrial conflict, and where they cannot avoid them, the events are presented as 'just happening' with no real attempt at explanation. [...]

We must be careful to specify the limits of this indoctrination. It is rarely direct, though the daily oath to the U.S. flag, or the granting of holidays to children in Britain if they will cheer visiting royalty, clearly come into this category. More usually, dominant-deviant issues are not presented at all to children. The essential point is 'the realities of the political process' (to use Litt's phrase) and the populist deviant tradition of the lower class are ignored in the classroom. Presumably the working-class child learns the latter from his family and peers; certainly he experiences something of the former when he enters the world of work, so his manipulated socialization is only partial. We may aptly describe these socialization processes as the mobilization of bias (the phrase of Bachrach and Baratz, 1962). [...] Hence we can see agencies of political radicalism, like the trade unions and the British Labour Party, struggling against their opponents' ability to mobilize the national and feudal symbols to which the population has been taught to respond loyally in schools and in much of the mass media (McKenzie and Silver, 1968:245). Thus the most common form of manipulative socialization by the liberal democratic state does not seek to change values, but rather to perpetuate values that do not aid the working class to interpret the reality it actually experiences. These values merely deny the existence of group and class conflict within the nation-state society and, therefore, are demonstrably false.

Thus there are strong suggestions that the necessary mixed model of social cohesion in liberal democracy should be based more on Marxist conflict theory than sociologists have usually thought. A significant measure of consensus and normative harmony may be necessary among ruling groups, but it is the absence of consensus among lower classes which keeps them compliant. And if we wish to explain this lack of consensus, we must rely to some extent on the Marxist theories of *pragmatic role acceptance* and *manipulative socialization*. Of course, the existence of contrary harmonistic processes is feasible. Alongside coercive processes there may exist elements of voluntary deference, nationalism, and other components of normative integration in liberal democracy. It is often difficult to distinguish the two. Yet sociologists can no longer assert that these elements produce value consensus between social members and value consistency within them. Thus whatever 'legitimacy' liberal democracy possesses is not conferred upon it by value consensus, for this does not exist.

However, these results do not contradict all such affirmations of the legitimacy of social structure. Though I have demonstrated the existence of present-day false consciousness, this is insufficient as a total explanation of pragmatic role acceptance. For the reason why most working-class people do 'accept' (in whatever sense) their lot and do not have consistent deviant ideologies, we must look back to the historical incorporation of working-class political and industrial movements in the 19th and 20th centuries within existing structures. Dahl's historical analysis would lead to the same conclusion as that of Marcuse, that the institutionalization of class conflict has resulted in a closing of the 'political universe.' But, of course, whereas Marcuse stresses that this process was itself dominated by the manipulative practices of the ruling class, Dahl has stressed its elements of genuine and voluntary compromise. Clearly, the historical as well as the present-day theory must be a 'mixed' one. Yet one obstacle to the development of a more precise mixed theory in the past has been the failure of most sociologists to take the Marxist tradition in social theory seriously. In particular, they have dismissed the crucial concept of 'false consciousness' as being non-scientific. Yet in this paper we have seen fulfilled two of the preconditions for an empirically-grounded theory of false consciousness. First, we saw quite clearly a conflict between dominant and deviant values taking place within the individual. Second, we found some evidence of the alternative precondition, the actual indoctrination of dominant values. Thus the third precondition, the ranking of conflicting values by an analysis of 'who gains and who loses', can be investigated, and some relevant suggestions have been made here. The central argument of this paper is that the debate between harmonistic theories and Marxist theories must be an empirical one. The way is open to further empirical investigations.

References

Abrams, P. 1963, 'Notes on the uses of ignorance,' *Twentieth Century* (Autumn):67–77.

Bachrach, P. and M. S. Baratz, 1962, 'Two faces of power,' *American Political Science Review*, 56:947–52.

Berelson, B. R., P. F. Lazarsfeld, and W. N. McPhee, 1954, *Voting*, University of Chicago Press.

Bettelheim, B. and E. Sylvester, 1950, 'Notes on the impact of parental occupations,' *American Journal of Orthopsychiatry*, 20:785–95.

Blauner, R., 1964, *Alienation and Freedom*, Chicago University Press.

Cannon, I. C., 1967, 'Ideology and occupational community: a study of compositors,' *Sociology*, 1:165–85.

Caro, F. G. and C. T. Pihlblad, 1965, 'Aspirations and expectations,' *Sociology and Social Research*, 49:465–75.

Dahl, R. A., 1967, *Pluralist Democracy in the United States: Conflict and Consent*, Chicago: Rand McNally.

Durkheim, E., 1964, *The Division of Labor in Society*, New York: Free Press.

Form, W. H. and J. Rytina, 1969, 'Ideological beliefs on the distribution of power in the United States,' *American Sociological Review*, 34:19–31.

Free, L. A. and H. Cantril, 1967, *The Political Beliefs of Americans*, Rutgers University Press.

Giddens, A., 1968, '"Power" in the recent writings of Talcott Parsons,' *Sociology*, 2 (September):257–72.

Goldthorpe, J. H., D. Lockwood, F. Bechhofer, and S. Platt, 1968a, *The Affluent Worker: Industrial Attitudes and Behaviour*, Cambridge University Press.

Goldthorpe, J. H., D. Lockwood, F. Bechhofer, and S. Platt, 1968b, *The Affluent Worker: Political Attitudes and Behaviour*, Cambridge University Press.
Haer, J. L., 1956-7, 'Social stratification in relation to attitude toward sources of power in a community,' *Social Forces*, 35:137-42.
Hess, R. D. and J. V. Torney, 1967, *The Development of Political Attitudes in Children*, Chicago: Aldine.
Himmelweit, H., A. H. Halsey, and A. N. Oppenheim, 1952, 'The views of adolescents on some aspects of the social class structure,' *British Journal of Sociology*, 3:148-72.
Kornhauser, W., 1965, *The Mental Health of the Industrial Worker*, New York: Wiley.
Leggett, J. C., 1964, 'Economic insecurity and working-class consciousness,' *American Sociological Review*, 29:226-34.
Lenski, G., 1963, *The Religious Factor*, New York: Anchor Books.
Lewis, L. S., 1964-5, 'Class consciousness and the salience of class,' *Sociology and Social Research*, 49:173-82.
Lipset, S. M., 1964, *First New Nation*, London: Heinemann.
Lipsitz, L., 1964, 'Work life and political attitudes: a study of manual workers,' *American Political Science Review*, 58:951-62.
Litt, E., 1963, 'Civic education, community norms and political indoctrination,' *American Sociological Review*, 28:69-75.
McClosky, H., 1964, 'Consensus and ideology in American politics,' *American Political Science Review*, 58:361-82.
McKenzie, R. and A. Silver, 1968, *Angels in Marble: Working-class Conservatives in Urban England*, London: Heinemann.
Manis, J. G. and B. N. Meltzer, 1954, 'Attitudes of textile workers to class structure,' *American Journal of Sociology*, 60:30-5.
Marcuse, H., 1964, *One-Dimensional Man*, London: Routledge & Kegan Paul.
Mercer, D. E. and D. T. H. Weir, 1969, 'Orientations to work among white collar workers,' in Social Science Research Council (eds), *Social Stratification and Industrial Relations*, Cambridge: Social Science Research Council, pp. 112-45.
Mizruchi, E. H., 1964, *Success and Opportunity*, New York: Free Press.
Nordlinger, E. A., 1967, *The Working Class Tories*, London: MacGibbon & Kee.
Ossowski, S., 1963, *Class Structure in the Social Consciousness*, London: Routledge & Kegan Paul.
Parkin, F., 1967, 'Working class conservatives: A theory of political deviance,' *British Journal of Sociology*, 18:278-90.
Rose, R., 1965, *Politics in England*, London: Faber.
Rose, R., 1969, *Studies in British Politics*, London: Macmillan, 2nd ed.
Scanzoni, J., 1967, 'Socialization, *n* achievement and achievement values,' *American Sociological Review*, 32:449-56.
Selznick, G. J. and S. Steinberg, 1969, 'Social class, ideology, and voting preference,' in C. S. Heller (ed.), *Structured Social Inequality*, New York: Macmillan, pp. 216-26.

Sigel, R., 1965, 'Assumptions about the learning of political values,' *Annals of the American Academy of Political and Social Science*, 361:1-9.

Stephenson, R. M., 1958, 'Stratification, education and occupational orientation,' *British Journal of Sociology*, 5:42-52.

Turner, R., 1964, *The Social Context of Ambition*, San Francisco: Chandler.

Veness, T., 1962, *School Leavers: their Aspirations and Expectations*, London: Methuen.

18   The structured communication of events

Stuart Hall

In modern advanced capitalist industrial democracies, such as Britain
today, mass communications systems play a critical ideological role.
The only comparable institution in earlier times would have been the
Church, in the period when Catholicism was the only universal religious
institution, integrating, within a common set of beliefs, practices and
doctrines, and through its hierarchy, offices and organizations, the
mightiest and the lowliest in the land into a single religious system.
Considered 'sociologically', the modern mass media help to integrate
the different regions, classes and cultures of a complex society like
Britain — if only by providing one region or class with information
about and images of how 'the others live' and how important events
affect them. This is a critical function, since our society is complex and
diverse and it is difficult for the mass of the population, who are not at
the centre of power and decision-making, to get — from their own
limited, differentiated experience — some knowledge of trends, movements and developments in British society *as a whole*. Compared with
other similar societies in western Europe and North America, the
British system of mass communications (taking the national press and
the broadcasting authorities together) is very densely concentrated.
Not only 'news' and 'information', but images and a sense of what is
relevant or 'important' — what is preoccupying the nation today — knit
British society together from Land's End to John O'Groats every day.
Through their choice of what to report and what to show, the media
help to 'set the agenda' of public issues each day — and, by and large,
to set it *nationally*. Of course, when we say that the media help to
'integrate' society, we must mean simply that they maximize the
knowledge of and contact between different and varying groups in
society. It used to take weeks for 'news' to reach outlying regions from
London, and perhaps months for a Papal Bull to reach the English

Source: This is an extensively revised and updated (1981) version of an
article which first appeared, under the same title, in *Getting the Message
Across*, Paris, © Unesco, 1965. Stuart Hall is Professor of Sociology,
The Open University.

269

province of the Catholic Church from Rome. It doesn't necessarily follow that, because people are now 'in contact' with each other, and with the centre, that they therefore 'agree' with each other more. The 'news' that unemployment is considerably higher in the North-West or in Scotland than it is in the South-East gives people a better picture of the employment patterns across the country as a whole. It may not necessarily make people in Glasgow feel more 'bound to' or 'in common with' those who are faring considerably better than they are, elsewhere.

When we speak of 'news' and 'better informed', we must bear in mind what *kind* of information this is. First, it is 'news' in the narrow sense: actual information about what is happening in Britain and in the world. But it is also 'images' and 'pictures' of the world which we receive – and these are a powerful stimulus to knowledge. Then it is 'knowledge' about how people behave, what they are thinking and talking about, how fashions – in clothes, or life-styles or speech or ideas – are changing. Finally, it is 'news' about how opinions *about* events are changing. It would be better to call all this, not 'information' in the strictest sense, but *practical social knowledge*. We may 'learn' as much about what we think northern working-class communities are like from watching *Coronation Street* – though we don't go to it for 'information' or to be 'educated' – as we do from *Nationwide* (which probably contains more 'entertainment' than 'hard news').[1] Rather than saying, simply, that the media 'inform and educate', it would be better to say that they add to and shape our general social knowledge – our 'pictures of the world' – about events in our society and other places.

Again, looked at 'sociologically', the mass media bridge a number of crucial gaps in our society. The kind of 'social knowledge' which the media transmit connects what may be broadly defined as two divided groups in society. First, it bridges the distance between the 'powerful' and the 'powerless'. The mass of the media audience is composed of ordinary citizens who have little day-to-day access to or information about high policy and strategy, or decisions and events which are likely, sooner or later, to affect their lives in a very immediate way. Second, it bridges the distance between those who are 'in the know' – the 'informed' – and those who are, in terms of how power operates, 'ignorant'. We have spoken of these as two, apparently different, groups. But you will see that they frequently overlap. Those who take national decisions every day also tend, for complex reasons, to be more 'in the know'. Those who don't may be well educated, but they don't have much access to the sort of privileged knowledge we are talking about here. Another way of putting this point is to say that the mass media operate within and are shaped by the way *power* and *knowledge* are distributed (unevenly) across society.

In this article we are particularly concerned with 'news' (broadly defined) about major national or international events – events with a political, industrial or social significance.[2] A substantial proportion of media time and massive technical, social and financial resources are given over, in our media systems, to this area of 'practical social knowledge'. But what is 'news' – who says that what we get *is* 'the news'? We can look at this question in two ways. First, by way of a general definition; then, in terms of the practice of those who package information and knowledge into news. Metaphorically, we can imagine a 'steady state' in the world, where, between one day and another, absolutely *nothing* changes. Life goes on exactly as it did before. In the strict sense, there would be nothing 'new' to report. And there is an apocryphal story that, in the days of Lord Reith when BBC news announcers still appeared in dinner jackets and black bow ties, an announcer *did* indeed appear one night and say, 'There is no news today.' The point is that 'news' is, literally, information about *how things have changed* since we last took stock of the state of the world. Usually, though not always, changed *for the worse*. That is why there is so little 'Good News' and why Bad News is almost always 'news'. Of course, this news about changes, new developments, may take different forms. It may tell us about something which is a bolt from the blue – totally unexpected: an earthquake in southern Italy and its consequences. It may tell us about a shift of direction in something we already know about: the resumption of hostilities in the Middle East or a new turn in the Government's economic strategy. It may tell us about something which is everyday in other places, but 'news' to us: Did you know that there are still millions starving in Kampuchea? Did you know that thousands of Palestinians are still living in transit camps? Whatever it is, the news will come to us as something rather unexpected, something out of the ordinary, unpredictable. It breaches the ordinary expectation in the back of our minds that 'things are simply going on as they were before'. In this sense, the news may prepare us for changes in the world – but it almost always 'surprises' us to some degree (and therefore perhaps un-nerves us, because the world always turns out to be less stable, predictable and safe than we expected or hoped).

This general definition helps to explain the practice of newsmen and journalists, and the 'news values' which they use to select what and what not to tell us about.[3] If the news is about change – then the biggest, most dramatic, most unexpected, most far-reaching changes will be the most important 'news items'. Natural or human disasters which affect large numbers of people, conflicts which break out into open violence, dramatic shifts in policy or in who holds power, the dramatic rise and fall of important people and governments, major breakthroughs, unexpected resolutions or compromises tend to float 'naturally' to the top of the news agenda. Against the stable background of a world in 'steady state', disaster, conflict, controversy and sudden reversals will always rank high in what is considered 'newsworthy'. There is no point in blaming the news-reader because what he or she tells us disturbs the even tenor of our lives. Dramatic shifts of direction is the main criterion of 'newsworthiness'; but it isn't the only one. The news is also *ethnocentric*: a disaster in foreign places, which doesn't involve Britain, will rank lower than a lesser disaster which touches this country directly, because it is less relevant to us (or so news editors judge). You know the joke about the news report which ran, 'Thousands die in earthquake disaster. Three Englishmen injured.' It has more than a grain of truth to it. The news is also strongly oriented to power and to powerful or prominent people and personalities. Power, of course, matters, since a powerful decision taken by twenty people in the Cabinet room may have consequences for the whole population. So the news is fascinated by power — and by people who wield power, including the sort of power that attaches to prominent personalities like sports-people or entertainers. Some parts of the news will have a more 'celebratory' character — even if no dramatic turn of events is involved. National occasions, like the State opening of Parliament — rituals which involve the public with the symbolic life of the powerful and the nation — will rate a place in the news, though they involve nothing unusual, and happen regularly, to time, every year. But the single, most important cluster of news values is that which includes disaster, conflict, controversy, change and dramatic reversals, and violence.[4]

Now there are a number of operational fictions about this process of 'providing social knowledge' in our society. I want, briefly, to consider two. The first operational fiction is that this kind of information is, essentially, *factual* or largely based on fact. Because television, especially, can transmit not only information *about*, but actual 'live' pictures of, events in the world, it is widely considered to 'show us what actually happens', to open a 'window on the world', and to bring us knowledge relatively 'pure', uncontaminated by opinion. This is what we might call the naturalistic view of television information. It is therefore held to contribute to the 'free flow', or circulation of information in our society. This notion of 'free flow', in turn, is underpinned and reinforced by the substantial constraints which are placed on broadcasters in our system, in order to ensure that they don't contaminate 'the facts' illegitimately with their own opinions. These constraints are enshrined in the requirements that this sort of information on television must be 'objective', 'balanced' and 'impartial'.[5] 'Objectivity' means that the broadcasters must report what they think or discover are the 'facts of the case', and not mix them up with their personal views about it. 'Balanced' means that, if there are two sides to a question, or two major opinions about it, these must be given a fair hearing. 'Impartial' means, however, that even though each side to a controversy may express a very strongly held view, the *broadcaster* must not get involved in judging between them, or expressing a personal view about which side is right. These operational fictions and practices are intended to prevent broadcasting, which is a powerful instrument, from playing an illegitimate role in influencing decisions about things which governments, politicians or the people ought to decide. It constrains the broadcaster from exploiting his or her powerful 'right to communicate'.

And since the day-to-day responsibilities for broadcasting rest with officials of the broadcasting companies and authorities, who are not (except for the respective chairpersons) political appointees or in the pay of the government, the constraints are held to secure two things: first, that broadcasting is 'independent' of the political system; second, that broadcasting can function as an independent source of information for the people, and operate (like the press) as a sort of 'fourth estate'.[6] Of course, in practice, these relations are subject to extensive and delicate negotiation. But on the whole, these factors, taken together, are held to ensure that broadcasting is a 'free, independent and accurate' source of practical social knowledge.

The alternative opinion is a minority one, but is strongly held in some quarters and has grown as a point of view in recent years. It demonstrates the massive opportunities which the broadcasters have to decide, select, present and communicate. It identifies the frequent recurrence of powerful views, favourably presented, on television, and the infrequent presentation of alternative or minority viewpoints. It points to the financial reliance of broadcasting on government, and the close relations between broadcasters and the powerful sources of their information. And it argues that, far from being independent, broadcasting is frequently and perhaps systematically 'biased' in its presentations.

In what follows, I want to consider the implications of these two views — 'free and independent' versus 'biased' — and to present an alternative. To sum up the argument briefly, at this stage: I would argue that there are several powerful reasons why the 'free and independent' picture is an *inadequate* way of understanding how broadcasting works and what it does — though it is not wholly wrong. I also want to argue that the simple notion of 'bias' — charging broadcasters with illegitimately expressing their own opinions or with 'tilting' the balance of the news — is also inadequate, though, again, not wholly incorrect. Instead, I want to replace *both* with a view of the communicative process as a necessarily *structured process*. By this I mean that communication of the kind I have been describing takes place within, and is therefore strongly influenced, shaped and determined by, the structures within which it functions. Second, that broadcasting is not a thing ('free' or 'biased') but a *process* – which takes place over time, involves certain patterned relations between the groups involved, depends on the way in which a number of social practices are linked together, and has certain predictable and identifiable kinds of outcome. These outcomes are not simple but complex. Nevertheless, they are not *random*. If we understand the structures, the relations, the practices, the ideas or ideologies which inform them, the conditions in which they operate, the other parts of society to which they are related, we can begin to identify those patterns – and thus understand better this type of communication as a social process. That is why I call the provision of social knowledge through broadcasting a *structured process*.

I now want to present a number of different aspects to support this argument.

Let us start with the 'free flow' of information – broadcasting as an 'open circuit'. It is true that broadcasting often reports on what people are doing and saying – and that this 'news' is transmitted back, via the media, to them and masses of other people like them. However, there is no sense in which the broadcasting institutions and the people, the audience, can be *equal* partners in this circular exchange. Broadcasters not only manage and monopolize the *means* (technical, social, financial) for finding out *and* for transmitting information. They must always constantly *select*.[7] There are millions of important events in the world occurring every minute. There is only half an hour of news, and perhaps ten major items. It is not only which item, in which order, but also *what aspect* of an event to report which is the broadcaster's responsibility. Every journalist's report passed back from the field is a selection from 'all that happened'. From this pool of information, only very few items can be selected. The reporter or cameraman has chosen one or two aspects to report on. From this, the news editors must select a few seconds, at most, to show. Items must be edited, shaped for the bulletin. They must be fitted to the length, style and format of programmes. Commentary and supporting pictures or information must be selected. The selected items must be ranked into an order. Links must be established between items. It is true that, in one sense, the 'news' passes from people back to them. It is even truer that it is the broadcasters who initiate and structure the circuit of communication – what they don't put into the circuit will not pass round. This process of 'initiating' communication is determinate and involves extensive editorial interventions, many practices of *shaping* and *selection* that are based not only on the technical means available but on *judgments* –

e.g. ideas of what is 'important' and 'relevant' and 'newsworthy' and 'dramatic', and what is not. What seems at first to be a naturalistic process (showing the world as it is) is now revealed as a very complex social practice: the practice of *making the news* − of *producing* information. What seems at first to be a perfect circle can now be seen as a circuit established between *unequally weighted* elements. Broadcasters communicate; audiences 'receive' their communications. 'Free flow' is really *structured* flow.

Let us look a little more closely at these practices of *producing* and *receiving* information. An event has taken place: a government has been overthrown. But how is that 'fact' to be shown? You cannot show it *all* − partly because it has probably been in preparation over many months, partly because there may have been no reporters on the spot during that time, partly because you can never film everything, partly because there isn't time to show everything, even if you had it. So perhaps a very few filmed sequences or shots, plus a very few minutes, at most, of reportage or commentary will have to 'stand' for the event in the bulletin: a few bursts of gunfire, plus a shot of tanks rolling into the courtyard of 'Government House', plus commentary. Of course, this is an accurate picture of 'how it happened' in the sense that the pictures are not fabricated and the reporter on the spot is telling us as accurately as possible 'what happened'. But in a larger sense − in terms of all that led up to the overthrow, the complex factors involved, the different issues and factions at work, its outcomes within the next few days, its long-term consequences for the balance of world power, its effects on our lives − almost everything of *significance* has had to be left out; and what *is* shown will have somehow to 'represent' what actually happened but can't be seen. Television cannot therefore 'mirror' or 'reflect' what happens in the world. It has to translate events into stories − words and pictures. Later on, in a Current Affairs documentary, things might be explored more fully, over a longer time-span (but even then, the representations remain necessarily selective and partial). What was reported in the first place will probably be re-shown and will constitute the 'factual basis' for, say, a studio discussion between different experts.[8] Television, then, cannot be comprehensively accurate − not because journalists are 'biased' but because it isn't possible, objectively. They must *represent* the world. They translate complex historical events into 'scenarios of action'. They must connect one event with another by the use of some implied explanatory logic. By definition, broadcasting is in the very complex business of making events in the world seem something. They produce meaning about the world. This is a *social*, not a natural, practice: the practice of signification.

But events in the world are notoriously ambiguous. They don't *mean* any one thing, on their own. Certainly the Soviet tanks *are* in Kabul — and the camera shows them to us. But what does the 'invasion of Afghanistan' mean? Soviet penetration or the result of covert American interference? A progressive or regressive move? Expansionist or defensive? Popular or unpopular in Afghanistan — and among whom, and how many? It doesn't matter, for your purposes, what you think about the Soviet invasion. You can be sure that, even if the same actual pictures are transmitted, the event will be differently 'represented' and mean something different on television in Moscow, Washington, London and Karachi. Very few 'facts' — especially about conflict or controversial events — ever reach us in the form of absolutely 'pure information'. We would not know what to do with them if they did. They are constantly made to mean something by being mapped into or placed in some *meaningful explanatory context.*[9] This is *not* the same thing as 'expressing an opinion'. The broadcaster may express no overt 'opinion' — certainly not his own view — but he *must* be making use of interpretive frameworks, otherwise the words and pictures would not make sense and the news would mean nothing to us. Producing the news means interpreting reality. Making things mean something is, by definition, an interpretive process. Whether they know it or not (or like it or not), broadcasters are constantly interpreting the world to us, defining the events they document, *defining reality*. This has little or nothing to do with overt or conscious bias. But it is also the case that the more unconscious these interpretive procedures are, the more we deny they exist, the less we reflect on where these interpretive schemas are drawn from and question the assumptions built in to them, *the more powerful they are*. They continue to shape and define reality — but they do so out of awareness and become 'taken-for-granted', and thus operate, as they say, 'behind men's backs'.

We can now consider the 'flow' of the communication circuit in a rather different way. Broadcasters define what is news, select the news, order, edit and shape it, translate events into their representative images, transpose happenings into a limited number of words and pictures to make up a 'story', and make use of interpretive schemas in order to define social reality to us. We call this the *encoding* process: news is not 'reality', but representations of reality encoded into messages and meanings.[10] It is, however, then often assumed that this *encoded reality* will pass in a transparent or unmediated way to the audience. The only breaks in this communication circuit are conceived to be circumstantial (is the audience watching?) and technical (can people literally understand what they are seeing and hearing? Is the editing too abrupt or sophisticated? Is the language too complex?). In fact, just as encoding reality is a social practice (or set of practices), so is 'receiving the message'. The audience or receiver must also deploy certain interpretive frameworks in order to 'get the message' and so 'take the meaning'. This, too, is not a natural but a *social* practice. Broadcaster and receiver must share a common language: the news in Chinese would make little sense on ITN. They must share the perceptual apparatus which allows the receiver to 'decode' the lines and dots transmitted by electronic impulse on a flat screen as 'representing' a recognizable set of objects and people in the world: that 'dark mass' *is* a Soviet tank. But, clearly, the audience must also share, to some degree, the interpretive frameworks or codes which the broadcaster is using, and a great deal of general social-knowledge-at-hand. If you don't know what the word 'inflation' means, or that there is a government strategy about it, what sense would you make of a few dots and lines on your screen, with a voice-over saying, 'There has been another sharp rise in inflation this month'? 'Soviet tanks rolled into Afghanistan today' will mean little or nothing without some sense that this affects the balance of power between East and West. The broadcaster will have to *assume* a great deal of background, contextual knowledge of this kind — he can't go back to the beginning of modern international relations each time there is a new turn of events. The broadcaster must assume this knowledge in the audience, and the audience will have to have it, to make sense of what is shown and heard. Meaning depends on the shared frameworks, shared codes, shared knowledge-in-use, shared interpretive frameworks between communicator and receiver. Otherwise, information will not pass from A to B — and there will be no circuit. If A 'encodes', then B (the audience) must 'decode'. Each is a social practice. Both depend on a massive background of shared assumptions.

In much of the news, much of the time, there *are* such shared perspectives. This is where we may make use, as a descriptive term, of the concept of *consensus*. The broadcaster takes-for-granted consensual background knowledge and frames of reference in the audience. But we must be careful not to extend this meaning too quickly to the other meaning of 'consensus' — to imply *agreement*. I may perfectly well understand what the Prime Minister is saying on the Nine O'Clock News. I just happen to disagree profoundly. There is a difference between understanding the *literal* meaning of words and images (denotative meaning), and either understanding or, more significantly, agreeing with the *interpretive* meaning (connotative). The line between these two is hard to draw precisely, but it is a useful practical distinction.[11] And you can see that there can be 'consensus' on the literal meaning at the same time as there is divergence or conflict about its interpretation. This is especially the case where what is being reported is *conflict* or *controversy* (the very heart of news) — above all, when it is conflict or controversy about important matters which touch, but also *divide*, the nation. For, in such cases, there is not likely to be much 'consensus', in the second sense, among different groups in the audience.

This affects very directly what we may call the 'objectivity' of the broadcaster. Where the broadcaster can assume a general consensus about an issue or event – both the broadcaster and the great majority of the nation have agreed to define the issue in *that* way – his 'objectivity' is secure. This may be, but isn't always, the case with foreign affairs. Would *anyone* have accused a BBC announcer of lacking 'objectivity' if he had described a German bomber brought down by anti-aircraft fire in 1940 as an 'enemy plane'? But the closer you get to home, and the more conflict or controversy is involved, the less the broadcaster can assume a 'consensus'. This is the broadcaster's dilemma – and, again, it doesn't have much to do with 'bias' as such. To call workers on strike 'militants' will be welcome to the Government (trying to keep wage demands low) and the employers (trying to keep production profitable and going) – and it may be accepted by a majority of the audience (who are adversely affected by strikes). For exactly the same reason, it will be seen as 'biased' by the union involved in the strike and deeply resented by the workers (who may have been reluctant to strike, and think they have a just cause).[12] The broadcaster cannot help but be caught in this crossfire.[13] Conflict and controversy is the daily bread of broadcasting. It is also the broadcaster's deadliest enemy, because it exposes the practice of 'making meaning' for what it is. It undermines the fiction of 'pure fact' and 'perfect objectivity' by showing that this objectivity rests on certain conditions (e.g. the existence of a consensus on an issue). When those conditions are not met, the conditional, problematic nature of broadcasting's 'objectivity' becomes visible.

Objectivity is another (more polite or convenient) name for *consensus*. The broadcaster can be 'objective', provided the consensus holds. When it breaks, he is in trouble. It also follows that, in order to preserve 'objectivity', broadcasting is constantly driven to take up a consensual position, to find consensus (even if it doesn't exist), and, when the chips are down, to produce consensus. If the broadcaster can presume that the majority believe all strikers are 'militants', he can use this interpretive category with impunity; but, on many issues, what the consensus actually *is* is extremely hard to determine. On controversial questions it is constantly shifting. It is influenced by many factors. In such cases, broadcasters are inevitably involved in the delicate work of assessing and judging where the 'balance of opinion' falls: or within what permissible *range*. In periods like the 1970s, when public opinion was shifting very markedly, this is a complicated affair. Broadcasters also decide who best expresses it, which viewpoints have to be represented by right, which are so marginal that they can be excluded. This task of exploring the consensus is made more difficult because conflict-situations often involve a struggle as to which 'definitions of the situation' will prevail. Some will inevitably benefit more than others from where the consensus is presumed to lie. To define a strike in terms of 'militancy', or picketing exclusively in terms of its 'violence', must bring aid and comfort to the Government and employers, and not to pickets or strikers. Again, this has little or nothing to do with 'bias'.

What's more, such 'definitions of the situation' *matter*. If they prevail, and become consensual, they may — for example — make people more willing to support anti-union legislation, more hostile to strikers. How people define situations affects what they do, what policies they are willing to support. Definitions therefore become factors in how conflicts are resolved. They affect the balance of social forces. But this is a critical stake in any struggle, for it affects the ability of one side or another to claim popular support for its policies, and to represent the 'national interest'. By assuming a certain definition as 'consensual', broadcasters will help to *make it more so* (a 'self-fulfilling prophecy'). If *every* strike is ascribed to 'union militancy', this will tend to become the prevailing, taken-for-granted definition. It will have become consensualized — a process, not a thing; and one in which broadcasting plays a determinate role. By 'shaping the consensus', broadcasting will have helped to *manufacture consent*. It can then be summoned up as an already established fact: 'The great majority of the British people are opposed to strikes and trade union militancy . . .' The contested proposition has become received wisdom. Opponents of this view will now have to argue their case against the background of an apparently universal agreement (consensus) that 'to strike is to be militant' (where 'militant' = bad, 'moderate' = good). I have chosen this example because the media language of industrial relations in the 1970s was saturated by the use of these two apparently descriptive, highly emotive and politically-charged words — the contrast between 'militants' and 'moderates'. The media come to have a vested interest — objectively — in 'the middle ground',[14] in *moderation*. It is in this sense that we can say that the media do not only reflect what the consensus is on any issue but help, in a number of ways, to construct consensus, to shape and influence it. It is a difficult fact of life for broadcasters to live with.

To return for a moment to the relation between communicating and receiving, 'encoding' and 'decoding': it can now be established that the 'communication' of social knowledge does not work like an open channel in which facts or events 'speak for themselves', and communications transmit the single, unproblematic meaning of them down the line, to be received in exactly the same way at the other end. Instead, broadcasters must interpret events, select the explanatory framework or context in which to set them, privilege or 'pre-fer' the meaning which seems to make sense to them, and thus encode a meaning. Audiences, like broadcasters, also stand in their own (very different) positions, relations and situations, have their own (again, different) relationship to power, to information, to sources, and bring *their* own frameworks of interpretation to bear in order to get a meaning, or *decode* the message. Rather than 'perfect transmission' or 'free flow', we can identify *three* optional typical positions in which an audience can stand to the meaning offered.[15] Audiences can take the meaning with which events have been imprinted and encoded. In that sense, they align their frameworks of interpretation with those of the communicators, and decode within the dominant, preferred or 'hegemonic' definition of events. Or they can take the global meaning which is offered, but make exceptions to it which modify it in the course of relating it to their own situation. An example here would be if an audience shares the dominant definition, 'Strikes are ruining the nation', but applies it to their situation in the form, 'However, *we* are badly paid and would be justified in going on strike for better wages'. Here, the dominant definition has been *negotiated*. Third, the dominant meaning may be perfectly understood, yet the meaning read or decoded in the opposite way. Someone on strike might well read that definition as, 'They *would* say that – it suits their book. I don't agree that strikes, rather than bad management or low investment, are the cause of our economic ills.' Here, the audience is decoding *oppositionally*. There is no way in which broadcasters can *ensure* that audiences will decode events within the hegemonic framework, even though they initiate the communication circuit and therefore have first go at 'making sense of the world'. There is, therefore, no 'perfect' communication, no pure transparency between source and receiver. The perfectly transparent medium would be the perfectly censored one – or one in which the only ideas available with which to make sense of the world were the *dominant* or 'ruling' ideas. Since events can mean more than one thing, and groups will define events differently according to their interests or social positions, and conflicts inevitably divide society precisely around which definition of social reality will or ought to prevail, mass communication systems in our sort of society will always remain what Enszensberger calls 'leaky systems'.

But now we must ask where the interpretive frameworks and the 'definitions of situations' which the broadcasters deploy *come from*? This is a more complex question than might first appear. The media are required to be 'balanced' as well as objective. This ensures that, with respect to any conflict or controversy, *more than one view* will be represented. In this sense, public affairs communication is structured very much on the model of the 'two-party system'. There are always at least two sides, two views – with the media as the neutral and impartial chairperson or 'Speaker' in the middle, moderating the debate. This prevents a single, monolithic view prevailing, and ensures a degree of pluralism or diversity. However, we need to explore further how 'balance' and 'impartiality' actually function in practice.

Since the broadcasters should, in the words of one important guideline, always be the last, if ever, to express a view, the views of a conflict which *are* represented must arise *outside* the media. On political events, they will be the views of the two major political party spokespeople: and they will be *quoted* (verbally or visually) – often verbatim, on camera – as a sort of witness to the broadcaster's objectivity. It is the 'Minister of Employment', not the BBC or ITN, who holds that 'Pickets are not typical, in fact they are very untypical of the way that the average British worker or trade unionist thinks.' On industrial disputes, both employers and trade unionists will also be given time to offer their definition of what is occurring. This does indeed preserve the broadcaster's impartiality. At the same time, it means that the established voices of powerful corporate groups will usually have, of right, the first opportunity, and at length, to define a conflict situation. The powerful become the 'primary definers' of conflict. They have access to the topic, they set the terms of the debate, they establish what is 'relevant' to the way the topic will be developed, and what is 'irrelevant'. Thus, in difficult economic circumstances, they can define a strike as 'threatening to an already weak economy'. This becomes the 'preferred' definition of it (consensual). Others, who (as we will show) necessarily come later, have to debate the issue *in these terms*. They will find it exceedingly difficult to establish, as an equally plausible way of debating a strike, the issue of 'low pay', or of 'comparability'. The *primary definition* of a topic carries enormous credibility and authority, and is hard to shift.

Of course, alternative views will also be represented. But they will tend to put a case *within the terms of reference* of the primary definition. It is much harder to break an existing set of reference-points and to set up an equally credible alternative. To take another example, if the definition of problems experienced by black groups in the society which prevails is, 'The cause of the problem is that there are too many of them over here', then the accredited alternative view is likely to be: 'The numbers are not as high as official sources say.' You will see that these views *differ*. You will also see that they also *agree*, in so far as they are operating on the same premise or assumption – that the problem *is a matter of numbers* (too high *v.* lower than is thought).

Race problems then become, by definition, *a problem of numbers*. Once this definition is in play, a hundred programmes will play infinite variations on this theme, without once challenging the underlying assumptions or the logic-in-use which flows from them. It would take an exceedingly long and skilful campaign to displace the problematic of the numbers game and replace it with an alternative framework — such as, 'The basic problem is not numbers but the hostility of whites towards blacks.'

Such radical shifts are few and far between. And when they occur, it tends to be because the terms have shifted within the élite itself, or because society is clearly evenly divided.[16] In the late 1970s, the dominant solution to our economic difficulties was said to be an 'incomes policy'. Since this was defined by the state as 'in the national interest', it was taken over, and provided the baseline for media coverage of a wide range of economic and industrial issues. Now that this panacea has been replaced by 'the need to control the money supply', it is *this* which provides the unstated premise of such media reporting. An interviewer would be judged impeccably impartial if she framed a question on the premise, 'Of course, since you can't exceed the Government's cash limits . . .' But this is because neo-Keynesianism, to which, in different ways, *both* Labour and Conservative Governments, pre-Mrs Thatcher, subscribed, has been replaced by a new monetarist orthodoxy. Shifts of framework *within* the echelons of power *do* get rapidly transferred as the baseline of 'reality' in the media, for it is part of their business to be sensitive to such shifts. Sources *outside* the matrix of power find it extremely difficult to break or change the terms of debate. Thus, while it is true that a single, monolithic definition almost *never* prevails unchallenged — media definitions, in this sense, are 'plural' — the *range of permissible definitions* is systematically limited (i.e. not 'pluralist' in the full sense). The media are not 'in the pay' of any particular party or group — and broadcasters jealously guard this independence. This does not contradict the fact that the media are oriented within the field of force of the powerful, their definitions systematically inflected towards how the powerful forces in society define political reality.

This is a matter of *structure*, not of personnel. Indeed, it exposes the inadequacies of the concept of 'bias'. 'Bias' must operate in a hidden or covert way. But the orientation of the media within the complex of power is a matter of broadcasting's *position* (not of the broadcasters' biases) — and functions quite openly and above-board. By definition, it is the powerful who define events — that is what we mean by calling them 'powerful'. Since they are publicly charged with responsibility for the conduct of affairs, they are the accredited, legitimate, authoritative sources of news. Since their decisions and actions will affect the whole population and the nation's future, no responsible broadcasting authority could regularly ignore them. And since broadcasting must not, itself, be seen to be influencing opinions, but must quote accredited sources external to it, it must indeed *rely on them* to establish the terms of debate, otherwise it might well (as it has been, on occasion) be thought to be usurping the process of public and political accountability. Their definitions of the situation will inevitably set the terms in which issues are debated and decided. There is nothing 'hidden' or covert about this.

The media are not, however, merely the ventriloquists of power, because they are required to 'balance off' official views with alternative ones. But, just as broadcasting has first to define the consensus in order to invoke and operate it, so it too must *define* what is 'balance'. Again, the analogy of the parliamentary system is relevant. Those who have a *required* 'right of reply' will tend to be drawn from 'the other official side, the opposition', within the complex of power. The 'balance' to a Government view is an 'Opposition' view. The 'balance' to an employer's view is a trade union leader's view. This will ensure 'pluralism' in the debate. But it will also systematically limit and *restrict the range* within which 'balance' is permitted to move. Though statement and rebuttal ensure vigorous, sometimes sharp, democratic debate, it is also, often, a conversation among groups who have many fundamental points of reference in common. Today's Shadow Minister of Employment will inherit the country's industrial problems of tomorrow. Both the Chancellor and his 'Shadow' have tinkered with monetarist solutions. Both Ministers of Labour believe in the necessity to 'restrain trade union power', though they differ as to means and degree. Let us not simplify the issue. *Debate*, not the monolithic presentation of a single view, is what characterizes British 'current affairs' television. That is why the simple conspiracy view lacks credibility. But let us not exaggerate the 'pluralism'. The range within which debate can move, before coming up hard against those limits which define non-consensual views as 'extremist' or 'irresponsible' or 'sectional' or 'irrational', is exceedingly restricted, and the limits are systematic — *structured*, not random.

When the media move outside these permissible limits, they encounter troubled waters.[17] If they range too widely, they will be accused of giving extremist views or minority opinions credibility. In any case, they know the accredited sources well, but beyond the corporate circle of power and influence, the movement of opinion is very much uncharted territory. On controversial issues relating to police powers, for example, the Home Secretary, his 'Shadow', the Chief Constable, the Police Federation have access to the topic, as of right.

The National Council of Civil Liberties may or may not be called upon to express a view — and will clearly be signalled as a minority pressure-group. The pecking-order within the system of power is well defined. Outside it, how is the broadcaster to know who should count? When does the 'Alternative Economic Strategy' of Labour's left-wing become credible enough to be an accredited alternative to Conservative and Labour economic policy? When is CND 'legitimate' enough to put its views as a credible alternative to those of the Minister of Defence? These are matters of extremely fine judgment, and how broadcasters settle them will help not to reflect, but to *construct*, 'balance'. Alternative viewpoints are sometimes 'put' on behalf of some pressure-group, not in its own voice, but through the mediation of the questioner or interviewer. You will often hear Sir Robin Day say to a minister, 'Of course, some people would say . . .' But in such cases, the media are playing a critical *mediating* role. Those whose views are 'put' will enter the debate, albeit in an indirect way. Those who don't register on the broadcaster's sensitive political seismograph will not. Like 'objectivity' and 'impartiality', 'balance', too, is not a fact but a process. It is the result of a   social practice. It takes place within a very definite system or structure of power.[18]

The concepts 'balance' and 'consensus' are, therefore, closely inter-linked. 'Consensus' does not imply a unified, single position to which the whole society subscribes. It means the basic *common ground*, the underlying values and premises, shared between two positions which may, in their detail, sharply diverge. 'Consensus' depends on structured disagreement — all those shared premises which enable 'Tweedledum and Tweedledee to *agree* to have a quarrel'. 'Balance' is therefore *framed by consensus*. Labour and Conservative deeply disagree as to the right economic policy. But they both subscribe to the two-party system.[19] The 'consensus' is the underlying premise (two-party govern-ment) which *frames* the disagreement over particular policies. It is within the limits of this consensus that broadcasting, typically, ranges. A revolutionary group which seeks to overthrow the two-party system is *not* one element in a 'balanced' debate because it does not share the consensus on the fundamental character of the political system. Groups which are not as 'far out' as that, but which are not 'central to the system', will be marginal to the consensus — and therefore marginal to how 'balance' is regularly operated in the media.[20]

On the whole, the media are scrupulously fair, impartial and 'balanced' within the terms of reference of the consensus, as we (and they) have defined it. Thus they are not, on the whole, 'partial' to Government or Opposition party. But they are 'partial' to the system, and to the 'definitions of political reality' which the system defines. Otherwise they would be in danger of becoming a sort of 'party in exile' — with their own powerful voice! Broadcasting cannot commit itself as to whether A or B's industrial policy will keep the wheels of industry turning. But it *is* committed to 'keeping production going', because both A and B define this as 'in the national interest'. What, at any time, can be credibly defined or affirmed to be 'in the national interest' becomes the *base-line* from which the broadcasters have to work. A former distinguished Director-General of the BBC, Sir Charles Curran, once put the point succinctly: 'Yes, we are biased — biased in favour of parliamentary democracy.'[21] Once you think about it, could the situation be any different? Could a broadcasting authority survive for long in Britain if it were 'biased in favour of one-party dictatorship'? Could it even plausibly arise or survive? This does not mean that the limits within which 'balance' currently operates could not be widened or extended. But the 'consensual' character of broadcasting does not arise from 'bias' in the normal sense of the term, but is a structural condition on which the whole broadcasting operation depends.

We have used the analogy of 'parliament'; but in fact it would be better to think of broadcasting as functioning on the analogy of *the state*. Like the state, it must take the ground of the 'national interest'. It must stand apparently outside and above the play of partisan interest. It must balance off conflicting interests. Its personnel, like those of the state, must be 'neutral', but committed to the 'system as a whole'. The parallels are even closer. For, since broadcasting must not become a 'state within the state', it must take its 'definition of political reality' *from* the state. What the state defines as 'legitimate' is 'the reference point of the mode of all reality shown on television'. Of course, broadcasting has other countervailing responsibilities which make this reproduction less than monolithic. For it must *also* deal with conflicts (even if at the inconvenience of those in power), report trends which might be 'bad news' for the state, reflect to some degree divergencies of opinion in society at large, question and explore offical views, test the coherence and internal contradictions of official policies. This helps to keep broadcasting 'open', and frequently creates a condition of 'cold war' between broadcasters and politicians. This helps to widen the way the 'consensus' is reflected and constructed by the media — but it does not displace their fundamental orientation. What is defined as 'legitimate opposition' has access, by right, to the debate on television. What lies on the margins of the state's definition of consensus will be marginal to television's discourse. What threatens the integrity of the state, especially if by violent means, is unshowable on television, except by express permission (e.g. interviews with spokesmen for the IRA). The state, ultimately, *defines the terrain* on which the representations of the world in television are constructed.

Does this mean that television is simply — as some have suggested — an 'ideological apparatus' *of* the state? In some countries it virtually is. But in Britain, broadcasting — like the law — is regulated, in relation to the state, by way of the classic doctrine of 'the separation of powers'. It could not otherwise fulfil its required function to be *both* an 'impartial source of knowledge' *and yet* 'part of the system'. Curran made the acute observation that 'the BBC's position is one of quasi-judicial impartiality'. Despite real differences of organization and financing, so is the ITV complex, where matters of political controversy and balance are concerned. This does *not* mean, as Curran implied, that broadcasting is wholly autonomous, subject only to external influence and pressure. But it is formally independent — relatively autonomous. During the General Strike (1926), in the BBC's infancy, Lord Reith argued persuasively that it was in the Government's best interest not to commandeer the BBC, as Churchill wished, but to leave it as an independent source of information. He laid on broadcasting a double injunction: to be 'allowed to define its position in the country' *and* to be 'for the Government in the crisis'. He squared the circle of this apparent contradiction in a subtle and delicate formulation: 'since the BBC was a national institution, and since the Government in this crisis were acting for the people, the BBC was for the Government in the crisis, too.'[22]

We have been arguing, then, that neither of the dominant explanations — 'independent and impartial' or 'biased' — are adequate, for they cannot grasp the *determinate relationship* in which broadcasting stands in our society. Only the concept of determinate structure will allow us to do so.

Throughout the paper, we have been discussing the *ideological* role of the media.[23] This is a difficult term to define precisely, but we have used the concept in a fairly simple way. By 'ideology' we understand, not highly systematic and coherent 'philosophies' of society, but the sum of the available ways in which we interpret, define, understand and make sense of social reality. In every society, the range of available ideologies will be limited. Moreover, these 'practical understandings' are not discrete ideas, but are linked into chains of explanations. They are not 'free-floating', but are structured, shaped and distributed in determinate ways. Though, in one sense, they are just the 'ideas in people's heads' about what society is and how it works, these 'ideas' arise from the way society is organized; they are historically shaped; they are transmitted and diffused through complex social organization and by the use of sophisticated technical means.

Moreover, they have *practical effects* because they are the ideas which organize social groups and classes into action, influence how they define reality, how they perceive conflicting social interests, and therefore what people do, who they support, what policies they back. Ideologies enter into the social and material organization of society, and influence practical outcomes. They are or can become materially effective. It therefore matters profoundly which ideas or 'ideologies' gain credibility, are constantly used to define and provide understandings of problems, appear, between them, to provide an adequate guide or map for us of the social world, and thus *become consensual*. The quasi-monopolistic position of broadcasting in our society gives it a profound cultural power over which ideas constantly circulate, which are defined as 'legitimate' and which are classified as 'irrelevant' or 'marginal'. This is a matter of ideological power — and the institutions like broadcasting and the press, which command the means of 'defining reality', will, inevitably, play an ideological role, however inconvenient this fact of life is to the broadcasters. We have tried to show why our broadcasting system *cannot*, by definition, circulate a single, simple, monolithic set of 'ruling ideas' about the social world. But we have also shown why broadcasting itself is and must be an ideological practice, and why there is a systematic tendency for the 'definitions of the situation' which broadcasting constructs to be ones which favour the prevailing social, political and economic arrangements of the society of which it is a determinate part.

Notes

1 *Nationwide* has been studied in two recent monographs: *Everyday Television* and *The Nationwide Audience*, by C. Brunsdon and D. Morley, British Film Institute, 1978, 1980.

2 There have been several recent studies of news: see P. Schlesinger, *Putting Reality Together* (Constable, 1978); Michael Tracey, *The Production of Political Television* (Routledge & Kegan Paul, 1977); P. Golding and P. Elliott, *Making the News* (Longman, 1979); Glasgow University Media Group, *Bad News* and *More Bad News* (Routledge & Kegan Paul, 1976, 1980); Stanley Cohen and Jock Young, eds, *Manufacture of News* (Constable, rev. ed., 1981).

3 On 'news values', see J. Galtung and M. Ruge, 'The structure of foreign news', *Journal of Peace Studies Research*, vol. 1 (1965) (and references in n. 2).

4 On the integrative function of rituals, see S. Lukes, 'Political ritual', *Sociology*, vol. 9, no. 2 (1975).

5 The most important formulation of these requirements is in the BBC's internal briefing document, *Principles and Practice in News*

and *Current Affairs* (1972). See the discussion of them in S. Hall, 'Broadcasting, Politics and the State: the Independence/Impartiality Couplet', IAMCR Conference Paper, Leicester (1976) and G. Tuchman, 'Objectivity as a strategic ritual', *American Journal of Sociology* (1971–2).

6   For a sophisticated official statement on 'independence in practice', see articles by Sir Charles Curran in the *Listener* for 20 June 1974, 14 May and 18 November 1976. For the case on 'bias', see *Bad News* and *More Bad News* (see n. 2); and J. Downing, *The Media Machine* (Pluto, 1980).

7   On 'selectivity', see the longer version of this article in *Getting the Message Across* (UNESCO Press, 1975). Also ibid. on the 'passage of a topic' from News to Current Affairs.

8   On the more 'explanatory' form of Current Affairs, see Hall, Connell and Curti, 'The Unity of Current Affairs Television', *Cultural Studies* (University of Birmingham, Centre for Cultural Studies), no. 9 (spring 1976).

9   On the 'interpretive work' of broadcasting, S. Hall, 'The rediscovery of ideology: return of the repressed in media studies', in M. Gurevitch, A. Bennett, J. Curran and J. Woollacott, eds, *Culture, Society and the Media* (Methuen, 1981).

10 See S. Hall, 'Encoding and decoding in the television discourse', in Hall et al., eds, *Culture, Media, Language* (Hutchinson, 1980).

11 On the 'denotative' and 'connotative' distinction, see ibid.

12 For recent studies of media coverage of industrial relations, see *Bad News* and *More Bad News*, and Downing, op. cit., and Beharrell and Philo, eds, *Trade Unions and the Media* (Macmillan, 1977).

13 On the broadcaster's dilemma, see S. Hall, 'The limits of broadcasting', *Listener*, 16 March 1972; and Golding and Elliott op. cit.

14 See K. Kumar, 'Holding the middle ground', *Sociology* (1975).

15 For 'typical decoding positions', see Hall, 'Encoding and decoding', based on F. Parkin, *Class Inequality and Political Order* (Paladin, 1972).

16 In the two most famous occasions – Suez crisis in Britain and the Vietnam War in the US – both the nation and the political elites were, in the end, so publicly divided that the broadcasters could assume a 'split consensus'.

17 On 'permissible limits', see S. Hall, 'Deviance, politics and the media', in Rock and McIntosh, eds, *Deviance and Social Control* (Tavistock, 1974).

18 'It [the BBC] is not only within the Constitution: it is within the consensus about basic moral values', BBC, *Principles and Practice*.

19 'The basic principle of BBC News is that a mature democracy is an informed (not guided) democracy. The BBC takes it for granted that the parliamentary democracy evolved in this country is a work of national genius to be upheld and preserved. The BBC's primary constitutional role is that of supplier of new and true information

as defined above', *BBC General Advisory Council Minutes*, 1976, quoted in Schlesinger, op. cit.

20 R. Miliband, 'Impartiality and objectivity in this sense stop at the point where political consensus itself ends', *The State in Capitalist Society* (Weidenfeld, 1969).

21 Curran, in 'Broadcasting and public opinion', *Listener*, 20 June 1974.

22 For a discussion of the BBC in the General Strike, see Asa Briggs, *The Birth of Broadcasting* (Oxford, 1961). Referring to Reith's Memorandum, Briggs comments: 'It clarifies the desire of the BBC to convey "authentic impartial news" while at the same time remaining in every sense of the word, "an organization within the constitution"' (p. 366).

23 On the 'ideological' role of the media, see Hall, 'The rediscovery of ideology'.

SECTION 6

Geography and Policy

Introduction

James Anderson

The geography of social processes is very uneven. Spatial patterns change over time. Charting and explaining these changing patterns is the main concern of the geographer. Combating their adverse effects, such as imbalances between houses and people or people and jobs, is a concern of the policy-maker, and sometimes the two concerns merge as when geographers are employed by urban and regional planning bodies. The six short articles in this section address these concerns, some focusing partly on the 'inner city problem' in Britain, though their implications are much wider.

Regions, cities and local areas vary greatly in character. Aberdeen grows with the North Sea oil industry and experiences shortages of labour and housing, while in towns like Consett and Corby, where steel plants have closed down, people cannot find jobs and houses cannot be sold. National and international phenomena such as economic booms or recessions affect all parts of a country, but some parts prosper or suffer more than others.

Sometimes social changes involve a major shift in basic geographical patterns. As Hobsbawm shows (Section 2), Britain's industrial geography was transformed in the period 'between the wars' when the older heavy industries of the North and West declined and new industries such as cars, aircraft and electrical engineering grew up in the Midlands and South-East. A similarly basic geographical transformation is under way in the United States. New industrial investment and population have shifted from the 'frost belt' of the Northern states to the 'sunbelt' that runs from Georgia and Florida through Texas to California. This shift also involved the rise of new industries, though traditional ones such as textiles were also attracted south by the cheaper, less unionized labour — the 'sunbelt's' cultural and political 'climate' is perhaps more important to investors than its sunshine. Its growing economic importance was

291

reflected in national politics when Georgia provided the American president in the late 1970s.

The changing relative importance of different industries and regions may thus involve cultural, social and political as well as economic factors, and it is sometimes referred to as 'the uneven development of capitalism'. It underlies the geography of all capitalist societies. The articles in this section, though relating directly to Britain, may therefore have at least some relevance to countries with a similar type of society, such as America. On the other hand, they do not apply to other types of society such as feudalism, or the so-called 'socialist' or 'state-capitalist' countries of Eastern Europe, where 'unevenness' is produced by different social mechanisms.

The spatial patterns involved in 'uneven development' are often complicated. For example, within the traditionally prosperous South-East there are areas like London's dockland which have more in common with economically depressed cities like Liverpool or Glasgow, while within depressed regions such as Northern Ireland or South Wales there are pockets of relative prosperity. Such patterns typically result from some combination of the different social processes studied by other social science disciplines, and geographers draw on them to explain spatial patterns and the problems in particular areas.

Here an important issue is the extent to which an area's problems can be explained by factors within the area itself. The assumption that they can be is challenged in several of our contributions. It was implicit in some 'inner city' policies such as the Community Development Projects which were set up around 1970 in some deprived urban areas to help local people to find solutions to the problems facing them.

Our first article, 'The Making and Breaking of Five Industrial Areas', brings together research findings from five of these Projects in different parts of Britain. It shows that, contrary to the initial assumption, the solutions were not to be found within the areas themselves, for their problems were not due mainly to local causes. Each of the five areas is in many respects unique, but nevertheless they all experienced similar patterns of growth and decline because of common national and international factors. Furthermore, within each area industrial decline set off similar 'chain reactions' of social deprivation and environmental dereliction, consequences which are discussed in later articles on 'inner city' policies and urban planning.

But first, how should the geography of decline be explained? Reading no. 20 was specially commissioned from Doreen Massey, who has done substantial research into the geography of industrial change; she demonstrates that the explanation has to be in terms of two different, though interacting, processes. First, and typical of much geographical explanation, there are changes in the geographical setting within which an industry operates — transport costs change, for instance, or women's employment patterns alter — for reasons quite external to the industry in question. Second, and often more important but frequently ignored in geographical explanations, are changes within the industry itself. Taking several industries, Massey shows how in the competition for profits the 'internal' and 'external' processes interact, how industrialists both introduce new techniques of production, for example, and at the same time seek to take appropriate advantage of the existing inequalities between areas.

In so doing they help to create new inequalities, and the 'inner city problem' is one result. The next two articles discuss government responses to it. Bob Davis and Judy Green (no. 21) criticize the policy of relying on small firms for an economic revival in these areas. They argue from a marxist viewpoint that there are no politically neutral solutions to the problem of industrial decay and unemployment, and that to pose the problem as one of regions ('distressed') or areas ('the inner city') is to divert attention from the failings of capitalism as a social system.

In contrast, Peter Walker, MP (no. 22) gives a Conservative view of the problem, and he also deals at greater length with its social aspects. Secretary of State for the Environment in the early 1970s, he provides a fascinating insight into the thinking of an important policy-maker, particularly on the threat to social order from crime and racial conflict, though ten years later actual Conservative policy was less benign toward inner city communities.

Reading no. 23 indicates that Conservative policy, particularly for 'enterprise zones', was now more laissez-faire in character and implied that urban planning was to blame for inner city decay. But property developers also play a part and Bob Colenutt, a geographer who has studied property development and the conflicts involved, outlines the relationship between planners and developers and how it varies in different types of urban area.

Finally, we include a short extract from a trade union publication on the dangers of racialism and what trade unionists should do about it (no. 24). Written by the local Trades Council in response to a series of racist attacks and murders in an inner city area of East London, it shows that it is not just social scientists or policy-makers who have social theories. So too do the grass-roots participants in social processes, and their ideas as well as their actions are part of the reality which social science has to explain.

19 The making and breaking of five industrial areas

Community Development Project

This extract is from a study of industrial decline and its consequences in five different places in Britain: *Batley*, a town between Leeds and Huddersfield in West Yorkshire, *Saltley*, just east of Birmingham's city centre, *Canning Town* in the east end of London, *Benwell*, west of Newcastle, and *North Shields* at the mouth of the river Tyne. On the surface, all that these areas have in common is that they contain a high proportion of people said to be 'multiply deprived' — in other words, each area is dogged by unemployment, bad housing and poverty.

Batley, Benwell, Canning Town, North Shields and Saltley are not otherwise alike. Each has its particular social, historical and industrial background. Each presents a different housing mix, some with high proportions of council stock, others with mainly private housing. The people in them vary too; some areas have significant numbers of Commonwealth immigrants, others not; some house a mainly young and transient population, in others it is older and more stable.

Beneath all these variations there are crucial similarities. All the areas were, at one time, major centres of production. There was shipbuilding and shiprepair in North Shields, arms and heavy engineering in Benwell, heavy woollen textiles in Batley, vehicles in Saltley, and the docks and associated port industries in Canning Town. But now they have all become depressed areas in their different ways. The story of these places reveals processes at work within the British economy, processes which produce dereliction, redundancies and decline.

The fortunes of each community are intimately related to the state of local industry, which in turn is dependent on processes at work in the wider community. As the economic role of each area changes over time, so the basis of the local community is transformed. The symptoms of 'deprivation' appear as industrial change shifts areas that were once important industrial centres to the periphery of the economy.

Source: Extracts from the Introduction and ch. 1 of *The Costs of Industrial Change*, January 1977, produced by CDP Inter-Project Editorial Team. Copies available from the Home Office (Urban Deprivation Unit), Horseferry House (Room 137), Dean Ryle Street, London, S.W.1.

Growth

The history of the five areas is part of the history of industrialisation in Britain. The uniqueness of this industrialisation stemmed from the fact that Britain was the *first* industrial nation. The social changes that made industrialisation possible had been proceeding for many decades before there was any significant change in technology or methods of production. New capitalist social relations had already replaced the elaborate systems of feudal controls which had been effectively destroyed in the seventeenth century. A century or more of foreign wars had led to British domination of much of the world, and a virtual monopoly of foreign colonies as compared with other European countries, and these colonies were to provide dramatically expandable markets for the new industries.

The first phase of industrialisation saw these advantages exploited. The cotton industry brought men and machines together in a new, disciplined and oppressive system of production based on the use of machines within factories – a way of organising work that became characteristic of advanced industrial capitalism. Manchester, the pioneer city of this first phase of the industrial revolution, grew tenfold between 1760 and 1830 as workers migrated in from the rural areas.

Most manufacturing industry in the first half of the nineteenth century, however, was still organised largely on the basis of domestic production, small workshops or handicrafts. It was only in the second phase of industrialisation with the growth of railways, shipbuilding, and large-scale capital goods industries that factory organisation of work and the application of machinery to production spread to a wide range of industry.

This second phase of industrialisation began with the great period of railway building and investment. 6,000 miles of track were laid between 1830 and 1850 [. . .] The rise of the railways together with shipbuilding stimulated the growth of the iron, steel and heavy engineering industries, firstly for the home market, but later increasingly for the overseas market. For as competition in these sectors from European and American industrialists increased towards the end of the nineteenth century British industrialists were able to evade it and continue to expand by exporting to the Empire. In this way the military supremacy which had provided the markets, enabling the first phase of industrialisation to get under way, came to lay the basis for a long-term decline in British industry once it was faced with powerful competition, a decline which would only be recognised long after the process had already begun.

It was this second phase of industrialisation that turned these five areas for a time into 'boom towns' [. . .]

The making and breaking of industrial areas — a model

The history of our five areas can be divided into three broad phases — *growth, maturity* and *decline*. To some extent this division is arbitrary and inevitably it over-simplifies the complex historical reality of industrial and social change. Nevertheless it does help to explain the processes underlying these changes, in particular the inter-action of industrial and population change over time. Each area is specific in its details, the timing of events and phases vary, and external factors, like land values or state intervention, play different roles in each case. No model can do justice to the complexity and variety of the real situations, but it can point up the important and far-reaching implications of industrial development and decline for the lives of people and their communities. To this end we set out here a simple version, an ideal-typical model of what happens in the creation and decline of areas like Batley, Benwell, Canning Town, North Shields and Saltley.

Industry	*Community*
Growth	
Firms locate in the area on green field sites. (The capital to set this up comes from profits made elsewhere, therefore contributing to the decline of some older working class area.) The industry expands and employment grows. All the available land is filled up.	A new population moves into the area. The new housing is partly financed by investors with a stake also in the new industry and so in ensuring that there is an adequate supply of labour available locally. Many of the new population have come from other areas of the country, where industry/agriculture is in decline.
Maturity	
Local firms remain profitable. Few firms leave the area and new growth slows. (Meanwhile, a new generation of industrial investment is being laid down elsewhere on green fields, partly financed by the profits from local industry.)	Employment remains at a fairly stable level. The local population is well established and settled. There is little turnover of population, as local employment and housing opportunities are still relatively good.
Decline	
Local industry begins to decline. There is little new investment in existing plant. Employment is cut. The traditional manufacturing sector continues to decline, pro-	The housing stock is beginning to deteriorate and many of the better paid and more skilled workers move out to newer working class areas. The reduction in job opportunities locally is an additional

viding fewer and fewer jobs — especially skilled jobs. Several firms close altogether, leaving vacant sites.

Vacant sites remain derelict or are developed for warehousing, distribution or offices — for which the area is attractive because of its relatively central location. No new manufacturing enterprises comparable to the traditional industries are attracted to these sites as they are relatively expensive to buy, rent and develop, and also because there is now relatively little skilled labour available locally.

But the availability of cheap, old premises, together with a pool of low income workers, does attract an inflow of small-scale, low wage, low productivity industry.

factor encouraging out-migration. More lower paid and less skilled workers move in from older working class areas.

Rate of out-migration increases. Workers who lose their jobs in local industry cannot find equivalent jobs as local manufacturing employment continues to decline; they remain unemployed or find jobs outside the area. The housing stock is in a poor condition. The continued shift to a lower income population means that the deterioration of the housing accelerates, as the residents are less able to afford improvements or the rent necessary to attract investment in improvement.

The emigration of younger, more skilled workers continues, leaving behind an increasingly unskilled, badly paid, insecurely employed or unemployed, and badly housed population.

Decline

The symptoms of industrial decline — derelict land, empty factories, run-down housing, unemployed workers — are painfully apparent in Batley, Benwell, Canning Town, North Shields and Saltley today. Yet their present state is the result of a process that has been going on for many years — in some areas for three-quarters of a century. [. . .]

The industrial decline of each area started for different reasons and at different times, and has proceeded at varying speeds. The first signs of stagnation and decline were evident in the north-east by the turn of the century, while in Saltley the new phase of investment in the motor industry staved off decline until the 1950s.

The traditional industries of North Shields had suffered a major collapse by the 1930s. The dramatic decline of local shipbuilding was highlighted by yards closing in the Howdon and Willington Quay areas, next to North Shields. Benwell's local industry underwent more gradual decline, interrupted by the booms of the two wars and the severe slump between them. A more rapid collapse with many closures began in the 1960s.

The textile industry in Batley, after reaching its peak in the First World War, declined steadily from then onwards. In Canning Town many firms were subject to takeovers and mergers from the early 1900s onwards in the face of falling profitability. Some of these mergers laid the foundations of what are now multinational companies. As in Saltley, serious economic decline in Canning Town has only become apparent relatively recently.

The disparate rate of change in the industrial bases of the different areas is reflected by the fact that in 1966, the traditional sector in North Shields provided less than a fifth of all jobs (shipbuilding, docks); less than two-fifths in Batley and Benwell (textiles and engineering respectively); but three-quarters of all jobs in Canning Town and Saltley. In general though, jobs in the traditional industries have been disappearing steadily in all five areas over the last forty years, and this trend has accelerated in the last ten years especially where the traditional sector had been large. A relatively small number of companies are responsible for cutting these jobs. They are often established firms, frequently the subsidiaries of major corporations pursuing rationalisation policies. In some areas less than half a dozen firms have been responsible for three-quarters of local job losses. In Canning Town, for example, just six companies — P&O, Tate & Lyle, Unilever, Harland and Wolff, Furness-Withy and Vestey's — accounted for three-quarters of the job losses there between 1966 and 1972.

Decline has not been a simple process. The collapse of the old industries is only one part of it, a part which has set up a long chain reaction. The surplus of unemployed workers, empty land and buildings left behind by the collapse of the traditional industries were soon exploited in new ways by new enterprises. Now both old and new industries exist side by side. This bank of underused resources — land, buildings and labour — which many investors have cashed in on, has been converted to a range of new industrial and non-industrial activities. These activities have not been so rewarding for the local workers.

Some new manufacturing firms are coming into all the areas. These are attracted to the older premises, which they can either rent cheaply or buy and convert at little cost. The premises vacated by older firms — often too small for modern manufacturing enterprises — can be highly suitable for smaller, labour-intensive firms. Contrary to what many people think, these old buildings are not worthless relics of a by-gone age, but money-making assets. Many firms newly arrived in the five areas are mainly interested in cheap premises; they may want a lot of cheap storage space, making minimal commitments of investment, and are often fly-by-night operators. Near Benwell, on the edge of the city, there is a small area mainly occupied by used-car lots and small clothing wholesalers.

Others of the new industries are actually labour-intensive. Using relatively primitive equipment, they aim to make a quick profit out of exploiting cheap labour. Many of the firms have themselves been pushed out of other city centres by redevelopment, fleeing to Batley, say, from the heart of Leeds or Bradford; sometimes they will only stay for a short time before they are moved on again. The firm of Spiralynx in Canning Town is typical. It moved into the area in the late sixties, after being pushed out of Tower Hamlets by redevelopment. Its business is to manufacture beds, which are then sold to highly reputable bedding firms, thus enabling them to reach a 'respectable' market, including local authorities and hospitals who would not otherwise buy them. Many of the workforce of 200, who are not unionised, are immigrants. Like most of the new manufacturing jobs, work at Spiralynx is insecure, low paid, and in poor conditions. Many such firms pay below even the poor minimum rate made compulsory by Wages Council legislation. They occupy an increasing share of the old industrial buildings and provide a growing proportion of local employment.

Of the land released by the decline of the older industries, much has simply remained derelict. In each of the five areas, there are large tracts of ground lying empty — visible reminders of the desertion of the areas by their traditional industries. Over a third of Saltley's industrial belt has lain empty for years and is still unused. Like most of Benwell's vacant land, this is owned by British Rail and the Gas Board, once important local employers. Vacant sites once used for docks, the production of cars, or mining, are in other cases redeveloped as unit industrial estates, sometimes renamed 'industrial parks', with property consortia often heavily involved. But it is clear that where private enterprise has taken on the job of redeveloping old sites for new industrial uses few jobs have been created as a result. The profits seem to lie not in creating alternative jobs in manufacturing to replace those lost from this land, but in preparing sites and premises for warehousing and distribution.

Thus the costs of industrial change are borne by local working-class communities. These communities grew up in response to the demand for labour from new industries, yet over time changes in these industries have destroyed their original role. The decline of each area's traditional industrial structure sets off a chain reaction of economic and social consequences, undermining every aspect of life in the local community, which increasingly serves as a 'reservoir' of unemployed and underemployed workers to be tapped only in times of boom, and as a source of workers for low-paid service activities over a widening area of each conurbation.

Up to the mid-sixties all five areas still had significant numbers of workers both living and working there. Manual jobs, in particular, were done by local residents, although the higher-paid managerial and supervisory jobs were performed usually by commuters from outside. In 1966, half the working population of Batley, Canning Town and North Shields still worked locally. Of the residents of Benwell and Saltley, traditionally more integrated into a wider employment network, rather fewer worked for local firms.

Since then, thousands of local jobs have been lost. Many firms have closed down altogether, and productivity drives in those remaining have meant the loss of many more jobs. As rationalisation brought widespread redundancies, workers with skills acquired over a lifetime, often with one employer, found they counted for nothing. With little comparable work available, they either remained unemployed or were forced into lower-paid, less-skilled work where that existed.

After 1966 unemployment rates in the five areas rose and remained consistently above the national average. At each slump the rate rose more rapidly, and at each boom it was slower to fall.

So now it is the people who live in areas like these five who are the waitresses, porters and cleaners in the centres of London, Birmingham, Newcastle and Leeds. It is not just the private sector that uses them in such low-paid, unpleasant and low status jobs. State agencies have also taken advantage of their availability to provide services on the cheap. The expansion of government services in the fifties and sixties means that many residents in these areas are now employed in hospitals, local authority social services departments, schools and colleges and the DHSS — as cleaners, home helps, canteen workers and clerical workers. They provide an important source of work for people in Batley, Benwell and North Shields, and to a lesser extent in Canning Town and Saltley.

Many of the workers drawn into these expanding fields of work were women. Many had not previously worked outside the home, but others — like Batley's women textile workers whose numbers declined at a rate of 3.4% a year between 1959–69 — had been thrown out of jobs in the traditional industries. Without the growth of the service sector, local unemployment in such areas would have been much higher. As it was, this growth disguised the full extent of job loss without compensating the workers in any way for their loss of skills and wages. Even this 'safety net', however, is now fast disappearing as the public sector is cut back.

In the five areas, the process from the creation of a working-class community to 'deprived area' status has taken less than a century. The last decade in particular has seen marked changes in their local populations, accompanying the basic economic changes in each area.

The depression of the 1930s brought long-term unemployment to the areas, especially on Tyneside, and many workers left their homes and localities altogether in search of work in the midlands and south east. In recent years people have left in much greater numbers to escape the declining employment situation and generally deteriorating state of local housing. In spite of often high rates of in-migration, most of the areas show a net population decline since 1966. This is most marked in Benwell, which has lost a quarter of its population, and in Canning Town, which has lost over a fifth. In both areas major housing redevelopment programmes have exaggerated the fall of population, but the underlying trend is clear. The total population loss figures disguise the selective basis of population changes. Most of the loss has been of younger, more skilled workers.

The significance of these changes is shown by the fact that the present rate of population change in the older areas of Newcastle is at least as great as that which occurred during the Industrial Revolution when the working-class community of Benwell was created. The five areas were built during the Industrial Revolution to provide labour for the new and growing local industries. Now this role has been undermined by the decline of these industries locally, and the older working-class communities are left to carry the costs of industrial change by companies in no way accountable to the local people.

20   The geography of industrial change

Doreen Massey

The geographical distribution of industry (both manufacturing and services) and of employment is constantly changing. New regions are constantly being invaded for the first time by modern industry while others, which maybe for generations had been major centres of employment, are deserted. Today, while multinationals set up plants in the Third World, some of the oldest industrial areas are losing jobs at a frightening rate. Areas which were once the centre of industrial development are reduced to 'problem' regions. The same kinds of shifts can be seen in the United Kingdom over the last two or three centuries. In the seventeenth century and most of the eighteenth the prosperous regions were in the South and East of England, which flourished on trade and agriculture. From the end of the eighteenth century, however, the new industries of the Industrial Revolution took over in economic importance. But they were located in the North of England, in South Wales and in Central Scotland. It was here that employment grew (though working conditions were appalling), while the agricultural areas in the South suffered relative poverty, unemployment and outmigration. But this pattern, too, was to undergo a change. The industries of Britain's nineteenth-century dominance began to decline and the new industries of the inter-war and post-war period established their factories in the South-East and the Midlands. So the old industrial areas became the new problem regions.

These 'problem regions' are of course still with us. They are the industrial parts of the present Development Areas. But since the 1960s there have been some further changes: unemployment has been rising in the previously prosperous Midlands and South, some industries have been shifting the balance of their employment towards the Development Areas, while unemployment rates in inner cities in all parts of the country have risen dramatically.

The last few centuries, therefore, have seen some major shifts in the

Source: article commissioned for this Reader. Doreen Massey is SSRC Fellow in Industrial Location and Senior Research Fellow, Department of Geography, London School of Economics and Political Science.

pattern of industrial development in this country. Moreover, within these larger movements there are continual smaller changes, as particular industries (and maybe therefore particular areas) grow and decline or change locations.

The analysis of locational change

The issue which this article is to address is how to analyse this changing geography of industry, this shifting spatial distribution of employment. It is important to recognise that this is a broad issue, one which must be set within a wide overall context, for the way in which a company chooses to locate its plants is part and parcel of the way in which it attempts to maximise its profits, to compete with other firms and sectors. We must therefore understand both the pressures which firms and industries are under in their chase after profits, and the ways in which they can use location to increase those profits.

This section outlines a very general approach to the analysis of industrial location change. The argument is that such change occurs as a result of the interaction of two different processes. On the one hand, there may be changes in industry itself, leading to a change in the demands it makes of a location (we shall call this set of demands an industry's requirements of production). On the other hand, the locational opportunities themselves may change. For example, there may be shifts in the distribution of the population, changes in comparative wage-levels between areas, or changes in relative distances caused by developments in transport and communications. So both the requirements of production and the geographical environment of an industry may undergo change. Both must be examined.

The next questions are what determines the requirements of production, and why should they change over time? It is perhaps easiest to think in terms of an example. Why, for instance, has the geographical distribution of employment in the clothing industry changed so much within the last fifteen or so years? Over that period, while total employment has been falling, there has been a noticeable shift in its locational pattern. Urban areas and the traditional centres of the industry have experienced major falls in employment. The three conurbations of London, West Yorkshire and Manchester, traditional bases of clothing manufacture, saw their share of national employment in the industry fall from 51 per cent in 1959 to 39 per cent in 1971. On the other hand a number of peripheral regions and rural areas (the South-West, the northern region of England, parts of East Anglia, Wales and Scotland) increased their number of jobs in these industries, and increased even more their share of the total. There has thus been a double shift, from old regions to new and from large urban areas to smaller towns and more rural areas. Why?

To understand this changing pattern it is necessary to stand back and analyse the position of the clothing industry in the wider national and international economies, and to understand the pressures which employers in that industry (for it is they who make the locational decisions) have been facing. Above all, over the long term, but particularly over the last ten or fifteen years or so, the clothing industry has come under increasing pressure, from a number of sources, to cut its costs of production. Sections of this industry have suffered from imports which could out-compete the products made in Britain largely because they were cheaper. Moreover, at the same time as the UK-based clothing industry was losing some of its share of the home market, that market itself was slowing down in its rate of growth. So the combined result of national and international economic circumstances has been that the clothing industry in the UK has come under enormous pressure to cut costs. If it was going to survive, therefore, the industry had to respond to these pressures. It did so, and it did so in a whole variety of ways. The way in which these pressures to cut costs could be responded to varied between different parts of the sector.

In a few parts of the industry it was possible to achieve some reduction in the costs of production by increased mechanisation. This was not a major factor in the clothing industry, but it enabled two kinds of savings. First it allowed the same amount of output to be produced by fewer workers, and second, in some cases, it allowed for those workers themselves to be less skilled, and therefore paid lower wages. Such a strategy was, however, possible only in those parts of the industry where the production process is relatively simple and standardisable (and therefore easier to mechanise) and also where mass production is possible. But it was less feasible in other parts of the industry, for instance where the production process is less easy to mechanise or where the production runs are too short to make mechanisation worth while (for instance, in some of the more 'fashion-oriented' parts of the industry).

There were also, however, other factors which further influenced the ability to lower costs. The industry is made up of a vast variety of different kinds of companies, from small, single-plant, individually-owned concerns, through medium-sized companies with one or two plants, to multinational conglomerates. The different scales and capacities of these different companies influenced the ways in which they could respond to the intensifying competition. Moreover, these differences in company structure tended to mirror those in production characteristics. For it is in the more easily mechanisable and mass production parts of the industry that big companies are most important. This in itself is of course no accident. It is precisely because they can take advantage of economies of scale and the possibility of more advanced production techniques that larger companies choose these parts of the industry to enter. Conversely, smaller firms are more able to set up and survive in the other parts of the industry. These two differences – in the kind of ownership structure and in the nature of production techniques – thus reinforce each other in their effects.

We can see then that the technical characteristics and possibilities in the sector combined with the kind of company structure influenced the ways in which different parts of the industry could respond to the increasing competitive pressures. Big firms were able to increase mechanisation, cut down on amounts of labour to produce any given level of output, and in some cases 'de-skill' the labour force a little and therefore lower wages. For small firms in the less mechanisable parts of the industry these options were not open. For them, it was necessary to cut costs, but without the advantage of mechanisation and/or mass production. There were, however, some changes that could be made which did not involve major changes in the production process or require major investment. These could therefore be adopted by both big and small firms. They involved getting more work out of the labour force within the existing production process (an intensification of the work process), together with an attempt to hold down wages, in part through employing different kinds of workers. A whole range of developments took place.

Even without major mechanisation it was possible to speed up the work process through the use of small-scale gadgets and machinery (automatic needle-threaders are a good example); all kinds of schemes, such as various forms of incentive-payment, were devised to get more work out of the workers in a given time, and where possible the production process was further divided up, again increasing its speed (and also its monotony). At the same time, wage increases in the clothing industry fell behind those in manufacturing as a whole, and there is evidence of a shift in the type of worker employed, with an increasing use of the more vulnerable sections of labour (in this case especially immigrants and married women) and forms of labour organisation (such as homeworking), all of which reduced the bargaining power of the workforce and enabled the employers thus to hold down wages and overall costs.

We have so far considered two factors (technical change and company structure) in the determination of the response to increased competitive pressures. Both concern production. But, as was said at the start of this section, there are two sides to the formation of locational patterns. For at the same time as these changes have been occurring within production, there have also been changes in the locational opportunities available to the industry. A number of things were going on. First, the long-term increase since the last war in the employment of women has put pressure on the availability of female workers. But it has been a pressure which has varied geographically; it seems to have been particularly strong in urban areas and even more especially in London. For it has been in these areas that service industry — much of it employing women — has expanded most. In these areas, the clothing industry, as a traditional and not very attractive or trendy employer of women, has come up against increasing competition for labour, and this precisely at a time when it is needing to reduce labour costs. In other parts of the country, however, the availability of female labour has increased and its relative cost reduced. One obvious example is the old heavy industry areas, once dominated by sectors such as coal-mining. Here the collapse of employment for men has made it both more possible and more necessary for women to go out to work. The female activity rates in such areas were until relatively recently extremely low, so the women now coming on to the labour market are inexperienced in matters such as trades union organisation. They constitute another kind of potentially vulnerable workforce. Finally, since the mid-1960s, costs in general in these regions were reduced by the operation of grants and subsidies available as part of the government's regional policy (though these were decreased later in the 1970s).

There was, then, geographical variation in the pressure on costs. And once again this affected the different parts of the sector differently. At one extreme there were hundreds of small firms stuck in London. Without the capital to invest in modern methods of production, and anyway with the applicability of mechanisation limited by the nature of the part of the sector in which they were operating, and often, very importantly tied to the fashion market of London, these firms were also facing considerably increased competition for their labour. Many of them went under, others survived by the kinds of methods described earlier, by intensifying the labour process, and holding down wages, the second of which could be done only by employing non-unionised and highly vulnerable labour. The big companies, however, were in a very different position. They had the capital and the geographical flexibility to seek locations in other regions. Many of them left the urban and traditional areas of the industry and went off in search of cheaper labour. Within the UK, as we have seen, such labour was available in the Development Areas, and also in smaller towns. Everywhere, the labour sought has been mainly female, unorganised and without any tradition of working in the clothing industry. (It should also be pointed out that the very big firms were able to move to the really cheap labour areas in the Third World — and thereby themselves become part of the problem of low-cost imports.)

The net result of all these complex and interacting processes has been the changing geographical distribution of employment described earlier. There have been massive losses of jobs in the cities as a result of small firms going out of business or contracting, because large firms move out to areas of cheaper labour, and work becomes intensified. There has also been a decline in working conditions. Clearly, we see here one of the components of the 'inner city problem'. In other areas, there has been an at least relative gain in employment. But the gain has been of low-paid jobs, since cheap labour was precisely one of the attractions of these areas. Nor have these areas gained as many jobs as the urban areas have lost, even in individual moves, since the change in location has often been the occasion for changes in production to reduce the amounts of labour required.

All that is a fairly complicated story. It would probably be helpful now to systematise it into a framework for explanation. The diagram indicates the main stages in the explanation, and the main directions of causality.

changes in
economic
conditions

$\downarrow$

changes in industry's
requirements of
production, leading
to changes in its
locational requirements

$\downarrow$
$\uparrow$

changes in
industry's
geographical
environment

It is perhaps useful to note a few points about this approach to the explanation of the geography of industrial change. Most of them can be illustrated from the case of the clothing industry.

First, it makes clear that the source of spatial differences and regional inequality within a country lies in the nature and the requirements of production itself.

Second, the geography of industry within a particular country, and the nature of that country's regional problems, etc., cannot be explained by an analysis which is confined to that country. The analysis must take account of the country's relation to the international economic system.

Third, the approach makes clear that all kinds of factors are important in explaining changes in industrial location. In particular both the organisational structure of industry and its technological characteristics will be important influences.

Fourth, however, none of these individual factors are independent. The organisational structure of an industry and its technological requirements may be interrelated, and each can change in response to the nature of competition and the requirements of profit-making.

By following through the diagram it is possible to understand some of the geographical changes which have been going on in other sectors of the UK economy since the mid-1960s. That period is important, for it was then that the British economy first began to feel seriously the effects of its declining international competitiveness. Different industries were affected in different ways by this worsening national situation. One of the responses, particularly in the early period when the world economy as a whole was relatively buoyant, was an attempt to reorganise certain sections of British industry in order to make them more competitive and to increase their profitability. Sometimes this happened through market and competitive processes, sometimes it was encouraged and aided by government policies. In many cases it had important geographical consequences.

One industry where government reorganisation was important was electrical engineering and electronics. Here, changing economic conditions had a number of effects. First there were the effects on the production process. These varied between different parts of the sectors. In some parts, the loss of markets left the industry with too much capacity for profitable production. This was especially true of heavy electrical engineering. Closures and rationalisation were therefore clearly necessary. In other parts of electrical engineering the main requirement was to cut the costs of production. This was achieved in a number of ways. Sometimes standardisation and further mechanisation enabled labour costs to be reduced; sometimes the same effect was achieved by changing the nature of the product, for instance from electro-mechanical to electronic. Finally, in electronics there was an increasing emphasis on, and development of the technology of, mass production. This often meant that increasing proportions of the production took on an assembly form. And these parts of production, again, were often performed by labour with no engineering skills, and frequently employed at very low wages.

Second, these changes in the production process were accompanied by changes in organisational structure. Companies in electrical engineering and electronics were prominent in the merger boom of the late 1960s. The mergers were necessary for different reasons in different parts of the sectors. In electrical engineering, which in general was on the decline, they were often necessary in order to co-ordinate the rationalisation process; in order to ensure that no companies actually went out of business. In electronics, by contrast, mergers were often necessary to increase the financial size of individual firms in order to enable them to cope with the investment needed for changing technology. The two aspects of change, therefore, in production technology and in ownership, were both essential to each other and enabled a change in the production requirements and possibilities in these sectors. What they did was to reinforce the changing nature of these industries' demand for labour. In terms of production workers, there has been a reduction in the number of workers needed for any given level of output, and a decline in the proportion of skilled workers because of both the decline and the changes in production in electrical engineering. This general acceleration in the process of de-skilling has led to an increase in the importance of semi-skilled and unskilled workers. Finally, the increasing importance of electronics has led to a growth in the importance of technical workers and of workers in research and development.

What these developments mean is that the labour-related 'location factors' relevant to the pattern of employment in these industries are also changing. First, the distribution of skilled manual workers has become less important, and that of unskilled and semi-skilled workers and of highly-trained and highly-paid technical and scientific workers has become more so. There is in the United Kingdom at present geographical variation in the distribution of all these 'factors'. Indeed, if there were not, they would not be operative location factors. Technical and research workers are overwhelmingly concentrated in the outer metropolitan areas of the South-East of England. The skilled manual workers, whose importance is declining, are located mainly in the old industrial conurbations and regions. Finally, there is also geographical variation in the distribution of unskilled and semi-skilled workers. In contrast to skilled workers, however, unskilled and semi-skilled workers are 'available' almost everywhere – especially at a time when there is such a high level of national unemployment. So it has not been simple availability which has operated as a location factor, but cost. And what cost has meant has been both actual wage levels and the level of such things as trades union organisation, absenteeism and militancy. And, as we saw in the case of the clothing industry, such workers are available – and in some cases have become both cheaper and *more* available – in Development Areas and small towns.

We have, then, both new requirements and possibilities of production and geographical variation in the distribution of these requirements. What kind of industrial location pattern is being evolved as a result of the interaction between these two sides of the equation?

Probably the most important is that which is based on the geographical separation of control and research and development functions from those processes of production that do still require a skilled labour force, and of these in turn from the increasingly important element of automated and assembly work, for which only semi-skilled and unskilled workers are needed. The geographical organisation of production, in other words, takes the form of a locational hierarchy. It should be noted that the existence of such hierarchies is dependent on both the factors mentioned in the framework. Both changes in production technique and changes in organisation (mainly increasing size of individual companies) have been necessary for the establishment of this form of use of space by industry.

Taking, as it were, the bottom end of the hierarchy first, the automated and assembly stages of production increasingly seek out the areas of cheaper and less militant (female) unskilled and semi-skilled labour. Often this means that they locate in areas where there are workers with little or no previous experience of going out to work for a wage, for instance old coal-mining areas where, as we have already mentioned, the female activity rates have been historically very low. The nature of employment for men (the fact that it was shift-work, and the burden of domestic labour which it implied) had for long been a deterrent to women taking up paid employment. There has also historically been very little opportunity for women to work for money in such regions. Another typical location for these assembly stages of production has many of the same characteristics. Small seaside towns and tourist resorts are a very popular locational choice.

Those processes of production which are not yet reduced to assembly work, and which do still require skilled manual workers, are still typically located in the old centres of skilled labour. Such regions include primarily the nineteenth-century industrial towns and conurbations. The important characteristic of this type of production, and therefore of employment in these areas, is of course that it is declining. And it is declining for a number of reasons. First there was a loss of jobs as a result of the closures resulting from overcapacity in electrical engineering. Second, there are reductions in workforces as a result of changes in production processes. Third, what new investment there is, for instance in electronics, no longer requires such locations for production. It no longer needs the amount of skilled manual labour that it used to; it is freed from its ties to skilled labour; so the new investment is going elsewhere, to the 'assembly-stage' regions of the hierarchy. Here, clearly, is another reason for inner-city decline.

Finally, at the top of the hierarchy are the metropolitan regions, excluding the inner cities of those regions. These areas are typified by the presence of managerial and highly-paid jobs, and of research and development. The major area of such employment in this country is that around London and the South-East, but there are also smaller concentrations in the north Cheshire region just south of Manchester, and around Edinburgh.

So electrical engineering and electronics faced rather different conditions from the clothing sector and behaved rather differently. There were bigger changes in production and more company reorganisations, especially mergers. We could, with more space, see how other industries behaved differently again. The service industries, for instance, began to establish their own kind of production hierarchy, retaining the higher-paid professional jobs in the South of England and decentralising clerical and more routine work.

Conclusions

Putting all these changes together, we can see some of the geographical implications of the reorganisation of parts of the British economy, a re-organisation which itself is part of the capital's response to the problems of falling profits and declining international competitiveness. It should be clear not only that these changes produced a different spatial pattern of employment, but that 'geography' was an important factor in the changes themselves. In effect, not only has British industry been going through a period of 'restructuring', but also this has involved a significant 'restructuring' of the working class. And the fact of geographical variation in the labour force has been an important element in this process. The ability of firms to shift locations as they change production technique often makes it impossible for unions to defend existing jobs and conditions of work. It also sets up one group of workers in competition with another. So geographical mobility and variation are actually part of the process of industrial change. We can see also that 'the spatial surface' which industry faces at any given time is itself a product of, among other things, the previous industrial history. The availability now of a female, 'green' labour force in the old industrial areas of Britain is a good example. So geography and geographical variation play a complex role in the process of industrial change: the geography of a country or region is a result of its previous history, it is an active ingredient in the present processes of industrial change, and it is a condition of future production.

The examples in this paper also illustrate how different companies and industries use space in different ways. There was one obvious contrast in the clothing industry example. Here the small companies were often effectively trapped in one location, and had to do their best to cope within the opportunities and constraints of that location. The big companies in the same industry, however, were locationally flexible in a way which enabled them both to adopt other, and often more effective, ways of cutting costs, and through that spatial strategy itself further to strengthen their position in comparison with the small-firm part of the sector. The big electronics firms were different again. They incorporated geographical variation into their process of production by actually separating out the different stages of activity and locating each in its most favourable region or area. In each of these three different examples, space or geography operated as a different kind of constraint and/or opportunity. In each case, locational strategy was an integral part of the overall process of maximising profits, but in each case the geographical variation was used or responded to in a different way.

Finally this discussion enables some light to be thrown on a couple of political issues concerning industrial geography.

First, there is a tendency in both social science and political debate to look for the causes of an area's growth or decline entirely within that area itself. One of the clearest cases of this in recent years has concerned 'the inner city'. Over and over again attempts have been made to explain their loss of manufacturing employment by the characteristics of the cities themselves. Sometimes it is the planners who are blamed, sometimes the high price of land, sometimes the workers themselves (for not being sufficiently skilled). Some of these attempts at explanation are in any case dubious. The previous examples indicate that, at least in these sectors, to the extent that manufacturing industry moves out of the inner city in search of a different labour force it is to find cheaper, *less* skilled and less organised workers. But such explanations are also inadequate in a more general way. As we have seen, the decline of the inner city is bound up with more major changes going on in the economy as a whole. The workers of the inner cities are among the victims of industry's attempts to increase its competitiveness and fight off falling profitability. It is in the cities that a lot of the older factories are located, and these are often the first to go in 'rationalisation' programmes. In other cases, where there has been new investment, it has taken place in other areas and often been coupled with closure of older plants in the conurbations. 'Local characteristics' are not unimportant in these processes. The level of land prices *has* often been important, for instance (though as much because firms can take advantage of them by selling land they own as because rents are too high). And the characteristics of the workforce *may* be influential (though more because of its strength and its wages than because of any lack of skills). But such factors operate within a broader context, and since the mid-1960s this context has been dominated by the declining competitiveness of British industry. To look solely within the inner cities for the causes of their employment decline is a geographical version of blaming the victims themselves for their fate.

The second, and related, issue is that geographical inequality and the associated problems of 'depressed' areas are too often interpreted in terms of competition between regions. In recent years the Development Areas and the inner cities have been seen to be in conflict in attracting jobs and in winning political support in the form of aid programmes and subsidies. In particular, representatives of inner cities outside Development Areas have blamed the operation of regional policy for their loss of jobs. There are two issues here. First, it is wrong simply to attribute urban decline to regional policy. The most obvious evidence of this is that the cities of the Development Areas have suffered a similar decline. The examples earlier in this paper show how the inducements of regional policy in fact *combined* with the changing demands of industry to produce a change in the distribution of employment. To return to our initial formulation, it was not just the change in the geographical environment (through regional policy), but also the developments in production which enabled the geographical shift in employment patterns. But the second, and more important, issue is that to see the problem in this way is to interpret it simply as a matter of distribution, as a question of who (i.e. which part of the country) gets what. Such interpretations are almost always divisive. What is more, they enable the real problems to be ignored. While those in the inner cities argue that regional policy is taking their jobs, while workers in one region argue for more regional aid at the expense of another, the real problems − the *total* shortage of jobs and the fact that in its shifting search for profits capital continually and necessarily creates inequality between areas − run the risk of being ignored.

21 Inner city policy: a marxist comment

Bob Davis and Judy Green

The inter-war crisis of capitalism gave rise to an account of economic problems in terms of 'distressed areas' or 'regions'. The current crisis has produced a view of urban problems, particularly related to so-called 'inner cities'. [. . .]

The 'inner city problem' has now replaced the 'regional problem' as the focus of interest and involvement for government, academics, and a range of voluntary agencies. Initially, official ideas about the 'problem' revolved around housing stress, environmental dereliction, decay and re-development. More recently, it is the employment aspect which has been emphasised.

Central government — perhaps belatedly — came to acknowledge the importance of industry and employment. Secretary for the Environment Peter Shore's speech in Manchester in September 1976 appeared to set the scene for the reversal of post-war policies which had encouraged the dispersal of jobs and people from the cities and the concentration of new manufacturing investment in out-of-town industrial estates and New Towns. Future policies had to deal with causes, not symptoms, of decline, and therefore with jobs: 'The opportunity to attract industry back to the inner areas now exists in a way in which it did not a decade or so ago.' But how was industry to be attracted back?

> Part of the [current inner city problem] is due to the forces which have led new *private investment* [our emphasis] in factories and housing to the growing towns and suburbs rather than in the cities.

So

> I see it as the job of central government first to ensure that all its own policies are consistent with our inner city strategy, and secondly

Source: 'The political framework: a marxist view', in Martin Loney and Mark Allen (eds), *The Crisis of the Inner City*, London, Macmillan, 1979, extracts from pp. 38–43, 45, 47–52.

to provide the framework and flexibility for local government to foster confidence in the inner cities so that *private investment* [our emphasis] is promoted.

The debate gathered momentum and a new policy package began to emerge. In February 1977 Shore, in announcing that at least £100 million would go to the inner cities to improve their local economies, stressed the need to preserve existing jobs and encourage the growth of new firms by providing a more suitable context for private industry to flourish: services must be better integrated and the environment improved because 'The flow of private investment, whether for commerce, industry or housing, depends among other things on raising the level of the environment'. Inner city policy was beginning to take on a definite — and rather familiar — form. The actual programme for the inner cities which was put together in 1977 included special 'partnerships' between government and local authorities in selected areas in order to establish 'inner area programmes aimed at keeping and attracting jobs' by means of such measures as creating advance factories and improving the environment. These moves were formalised in June 1977, with the publication of the inner cities White Paper which proposed that local authorities should have new powers to assist industry through loans, grants, and the construction of industrial improvement areas. The problems the White Paper identified were seen as having their roots in economic issues:

the decline in the economic fortunes of the inner areas often lies at the heart of the problem . . . [there has] not been enough investment in new manufacturing industry to counterbalance . . . job losses.

Local authorities were to be the agents for action — but 'authorities with inner area problems will need to be entrepreneurial in the attraction of industry and commerce.' This involved a special effort towards the private sector. In order to strengthen the economy of inner areas, authorities needed to

stimulate investment by the private sector, by firms and by individuals, in industry, in commerce, and in housing. The resources and energies of small and medium size firms are essential if real progress is to be made and the diversity, and vitality, for so long characteristic of inner cities, is to be restored.

[. . .]
The urgency of the jobs situation was not lost on the government. But far from representing a genuine 'intervention', the new inner city

policies did not challenge current trends in the private sector of industry at all — rather, they leant over backwards to accommodate them. [. . .]

The relaxation of controls over the exploitation of the inner cities [for the benefit of private industry] was matched in its cynicism by the paltry public expenditure effort on them. Massive expenditure on the cities — despite the scale of their problems and despite all the ballyhoo — just could not be afforded. [. . .]

Mr Shore had obviously been listening to the advice of big capital, which seemed to be saying 'do something but not too much'. The *Financial Times* (10/2/77) welcomed the low level of expenditure on the inner cities:

> The Government's new approach to the problem of inner city decay, as described by the Secretary of State for the Environment . . . adds up to nothing very much. This is only partly to be regretted, since there has been a very real danger that Mr Shore would persuade the Cabinet to allow him to announce the expenditure of further hundreds of millions of pounds on the impossible task of stemming the outward flow of people from city centres to the greener suburbs.[. . .]

Not only was 1977 'the year of the inner city', it was also the year the Labour government resurrected the small businessman and made him the new hero of the day. A variety of new government measures were processed during 1977-8 to help small businessmen, including favourable treatment in successive budgets. [. . .]

For some time, it has been clear that, although the large traditional employers have been running down their manufacturing investments in the older urban areas, this does not represent a straightforward withdrawal by capital. Capital has found new uses for the inner city — or, more precisely, for its people and its land.

The inner areas of cities like Newcastle have recently seen a new generation of back-street sweatshops mushroom, attracted by cheap labour and cheap premises left behind by the more mainstream industrial activities. Similarly, large tracts of land have become available as former industrial sites are cleared. [. . .]

Under the present system, industrial investment will take place only on capital's own terms. [. . .] Small firms are being given the run of the inner city areas that no one else wants. [. . .] But clearly small firms offer no solution to the unemployment problems of local areas. All the effort directed at the small firm can be wiped out by one closure of a major manufacturer. [. . .]

The implications for the workforces of the inner cities or older industrial areas are that they are being softened up for a fresh round of exploitation — as and when needed. With worse wages and conditions and less security compared to mainstream labour market activities, they suffer all around. In addition, of course, trades unionism and workplace organisation are less well developed in the small business sector. [. . .]

Harold Lever [in charge of the Labour Government's small firms policy], in a 1978 debate in the House of Commons on the impact of the employment protection legislation on small firms, said that although he endorsed the purposes of employment protection laws, he was anxious to ensure that they were achieved 'with the minimum of difficulty for smaller firms'. The interpretation widely given to this was that the government would act to cushion small businesses against the Employment Protection Act and other employment reforms won by the working class — and passed by a Labour government — in the 1970s.

We would suggest that, in the long run, the industrial strategy as a whole is opposed to the interests of the working class. It is designed to usher in a new era of exploitation, not emancipation. The last Labour government was the capitalist state's handmaiden in helping to achieve this. The whole strategy deliberately excluded any socialist alternatives. It did not address itself to the fundamental issues of the ownership and control of the means of production, distribution and exchange.

Just like the earlier regionalism (which in the interwar crisis gave an account of economic problems in terms of 'distressed regions'), the inner city strategy serves to divert political activity and attention from the overall operations of the capitalist system towards the particular problems and alleged peculiarities of places and people. Also, like regionalism, a whole fresh range of committees and tripartite consultative bodies serve to enmesh and incorporate Labour leaders — councillors, trade unionists, community groups — into acceptance of the state's definition of the nature of the problem, its proposed solutions and, by extension, its own authority and legitimacy.

There are further parallels with regionalism and its view of the working class, for the inner city perspective has a strong 'blame the victim' element. [. . .]

In his speech at the Bristol 'Save Our Cities' conference, Shore alluded to the social considerations lying behind the inner cities initiatives — including crime. And the White Paper reiterated not only the theme of an 'unbalanced' population (skilled workers migrating out, leaving behind a pool of less skilled workers who by implication cannot cope) but also the idea of 'collective deprivation', manifesting itself in a 'pervasive sense of decay and neglect' in some inner areas. It was this which, in fact, provided 'an important argument for tackling inner city deprivation on an area basis and for discriminating in favour of the inner areas in the working out of public policies and programmes'. Their decline needed arresting too, for fear of contamination — 'the heart of our cities would suffer as the surrounding inner areas went further downhill'. [. . .]

There is of course a crucial dimension lacking from this account, which is the class struggle. Restructuring involves — in fact, is part of — the class struggle. There is no inevitability about the outcome. Labour organisations can fight the industrial strategy of the capitalist state. Whether they do, and how they do it, will affect the overall outcome and is not something we can speculate about here. One thing about the reversal of policies towards the small business sector of petty bourgeois capital that is sure is that the conditions for the pursuit of capital accumulation and growth are being recreated for this sector of capital at this moment in time. But that, of course, sows the seeds of its own reversal, as it entails yet another process in the historic conflict between capital and labour.

True to the traditions of bourgeois reformers, the problem is defined not as one intrinsic in capitalism, but as inherent in peoples, as one of social and political order and the integration of the growing underclass into civil society. [. . .] With a historical perspective, the problem can be seen as nothing new — though its guise has changed slightly. The overall problem is deeply political. It is our contention that there can be no easy technical, administrative or politically neutral solutions to the major social and economic problems which underlie, and cause, the 'regional' or the 'inner city' problems.

22 Inner city problems and policies: a Conservative view

Peter Walker

The city is the most important of our products. It was Winston Churchill who once said, 'We shape our cities and then they shape our way of life'. Britain's urban problems are aggravated because of the way the majority of our cities developed in the early stages of the Industrial Revolution. These cities contain old housing, old factories and old civic buildings. Their rivers have been allowed to become polluted and they suffer from a lack of any total concept or vision. The western world faces problems that arise because a society with a disorganised mixture of competing objectives is unable to provide a high quality of life. The several self-interests do not add up to common benefit. It is the way we tackle the problem of improving the quality of city life that will determine whether our cities will prove to be the death or the revival of our civilisation.

The people who live in the most deprived areas of our major cities have a bad record of voting, perhaps because over the years they have felt that voting for one party or another did not make very much difference. In these areas communications are bad: many of the people do not read widely, they do not listen to the news programmes, and they concentrate upon lighter entertainment if they have television. They do not feel they have much power to influence authority, for what complaints they have made in past years have sometimes been listened to but seldom acted upon. The officers of local authorities and government departments appear to them rather remote, both physically and culturally. They have reached a stage of permanent despair in which there is little hope, and as hope disappears tacit acceptance takes its place.

Ignorance of the facts

I was not only the first Secretary of State for the Environment in

Source: 'The political framework: a Conservative view', in Martin Loney and Mark Allen (eds), *The Crisis of the Inner City*, London, Macmillan, 1979, pp. 9–18, 21.

319

Britain but the first person to hold such a position in any democracy, and I was excited by the possibility of using the resources of a large department to improve radically the condition of our inner city areas. I quickly discovered that the realities of inner city life in Britain were relatively unknown to both local and central government: it was known how many people were on social security in certain localities; there was an awareness of areas of high unemployment and areas where the crime rate was high; but there were no plans to transform these areas.

Primarily, there had been no assessment of what was necessary to improve housing conditions. Certain areas were scheduled for demolition, a process that tended to add to a locality's misery for a considerable period of time. The bulldozer was used not just on houses that needed to be replaced but on countless thousands of houses that could well have been improved and would have provided far pleasanter houses than the multi-storey blocks to which their occupants were transferred. There was no accurate information about those people who needed social security and other benefits but were not obtaining them. There was no basic measure of the horrific conditions that currently existed or of the quality of life that it was so desperately important to obtain. I was determined to discover the scope of the problems and then to pursue policies that would transform the reality of today, ghastly and awful as it is for many communities, into a decent and tolerable life in the future.

The inner city studies

I decided to examine the underlying problems in six urban areas. Three of these areas were to be complete towns — Sunderland, Rotherham and Oldham — and three of them districts of major cities which were known to suffer from multiple deprivations — Liverpool 7 and 8, Birmingham Small Heath and the London borough of Lambeth. I decided that this was not an inquiry that should be in the hands of officials, because I felt that it was important that from the very beginning politicians, and politicians with power, should be immersed in the study. I asked that each of these inquiries should be under a steering committee of three people: a minister from my department, the leader of the local council (being the person with most political power in the locality concerned) and a senior partner of a major firm of consultants on urban problems. I took the chair at the inquiry looking into a district of Birmingham. Others of my ministers took the chair at each of the other inquiries. The six leaders of the councils agreed to take their place, and six different firms of consultants were chosen so that we would get a genuine diversity of ideas, observations and solutions from the reports. The store of knowledge thus obtained would enable us to tackle vigorously and competently the problems of our cities.

It is a matter of deep personal regret that within a few months of starting these studies I was moved to another department to become the Secretary of State for Trade and Industry. I regret even more that, thereafter, these studies took a lower priority in the work of the Department of the Environment. Ministerial interest gradually lessened and when the reports finally appeared, with little publicity or comment, they remained almost totally unknown, not only in the country as a whole but even in the towns and localities upon which the reports were based. Nevertheless, they have provided a fund of knowledge for future ministers to draw upon, for they do show the way to future progress, and even more devastatingly they point out the terrible mistakes of the past and the present, demonstrating clearly our continuing failure to provide the resources that are needed.

The Liverpool study covers a district that has all the problems associated with the worst of our inner city areas — the district known as Liverpool 8. Liverpool 8 contains 9.6 per cent of the population of the city but it has a much higher incidence of the worst urban problems. At a time when the city was suffering from an unemployment rate of 8 per cent, Liverpool 8 had a rate of 11 per cent and the worst ward a rate of 18 per cent. Whereas 4 per cent of the population of Liverpool as a whole are immigrants, Liverpool 8 has 8 per cent and the worst ward 13 per cent. Liverpool has a far greater concentration of families with large numbers of children. In Liverpool as a whole 6 per cent of the families have more than four children. In Liverpool 8 the figure is 9 per cent. The number of educationally subnormal children in the worst district of Liverpool 8 is almost twice the figure for Liverpool as a whole. The proportion of adults who are mentally ill in the city as a whole is 0.5 per cent: in Liverpool 8 it is 2.8 per cent, in the worst ward 4.5 per cent.

The housing conditions in Liverpool 8 are very much worse than in the rest of the city. There are over 1.5 persons to a room in only 3 per cent of the households in Liverpool, but in the worst ward of Liverpool 8 the figure is 9 per cent. In the city as a whole 71 per cent of the population have a bath, an inside toilet and hot water, but only 43 per cent of the people in Liverpool 8 have such fundamental facilities. As to the housing stock in the area, 8 per cent is either due for clearance or has been scheduled as having a short life of only 15 years or less. Future plans for redevelopment will result in the closure of over 100 of the 180 businesses in the district.

With 9.6 per cent of the total population of Liverpool living in an area of such multi-deprivation, one would anticipate that much more than 9.6 per cent of Liverpool's expenditure would be put into the area. The inner city study discloses the horrifying fact that in this part of Liverpool they do not even obtain the 9.6 per cent of the expenditure which they would get if they were just getting the average allocation for the city as a whole, for they obtain only 6.1 per cent of the money available. The basic principle of the greater the problems the less the effort is, I am afraid, typical of many of Britain's cities. [. . .]

The crime figures for our cities are alarming, and accelerating. In the Inner London area in 1973 one in every 25 children between the ages of 10 and 16 was arrested. This proportion has grown worse since. In 1975 in the Metropolitan Police area young people between the ages of 10 and 16 accounted for half the arrests for burglary and a third of all the arrests.

The accelerating decline

What are the underlying problems that create these conditions? There is the growing problem of unemployment, a problem that increases as our public transport system breaks down. Many lower income families living in inner city areas are unable to provide their own transport, and as public transport ceases to function they become immobile. A second problem is the crime rate itself, for not only is it increasing and self-reinforcing but it creates further problems which encourage delinquency. It is very difficult to attract new businesses to areas of high crime rate. Businesses that are perpetually burgled and have to have windows barricaded find other locations. More people become unemployed and the crime rate rises. This particularly affects young people.

These districts contain a large proportion of elderly people who have nowhere else to move to and are trapped in the locality. They are the reception areas for those who move to our bigger cities, be it from Glasgow, Cork or Bombay. They are areas where there is very little proper professional advice available. The best solicitors do not site their offices in such localities, so the quality of legal advice is inferior. Doctors prefer to live and work in pleasant areas rather than where their professional skills are most needed.

Fundamental to the improvement of life in our inner cities is the task of creating better job opportunities. A combination of high unemployment and low earnings brings about a rapid deterioration in the quality of life in these areas. As jobs become scarce longer journeys are needed to obtain work, and as public transport breaks down job opportunities are reduced. As the price of public transport increases the expense of travelling considerable distances becomes a factor in still further reducing living standards. The necessity for mothers to work longer to supplement the family income means that the children receive less attention and the likelihood that children will play truant and commit petty crimes is correspondingly increased. The prospects of employment and good earnings are worse for the unskilled than the skilled, worse for black than white, worse for the school-leaver than those already established in their jobs. The inner city areas contain, predominantly, the unskilled and the blacks, and they also have a very substantial volume of school-leavers in proportion to their total populations. The difference between the aspirations and the qualifications of many of the young people represents a basis for discontent.

A positive programme for full employment

A positive programme for improving employment opportunities in the inner city areas is urgent.

1   The government's industrial development certificate powers should be applied so as to benefit selected areas. At the present time they are applied to benefit whole regions of the country – the northwest, the north-east, Scotland and Wales. There are districts in Birmingham and London in which unemployment is so high that it is imperative to direct more industrial and commercial activity to them. Selected districts of our major cities should, like the regions of high unemployment, be designated into regions where industrial development certificates will no longer be required.

2   The government's job creation programme should concentrate on the inner city areas with high unemployment as well as the regions of high unemployment.

3   The effects on job opportunities should become a far more dominant factor in decisions about redevelopment. In far too many parts of our major cities reconstruction programmes have meant the elimination of many small businesses and their replacement with housing, educational and recreational facilities which provide no work for the people concerned.

4   In looking at future land designation for planning purposes and in the allocation of land which central or local government already has in its ownership, the provision of space for commercial and industrial activities should be an important consideration.

5   Small business advisory services should be developed in inner city areas with high unemployment. As Secretary of State for Trade and

Industry I instituted such a programme when I realised how many of the small firms which contribute so much to our employment and export prospects did not have available to them the same range of information and knowledge that the larger firms naturally possessed. They were not as aware as the larger firms of the availability of different forms of government aid and government grants. Nor were they aware of the range of government export services. They were ignorant of some important and up-to-date methods of marketing. The provision of an advisory service to small firms and small industries is highly cost-effective: it is relatively cheap to run and the benefits of the expansion of these small businesses more than compensate for any public expenditure involved.

6   We should take advantage of unemployment in the construction industry to transform the built environment of our inner cities. When in 1971 I was faced with rising unemployment in the construction industry, I persuaded the then Conservative government that it was an absurdity when there was so much to be done that these men should be idle and drawing unemployment or supplementary benefit. I increased to 75 per cent the improvement grants for modernising older houses and saw to it that the grants for the clearance of derelict land and slag heaps were increased. The unique scheme of 'Operation Eyesore' was started, whereby any local authority that had a dirty building, a derelict site it wished to landscape, or indeed any other eyesore, could obtain a substantial grant to remove it. This was given on condition that the work was completed within two years – the two years in which there would otherwise have been high unemployment in the construction industry.

7   We should substantially improve training facilities within the areas of high unemployment in our inner cities.

8   We must see that in these areas the schools and other educational facilities place a far greater emphasis on preparing people for the work opportunities that are likely to exist.

9   We must provide better schools. If we are to revive these areas, less crime and better schools are the best way to bring back the future leaders, the future managers, and the middle classes in general to these localities. Such people will not live in areas of high crime and bad schools. Frequently the areas with the worst housing also have the worst schools. A Ministry of Education inquiry showed that whereas over the whole country 40 per cent of school buildings tended to be inadequate the corresponding figure for areas of bad housing was nearly 80 per cent. The EPA (Educational Priority Area) report on primary schools showed that in the London project area 25 per cent of children change schools during the school year. The teaching staff in urban stress areas also shows a high turnover rate and only a small proportion of teachers have more than five years' experience. A large majority of teachers in these

schools come from middle-class or white-collar backgrounds and live outside the areas where they teach. Attainment tests suggest that there are many more lower-attaining children in the urban stress areas than elsewhere, while a high proportion of children have serious linguistic difficulties. The problems caused by past immigration will be with the schools for a long time. What is essential is to provide a more extensive programme of English-teaching for immigrant children. The social problems created by immigrants' inability to communicate with the rest of the community are self-evident. If this prevents them getting jobs it will only intensify the cycle of deprivation.

10   We must organise local government finance in such a way that the declining inner city areas are not the areas where local taxation is at its peak. One of the disasters of the United States has been that high local taxation in the inner cities has pushed out industry and commerce and the more prosperous people. Inner city areas have to meet the high costs that follow from poverty and bad housing, which means that the amount of tax they have to raise per head of the population is very much higher than elsewhere. In these areas the child population is normally much higher, which means that they also have more schoolchildren to support. As industrial firms and the more prosperous families move away, they deprive the areas of major sources of revenue and so add a still greater burden to the already impoverished people that remain. It is vital that whatever system of local government finance is adopted it is one that prevents this scenario.

11   Crime-prevention must be increased in these areas. The relationship between crime and high unemployment must be recognised. The two are very closely interlinked. In areas of high crime, job opportunities decline swiftly; in areas of high unemployment, crime increases swiftly. There could not be a more vicious circle. It is vital therefore not only that crime prevention is increased in such areas but also that jobs are provided so that the young do not turn to crime, as they always have done in areas of unemployment. In inner city areas three times as many major crimes are committed as in other parts of the cities. But even this is not a true index of the realities of crime in those areas, for the statistics of crime tend to be the statistics of arrests. For much of the petty crime in these districts there are no arrests. There is a mass of vandalism — to public housing and to commercial premises — which is seldom detected and for which there are few arrests but which does immense damage and harm to the prospects of the locality itself. In New York crime is so bad that there are many localities into which the police hardly go. It is vital, if our inner city areas continue to decline, that we do not create no-go areas. [. . .]

The urgent choice

The problem of our inner cities is caused by their concentration of people living on the economic and social margins of society. This concentration is increasing. The economic and social conditions are deteriorating. The problem of the inner city is the most serious social problem facing British government. Urgent action is needed if the problem is not to become as intractable as it has in the United States.

The cost of failure to solve the problems of our cities will be paid in lives of misery for many of the inhabitants. The reward of well thought out, dynamic policies could be cities of beauty and opportunity where men and women can decide for themselves how they will work, live and enjoy their leisure.

There is a reward of such magnitude that it should command the highest priority in any political party.

23   Planning and the property market: conflict or co-operation?

Bob Colenutt

The geography of our towns and cities and the quality of the urban environment is shaped by the property market in land and buildings and by local authority planning. In some areas the environment has got markedly worse in recent years, and even where it appears reasonably good there may be sharp local disagreements over how land or buildings are used. In some cities large areas have been redeveloped and transformed against the expressed wishes of most local people.

How can this be? After all, local people elect the local councils which are responsible for planning, and the United Kingdom has had a comprehensive system of town and country planning for over thirty years. Are the planners to blame, or does the fault lie in the way the property market operates? Sometimes it is 'property speculators' who are blamed, but if they are responsible, why don't the planners intervene? All these questions boil down to one central one: What is the relationship between planning and the property market?

This article begins by describing the functions of the planners and their general relationship with property developers. Then it examines how this relationship differs in three different types of area and how the 'balance of power' between planners and developers might be changed.

Planners and developers

Local authority planners have two main responsibilities. First, they prepare plans which show where different types of property development can take place. These plans take into account the views of local people and they include maps showing the desired pattern of land uses and transport links, and the policies which are to be used to achieve the aims of the plan. Second, the planners assess development proposals

Source: article commissioned for this Reader. Bob Colenutt is Research Officer, Joint Docklands Action Group, London.

submitted by developers, builders or private individuals. These 'planning applications' are judged against the local authority's plan for the area and other council policies, and the final decision is normally taken by a committee of councillors. Thus the main point of contact between developers and planners is when planning applications are submitted. Applicants are concerned to get their proposals approved as quickly as possible, while the planners try to ensure that development corresponds with council plans and policies.

In some cases, particularly when a big development scheme is contemplated, a developer may approach the local authority and the planners will co-operate in drawing up a 'planning brief' for the site to provide guidelines for the developer when submitting a formal planning application.

The relationships between planners and developers become clearer if we look at areas with different potentials for development. In 1980, the Property Advisory Group — a committee of financiers, developers and property experts appointed by the government — distinguished three types of development area.

1   Areas where the private sector wants to invest and does not seek special incentives from local authorities. In these areas, primarily located in central London and the South-East of England, there is strong demand for property even during national economic recessions. Here investors are only too anxious to find buildings and land to invest in, and they object to delays or restrictions in taking advantage of these opportunities.
2   Areas in which the private sector will invest provided the public sector, in the shape of local councils or the government, takes a share in the risk or makes considerable prior infrastructure investment. These areas are located in city centres outside South-East England and in some industrial estates around the big cities.
3   Areas where private investors are extremely reluctant to take risks even where local authorities or government departments are prepared to underwrite infrastructure costs. Parts of Glasgow, Liverpool, East London, Newcastle and other inner city areas fall into this category.

Under the circumstances where parts of the country are besieged by pressure for development and other parts cannot attract private investment at any price, the strategies and activities of the planners vary widely.

Planning in areas of high demand

In the high-demand areas such as central London, planners must either accommodate demand pressures or formulate policies for restraining or deflecting unwanted development. Policies for preventing development in the 'Green Belt' or for decentralizing offices and industry, which have been associated with British planning since the 1950s, are typical responses to the concentration of demand for development.

The key question that arises in the high-demand areas is this – To what degree do the plans reflect the requirements of developers and investors and to what extent do they reflect the needs of local residents? The planners will often argue that the pattern of development undertaken by the private sector will 'benefit the community'. But in local plans for central city areas or suburban centres it is exceptional to find an explanation of *how*, or to what extent, local people will benefit from the planned development.

We often need to look at the history of these local plans to discover their real aims. A good example is the history of the Cardiff Centre Plan documented by Bob Dumbleton in a booklet appropriately called *The Second Blitz*. In 1965, the Cardiff City Council hired planning consultants Colin Buchanan and Partners to prepare an entire transport and economic development strategy for the city. Buchanan came up with proposals for 36 miles of urban motorway, a redeveloped and enlarged city centre, and five new suburban shopping centres. Quite apart from the destruction of 3,300 homes by the motorways and the drastic impact of the new shopping centres on local shopping parades, the plan was based upon highly speculative assumptions about shopping demand and car ownership. Yet demands from local residents for a public inquiry were turned down by the Welsh Secretary of State.

The Council advertised for a developer for the town centre redevelopment and selected Ravenseft Properties, a subsidiary of Land Securities Investment Trust, the largest property company in the UK. Ravenseft and the Council produced a planning brief in 1968, later amended in 1969, called the Centreplan. This plan contained one million square feet of new office space, a new shopping centre, large multi-storey car parks and an exhibition hall. The Council would assemble the land and lease it to Ravenseft who would undertake the redevelopment.

An inquiry was held into Centreplan, but the Welsh Office made only minor alterations to the land use proposals. In 1971, ten days before the local elections, the Council signed with Ravenseft. The plan obscured the financial issues – the costs, risks and deals – involved. But in the end it was these that killed Centreplan. With virtually nothing built four years after the contract was signed, Ravenseft pulled out and Cardiff Council cancelled the contract in 1975. The Centreplan – described by the consultants and developers as the 'most exciting development of the decade' – evaporated because of the collapse of the property market in 1974. But enormous damage had been done: land and buildings awaiting redevelopment were blighted and new roads had been partially built.

Cardiff Council tried to pick up the pieces by producing a less ambitious plan focusing on just four major city-centre sites. Again developers were invited to tender. This time the Heron Corporation was chosen, and rapidly obtained planning permission for two office blocks and a shopping centre. Again the Council was to play a leading role as assembler of land and provider of car parks; all provided on very favourable terms to Heron.

The devastation of Cardiff city centre is a monument to 'demand-led' local planning in which the plan is derived from estimates of private sector demand. Three vital ingredients were missing from the plan. First, an assessment of what was needed by the residents of Cardiff; second, an appraisal of the financial viability of the Ravenseft plan, and third, an assessment of who would benefit and who would lose out.

The Cardiff story is not unusual. Similar processes have taken place in Swansea, Port Talbot, Newcastle, North Southwark in London, Wapping in London's Docklands, Croydon, Brighton and Edinburgh – just to name the cases which have been documented. They show that there is a weak correspondence between the gains for developers and investors and the benefits for local residents, and that invariably the costs and consequences of 'demand-led' plans are not assessed. Indeed, the economics of the property investment and the distribution of land ownership are politically sensitive issues and as such are often 'hidden' by the planners themselves.

Planning gains

Local councils also accommodate development pressures by negotiating so-called 'planning gains' from developers of particular sites. If the profits from a development scheme are large, then local councils can often persuade developers to provide landscaping, open space, public rights of way or housing units in exchange for planning permission for the main commercial development. Although it is illegal to require these 'extras' unless they can be justified on strictly planning grounds, it is nevertheless common for planners to negotiate planning gains. There is a very fine line between offering a bribe to the council in order to get planning permission and entering into a planning gain agreement; often planners may wonder if they are being bribed, while developers may think they are being blackmailed.

As for 'the community' which is supposed to be the beneficiary of such agreements, there are serious drawbacks to the planning gain approach. First, the extras are entirely dependent on the financial viability of the overall development which, as in the Cardiff case, is often in serious doubt. Such schemes are extremely sensitive to economic cycles and interest rates and, even when started, take years to complete. Second, the planning gains may not be what local residents want or may be located in quite the wrong place. A planning gain that makes a good addition to an office block, such as a car park or an exhibition hall, may be of no benefit at all to residents of the area. Even a community hall or play-space may be worthless if it is located on the wrong side of a busy main road or away from where residents live.

London contains some bizarre reminders of the failure of the planning gain approach. Around some of London's most famous office landmarks such as Centre Point, the Euston Centre or the IPC Tower at Blackfriars Bridge, you will find empty shop fronts, unfinished landscaping, deserted plazas or unused underground car parks – each intended to be the extras that would make the main development more palatable to the local planning authority.

Developers and their advisers generally have more 'leverage' than the planners, and the latter are often unable to find a solution to the conflicts between the pressures from developers and the needs of local residents. We have seen that local plans are often formulated around the proposals of developers, and massive public protest would be required substantially to modify the plans of a council committee to this type of planning: normally only minor changes can be achieved. Often discussions take place between planners and developers well before the public hears about the scheme. Once the scheme has been made public, the planners can offer interested residents only minor modifications. Only where a council has itself got an alternative strategy, or is willing to listen to alternatives, can public consultation make an impact.

Planning in areas of moderate demand

Whereas in high-demand areas many sites may be regarded as 'prime' investment locations, in areas where demand is lower there are very few prime sites; most will be either 'secondary' or of no interest at all to investors. In these areas demand for property is variable and uncertain. In boom times, demand will pick up, but this can be short lived, as the Cardiff example showed. Investors will be highly selective in ensuring that the location, quality and user of the building are all just right. Local authorities have to work much harder to attract new investment and will often have to bear a proportion of the financial risks in order to get the developer or finance house to commit themselves. Thus, in medium-demand areas with developers and investors needing the help of local authorities to realize their schemes and with local councils dependent upon developers to implement local plans, a close relationship between the two is established.

The role of local authorities working in close relationship with developers, local landowners and businesses is not only to prepare plans and expedite planning applications, but to channel land, grants and other incentives towards potential investors or firms that might come into the area. Thus, land may be bought by the local council using its Compulsory Purchase powers and leased back to developers, or sites may be assembled by the council, enabling redevelopment to take place on a comprehensive basis. Small firms can attract grants for improvements to their buildings (under the Inner Urban Areas Act) or in the Development Regions of Wales, Scotland, the North-East or Northern Ireland, developers and businesses can obtain substantial subsidies to encourage them to invest. The new Ford plant in South Wales, for example, received a subsidy of many millions from the government.

On a more modest scale, local councils may offer council houses to 'key workers' in local companies, help firms with loans or give advice about development sites.

Thus the function of local authorities in areas of moderate demand is to minimize the financial risks taken by investors. The risks of putting up private factories, shopping centres or private housing estates are often borne by the public. Public subsidies range from virtual gifts of land and property to financial partnerships between local councils and developers on individual schemes. And when local councils are suffering cut-backs, they are prepared to go to considerable lengths to entice private investors. In a recent case, the county planning officer said that in order to get the 1980 Birmingham City Centre Plan implemented, the council were 'virtually giving away land to developers who were prepared to follow the plan'.

The public outside the town hall and indeed most backbench councillors have little influence over the agreements and arrangements reached between planners and developers. The terms and conditions of council land and property sales, or the details of leases granted to developers, are normally known to just a handful of council officers and councillors. It takes very persistent questioning and investigation for councillors, let alone residents, to find out what is going on — and if they do it is usually too late to influence the agreements.

Planning in depressed areas

The third type of area poses even more serious problems for councils and local residents. In regions of economic decline where industry has closed down leaving large areas of land derelict and blighted, there is little demand for land and property. Investors not only regard such areas as very high risk but attempt to move whatever residual investment they have there out as fast as possible.

Planners and the public are placed in an impossible position. Developers and businesses may be unwilling to invest whatever the incentives offered. No amount of protest by residents is likely to help. Even the best intentioned local plans are unlikely to be implemented.

In much of Glasgow, parts of West Yorkshire, South Wales, Belfast, Merseyside, or London's East End, or in dying mining towns or towns where steel plants have closed, local plans are virtually meaningless — unless backed up by substantial public resources which can carry forward the plan from land reclamation to redevelopment.

Private investment regards such areas as bad risks because of a combination of low demand, high costs of land reclamation, a poor environment and low incomes. Large areas of the country are, therefore, effectively 'red-lined' by banks, pension funds and insurance companies. In the same way that building societies will not lend money for properties within specific run-down areas of cities, so financial institutions regard housing and commercial development a bad risk within the depressed regions of the country and the normal practices of local authorities in minimizing the risks to private investors are generally inadequate to counteract this.

The government has resorted to two new approaches to such problem areas. They have announced the creation of eleven 'Enterprise Zones'. These are zones of up to 500 acres where sweeping subsidies and tax concessions will operate. Modelled loosely on tax-free zones in Hong Kong, Hamburg and Shannon Airport, the idea is to offer exceptional enticements to private investors in the hope that businesses will come into the Enterprise Zones and jobs will be created. A particular feature of Enterprise Zones is that there will be only minimal planning controls, and applying for planning permission will be virtually a formality — the implication being that 'the planners are to blame' for the previous lack of investment.

The underlying assumption of the Enterprise Zones is that economic regeneration can be stimulated by tax concessions and the removal of 'red tape'. Depressed areas, it is argued, can be revived by the private sector if the conditions are 'right'. To some extent, the Enterprise Zone idea has been propagated as a political answer to those who say that only massive investment by the public sector can save blighted inner-city areas and abandoned industrial towns. It remains to be seen whether the Enterprise Zones will attract substantial *new* investment, but most depressed areas are not covered by them.

Similar weaknesses are apparent in the government's proposals to set up 'Urban Development Corporations' in the Liverpool and London docklands. Again the object is 'urban regeneration' and again the means is to concentrate revival on relatively small areas where 'red tape' will be reduced to a minimum. In Urban Development areas, government officials will take over planning from the local councils. Government money will be pumped into land acquisition and reclamation and, once the land is prepared, it will be sold off on favourable terms to the private sector. Again the assumption is that the private sector can make regeneration happen with the government acting as a 'pump primer'.

In both Liverpool and London, the government has put much of the blame for the decay of the inner areas on the local authorities. The aim of the Urban Development Corporations is to show that with control centralized in small 'dynamic' authorities a more streamlined and efficient development machinery can be created which will give greater encouragement to the private sector than would elected local councils. Both Enterprise Zones and Urban Development Corporations are variations of the 'demand-led planning' that we saw in action in Cardiff. The incentives and machinery are different, but the ultimate reliance on private investment and the moulding of plans around that goal – whether by streamlining planning or doing away with it altogether – are identical. It is doubtful, however, whether demand-led planning can alter the criteria of private investors. Very few additional sites can be brought within their scope by this means.

Public development finance is therefore the only long-term answer to the problems faced by the depressed areas. Comprehensive public investment for houses, schools, factories, shops, parks and offices is desperately needed. If it does not take place soon, many more communities will literally die away.

The 'balance of power' in property development

The three types of area we have looked at illustrate the different ways in which the private sector holds the balance of power in the planning and development of towns and cities. Planners and local councils tend to play a rather subservient role to landowners, developers, investors and other businessmen.

The main reasons for this imbalance are:

1   Financial institutions and businesses largely determine what type of investment takes place and where it takes place. They decide on their own criteria what are prime sites or high-risk sites. There is nothing that

planners can do to alter these conditions and only a limited amount
that can be done through planning to alter the market demand for sites
and buildings.

2   Landowners and developers are able to put considerable pressure
on local councillors and planners (and government as well) to 'bend'
local plans and investment programmes in directions favourable to the
private sector.

3   Although there are important exceptions that we consider below,
local councils generally do not have either the political will or the
resources to become developers. They are restricted by central government in their powers and finance to buy land and develop buildings
themselves. Faced with cuts in local government expenditure, many
councils are being forced to sell off the very resources of land and
property that make 'positive' planning possible and, in the absence of
alternative sources of funding, they are being forced to depend heavily
on the private sector.

But the way in which these factors exert themselves in the three
areas varies considerably. In the high-demand areas, planners have much
more leverage over developers than in low-demand areas and thus are
able to extract planning gains more easily. Conversely, in depressed
areas, the planners, far from being able to exercise their powers more
freely, are being required by the government to relinquish them in the
hope that a reduction in planning will provide greater incentives to
private investors.

So far, a rather one-sided picture of the achievements of local councils
in planning the urban environment has been painted. There are in fact
many examples of high quality public developments, but they have
come about under special circumstances.

Specific legislation exists to enable local authorities to build schools,
to enable Health Authorities to build clinics and hospitals, and to allow
councils to build housing, hostels and homes for the elderly and disabled.
Similarly, New Town Acts and Town Development Acts have enabled
extensive public development to take place. But it should be stressed
that under this legislation the public sector has not been operating in
direct competition with the private land and property market. Thus
there is little 'distortion' in most of the public schemes that have gone
forward — most were built in the location and with the design that was
needed. The major exception is in the field of public housing, where
land costs and restrictive legislation have had a considerable impact on
the location, density and design of council housing estates.

We do not have to look far to find examples of outstanding public
schemes. Primary schools built in the 1960s and 1970s under the

Education Acts — low rise and with imaginative designs — can be found in most towns and cities. Some of the London County Council's post-war housing estates such as the Lansbury in East London and its recent so-called 'infill' schemes are very popular with residents. Some towns on the outskirts of the conurbations which were developed under the 1952 Town Development Act such as Swindon or Droitwich are very successful. They include both housing, shops and industrial estates. Many councils have bought run-down housing and have rehabilitated it: old Georgian or Victorian terraces have been renovated, often to a very high standard, instead of being pulled down or left to decay.

The latest generation of 'new build' council or housing association estates since 1970 are often highly acclaimed. In London, outstanding new developments include the Setchell Road Estate in Southwark, the Foundling Estate in Bloomsbury and the Alexandra Road Estate in Camden.

However, the issue of the balance of power is not really raised until public development conflicts with the demands of the market. When high land costs prevent public schemes going ahead or when Compulsory Purchase Orders are resisted by powerful landowners, local authorities have to fight to get their schemes approved by government. Similarly, where legislation allows local councils to *intervene* in the market, that is where the conflict between councils and the market can be best observed.

One such area of intervention is the use of conservation powers. Councils have wide powers to preserve buildings and declare conservation areas. Often this can lead them into conflict with property owners and developers and it takes considerable determination and political will to pursue conservation policies rigorously. Yet successful schemes have been followed through in Bristol and Chester town centre. In London, the preservation and restoration of the Covent Garden market was achieved in the face of intense pressure to demolish the market buildings for an office development.

Another area of intervention is the power given to local authorities under the Inner Urban Areas Act to declare Industrial Improvement Areas and to give grants and loans to firms for improvement and construction of industrial and commercial buildings. Rochdale and Newcastle have been able to bring decaying industrial areas back to life when the market had given them up for lost.

Finally, and most important, local authorities have powers, albeit severely limited by central government, to provide facilities which are normally provided by the private sector. In these cases, councils are in direct competition with market forces. Yet even here there have been some important successes. Gateshead has developed an International Athletic Centre, some authorities have built factory units or workshops, while others have set up co-operative businesses or given money to voluntary groups to start workshops or community projects.

However, when it comes to either turning down a large private development proposal or attempting to provide a facility in competition with developers, the imbalance of power is fully exposed. Not only can developers put considerable pressure on local authorities and government, but political pressure can be exerted to get the council to back down. For example, authorities such as Lambeth, Sheffield and South Yorkshire suffered vilification in the press because they attempted to maintain council services instead of cutting them or passing them over to the private sector.

Another example of the pressure that can be exerted when a local authority stands up against market forces is the Coin Street development in Lambeth, South London. In 1977 the council drew up a statutory local plan for the area which designated the Coin Street sites for housing, but the Secretary of State overruled the plan in favour of a 'mixed development' zoning which then enabled private developers to submit applications for a very large office complex. The sites in question were regarded by the property market and the government as 'too valuable' to be used for housing, even though this was the expressed wish of local residents, local councillors and the council itself.

There is thus a tendency for government to 'rectify' decisions or policies pursued by local authorities that run counter to the demands of the market. This is most obvious when there are conflicts over very expensive sites or valuable properties, but it can exist even in areas of 'moderate demand'.

Changing the 'balance of power'

The main reason for wishing to change the balance of power in the land and property market is to alter the range of interests that can benefit from planning decisions. There is a close relationship between the structure of power and the structure of benefits. Where local authorities or other public bodies have more control, they can regulate and distribute the benefits of planning more widely. In particular, deprived areas can obviously gain far more from interventionist and positive planning than from a planning system that is restricted to the negative action of simply preventing certain types of development.

What are the factors determining the degree of positive planning?

1   Powers to acquire land where and when it is needed by the com-

munity. Local authorities and public bodies cannot plan properly if they cannot obtain land of the right type in the right location.

2   Finance and building resources to enable land and buildings to be reclaimed, rebuilt or renovated in the public interest.

3   Strong negative powers over private development — if powers to say 'no' or to modify development are weak, planning will be largely ineffective.

4   Public participation at all stages in the planning and development of areas. There must be the widest and most open public debate. Plans, developers' schemes and financial agreements — all must be subject to public debate.

It is clear that none of these four conditions exists to any degree in the UK. Where they exist at all it is often in association with specific planning functions, such as for road building, rather than general planning functions. Planning is thus the servant and not the master of the forces shaping the urban environment. Whether we look at redevelopment in London or on Clydeside, the conclusion is the same. The blame for urban decay and environmental mistakes does not lie with the planners. It is true that mistakes have been made by them and that they have often been willing co-ordinators of the development process. But it is a process they largely do not control. Even their political masters, the elected local councils, have limited leverage and few resources to stem urban decay or provide an attractive alternative. The room for manoeuvre of planners and local councils, and ultimately of local residents, is determined largely by investors working through the property market. The financial criteria of the property market, expressed in terms of 'prime', 'secondary' and 'high-risk' sites, are at the root of the urban development process.

24   Racialism and the trade union movement

Bethnal Green and Stepney Trades Council

In Britain racialism has been ruthlessly and successfully promoted by the ruling class and built into their institutions and ideas. It has been used to hold down wages, to maintain bad working conditions, to boost profits and divide the workers. The legacy of an imperial history in particular has built up prejudiced attitudes towards coloured workers which are now endemic among the British working class.

Brian Nicholson, tally clerks' leader in the London Docks, wrote an important paper called *Racialism, Fascism and the Trade Unions* for the Transport and General Workers Union in 1974 which began to explore the 'taboo' subject of racialism within the trade union movement. He faces the harsh reality that racialist sentiment is already deeply rooted in the working class.

There is a paradox in the British labour movement. On the one hand leading figures in the trade unions have always been in the vanguard of opposition to racialism in domestic policy and abroad. The TUC itself has spelled out on many occasions its repudiation of discrimination and bigotry, of racist immigration policies, and the poison of the National Front and similar organisations. This vigorous anti-racialist approach is reflected throughout the movement, in Trades Councils, trade union branches and on the shop floor, among the activists in the movement who make up a small but vital minority. The attitude of these activists is well summed up in this statement from Jack Jones, then General Secretary of the Transport and General Workers Union, in the introduction to *Danger, Racialists at Work* (a pamphlet produced by Liberation after the death of anti-racist Kevin Gately on a demonstration against the National Front in 1974).

The Trade Union Movement was built on the rock of solidarity and brotherhood. Discrimination on the grounds of race, colour or reli-

Source: from *Blood on the Streets*, a report by Bethnal Green and Stepney Trades Council on Racial Attacks in East London, September 1978, pp. 30–5. (The authors are now the Tower Hamlets Trades Council.)

gion is completely contrary to these principles. The disgrace of discrimination and racialism clearly acts against all that is meant by trade unionism. It is surely right therefore that all good trade unionists should set their face against those who attempt to stir up trouble by trying to set worker against worker. Disunity and division can only develop if the racialists succeed. Their propaganda is an assault upon our conscience and good sense. In my view active trade unionists must do all they can to rebutt and rebuff racialists, anti semitic and discriminatory tendencies . . . the alarm is sounded to which we must respond in full measure.

There is again a small minority of active and openly racist bigots who spread their poison among the trade union membership in this country. It is idle to deny their existence, and the damaging influence they have within the movement.

The mass of workers in this country, however, particularly in this predominantly working-class area of London, probably take a more neutral view of race and immigration. There is often strong xenophobia, a worry about the unknown, a distrust of the stranger — especially people who look and behave differently from the traditional inhabitants of this close-knit, single-class East End community. While they do not particularly seek strangers as neighbours or as workmates, once they are here the strangers may be seen in a different light. Class or community interests can be recognised by most of these workers at times of struggle against a common enemy — the boss, the Council, the landlord — as more important than any distrust they may feel towards 'immigrants' in general. The coloured worker or tenant is gradually seen as 'one of our own'. It is this neutral mass of working-class people who can be won as potential allies to take a stand against racialist ideas, or swayed towards the racialist camp quite easily.

It is only at periods such as the present, when capitalism is in deep crisis, that workers' fears of economic insecurity, bad housing conditions and anxiety about unemployment can be stirred up by ruthless demagogues, and racist propagandists can provide a ready scapegoat — the immigrant. Areas where unemployment stands as high as 15 per cent and social conditions are particularly bad, like Tower Hamlets, are ripe for the racists' lies. Black workers get the blame.

Racialism splits and divides the working class with potentially disastrous consequences for organised labour on the shop floor. For the Trade Union Movement racialism is what Nicholson calls: 'the Trojan Horse within the working class' threatening that fragile unity in practice which turns organised labour into a social force, able to combine effectively against the employers' interest.

He warns that racialism is used classically as a rallying point for agitation by fascist organisations seeking to destroy the independent organised labour movement. The vulnerability with British trade unions on the race issue has grown as trade union officials and the rank and file leadership have tended to turn a blind eye to racialism in the workforce while supporting glorious resolutions against racialism at conferences and rallies. Increasingly it is realised that the trade unionist's job is not merely one of recruiting black workers into the trade union movement, but also of working specifically against the structures of discrimination in employment. Issues such as the over-representation of coloured labour in dirty jobs, in night shift work, and lack of opportunities for apprenticeships or promotion for immigrant workers is increasingly recognised as a key area for trade union organisation and action rather than a job for the Race Relations Act to tackle. Nicholson writes: 'Workers' unity cannot be built in a situation where the whites have the spanners and the blacks have the brooms.' Statistics show that proportionately more immigrants are trade union members than workers from the host community (the Bengali workforce in the East End is a rare exception to this rule). However, more and more white trade unionists are beginning to recognise that, as a consequence of the depth of racialist ideas among white working-class people, and the years of neglect or inadequate response by the trade union movement to racial harassment and discrimination, many black workers now are frankly sceptical about the commitment of the trade union movement to racial justice. They have little time for what Nicholson describes as 'existing trade union structures which appear to tolerate inferior conditions for immigrant workers as if they were as natural as a cold in winter.'

Many trade unionists still see immigrants as cheap labour and a major threat to their trade union struggles, to their wage levels and standard of living. The courageous stand of the Grunwick strikers and others has begun to nail that myth. It is clear that the immigrant community in East London for instance will have a great deal to contribute to the movement, and has already shown enormous guts and responsibility in its response to the racist onslaught. There is still a massive job to be done in combating the racialist ideas and attitudes that remain within the trade union movement in the East End of London. There is at least a commitment within the movement to that battle. While there is still widespread ignorance about workers' rights among the embattled Asian community here, at least a start is being made in the long process of unionisation.

The discrimination sub-committee of Tower Hamlets NALGO is beginning to examine racial bias in the Council's employment policies, in collaboration with the Trades Council and the Employment Committee of the Council of Citizens of Tower Hamlets (the local CRC).

During the winter of 1977 a fight for the rights of Asian workers led to Bethnal Green and Stepney Trades Council becoming involved in a building workers' dispute about a cut in wages at the Nat West Bank site in Alie Street, E1. The police arrested nine pickets who were warming their hands on a brazier in the bitter cold. The brazier had been used for nine weeks by striking firemen across the road from the building site without harassment. All the pickets arrested were Ugandan Asians. There were white strikers on three other gates to the site warming their hands in the same way who were not approached or stopped by the police. The Trades Council and the building workers' union UCATT protested strongly against what was seen clearly as racial discrimination as well as harassment of pickets in the police handling of this industrial dispute. Over £400 was raised to help pay off the fines and wages loss suffered by the pickets. The pickets were arrested for the 'wanton lighting of bonfires', an offence dating back to the 1830s, originally brought in to smash the 'Captain Swing' riots and the hayrick burning by oppressed agricultural workers at the time of the attempted repeal of the Combination Acts.

Blatant harassment of trade union pickets in industrial disputes with the law acting as 'company police' has been virtually unknown in the East End of London in recent years. Fears are growing that this episode might herald the start of a new police tactic, particularly if it is to be directed against coloured workers.

There is an added significance for trade unionists that the picket line where these pickets were arrested was some 30 yards from the place where the Amalgamated Society of Engineers, predecessor of the giant Amalgamated Union of Engineering Workers, was founded in 1851.

The area of work most Bengalis have chosen in East London, the rag trade, is notoriously difficult to organise, where many small family shops barely survive from season to season. However, considerable efforts are being made now by the Tailors & Garment Workers' Union to recruit Bengalis. Only the larger clothing factories tend to be organised by trade unions. Although trade union membership is very low among the Bengali community so far, NUT & GW shop stewards make a point of explaining to all immigrant workers in the organised shops that the union is a combination for all employees regardless of their background, set to protect their interests against the employer and that their union throughout its history has been built round successive generations of immigrant clothing workers. Following the murders of Altab Ali and Ishaque Ali (who was a member of the NUT & GW) the National Executive Committee of the union issued a powerful statement in English and Bengali condemning racist attacks:

Equality for all workers, irrespective of race, colour, national origin, creed or sex, has always been an important tenet of faith within the labour movement, so the continued attacks on working people because of their colour or national origins by racialist groups in the East End of London and elsewhere are alien to us.

We strongly condemn any arbitrary attempt to divide worker from worker and call upon our members to stand up and fight against racism at every level. An attack on any member of our Union is an attack on our basic principles and we can not stand idly by while our members are subjected to physical attacks and intimidation.

The understandable fear of the Bengalee community in the East End of London must be countered by efforts on the part of the authorities to ensure that the cause for their fear is removed. In this respect we cannot emphasise too much the need for the Government and the Police in particular to win the confidence of the Bengalee community.

The work of the Trades Council is particularly important and we urge our members from all sections of the community to participate effectively in their activities.

We call upon all workers in the clothing industry, irrespective of their ethnic origins, to join the National Union of Tailors and Garment Workers and to play a full role in its activities.

This was followed up by visits from Len Murray, TUC General Secretary, and Bill Keys, Chairman of the TUC's Equal Rights Committee, to the East End on the invitation of the Trades Council, and the publication of a major statement from the TUC, in four languages, on the race relations situation in East London, which was widely circulated through the Trade Union Movement in the area.

Conclusion

Racialism is a major threat gnawing at the entrails of the trade unions. The labour movement now has to take the fight against the divisive poison of race hate from the pious resolutions of Congress, union conferences and rallies and tackle the menace head on at the workplace and on the shop floor.

SECTION 7

The Individual and Society

Introduction

Clive Holloway

In the study of society, the individual tends to get lost in the crowd. We, as people, are the cannon fodder of the statistics and classifications in social theory — we become wage-earners, voters, unionists, or even tinkers, tailors, beggar-men or thieves. In some senses this is a fair and necessary kind of depersonalization. The workings of capitalist economics, or of democracy, require explanations in terms of social process, not of social beings. Yet somehow there seems to be something missing in any wide-ranging analysis of society which reduces a person to the status of a social unit.

One reason why a study of human nature, and of its individual variety, is needed for a complete account of society is that an understanding of personality allows us to 'round off' the picture provided by the other social sciences. It explores those variations in behaviour which go beyond the sociologists' social roles, or socio-economic classes. It allows us to analyse the differences between those whose perceptions of the world make them vote to the left or to the right, conform or rebel, stay sane or go mad, even when people are trapped within the same socio-economic niche.

There is another more urgent reason for studying human nature. The relationship between the individual and society is problematic, and needs some explanation of its own. Should we, for instance, regard the person as a miniature encapsulation of social process, a product of cultural conditioning? Or could we turn the tables and suggest that social process merely represents a mechanism for satisfying the inherent existential and biological needs of individuals? What role can we ascribe for consciousness — the uniquely human capacity for self-awareness? Is society a product of man's inventive intelligence, or is it a result of his unconscious drives, a product which the conscious mind can only gaze on — in awe or trepidation?

There are no simple answers to such questions. The relationship between the individual and society itself depends on which of a number of competing ideas about human nature are subscribed to. The study of individuals — their behaviour and experiences — lies in the realm of what may be described as the psychological sciences, but these represent no more than a conglomeration of disciplines which span the bridge between science and social science, and which propagate very different views on the relationship between man and the social environment.

In the first article of this section a number of different viewpoints are contrasted, ranging from those which explain human nature in terms of genetic endowment to those which suggest that human nature is no more than the habits and thoughts instilled by social conditioning. Their span runs from those conceptions of humanity which regard people as passive agents — victims of their own inheritance or of their social environment — to those which see people as conscious and active creators of their own social world. And there are those viewpoints which argue for the engagement of all these perspectives in a single and integrated model of man.

In an academic world, science and social science disciplines compete for the explanatory rights to human nature and it is therefore of the utmost importance to base any discussion on a clear understanding of the implicit beliefs and assumptions which lie behind the facts and explanations which any approach offers. In article 25, the characteristics of these different approaches are stated in perhaps their most programmatic, most provocative, form in a series of short extracts from the work of their most famous exponents, past and present.

In contrasting the ideas of 'individual' and 'society' we should be careful not to oversimplify the relationship between the two. People do not stand just as isolated units, generating within a vast, depersonalized social structure. Most of our dealings with the social world are conducted with people whom we know and within the context of the informal social groups among which we spend much of our lives — the family, neighbours, workmates or the street-corner gang. People negotiate their place in a world of other people. But the way in which people find a place in the social world involves, *inter alia*, an analysis at two different levels.

Within a wider context, we need to discover the structure of informal social worlds, and the social roles which those structures require. The behaviour of the individual only then becomes interpretable, because it must be seen as an attempt to live out one of those subscribed roles and to satisfy others within the enclosed social world that the role is being fulfilled satisfactorily. In article 26 Peter Marsh looks at the social world of the football terraces and shows how the seemingly aimless violence which occasionally erupts within it is explicable once we stop judging it as spectators, and enter the world of young fans, both on and off the terraces. The hooligan who so often appears on our television screens fulfils a particular social role in a social structure which gives both meaning and support to its individual members.

Yet we also need to explain how people adopt and adapt to these social roles, and how such roles are projected to other members of the group. The individual stands for a particular position within the social structure, and must maintain the appearances and satisfy the expectancies which that position demands. In article 27, Erving Goffman discusses how we judge each other in our social roles, and how we project an image of ourselves while forming impressions of others. He describes social interactions as a precarious exchange in which each participant attempts to reach behind the social façade of the other in order to evaluate the trustworthiness and reliability of his opponent as an individual.

In all of this — the necessity to consider the relationship between person, social group and society at large — there are profound methodological problems. If the other social sciences find difficulty in creating a value-free assessment of social process — if only because we live within the scope of its operation — how much more difficult it is when man, as scientist, turns his attention to himself. How is the psychologist to study man? The attempt to find a solution to this problem has, in the opinion of many, not been successfully achieved. In the last article in this section Isidor Chein explains how the psychological sciences have often ducked the problem, preferring to study only those circumscribed aspects of human nature that seem to be susceptible to orthodox methods of 'scientific' analysis. In doing so, Chein argues, they may have thrown out the existential baby with the scientific bath-water.

25 Human natures?

David Barash, Erik Erikson, Erich Fromm,
George Kelly, Mary Midgley, B. F. Skinner
and John B. Watson

25.1 Have we a nature?

Mary Midgley

Every age has its pet contradictions. Thirty years ago, we used to accept
Marx and Freud together, and then wonder, like the chameleon on the
turkey carpet, why life was so confusing. Today there is similar trouble
over the question whether there is, or is not, something called Human
Nature. On the one hand, there has been an explosion of animal behaviour studies, and comparisons between animals and men have become
immensely popular. People use evidence from animals to decide whether
man is naturally aggressive, or naturally territorial; even whether he has
an aggressive or territorial instinct. Moreover, we are still much influenced
by Freudian psychology, which depends on the notion of instinct.* On
the other hand, many sociologists and psychologists still hold what may
be called the Blank Paper view, that man is a creature entirely without
instincts. So do Existentialist philosophers. If man has no instincts, all
comparison with animals must be irrelevant. (Both these simple party
lines have been somewhat eroded over time, but both are still extremely
influential.)

According to the Blank Paper view, man is entirely the product of
his culture. He starts off infinitely plastic, and is formed completely by
the society in which he grows up. There is then no end to the possible
variations among cultures; what we take to be human instincts are just
the deep-dug prejudices of our own society. Forming families, fearing
the dark, and jumping at the sight of a spider are just results of our conditioning. Existentialism at first appears a very different standpoint,
because the Existentialist asserts man's freedom and will not let him
call himself a product of anything. But Existentialism too denies that
man has a nature; if he had, his freedom would not be complete. Thus

---

* For a good modern revision of Freudian views in relation to ethology,
see Anthony Storr, *Human Aggression* (Penguin Books, 1971).

Sartre insisted that 'there is no human nature . . . Man first of all exists, encounters himself, surges up in the world, and defines himself afterwards. If man as the Existentialist sees him is not definable, it is because to begin with he is nothing. He will not be anything until later, and then he will be what he makes himself.' For Existentialism there is only the human condition, which is what happens to man and not what he is born like. If we are afraid of the dark, it is because we choose to be cowards; if we care more for our own children than for other people's, it is because we choose to be partial. We must never talk about human nature or human instincts. [. . .]

I am suggesting that we badly need new and more suitable concepts for describing human motivation [. . .] It might seem that we know plenty about that much-described matter, human conduct. So we might, if we had always asked the right questions and had not been more anxious to deceive ourselves than to learn the truth. But we can always do with new questions. People like Nietzsche, Freud, and Marx, by asking new questions, have taught us much, and it is yet further questions, and a more intelligent connecting of questions, that we still need. [. . .]

Source: *Beast and Man: the Roots of Human Nature*, Methuen, University Paperback, copyright Cornell University, 1978, extracts from ch. 1, pp. 3–24.

25.2 People in the service of their genes

David Barash

As Samuel Butler pointed out, a chicken is but an egg's way of making more eggs. A more modern view might be that a chicken is a device invented by chicken genes to enhance the likelihood of more chicken genes being projected into the future. People are similar devices – temporary, skin-encapsulated egos, serving as complex tools by means of which their potentially immortal genes replicate themselves.

Natural selection is happening whenever some individuals produce more successful offspring than others, which is another way of saying that some genes are making more copies of themselves than are others. In other words, individuals and genes differ from other individuals and genes in their *fitness* – how successful they are at projecting copies of themselves into future generations. Those that are more successful we call more 'fit.'

The fit – not the meek – have already inherited the earth. This is not to espouse cutthroat competition or dog-eat-dog nastiness. The fact is that fitness may be achieved in many different ways, of which the most important are probably the least eye-catching — keeping the body going, avoiding temperature excesses, getting enough to eat and so on. Although success in all these activities requires a great deal of complex organization, and although a clear-cut goal is achieved — maximum fitness — neither the genes nor their carriers need have any picture of what they are doing, or why. They simply do their job, and natural selection does the rest. [. . .]

One of the new insights of sociobiology is that fitness, mediated by natural selection, is not limited to such relatively simple factors as the structure or functioning of a body. It also includes complex social behaviors, such as courting, fighting, associating with friends and caring for offspring. It turns out that, in general, individuals that function better socially are better perpetuators of their genes (that is, are maximally fit) and are more favored by natural selection than those who don't.

Notice that the focus in all our discussions is intensely selfish, focusing on the individual and not on the species. This emphasis runs counter to most people's conception of evolution: that it proceeds for the benefit of the species. This is a crucial point: it does nothing of the sort. [. . .]

As do all other living things, people get ahead in evolution by passing on their genes to the next generation. Every time a person reproduces, he or she passes on half of its genes to the child. [. . .] When these genes unite with the packaged genes from an individual of the opposite sex, somebody new is produced, carrying one-half of the replicated genes from each parent. There is only one way that natural selection can get a handle on the success of our genes: by the success of the bodies that carry them. Evolution is a process of gene replication, and it has no interest in what we do, except insofar as our behavior contributes, either positively or negatively, to this replication. And, in fact, everything we do, from relaxing, to working, fighting, eating — indeed, everything we do — does have consequences for reproduction, even though sometimes these consequences may seem small and almost inconsequential.

By reproducing, we replicate our genes. Parental behavior, then, in all animals — including humans — occurs because it represents the successful strategy of constituent genes in reproducing themselves. A genetic basis for intentional childlessness would have a dim evolutionary future indeed!

The plain fact is that genes have been selected for success in looking out for themselves, and they accomplish this by making copies of themselves. Making babies is their major way of doing that — although not the only way. [. . .] Even reproducing is merely a special case of the more general evolutionary requirement of selfishness. Parental love itself is actually but an evolutionary strategy whereby genes replicate themselves. They do so by inducing the parents (their bodies) to behave in ways that enhance the success of their offspring. That is, the love of parent for child is one way that genes look after copies of themselves, encapsulated within other bodies, called children. Of course, our genes don't think, much less plan strategies. But they act as though they do. [. . .]

Source: *Sociobiology: the Whispering Within*, Harper & Row, Souvenir Press, 1980, extracts from pp. 21-2, 24-5.

25.3 Are 'mental' traits inherited?

John B. Watson

Does the behaviorist mean to say that great talent is not inherited? That criminal tendencies are not inherited? Surely we can prove that these things can be inherited. This was the older idea, the idea which grew up before we knew as much about what early shaping throughout infant life will do as we now know. The question is often put in specific form: 'Look at the musicians who are sons of musicians; look at Wesley Smith, the son of the great economist, John Smith – surely a chip off the old block if ever there was one.' The behaviorist recognizes no such things as mental traits, dispositions or tendencies. Hence, for him, there is no use in raising the question of the inheritance of talent in its old form [. . .]

Why did Wesley Smith succeed in reaching eminence when so many sons who had famous fathers failed to attain equal eminence? Was it because this particular son inherited his father's talent? There may be a thousand reasons, not one of which lends any color to the view that Wesley Smith inherited the 'talent' of his father. Suppose John Smith had had three sons who by hypothesis all had bodies so made up anatomically and physiologically that each could put on the same organization (habits) as the other two.* Suppose further that all three began to work upon economics at the age of six years. One was beloved by his father. He followed in his father's footsteps and due to his father's tutorship this son overtook and finally surpassed his father. Two years after the birth of Wesley, the second son was born; but the father was taken

---

* And by this statement we do *not mean that their genetic constitution is identical.*

up with the elder son. The second son was beloved by the mother who now got less and less of her husband's time, so she devoted her time to the second son. The second son could not follow so closely in the footsteps of his father; he was influenced naturally by what his mother was doing. He early gave up his economic studies, entered society and ultimately became a 'lounge lizard.' The third son, born two years later, was unwanted. The father was taken up with the eldest son, the mother with the second son. The third son was also put to work upon economics, but receiving little parental care, he drifted daily towards the servants' quarters. An unscrupulous maid had taught him to masturbate at three. At twelve the chauffeur made a homosexual of him. Later falling in with neighbourhood thieves he became a pickpocket, then a stool-pigeon and finally a drug fiend. He died of paresis in an insane asylum. There was nothing wrong with the heredity of any one of these sons. All by hypothesis had equal chances at birth. All could have been the fathers of fine, healthy sons if their respective wives had been of good stock (except possibly the third son *after* he contracted syphilis).

Objectors will probably say that the behaviorist is flying in the face of the known facts of eugenics and experimental evolution — that the geneticists have proven that many of the behavior characteristics of the parents are handed down to the offspring — they will cite mathematical ability, musical ability, and many, many other types. Our reply is that the geneticists are working under the banner of the old 'faculty' psychology. One need not give very much weight to any of their present conclusions. We no longer believe in faculties nor in any stereotyped patterns of behavior which go under the names of 'talent' and inherited 'capacities.'

Source: *Behaviorism*, Phoenix Books, University of Chicago Press, copyright 1924, 1925, 1930 by J. B. Watson, extracts from ch. 5, 'Are there any human instincts?', pp. 93–113.

25.4   Behavior or cognition?

B. F. Skinner

The variables of which human behavior is a function lie in the environment. We distinguish between (1) the selective action of that environment during the evolution of the species, (2) its effect in shaping and maintaining the repertoire of behavior which converts each member of the species into a person, and (3) its role as the occasion upon which behavior occurs. Cognitive psychologists study these relations between organism and environment, but they seldom deal with them directly. Instead they invent internal surrogates which become the subject matter of their science. [. . .]

By its very nature operant behavior encourages the invention of mental or cognitive processes said to initiate action. In a reflex, conditioned or unconditioned, there is conspicuous prior cause. Something triggers the response. But behavior that has been positively reinforced occurs upon occasions which, though predisposing, are never compelling. The behavior seems to start up suddenly, without advance notice, as if spontaneously generated. Hence the invention of such cognitive entities as intention, purpose or will. [. . .] Because controlling circumstances which lie in an organism's history of reinforcement are obscure, the mental surrogate gets its chance. Under positive reinforcement we do, as we say, what we are free to do: hence the notion of free will as an initiating condition. (I think it was Jonathan Edwards who said that we believe in free will because we know about our behavior but not about its causes.)

When we do not know why people do one thing rather than another, we say that they 'choose' or 'make decisions.' Choosing originally meant examining, scrutinizing, or testing. Etymologically, deciding means cutting off other possibilities, moving in a direction from which there is no return. Choosing and deciding are thus conspicuous forms of behavior, but cognitive psychologists have nevertheless invented internal surrogates. Anatole Rapaport puts it this way: 'A subject in a psychological experiment is offered a choice among alternatives and selects one alternative over others.' When this happens, he says, 'common sense suggests that he is guided by a preference.' Common sense does indeed suggest it, and so do cognitive psychologists, but where and what is a preference? Is it anything more than a tendency to do one thing rather than another? [. . .]

'Intention' is a rather similar term. [. . .] Must the intention of the speaker be taken into account? In an operant analysis verbal behavior is determined by the consequences which follow in a given verbal environment, and consequences are what cognitive psychologists are really talking about when they speak of intentions. All operant behavior 'stretches forward' to a future even though the only consequences responsible for its strength have already occurred. I go to a drinking fountain 'with the intention of getting a drink of water' in the sense that I go because in the past I have got a drink when I have done so. [. . .]

Having moved the environment inside the head in the form of conscious experience and behavior in the form of intention, will, and choice, and having stored the effects of contingencies of reinforcement as knowledge and rules, cognitive psychologists put them all together to compose an internal simulacrum of the organism, a kind of Doppelgänger, not unlike the classical homunculus, whose behavior is the subject of what Piaget and others have called 'subjective behaviorism.' The mental apparatus studied by cognitive psychology is simply a rather crude version of contingencies of reinforcement and their effects. [. . .]

The appeal to cognitive states and processes is a diversion which could well be responsible for much of our failure to solve our problems. We need to change our behavior and we can do so only by changing our physical and social environments. We choose the wrong path at the very start when we suppose that our goal is to change the 'minds and hearts of men and women' rather than the world in which they live.

Source: 'Why I am not a cognitive psychologist', *Behaviorism*, vol. 5, no. 2 (Fall 1977), extracts from pp. 1–10.

25.5 Relevance and relativity in psychopathology

Erik Erikson

In every field there are a few simple questions which are highly embarrassing because the debate which for ever arises around them leads only to perpetual failure and seems consistently to make fools of the most expert. In psychopathology such questions have always concerned the location and the cause of a neurotic disturbance. Does it have a visible onset? Does it reside in the body or in the mind, in the individual or in his society?

For centuries this query centred around the ecclesiastical argument over the origin of lunacy: was it an indwelling devil or an acute inflammation of the brain? Such simple contraposition now seems long outdated. In recent years we have come to the conclusion that a neurosis is psycho- *and* somatic, psycho- *and* social, and *inter*-personal.

More often than not, however, discussion will reveal that these new definitions too are only different ways of combining such separate concepts as psyche and soma, individual and group. We now say 'and' instead of 'either — or', but we retain at least the semantic assumption that the mind is a 'thing' separate from the body, and a society a 'thing' outside of the individual.

Psychology is the child of medicine which had its illustrious origin in the quest for the location and causation of disease. Our institutions of learning are committed to this quest, which gives to those who suffer, as well as to those who administer, the magic reassurance emanating from scientific tradition and prestige. It is reassuring to think of a neurosis as a disease, because it does feel like an affliction. It is, in fact, often accompanied by circumscribed somatic suffering: and we have well-defined approaches to disease, both on the individual and on the epidemiological level. These approaches have resulted in a sharp decline of many illnesses, and in a decrease of mortality in others.

Yet something strange is happening. As we try to think of neuroses as diseases, we gradually come to reconsider the whole problem of disease. Instead of arriving at a better definition of neurosis, we find that some widespread diseases, such as afflictions of the heart and stomach, seem to acquire new meaning by being considered equivalent to neurotic symptoms, or at any rate to symptoms of a central disturbance rather than of a peripheral happening in isolated afflicted parts. [. . .]

Here we come to our first clinical postulates. That there is no anxiety without somatic tension seems immediately obvious; but we must also learn that there is no individual anxiety which does not reflect a latent concern common to the immediate and extended group. An individual feels isolated and barred from the sources of collective speech when he (even though only secretly) takes on a role considered especially evil, be it that of a drunkard or a killer, a sissy or a sucker, or whatever colloquial designation of inferiority may be used in his group. [. . .]

We are speaking of three processes, the somatic process, the ego process, and the societal process. In the history of science these three processes have belonged to three different scientific disciplines – biology, psychology, and the social sciences – each of which studied what it could isolate, count, and dissect: single organisms, individual minds, and social aggregates. The knowledge thus derived is knowledge of facts and figures, of location and causation; and it has resulted in argument over an item's allocation to one process or another. Our thinking is dominated by this trichotomy because only through the inventive methodologies of these disciplines do we have knowledge at all. Unfortunately, however, this knowledge is tied to the conditions under which it was secured: the organism undergoing dissection or examination; the mind surrendered to experiment or interrogation; social aggregates spread out on statistical tables. In all of these cases, then, a scientific discipline prejudiced the matter under observation by actively dissolving its total living situation in order to be able to make an isolated section of it amenable to a set of instruments or concepts.

Our clinical problem, and our bias, are different. We study individual human crises by becoming therapeutically involved in them. In doing so, we find that the three processes mentioned are three aspects of one process – i.e., human life, both words being equally emphasized. Somatic tension, individual anxiety, and group panic, then, are only different ways in which human anxiety presents itself to different methods of investigation. Clinical training should include all three methods. [. . .]

Source: *Childhood and Society*, Triad/Paladin, St Albans, 1977, copyright W. W. Norton, 1950, 1963, extracts from ch. 1, pp. 19–32.

25.6   The emergence of self-awareness

Erich Fromm

Man is the only animal who not only knows objects but who knows that he knows. Man is the only animal who has not only instrumental intelligence, but reason, the capacity to use his thinking to *understand* objectively — i.e. to know the nature of things as they are in themselves, and not only as means for his satisfaction. Gifted with self-awareness and reason, man is aware of himself as a being separate from nature and from others; he is aware of his powerlessness, of his ignorance; he is aware of his end: death.

Self-awareness, reason, and imagination have disrupted the 'harmony' that characterizes animal existence. Their emergence has made man into an anomaly, the freak of the universe. He is part of nature, subject to her physical laws and unable to change them, yet he transcends nature. He is set apart while being a part; he is homeless, yet chained to the home he shares with all creatures. Cast into this world at an accidental place and time he is forced out of it accidentally and against his will. Being aware of himself, he realizes his powerlessness and the limitations of his existence. He is never free from the dichotomy of his existence: he cannot rid himself of his mind, even if he would want to; he cannot rid himself of his body as long as he is alive — and his body makes him want to be alive.

Man's life cannot be lived by repeating the pattern of his species; *he must live*. Man is the only animal who does not feel at home in nature, who can feel evicted from paradise, the only animal for whom his own existence is a problem that he has to solve and from which he cannot escape. He cannot go back to the prehuman state of harmony with nature, and he does not know where he will arrive if he goes forward. [. . .] Man's existential, and hence unavoidable, disequilibrium can be relatively stable when he has found, with the support of his culture, a more or less adequate way of coping with his existential problems. But this relative stability does not imply that the dichotomy has disappeared; it is merely dormant and becomes manifest as soon as the conditions for this relative stability change.

Indeed, in the process of man's self-creation this relative stability is upset again and again. Man, in his history, changes his environment, and in this process he changes himself. His knowledge increases, but so does his awareness of his ignorance; he experiences himself as an individual, and not only as a member of his tribe, and with this his sense of separateness and isolation grows. He creates larger and more efficient social units, led by powerful leaders — and he becomes frightened and submissive. He attains a certain amount of freedom — and becomes afraid of this very freedom. His capacity for material production grows, but in the process he becomes greedy and egotistical, a slave of the things he has created.

Every new state of disequilibrium forces man to seek for new equilibrium. Indeed, what has often been considered man's innate drive for progress is his attempt to find a new and if possible better equilibrium. [. . .]

These considerations suggest a hypothesis as to how to define the essence or nature of man. I propose that man's nature cannot be defined in terms of a specific quality, such as love, hate, reason, good or evil, but only in terms of fundamental *contradictions* that characterize human existence and have their root in the biological dichotomy between missing instincts and self-awareness. Man's existential conflict produces certain psychic needs common to all men. He is forced to overcome the horror of separateness, of powerlessness, and of lostness, and find new forms of relating himself to the world to enable him to feel at home. I have called these psychic needs existential because they are rooted in the very conditions of human existence. They are shared by all men, and their fulfilment is as necessary for man's remaining sane as the fulfillment of organic drives is necessary for his remaining alive. But each of these needs can be satisfied in different ways, which vary according to the differences of his social condition. These different ways of satisfying the existential needs manifest themselves in passions, such as love, tenderness, striving for justice, independence, truth, hate, sadism, masochism, destructiveness, narcissism. I call them character-rooted passions — or simply human passions — because they are integrated in man's *character*. [. . .]

What all men have in common are their organic drives (even though highly modifiable by experience) and their existential needs. What they do not have in common are the kinds of passions that are dominant in their respective characters — character-rooted passions. The difference in character is largely due to the difference in social conditions (although genetically given dispositions also influence the formation of the character); for this reason one can call character-rooted passions a historical category and instincts a natural category. Yet the former are not a purely historical category either, because they are the result of the impact the various historical constellations have on the biologically given conditions of human existence.

Source: *The Anatomy of Human Destructiveness*, Cape, 1974, ch. 10, extracts from pp. 218–67.

25.7a   Psychotherapy and the nature of man

George Kelly

It is sometimes argued that a person in distress does not behave as he does when things are going well. This is true. When things are going well he tends to behave like other people, or according to the way the cultural anthropologist has written up the manners of his home town. But, for the psychologist who wants to understand the nature of man, which is better, to observe a person when he is conforming to the local rulebook, or to try to understand him when he has been thrown back on his own resources and no official rulebook seems to apply?

I am not saying that the nature of man is the nature of the extraordinary man. What I am saying is that the nature of man is revealed in his extraordinary moments, moments that may be illuminated in the course of his psychotherapy. And it is for this reason that I have no desire to be an applied psychologist or to agree that the mean of man's behavioral reactions in a conformity situation is an adequate measure of his basic nature. For to agree with this tenet is to agree that the psychology of man is a psychology of norms and static mediocrity. It is to concede that truth lies with the majority, and to join, I fear, in the clamor for a unified theory of psychology, as if truth were to be achieved by negotiations.

Psychotherapy, it must be conceded, may not provide us with the only opportunity to see man in the crucial moment when conventionalities have failed him and he is left with no resources other than his own nature. The nature of man may be exposed to observation on other occasions. Perhaps we can see his nature equally well when he faces death and looks back regretfully on a life of normal and conforming behavior. Perhaps we can see it as we look back over two or three thousand years of history in which the myriad of average, normal, conforming behaviors have been mercifully overshadowed by the signal achievements of men and peoples. Perhaps it can be seen in a kindergarten before discipline and socialization have set in. Perhaps it can be seen even in the laboratory, though the chances are that if it shows up there the subjects will be thrown out of the experiment. [. . .]

But wheresoever the nature of man may be observed in its nascent form, I am sure that the psychologist is nowhere more likely to run into its puzzling complexities and exasperating perversities than in his efforts to accomplish psychotherapy. It is there that one hopes to see the person struggling with changes in himself as he attempts to draw some compromise between the normalized psychological doctrines of the world around him and his own natural eagerness to reach out for what he is unable to attain. To cope with this problem is not always a very comfortable experience for a would-be scientist. Certainly it is not a very practical way for him to extend his bibliography, and this is perhaps the reason that clinical psychologists do not publish more than they do and why what they do publish seems so inconclusive. But dissatisfied as I am with the progress of clinical psychology, I am even more pessimistic about any science of psychology that cuts itself loose from the perplexing realities of psychotherapy. As Mark Twain once said, 'Every dog should have some fleas, lest he forget that he's a dog.'

25.7b Construing

George Kelly

Now suppose — just suppose — the prevailing psychology of our times was not a stimulus-response psychology or even a psychology of biographical determinants. Suppose it was instead a psychology that concerned itself with how men construe the world around them, and particularly with how they construe each other. Suppose this was not only the psychology employed by psychologists, but the psychology employed by all of us. That is to say, it would represent the psychological outlook of our culture and times. What difference would it make?

First of all, it would be a good idea to identify two levels of construing. The first would be concerned with events and with men treated as events. By that I mean we would construe men's behaviors rather than their outlooks. Another person would be simply another moving object on our horizon. This is one level of construing.

But then suppose there were a second level of construing. This would be concerned with construing the constructs of other men. Instead of making our own sense out of what others did we would try to understand what sense they made out of what they did. Instead of putting together the events in their lives in the most scientifically parsimonious way, we would ask how they put things together, regardless of whether their schemes were parsimonious or not.

25.7c   A psychology of man himself

George Kelly

It occurred to me that what seemed true of myself was probably no less true of others. If I initiated my actions, so did they. I suppose you might say that this position commits me to a psychology of man rather than of his circumstances. It is a psychology concerned with what we do and why we do it, rather than one that attempts to pinpoint the events that compel others to do what they do not choose to do. There is, I suspect, a lot of difference between these two psychologies. But so far, it must be said, there was nothing in my thinking that could be called a full-blown theory of personality — only a kind of convenient posture I assumed toward what confronted me.

But to believe that man is the author of his destiny is not to deny that he may be tragically limited by his circumstances. I saw too many unfortunate youngsters, some of them literally starving in that depression-ridden dust bowl, for me not to be aware of their tragic limitations. Clearly there were many things they might have liked to do that circumstances would not permit. But, nevertheless, this is not to say that they were victims of circumstances. However much there was denied them, there was still an infinity of possibilities open to them. The task was to generate the imagination needed to envision those possibilities. And this is a point of departure for a psychology of man. [. . .]

Source: B. Maker, ed., *Clinical Psychology and Personality: the Selected Papers of George Kelly*, Robert E. Krueger, New York, 1979, extracts from ch. 2, pp. 46–65, and ch. 10, pp. 207–14.

26 Life and careers on the soccer terraces

Peter Marsh

To most people in our society, the activities of the current generation of young football fans seem violent and destructive. Above all they are seen as being *senseless*. Violent behaviour is viewed as random and without reason. The rhetoric of this viewpoint is very familiar. [. . .] It is the rhetoric of the outraged, right-thinking, decent majority – of those who find a ready audience through the media channels.

My concern here is with a different rhetoric – not the moral panics of those outside of the terrace culture, but a story which emerges from the *inside*, from speaking to the fans on the terraces. This story from inside leads to conclusions radically different from those currently available in the raging debate on soccer hooliganism. And it's one which goes a little way towards an understanding of what is going on at football matches – as opposed to what people *think* is going on.

This story is not mine, it is that of the fans themselves. I introduce some concepts – some explanatory tools – in order to make it intelligible to those outside the soccer culture. Some people may quarrel with parts of this 'gloss'. But the story is still there. It exists in the everyday social talk and collective action of soccer fans from Southampton to Middlesbrough. And because it reflects the inside social reality of the terrace culture; because it is not some abstract product of a psychological model, it has to be taken seriously.

Perhaps listening to what fans have to say sounds 'unscientific'. You can draw very few graphs in this line of work. But the story speaks for itself. It is both intelligible and meaningful to anyone prepared to give it the attention it deserves.

> It's like an outing, the feeling of actually being on the terraces with a lot of people with a common aim in their minds, apart from violence, to help the team to win, to see the goals go in and to see a good game.

Source: Roger Ingram, Stuart Hall, John Clarke, Peter Marsh and Jim Donovan, *Football Hooliganism: the Wider Context*, London, Inter-Action Inprint, 1978, extracts from pp. 61–77, 80–1.

At away games then it's a feeling of actually being somewhere new, of sharing and looking at the other team's ground. And one of the most enjoyable parts, more than anything, is the actual travelling, going there on a coach with 40 or 50 other friends, sort of having a drink, having a sing-song, coming home. And I think the most exciting part is the real big F.A. Cup games or a large draw when it's so important to you that people actually come out with ideas like big red and white top hats or big flags or banners with certain slogans written on them to provide fun. I don't think in my experience there's much to compare with the atmosphere of being in a large group, all singing and chanting to support your team.

The order of the 'End'

Oxford United fans have a chant, '*Atmosphere, Atmosphere*'. It's within this atmosphere on the soccer terraces all over the country, that miniature social worlds exist and flourish. It is these social worlds which constitute a micro-culture within our society. And when we talk of culture we imply that within it there is order. Order rests upon shared meanings, and social roles and a system of rules – elements which have to be teased out of apparent chaos if we are ever to understand what football fans are doing and why they are doing it. Contained within this account of everyday events are both explicit and implicit references to the rules on which order rests.

There's an organised pattern of events, I mean you know what's going to happen. Bringing a knife, I mean, probably by your own supporters sometimes it's looked down on as being a form of, you know, cowardice. There's not many people will carry knives about, there's not many who set out to harm someone. Not many people have got that killer instinct, I mean once you've sort of kicked them to the floor and made them bleed, I mean that's it. It's left at that and they'll just say 'leave him' he's had enough. It's not very often it goes onto a point where he's kicked senseless. On an average it tends to be more like losing a couple of teeth or going home with a black eye or maybe a cut. I think people do after a time recognise the games that are going to cause trouble, they actually stand in the position within the ground where they know that there's not going to be much confrontation.

The search for order already begins to look promising. The notion of random irrationality is refuted by those directly involved in the action [. . .] With this in mind it might be profitable to examine those aspects of social order which can be directly retrieved from accounts that fans offer in conjunction with that much maligned tool of sociology and social psychology – observation. Looking at what happens raises questions concerning the nature of order (or lack of order) within distinct social groups. It directs attention to aspects of structure which require explanation. It leads one gently into the inside – to the position from which the route towards understanding opens up.

If you look closely at a particular 'End' over a number of Saturdays some very obvious points emerge. Fans stand in regular places and with the same people around them each match. Young boys, between 9 and 13 form a distinct sub-group, usually at the front of the terraces. The middle age range of 14 to 17, who form the bulk of any End, occupy the most central positions. Older fans generally stand to one side of the centre, but there is immense variation from ground to ground.

Perhaps the most noticeable aspect of an End is its cohesion. Despite the fact that there are isolatable sub-groups within it, action often achieves a very remarkable unity – especially in singing, gesturing and the chanting of bloodcurdling imprecations. If you've ever stood in front of a terrace of people who are chanting, *'You're gonna get your fucking head kicked in'*, the unity can appear quite alarming. Happily the threats are rarely translated into action. [. . .]

When you attend games and compare what you see with impressions gained from the press, it may come as a surprise to find that the terraces don't run with blood every Saturday or that injuries are rarely to be witnessed. You get the feeling that either you've been reading the wrong newspaper or you're at the wrong ground. The trouble is though, that switching to a different newspaper rarely makes much difference and travelling round the country to other grounds doesn't either. It's true, there are fights from time to time, and sometimes fans get hurt. But End-watching on a regular basis suggests that violence – in the sense of physically injurious encounters – is only a small part of the terrace action. Aggro is certainly there, but aggro is not quite what it may seem.

The aggro fans talk of is in effect a highly distinctive, and often cere-monial, system for resolving conflict.

They've got their area to stay in, if they come in our area then they've got to be moved. They've got to get back to their own side. But you get a lot of these kids saying 'Oh we're going up there . . . you know, we'll go up there and have a good scrap.' They're hoping that they'll just go up there and chase the other supporters round the ground and not get into any scraps, you know. They've already proved themselves superior without kind of sticking a boot in or sticking a fist in or anything like that.

Proving superiority is the object of this game, and that can be achieved without recourse to savage attacks or serious bloodshed. Consider this example of 'a fight' between two rival fans at Oxford United's ground:

Four Sheffield boys sit eating crisps on a pile of concrete slabs. A number of Oxford boys gradually move over and silently surround them. Taunts and subtle threats are made by the Oxford boys, and one of their number moves in closer to lead the antagonism. A Sheffield boy, who so far has been looking steadfastly at the ground in front of him, inadvertently glances up for a moment at the leading Oxford man. He is immediately accused of 'staring', and is challenged to stand up and fight. The challenge is ignored. Other Oxford boys now move in closer and become more vocal. The leading Oxford fan continues his taunting and starts to flick the reluctant Sheffield boy's hair and collar. At this point, the Sheffield boy leaps up, his face red with anger. Adopting a stance with feet apart and arms outspread, he faces his opponent. The two stand silently facing each other, while the onlookers step back a pace. After what seems to be a very long period of nothing happening, an intermediary in the form of an older Oxford fan arrives on the scene. He moves the younger Oxford fan out of the conflict area. The police, having been onlookers up to this point, *only now* grab the Oxford antagonist and push him roughly in the opposite direction. There is an almost audible sigh of relief. Everyone returns to watch the second half of the game, which has now been in progress for about ten minutes.

This, perhaps surprisingly, is extremely typical of events involving small groups of fans at football grounds. And it's not a phenomenon peculiar to Oxford United. Even at the biggest First Division grounds, the patterns of conflict and hostility are very similar. They are so routine and commonplace that they are taken-for-granted and unremarkable. The apparent inconsequentiality, however, masks the fact that it is in these rituals that 'honour' is satisfied.

Fans demonstrate aspects of character which meet with acclaim and social approval within their social world. Fighting and being part of any aggro that's going are useful pieces of self-presentation in this respect because, whatever else his failings, a fan who stands his ground is one of the boys. But whilst violence is sanctioned, and even demanded, the practice of violence is constrained by internal and informal social controls which apply equally in both individual face-to-face encounters and mass confrontations. In London there is a line of graffiti which proclaims that 'A little bit of violence never hurt anyone.' Whoever wrote it understood all about terrace aggro.

I'm not suggesting for one moment that people never get injured at football matches. Nor do I wish to imply that all is hunky-dory because there is order and control on the terraces. I raise the issue of fights and violence at this stage because it is in the episodes of conflict and antagonism that the presence of order is most strikingly revealed. But how is this order learned by those whose actions are constrained by it?

Roles – the career structure of the terrace

The football terraces provide an alternative career structure – an orderly framework for making progress in the society of the terrace. Unlike careers in the outside world there's no financial reward to be gained. The pay-off is in social terms. But the benefits are still tangible and real. To young working class kids for whom school, work or the dole queue offer little in the way of potential for personal achievement, the availability of an alternative world in which to become *somebody* is attractive. And so, boys of 9, 10 or 11 are drawn to the terraces by the prospect of immediate membership of a society which offers excitement, danger and a tribal sense of belonging. These are the 'Novices' or 'Little Kids' at the start of their apprenticeship.

> Yeah the little ones, you know, they all come up thinking they're hard, you know, and say if the big ones come in, you know, and start singing and that, you see all the little kids running off, starting to sing with them. If the big ones start to run they'll start to run just to act hard, you know, and they wait outside the pubs for them and that, and this is true, they do, some of them wait outside the Silver Sword for them, and they walk up with them just to think they're hard, just to talk and sing with them.
>
> They'll go up and do all the signs and they'll chant 'come on', 'up the aggro' and everything like that, and then as soon as anything happens they'll run everywhere and put everything into a panic and you don't know where you are.
>
> They go on looking for trouble then when they get it they don't want it and they leave other bigger ones to sort it out.

To older fans, Novices are a bit of an embarrassment because they don't really know what they are doing. Their knowledge of the codes of conduct is limited and superficial. But acquisition of appropriate knowledge and skill is made easier by the fact that there is a distinct model to which they are aspiring. The model is the 'hooligan' or, being less emotive, the 'Rowdy'. Rowdies are the energetic lads on the terraces. They are the ones who sing and chant the loudest, wear the most extreme forms of 'gear' and run around a lot. They are also the people magistrates describe as animals, morons and thugs.

Rowdies form the core membership of the terrace culture. Their average age is 15 or 16 and although there are no initiation rites or entry ceremonies – in fact any supporter can join in a superficial sense – the 'men' are separated from the 'boys' in situations which demand specific action. Only by matching up to the standards expected, and by demonstrating commitment to the commonly held values and ideals, can the Rowdy hope to be recognised by his peers.

> I mean it don't matter really if you lose a fight, so long as you don't back down. I mean you could end up in hospital but so long as you didn't back down you'd prove your case. I mean there's a lot of this not wanting to be called a coward in it. When you're sixteen or seventeen, before say you're courting steady and that, that's the time when you don't like being called a coward. And it's one thing that hurts you more than anything else you know.

Within the Rowdy group, career development proceeds partly through general statements of worth such as these but also through the pursuit of certain key status positions. One very favourable role is that of the fan who aspires to being an 'aggro leader' or, more colloquially, a hard-case. End-watching, again, helps to distinguish such individuals. They are the ones who will lead running charges at the opposition fans, both inside and outside the ground, and they will figure prominently in the scuffles and fracas which break out around the concourses of grounds lacking refined security fences and barriers. Being a hard-case gets you the best seat on coaches to away matches, Novices buy you beers and other fans show a satisfying deference. Such a position can be held, informally, without bullying or coercion. It does, however, require a certain degree of fearlessness.

> I think we were at Bradford City and we knew that right at the end of the match they were all going to come over the fences and over walls and everything and it were just going to be one helluva Custer's last stand. And there were about fifty or sixty who fought against something like three hundred. We never stood a chance but we knew that we couldn't really back down against them, and after we'd stood there on the hill and we'd been beaten, I mean you could see youths, Bradford supporters, carrying Chesterfield supporters out of the ground back to the buses. And you could see Chesterfield supporters carrying Bradford City supporters back to the buses, I mean after the fight I mean, you know, that were it.

That's how the hard-case builds his reputation. Again, he does it not by causing serious injury to other people, but by consistently demonstrating a determination to stand up for himself and his group. But his fearlessness is limited. For the total absence of fear is an aspect of character more typical of the Nutter than the hard-case.

> Well, for me somebody who's hard does not necessarily have to start the trouble or actually be the cause of it. Some people that are described as nutters or head-bangers may not necessarily be physically hard, it's just that they've got the nerve, more than anything else, to do something that is considered out of the ordinary, and that's what they get their reputation for − not so much being hard in the one-to-one confrontation or something, but actually having the nerve to charge into a situation that they know they're gonna come out the losers.

Nutters 'go crazy' or 'go mad' − they go beyond the fans' limits of acceptable and sane behaviour. In doing so, however, everybody else on the terraces comes to understand more clearly where those limits lie. In fact, the existence of Nutters is proof of the existence of order in the first place. If random action was the norm, Nutters would be indistinguishable from anybody else. But the fact that they are viewed, from the inside, as deviant, provides us with a very useful way of assessing the nature and extent of the informal terrace rules. We can look at what *shouldn't* be done, which is always an easier task than teasing out what *should*.

Typical of being nutty would be attempting to beat a fan on the ground to a pulp, or walking down a railway line to challenge, single-handed, a train full of rival supporters. Luckily for Nutters, and their victims, the terrace culture exercises considerable restraint on the activities of its deviants. In fights they are pulled away from rivals who have had enough and, when in peril on railway lines, will simply be carried to safety. Nutters do, however, provide entertainment. They are like Court Jesters. Everybody knows they are crazy and are prepared for the fact that they will do outrageous things. In any case, the career of the Nutter is usually fairly short. It is he who will run onto the pitch, and into the arms of a waiting policeman, every time the *Match of the Day* cameras are in evidence. He is a visible offender and an easy target for the forces of Law. [. . .]

One problem with being a Rowdy is that you are constantly under pressure to prove things. This applies particularly to Rowdies in specialised and status-laden roles. You have to keep demonstrating your manliness, your 'bottle' and your knowledge of what's what. It's easy to fall from grace. You can foul things up or be seen as a 'wanker'. And you have to keep wearing all that denim gear and Dr Marten boots and a scarf round your wrist even when you might be feeling a bit old for it and even when it's becoming a bit of a nuisance. [. . .]

> . . . It ended up, you was going up there and soon as you stepped in the ground they see we had white baggies on and boots and that's it, we were the troublemakers and they used to kind of watch us. When I went to Leicester, just because I rolled my sleeves up on me denim jacket as we got off the train — there was a special copper on that — you know, one of these plain-clothes boys — he got me over to the side and said, 'Look, I already know you're one of the leaders. If anything goes wrong today, if there's any trouble, you're gonna be the first one to be arrested.' That's just because of the clothes you're wearing, so that's one of the main reasons I kind of gave up wearing that.

The only way out of this dilemma is to 'graduate'. Graduates have moved on from putting on a show and 'mouthing off'. Having consistently demonstrated their personal worth and character in the Rowdies, they can now rest on their laurels. They are recognised by all other fans in the End as men of distinction who, when the chips are down, will play their part. But in the more routine rituals and ceremonial proclamations of masculine integrity they need no longer play any part. In fact they can *look* totally unremarkable.

> . . . these little kids are wearing this kind of uniform to make them look a bit hard, to make them look . . . when you get a bit older, maybe you don't need to look hard . . . Well you realise that, you know, kind of clothes don't make you anything.
>
> I think when you actually get to know the group of people that you go to the football with or actually know socially you don't need to conform to the expected standard, I mean you can be more of an individual because people accept you for an individual rather than just one of the boys.
>
> I mean if a fight starts then, well, like Saturday I mean, well then I had no choice — I just had to turn round and fight. But if a fight starts then I don't get out of the way of it. I used to go looking for trouble but I kind of realised that was a bit senseless.

The moral career structure, from apprenticeship through to graduation, and eventually retirement, is the social mechanism through which order is transmitted. It allows for rules to be learned and shared meanings realised. It allows for achievement and for sharing of collective pride.

And it's this that marks aggro off as a very special kind of violence. Life is orderly and fights are orderly. But there's a snag.

Exaggeration and internal rules

The reason that the social world of the football terrace exists and flourishes has a lot to do with the fact that kids are leading boring, routine, often alienated, safe and uneventful lives. Football offers an escape — but what to? Another routine and ordered existence? That's the problem. At the heart of the accounts that fans give concerning their social world is the realisation of constraint and regularity. But this makes the terraces less distinguishable from the weekday world. Fights may be 'safe', but safe fights never won anyone any glory. Somehow, excitement, danger and unpredictability must be reintroduced into the socially constructed internal order. This is done by what I choose to see as a *conspiracy* to deny the order that the rowdies know to exist. Events must be exaggerated — they must become larger than life. Bloody murder may never happen but there must be at least some foundation for its *anticipation.*

When I first started doing research work with football fans it was this conspiracy to exaggerate that I first encountered. It cropped up in conversations like this one:

Question: What do you do when you 'put the boot in'?
Fan A: Well, you kicks 'em in the 'ead don't you — heavy boots with metal toe-caps an' that.
Q: What happens then?
(puzzled look from fans)
Q: Well what happens to the guy you've kicked?
Fan A: He's dead.
Fan B: Nah! He's all right — usually anyway.

This sort of stuff is very confusing. Luckily, as we've seen, not all accounts are quite so enigmatic. But this exaggeration does crop up and the only way to make sense of it is to see how fans themselves cope with the problem. Doing it this way one can become aware of how much exaggeration is tolerated by fans before downright 'bullshitting' begins. In this next extract, one fan goes too far in pushing the excitement up — the reaction of his mates is very revealing.

Fan A: It's the name and the reputation. You go somewhere like today, we'll go down to Southampton, they'll say 'Millwall ah,' and they'll turn out in force, 'let's have a go at Millwall, we know they're going to bring some supporters.' If the other team, the home team, knows the away team's going to bring supporters they'll come out for a fight, half of them.

Fan B: It's a shouting match . . . it starts off with, but . . . you know, it gets kind of emotional don't it . . . Really good Millwall supporters, right, they can't stand their club being slagged down you know, and it all wells up, you know, and you just feel like hitting someone.

Q: How many people actually get hurt in those kind of things though?

Fan A: When we played Everton in the F.A. Cup I spent two weeks in hospital, I got seven busted ribs and a broken nose.

Fan B.   No, that's exaggerating. The young fellas, you know, they're giving each other verbal and that, you know, and they're running each other down, that's all harmless fun you know, even if they sort of have a little chase and chase one another round the grounds . . . But when it comes to people bringing out knives, that's out of order.

Fan A: But it's changed, it's changed, everything comes out now. Alright, fair enough, when we go away, I'll admit it, I do people in the eyes with ammonia, so what? Right? I got done at Everton, and since I've been there I've carried that ammonia with me all the time. There's no way I go away without that ammonia.

Fan C: Where is it now then?

Fan A: Today I haven't got it, right?

Fan C: Aah, I don't believe you. I don't believe you. If you take it everywhere why ain't you got it today?

Fan A,   'Cos I haven't been home to get it. Straight, that's the truth.

Fan B: No, you go down this train and ask everybody if they've had . . . a fight, you know, a batter with anybody at a football match and they might say we done this and we done that but they never actually done it. It's always 'we', you know, 'we', it's the group . . . Yeah, it's we done this but never actually they done it, the majority done it, you know? 'We', you know what I mean? Its never 'I'. [. . .]

Throwing ammonia around is defined as out of order. Such statements, again, confirm the presence of social order in the first place – an order in which fans 'giving each other verbal' is legitimate but bringing out knives and other weapons is not. It's possible to add, through social talk, a little spice to this order but there are further rules which operate to restrict the extent to which this can be taken. The 'bullshitter' in the last extract, which comes from a tape recorded session with some Millwall fans on a special train to Southampton, was subject to censure which eventually obliged him to stand alone in the corridor for the rest of the journey.

Orderly life on the terraces, then, rests upon active subscription to a set of sub-cultural rules. These rules are of two kinds. Firstly, there are prescriptive rules which dictate appropriate action. They imply concepts like 'ought' and 'should' — they dictate the things which 'are done' and 'not done'. Secondly, there are interpretative rules. These enable common definitions of situations and rest upon the existence of shared meanings. Thus, certain events will be classed as 'fights', 'bovver', 'provocation' and so on and will determine which of the prescriptive rules are applicable and relevant to the situation.

Discovering these rules can be fairly straightforward. At the simplest level you can ask questions of fans such as 'What is going on?' and 'What should one do?' Even more basically you can simply ask fans what the rules are and very often you will get replies which stand up to subsequent checking and validation.

Disruption of the internal order

The perspective that fans provide stands in direct contradiction to the dominant ideology current in our society — and dominant ideologies usually win. Having consistently failed to understand what fans are doing, we are progressively changing what, *in reality*, they actually do. In fact we are beginning to make them play the game we thought they were playing, but which they were not playing.

The reasons for this are fairly clear. The media, of course, play an important role in changing reality but this feeds down and affects the actions of other people involved in the world of soccer. The police, for example, are obliged to step up their intervention in what fans are doing. Perhaps surprisingly, I have found that the accounts that individual policemen give concerning what's happening at football matches are often similar to those offered by the fans themselves. The pressures of social outrage, however, oblige them to appear efficient and in control, and the resulting intervention which is unskilled, or seen by the fans as unreasonable, can add a new source of conflict. [. . .]

Perhaps in the end we will have to learn to live with a bit of aggro. It's not a popular thought. But anyone who advocates a passive Utopia in which boys and young men never enter into conflict with each other, never fight or engage in ceremonial 'rumbles', and never seek to 'make their mark' in informal social situations, can take little comfort from the history of our world. Whatever our view on aggression, and whatever our thoughts concerning an ideal society, we are forced to examine something other than the myths attached to the phenomena such as football hooliganism. Unless we want total chaos — unless we want to achieve the ultimate alienation of a vast chunk of the working class youth — we are obliged to look at a reality which exists inside the phenomenon, and which emerges in the story that fans tell. We may still not like it. But we can, at least, listen.

I'm afraid there's got to be some sort of outlet. You see, say in this area. When you leave school and you've got no qualifications, you've got a choice of two jobs: either become a labourer or down't pit. Now it doesn't leave a lot to the week, either to race dogs or fly pigeons. You're really limited. I think, council have banned pigeons in't back yard and say they banned goats, and you've got to find some sort of expression and . . . and physical expression, so violence has become an expression.

It's society innit, you know, if they didn't do it in football ground, you'd do it in pubs, you know, do it . . . It's just pride . . . pride . . . street corners and all that, you know. It's . . . in actual fact it's doing society a favour, its keeping 'em away, keepin' 'em at football grounds and you've got plenty of police on hand an' that . . . It is society a lot of it, you know, it's down to society.

27 The presentation of self

Erving Goffman

When an individual enters the presence of others, they commonly seek to acquire information about him or to bring into play information about him already possessed. They will be interested in his general socio-economic status, his conception of self, his attitude toward them, his competence, his trustworthiness, etc. Although some of this information seems to be sought almost as an end in itself, there are usually quite practical reasons for acquiring it. Information about the individual helps to define the situation, enabling others to know in advance what he will expect of them and what they may expect of him. Informed in these ways, the others will know how best to act in order to call forth a desired response from him.

For those present, many sources of information become accessible and many carriers (or 'sign-vehicles') become available for conveying this information. If unacquainted with the individual, observers can glean clues from his conduct and appearance which allow them to apply their previous experience with individuals roughly similar to the one before them or, more important, to apply untested stereotypes to him. They can also assume from past experience that only individuals of a particular kind are likely to be found in a given social setting. They can rely on what the individual says about himself or on documentary evidence he provides as to who and what he is. If they know, or know of, the individual by virtue of experience prior to the interaction, they can rely on assumptions as to the persistence and generality of psychological traits as a means of predicting his present and future behaviour.

However, during the period in which the individual is in the immediate presence of the others, few events may occur which directly provide the others with the conclusive information they will need if they are to direct wisely their own activity. Many crucial facts lie beyond the time and place of interaction or lie concealed within it. For example, the 'true' or 'real' attitudes, beliefs, and emotions of the individual can be

Source: *The Presentation of Self in Everyday Life*, London, Allen Lane, 1969, pp. 1–14.

ascertained only indirectly, through his avowals or through what appears to be involuntary expressive behaviour. Similarly, if the individual offers the others a product or service, they will often find that during the interaction there will be no time and place immediately available for eating the pudding that the proof can be found in. They will be forced to accept some events as conventional or natural signs of something not directly available to the senses. In Ichheiser's terms,[1] the individual will have to act so that he intentionally or unintentionally *expresses* himself, and the others will in turn have to be *impressed* in some way by him.

The expressiveness of the individual (and therefore his capacity to give impressions) appears to involve two radically different kinds of sign activity: the expression that he *gives,* and the expression that he *gives off.* The first involves verbal symbols or their substitutes which he uses admittedly and solely to convey the information that he and the others are known to attach to these symbols. This is communication in the traditional and narrow sense. The second involves a wide range of action that others can treat as symptomatic of the actor, the expectation being that the action was performed for reasons other than the information conveyed in this way. As we shall have to see, this distinction has an only initial validity. The individual does of course intentionally convey misinformation by means of both of these types of communication, the first involving deceit, the second feigning.

Taking communication in both its narrow and broad sense, one finds that when the individual is in the immediate presence of others, his activity will have a promissory character. The others are likely to find that they must accept the individual on faith, offering him a just return while he is present before them in exchange for something whose true value will not be established until after he has left their presence. (Of course, the others also live by inference in their dealings with the physical world, but it is only in the world of social interaction that the objects about which they make inferences will purposely facilitate and hinder this inferential process.) The security that they justifiably feel in making inferences about the individual will vary, of course, depending on such factors as the amount of information they already possess about him, but no amount of such past evidence can entirely obviate the necessity of acting on the basis of inferences. As William I. Thomas suggested:

> It is also highly important for us to realize that we do not as a matter of fact lead our lives, make our decisions, and reach our goals in everyday life either statistically or scientifically. We live by inference. I am, let us say, your guest. You do not know, you cannot determine scientifically, that I will not steal your money or your spoons. But inferentially I will not, and inferentially you have me as a guest.

Let us now turn from the others to the point of view of the individual who presents himself before them. He may wish them to think highly of him, or to think that he thinks highly of them, or to perceive how in fact he feels toward them, or to obtain no clear-cut impression; he may wish to ensure sufficient harmony so that the interaction can be sustained, or to defraud, get rid of, confuse, mislead, antagonise, or insult them. Regardless of the particular objective which the individual has in mind and of his motive for having this objective, it will be in his interests to control the conduct of the others, especially their responsive treatment of him. This control is achieved largely by influencing the definition of the situation which the others come to formulate, and he can influence this definition by expressing himself in such a way as to give them the kind of impression that will lead them to act voluntarily in accordance with his own plan. Thus, when an individual appears in the presence of others, there will usually be some reason for him to mobilise his activity so that it will convey an impression to others which it is in his interests to convey. Since a girl's dormitory mates will glean evidence of her popularity from the calls she receives on the phone, we can suspect that some girls will arrange for calls to be made, and Willard Waller's finding can be anticipated:[2]

> It has been reported by many observers that a girl who is called to the telephone in the dormitories will often allow herself to be called several times, in order to give all the other girls ample opportunity to hear her paged.

Of the two kinds of communication — expressions given and expressions given off — this report will be primarily concerned with the latter, with the more theatrical and contextual kind, the non-verbal, presumably unintentional kind, whether this communication be purposely engineered or not. As an example of what we must try to examine, I would like to cite at length a novelistic incident in which Preedy, a vacationing Englishman, makes his first appearance on the beach of his summer hotel in Spain:[3]

> But in any case he took care to avoid catching anyone's eye. First of all, he had to make it clear to those potential companions of his holiday that they were of no concern to him whatsoever. He stared through them, round them, over them — eyes lost in space. The beach might have been empty. If by chance a ball was thrown his way, he looked surprised; then let a smile of amusement lighten his face (Kindly Preedy), looked round dazed to see that there *were* people on the beach, tossed it back with a smile to himself and not a smile

at the people, and then resumed carelessly his nonchalant survey
of space.

But it was time to institute a little parade, the parade of the Ideal
Preedy. By devious handlings he gave any who wanted to look a
chance to see the title of his book — a Spanish translation of Homer,
classic thus, but not daring, cosmopolitan too — and then gathered
together his beach-wrap and bag into a neat sand-resistant pile
(Methodical and Sensible Preedy), rose slowly to stretch at ease his
huge frame (Big-Cat Preedy), and tossed aside his sandals (Carefree
Preedy after all).

The marriage of Preedy and the sea! There were alternative rituals.
The first involved the stroll that turns into a run and a dive straight
into the water, thereafter smoothing into a strong splashless crawl
towards the horizon. But of course not really to the horizon. Quite
suddenly he would turn on to his back and thrash great white
splashes with his legs, somehow thus showing that he could have
swum further had he wanted to, and then would stand up a quarter
out of water for all to see who it was.

The alternative course was simpler, it avoided the cold-water
shock and it avoided the risk of appearing too high-spirited. The
point was to appear to be used to the sea, the Mediterranean, and
this particular beach, that one might as well be in the sea as out of it.
It involved a slow stroll down and into the edge of the water — not
even noticing his toes were wet, land and water all the same to *him*!
— with his eyes up at the sky gravely surveying portents, invisible to
others, of the weather (Local Fisherman Preedy).

The novelist means us to see that Preedy is improperly concerned with
the extensive impressions he feels his sheer bodily action is giving off to
those around him. We can malign Preedy further by assuming that he
has acted merely in order to give a particular impression, that this is a
false impression, and that the others present receive either no impression
at all, or, worse still, the impression that Preedy is affectedly trying to
cause them to receive this particular impression. But the important
point for us here is that the kind of impression Preedy thinks he is
making is in fact the kind of impression that others correctly and incor-
rectly glean from someone in their midst.

I have said that when an individual appears before others his actions
will influence the definition of the situation which they come to have.
Sometimes the individual will act in a thoroughly calculating manner,
expressing himself in a given way solely in order to give the kind of impression to others that is likely to evoke from them a specific response
he is concerned to obtain. Sometimes the individual will be calculating

in his activity but be relatively unaware that this is the case. Sometimes he will intentionally and consciously express himself in a particular way, but chiefly because the tradition of his group or social status require this kind of expression and not because of any particular response (other than vague acceptance or approval) that is likely to be evoked from those impressed by the expression. Sometimes the traditions of an individual's role will lead him to give a well-designed impression of a particular kind and yet he may be neither consciously nor unconsciously disposed to create such an impression. The others, in their turn, may be suitably impressed by the individual's efforts to convey something, or may misunderstand the situation and come to conclusions that are warranted neither by the individual's intent nor by the facts. In any case, in so far as the others act *as if* the individual had conveyed a particular impression, we may take a functional or pragmatic view and say that the individual has 'effectively' projected a given definition of the situation and 'effectively' fostered the understanding that a given state of affairs obtains.

There is one aspect of the others' response that bears special comment here. Knowing that the individual is likely to present himself in a light that is favourable to him, the others may divide what they witness into two parts: a part that is relatively easy for the individual to manipulate at will, being chiefly his verbal assertions, and a part in regard to which he seems to have little concern or control, being chiefly derived from the expressions he gives off. The others may then use what are considered to be the ungovernable aspects of his expressive behaviour as a check upon the validity of what is conveyed by the governable aspects. In this a fundamental asymmetry is demonstrated in the communication process, the individual presumably being aware of only one stream of his communication, the witnesses of this stream and one other. For example, in Shetland Isle one crofter's wife, in serving native dishes to a visitor from the mainland of Britain, would listen with a polite smile to his polite claims of liking what he was eating; at the same time she would take note of the rapidity with which the visitor lifted his fork or spoon to his mouth, the eagerness with which he passed food into his mouth, and the gusto expressed in chewing the food, using these signs as a check on the stated feelings of the eater. The same woman, in order to discover what one acquaintance (A) 'actually' thought of another acquaintance (B), would wait until B was in the presence of A but engaged in conversation with still another person (C). She would then covertly examine the facial expressions of A as he regarded B in conversation with C. Not being in conversation with B, and not being directly observed by him, A would sometimes relax usual constraints and tactful deceptions, and freely express what he was 'actually' feeling about B. This Shetlander, in short, would observe the unobserved observer.

Now given the fact that others are likely to check up on the more controllable aspects of behaviour by means of the less controllable, one can expect that sometimes the individual will try to exploit this very possibility, guiding the impression he makes through behaviour felt to be reliably informing.* For example, in gaining admission to a tight social circle, the participant observer may not only wear an accepting look while listening to an informant, but may also be careful to wear the same look when observing the informant talking to others; observers of the observer will then not as easily discover where he actually stands. A specific illustration may be cited from Shetland Isle. When a neighbour dropped in to have a cup of tea, he would ordinarily wear at least a hint of an expectant warm smile as he passed through the door into the cottage. Since lack of physical obstructions outside the cottage and lack of light within it usually made it possible to observe the visitor unobserved as he approached the house, islanders sometimes took pleasure in watching the visitor drop whatever expression he was manifesting and replace it with a sociable one just before reaching the door. However, some visitors, in appreciating that this examination was occurring, would blindly adopt a social face a long distance from the house, thus ensuring the projection of a constant image.

This kind of control upon the part of the individual reinstates the symmetry of the communication process, and sets the stage for a kind of information game — a potentially infinite cycle of concealment, discovery, false revelation, and rediscovery. It should be added that since the others are likely to be relatively unsuspicious of the presumably unguided aspect of the individual's conduct, he can gain much by controlling it. The others of course may sense that the individual is manipulating the presumably spontaneous aspects of his behaviour, and seek in this very act of manipulation some shading of conduct that the individual has not managed to control. This again provides a check upon the individual's behaviour, this time his presumably uncalculated behaviour, thus re-establishing the asymmetry of the communication process. Here I would like only to add the suggestion that the arts of piercing an individual's effort at calculated unintentionality seem better developed than our capacity to manipulate our own behaviour, so that regardless of how many steps have occurred in the information game, the witness

* The widely read and rather sound writings of Stephen Potter are concerned in part with signs that can be engineered to give a shrewd observer the apparently incidental cues he needs to discover concealed virtues the gamesman does not in fact possess.

is likely to have the advantage over the actor, and the initial asymmetry of the communication process is likely to be retained.

When we allow that the individual projects a definition of the situation when he appears before others, we must also see that the others, however passive their role may seem to be, will themselves effectively project a definition of the situation by virtue of their response to the individual and by virtue of any lines of action they initiate to him. Ordinarily the definitions of the situation projected by the several different participants are sufficiently attuned to one another, so that open contradiction will not occur. I do not mean that there will be the kind of consensus that arises when each individual present candidly expresses what he really feels and honestly agrees with the expressed feelings of the others present. This kind of harmony is an optimistic ideal and in any case not necessary for the smooth working of society. Rather, each participant is expected to suppress his immediate heartfelt feelings, conveying a view of the situation which he feels the others will be able to find at least temporarily acceptable. The maintenance of this surface agreement, this veneer of consensus, is facilitated by each participant concealing his own wants behind statements which assert values to which everyone present feels obliged to give lip service. Further, there is usually a kind of division of definitional labour. Each participant is allowed to establish the tentative official ruling regarding matters which are vital to him but not immediately important to others, e.g., the rationalisations and justifications by which he accounts for his past activity. In exchange for this courtesy he remains silent or non-committal on matters important to others but not immediately important to him. We have then a kind of interactional *modus vivendi*. Together the participants contribute to a single over-all definition of the situation which involves not so much a real agreement as to what exists but rather a real agreement as to whose claims concerning what issues will be temporarily honoured. Real agreement will also exist concerning the desirability of avoiding an open conflict of definitions of the situation * I will refer to this level of agreement as 'working consensus'. It is to be understood that the working consensus established in one interaction setting will be quite different in content from the working consensus established in a different type

* An interaction can be purposely set up as a time and place for voicing differences in opinion, but in such cases participants must be careful to agree not to disagree on the proper tone of voice, vocabulary, and degree of seriousness in which all arguments are to be phrased, and upon the mutual respect which disagreeing participants must carefully continue to express toward one another. This debaters' or academic definition of the situation may also be invoked suddenly and judiciously as a way of translating a serious conflict of views into one that can be handled within a framework acceptable to all present.

of setting. Thus, between two friends at lunch a reciprocal show of affection, respect, and concern for the other is maintained. In service occupations, on the other hand, the specialist often maintains an image of disinterested involvement in the problem of the client, while the client responds with a show of respect for the competence and integrity of the specialist. Regardless of such differences in content, however, the general form of these working arrangements is the same.

In noting the tendency for a participant to accept the definitional claims made by the others present, we can appreciate the crucial importance of the information that the individual *initially* possesses or acquires concerning his fellow participants, for it is on the basis of this initial information that the individual starts to define the situation and starts to build up lines of responsive action. The individual's initial projection commits him to what he is proposing to be and requires him to drop all pretences of being other things. As the interaction among the participants progresses, additions and modifications in this initial informational state will of course occur, but it is essential that these later developments be related without contradiction to, and even built up from, the initial positions taken by the several participants. It would seem that an individual can more easily make a choice as to what line of treatment to demand from and extend to the others present at the beginning of an encounter than he can alter the line of treatment that is being pursued once the interaction is under way.

In everyday life, of course, there is a clear understanding that first impressions are important. Thus, the work adjustment of those in service occupations will often hinge upon a capacity to seize and hold the initiative in the service relation, a capacity that will require subtle aggressiveness on the part of the server when he is of lower socio-economic status than his client. W. F. Whyte suggests the waitress as an example:[4]

> The first point that stands out is that the waitress who bears up under pressure does not simply respond to her customers. She acts with some skill to control their behaviour. The first question to ask when we look at the customer relationship is, 'Does the waitress get the jump on the customer, or does the customer get the jump on the waitress?' The skilled waitress realises the crucial nature of this question. . .
> The skilled waitress tackles the customers with confidence and without hesitation. For example, she may find that a new customer has seated himself before she could clear off the dirty dishes and change the cloth. He is now leaning on the table studying the menu. She greets him, says, 'May I change the cover please?' and, without waiting for an answer takes his menu away from him so that he

moves back from the table, and she goes about her work. The relationship is handled politely but firmly, and there is never any question as to who is in charge.

When the interaction that is initiated by 'first impressions' is itself merely the initial interaction in an extended series of interactions involving the same participants, we speak of 'getting off on the right foot' and feel that it is crucial that we do so. Thus, one learns that some teachers take the following view:[5]

> You can't ever let them get the upper hand on you or you're through. So I start out tough. The first day I get a new class in, I let them know who's boss. . . You've got to start off tough, then you can ease up as you go along. If you start out easy-going, when you try to get tough, they'll just look at you and laugh.

Similarly, attendants in mental institutions may feel that if the new patient is sharply put in his place the first day on the ward and made to see who is boss, much future difficulty will be prevented.[6]

Given the fact that the individual effectively projects a definition of the situation when he enters the presence of others, we can assume that events may occur within the interaction which contradict, discredit, or otherwise throw doubt upon this projection. When these disruptive events occur, the interaction itself may come to a confused and embarrassed halt. Some of the assumptions upon which the responses of the participants had been predicated become untenable, and the participants find themselves lodged in an interaction for which the situation has been wrongly defined and is now no longer defined. At such moments the individual whose presentation has been discredited may feel ashamed while the others present may feel hostile, and all the participants may come to feel ill at ease, nonplussed, out of countenance, embarrassed, experiencing the kind of anomaly that is generated when the minute social system of face-to-face interaction breaks down.

In stressing the fact that the initial definition of the situation projected by an individual tends to provide a plan for the co-operative activity that follows — in stressing this action point of view — we must not overlook the crucial fact that any projected definition of the situation also has a distinctive moral character. It is this moral character of projections that will chiefly concern us in this report. Society is organised on the principle that any individual who possesses certain social characteristics has a moral right to expect that others will value and treat him in an appropriate way. Connected with this principle is a second, namely that an individual who implicitly or explicitly signifies that he has certain social characteristics ought in fact to be what he claims he is. In consequence, when an individual projects a definition of the situation and thereby makes an implicit or explicit claim to be a person of a particular kind, he automatically exerts a moral demand upon the others, obliging them to value and treat him in the manner that persons of his kind have a right to expect. He also implicitly forgoes all claims to be things he does not appear to be* and hence forgoes the treatment that would be appropriate for such individuals. The others find, then, that the individual has informed them as to what is and as to what they *ought* to see as the 'is'.

One cannot judge the importance of definitional disruptions by the frequency with which they occur, for apparently they would occur more frequently were not constant precautions taken. We find that preventive practices are constantly employed to avoid these embarrassments and that corrective practices are constantly employed to compensate for discrediting occurrences that have not been successfully avoided. When the individual employs these strategies and tactics to protect his own projections, we may refer to them as 'defensive practices'; when a participant employs them to save the definition of the situation projected by another, we speak of 'protective practices' or 'tact'. Together, defensive and protective practices comprise the techniques employed to safeguard the impression fostered 'by an individual during his presence before others. It should be added that while we may be ready to see that no fostered impression would survive if defensive practices were not employed, we are less ready perhaps to see that few impressions could survive if those who received the impression did not exert tact in their reception of it.

In addition to the fact that precautions are taken to prevent disruption of projected definitions, we may also note that an intense interest in these disruptions comes to play a significant role in the social life of the group. Practical jokes and social games are played in which embarrassments which are to be taken unseriously are purposely engineered.[7] Fantasies are created in which devastating exposures occur. Anecdotes from the past — real, embroidered, or fictitious — are told and retold, detailing disruptions which occurred, almost occurred, or occurred and were admirably resolved. There seems to be no grouping which does not have a ready supply of these games, reveries, and cautionary tales, to be used as a source of humour, a catharsis for anxieties, and a sanction for inducing individuals to be modest in their claims and reasonable in their

---

* This role of the witness in limiting what it is the individual can be has been stressed by Existentialists, who see it as a basic threat to individual freedom. See Jean-Paul Sartre, *Being and Nothingness* (London: Methuen, 1957).

projected expectations. The individual may tell himself through dreams of getting into impossible positions. Families tell of the time a guest got his dates mixed and arrived when neither the house nor anyone in it was ready for him. Journalists tell of times when an all-too-meaningful misprint occurred, and the paper's assumption of objectivity or decorum was humorously discredited. Public servants tell of times a client ridiculously misunderstood form instructions, giving answers which implied an unanticipated and bizarre definition of the situation.[8] Seamen, whose home away from home is rigorously he-man, tell stories of coming back home and inadvertently asking mother to 'pass the fucking butter'.[9] Diplomats tell of the time a near-sighted queen asked a republican ambassador about the health of his king.[10]

To summarise, then, I assume that when an individual appears before others he will have many motives for trying to control the impression they receive of the situation. This report is concerned with some of the common techniques that persons employ to sustain such impressions and with some of the common contingencies associated with the employment of these techniques. The specific content of any activity presented by the individual participant, or the role it plays in the interdependent activities of an on-going social system, will not be at issue; I shall be concerned only with the participant's dramaturgical problems of presenting the activity before others. The issues dealt with by stagecraft and stage management are sometimes trivial but they are quite general; they seem to occur everywhere in social life, providing a clearcut dimension for formal sociological analysis.

It will be convenient to end this introduction with some definitions that are implied in what has gone before and required for what is to follow. For the purpose of this report, interaction (that is, face-to-face interaction) may be roughly defined as the reciprocal influence of individuals upon one another's actions when in one another's immediate physical presence. *An* interaction may be defined as all the interaction which occurs throughout any one occasion when a given set of individuals are in one another's continuous presence; the term 'an encounter' would do as well. A 'performance' may be defined as all the activity of a given participant on a given occasion which serves to influence in any way any of the other participants. Taking a particular participant and his performance as a basic point of reference, we may refer to those who contribute the other performances as the audience, observers, or co-participants. The pre-established pattern of action which is unfolded during a performance and which may be presented or played through on other occasions may be called a 'part' or 'routine'. These situational terms can easily be related to conventional structural ones. When an individual or performer plays the same part to the same audience on different occasions, a social relationship is likely to arise. Defining social role as the enactment of rights and duties attached to a given status, we can say that a social role will involve one or more parts and that each of these different parts may be presented by the performer on a series of occasions to the same kinds of audience or to an audience of the same persons.

Notes

1   Gustav Ichheiser, 'Misunderstandings in human relations', Supplement to *American Journal of Sociology*, LV (September 1949), pp. 6–7.
2   Willard Waller, 'The rating and dating complex', *American Sociological Review*, II, p. 730.
3   William Sansom, *A Contest of Ladies* (London: Hogarth, 1956), pp. 230–2.
4   W. F. Whyte, 'When workers and customers meet', ch. VII, *Industry and Society*, ed. W. F. Whyte (New York: McGraw-Hill, 1946), pp. 132–3.
5   Teacher interview quoted by Howard S. Becker, 'Social class variations in the teacher–pupil relationship', *Journal of Educational Sociology*, XXV, p. 459.
6   Harold Taxel, 'Authority Structure in a Mental Hospital Ward' (unpublished Master's thesis, Department of Sociology, University of Chicago, 1953).
7   Goffman, 'Communication Conduct in an Island Community', University of Chicago, 1953, Ph.D. thesis no. 2149, pp. 319–27.
8   Peter Blau, 'Dynamics of Bureaucracy' (Ph.D. dissertation, Department of Sociology, Columbia University, University of Chicago Press, 1900), pp. 127–9.
9   Walter M. Beattie, Jr, 'The Merchant Seaman' (unpublished M.A. report, Department of Sociology, University of Chicago, 1950), p. 35.
10 Sir Frederick Ponsonby, *Recollections of Three Reigns* (London: Eyre & Spottiswoode, 1951).

28   The problem of the image of man

Isidor Chein

Sigmund Koch has remarked that 'psychology has been far more concerned with being a science than with courageous and self-determining confrontation of its historical subject matter.'[1] Koch pointed out how little scientific psychology has contributed to the humanities in the face of his conviction that 'psychology . . . *must* be . . . that area in which the problems of the sciences, as traditionally conceived, and the humanities intersect.' [. . .]

Yet the issue runs deeper than the service of psychology to the humanities. It concerns the nature of psychology itself, and, at the heart of this issue, I find the issue of the image of Man. Specifically, I suggest, we must choose between two images. The first is that of Man as an active, responsible agent, not simply a helpless, powerless reagent. Man, in the active image, is a being who actively does something with regard to some of the things that happen to him, a being who, for instance, tries to increase the likelihood that some things will happen and that others will not, a being who tries to generate circumstances that are compatible with the execution of his intentions, a being who may try to inject harmony where he finds disharmony or who may sometimes seek to generate disharmony, a being who seeks to shape his environment rather than passively permit himself to be shaped by the latter, a being, in short, who insists on injecting himself into the causal process of the world around him. If Man is said to respond to his environment, the word 'response' is to be taken in the sense that it has in active dialogue rather than in the sense of an automatic consequence.

The contrasting and the prevailing image among psychologists whose careers are devoted to the advancement of the science and among astonishingly large numbers of those concerned with behavioral orthogenics (guidance, counseling, psychotherapy, and so on) is that of Man as an impotent reactor, with his responses completely determined by two distinct and separate, albeit interacting, sets of factors: (1) the forces

Source: *The Science of Behaviour and the Image of Man*, London, Tavistock Publications, 1972, extracts from pp. 3, 5–14.

impinging on him and (2) his constitution (including in the latter term, for present purposes, momentary physiological states). Response is at all times and at every moment an automatic consequence of the interaction of body and environment. Man, as such, plays no role in determining the outcome of the interplay between constitution and environment. He is implicitly viewed as a robot — a complicatedly constructed and programmed robot, perhaps, but a robot nevertheless.

Note well that the issue is not simply whether behavior is purposive, not at least in some usages of the word 'purpose.'[2] One may conceive of Man as driven by powerful instinctual drives that impel him to seek particular ends; if the environment permits, the ends will be attained and, if not, a definite something else will happen. This model, commonly thought of as a purposive one, leaves Man a passive victim of the interplay between constitution and environment no less than do the nonpurpose stimulus-response models. Man, as such, has nothing to do with the outcome. He does nothing; things happen to him.

Nor is the issue whether one can reduce a human being to a state in which he is nothing more than a helpless passive reagent. Stupefy him, for instance, and drop him down an elevator shaft; his descent will not differ from that of any other physical body of the same shape. Nor is the issue whether there may not be reactions of the human body that are aptly described in the terms of the second image. Strike the patellar tendon, for instance, and, if the appropriate segments of the nervous system are intact and functioning and there are no physical restraints, there will follow a characteristic kick. The body is a physical body and, as such, it is utterly subject to physical law. The organism is a physiological system and, as such, it is utterly subject to physiological law; I am willing to take it as axiomatic that physiological law cannot be incompatible with physical law. I am similarly ready to take it as axiomatic that psychological law cannot be incompatible with either physiological or physical law. If it could be, the world would be reduced to chaos.

These are assumptions that I am not only willing to grant, but that I think are necessary to the scientific enterprise. They are not subject to disproof. Any apparent contradiction of them would only lead me to question the adequacy of our formulations of the relevant laws or the accuracy or sufficiency of the contradictory observations. To do otherwise would only be to put an end to inquiry and investigation — an end to science. They are not metaphysical or epistemological propositions at all, they are simply motivating assumptions of scientific inquiry.

I must assume that one who behaves is utterly subject to behavioral law and that the latter is not incompatible with either physiological or physical law. It does not follow that behavioral law is reducible to physiological or physical law, or that physiological law is reducible to physical law. A boiler system is subject to thermodynamic law, and it is also subject to mechanical law; but it does not follow that thermodynamic law is reducible to mechanical law. The concurrent relevance of two domains of law to one system does not necessarily imply that the two sets of laws are necessarily reducible to one of them. I am not saying that one set of laws is not reducible to another (such a ukase, too, would only put an end to inquiry), merely that it is not necessarily so; and I would very much want to encourage any line of inquiry that offered a promise of successfully accomplishing the reduction. Nor am I in any manner averse to the pursuit of investigations the aim of which is to determine how much of what seems to be behavior can be subsumed under physiology or physics.

I am, however, and it seems to me that any scientist ought to be, very much averse to the exclusion of observables on the ground that it is not apparent that the reduction can be accomplished. We should be equally averse if it were a certainty that the reduction is impossible. Our first responsibility, one that transcends all others, is to our observables. All our other commitments as scientists are deducible from this one, and only from this one. The law of parsimony, for instance, on which we place so much stock can only be justified on the ground that an unparsimonious explanation (one that postulates unnecessary entities, factors, forces, sources or forms of energy, intervening variables, and so forth) carries us unnecessarily far away from our observables.

To my mind, and this is the issue, we can only hold the second, the robotic, image by violating our cardinal obligation as scientists — to maintain faith with our subject matter, that is, to report scrupulously that which we observe and to observe fully without willful bias. [. . .]

I am charging that psychologists maintain the image of Man as a passive corporeal entity governed by a thermodynamic principle because of their philosophical precommitments and in flagrant disregard of contradictory information. To avoid misunderstanding, I want to put this charge in perspective before I present my argument.

Let me distinguish between a metatheory and a theory. My criterion for making this distinction is that the former does not lead to specific predictions the confirmation or disconfirmation of which would verify or contradict it. The properties of a good metatheory are that it provides a comprehensive frame within which phenomena can be efficiently ordered and relationships among phenomena parsimoniously expressed, that it offers the opportunity for and encourages the interrelating of all phenomena that come within its scope, and that it directs attention to the possibilities of phenomena and relationships among phenomena that might otherwise be missed. Most so-called theories are actually metatheories; if it is true, as has been claimed, that no theory has ever been abandoned because of factual contradiction, all theories are really meta-theories. With enough ingenuity, it is presumably possible to save any theory against factual contradiction by adding one or more postulates, making one or more well-chosen *ad hoc* assumptions, or, more vaguely, assuming the intrusion of some uncontrolled variables. In a sense, for instance, every bridge is a test of the principles of Newtonian mechanics, but I doubt if anyone has ever seriously questioned Newton's laws (which, incidentally, are tautologies to start with) on the grounds that bridges designed by the best of engineers have been known to collapse; one assumes instead (and quite properly, too) some defect in the materials and/or some unanticipated circumstances that generate stresses and strains that the bridge was not designed to withstand. The scientific fate of competing metatheories depends on how well they achieve the proper-ties described earlier in this paragraph, and one may regard a metatheory as validated to the extent that it possesses these properties to a greater degree than do its competitors.

In this connection, I hasten to add that we are concerned with the image of Man, not with a model. As used in scientific discourse, *models* are limited-purpose scientific devices that aid in exploring certain seg-ments of the data universe and testing certain propositions. A model is, knowingly, an analogical construction that ignores the differentiating data; thus, to the extent that the nervous system is comparable to a telephone network (one model of the nervous system), known properties of such networks ought to hold for the nervous system and certain parallel outcomes ought to be demonstrable for events in the nervous system and telephonic networks. In a sense, the model is used to test how far a particular analogy can be pushed in certain directions, but no one in his senses would assume that a telephone model of the nervous system commits him to the assumption that neurones are copper wires. By the same token, the failure of a model simply indicates that a par-ticular analogy cannot be pushed very far in certain directions; its success or failure does not demand a revolution in science or in scientific styles of thought. This, by contrast, is precisely what the Copernican and Dar-winian conceptualizations accomplished. They did not substitute one model for another. They revolutionized our image of the world and of Man's place in it. The images that these and other revolutionaries wrought and embodied in their metatheoretical stances gave direction and meaning to much of the subsequent course of scientific development. There were also changes in our image of the world and of Man's place in it that were not rooted in any new conceptualizations at all, but in the sheer process of discovery, for example, of the vastness of our universe and of universes beyond the up-to-then known universe.

I am quite willing to grant to the critic whose comments led me to the preceding discursus on the difference between model and image that many of the new images also led to much unproductive controversy (for instance, whether it is or is not possible to respect Man cast in the image of a glorified monkey), but must insist that the latter devolved around side issues typically involving distortions of the images and their logical implications. Controversy over the images that respects the rules of logic cannot be unproductive. The very nature of science is at stake.

The present essay is unequivocally intended as a contribution to psychological metatheory. It is not concerned with trying to establish psychological fact. I know that most psychological research, my own included, is in itself indifferent to the metatheoretical issues I shall be discussing. A research finding stands regardless of the metatheoretical frame of reference to which it is referred. Any alternative metatheoretical position that can neither assimilate it nor explain it away is, on the face of the matter, a defective metatheory. I also know that the majority of psychological researchers and teachers give little thought in their workaday lives to metatheoretical issues and that, in fact, they hardly seem to be concerned about maintaining any consistent view of these matters. Apart from the fact that inconsistency is itself likely to generate considerable confusion, there are, however, two major ways in which I think we go astray.

The first occurs when we try to integrate the various bits of accumulating psychological information into a more comprehensive coherent whole; it is, after all, one of the major facets of the business of science to integrate knowledge into coherent larger units. Countless researchers contributing vast numbers of bits of information do not produce a body of scientific knowledge if the bits of knowledge are unrelated to one another even though they may be systematically arrayed in a master file. The Sears Roebuck catalog and the collected volumes of the telephone directory would not be mistaken by anyone as contributions to science for all that they contain more facts per page, in highly accessible array, than any scientific tome I have ever come across.*

A special case of going astray for lack of attention to the pattern of the integrated whole is that, since we do not derive our research problems out of a vacuum, we do have some more or less vague and tacit notion of how the bit of information we hope to contribute will fit into the totality. Hence, our individual research projects, in themselves in different

* I believe that I first came across the example of the telephone directory as a nonscientific body of systematized knowledge in a lecture by Professor Morris Raphael Cohen.

to the metatheoretical issues, are presented in a language and conceptualized in terms that are consistent with our metatheoretical frames of reference. The individual research project thus carries within itself a tacit directive as to how it should be dealt with in a larger integration.

Consider, for instance, research on conditioning. The basic phenomena are interpretable in terms of perceived contextual relationships and relevant motivation. Typically, however, the concepts and phenomena are presented in terms that are more or less explicitly reminiscent of wired switchboards or hydraulic erosion. That is, conditioning, taken as the prototype of all learning, is presented in terms that pre-suppose a robotic image of Man. Even when motivation is introduced in the model, it is only to admit a factor that affects the openness of neural pathways. To be sure, the robot image implicit in conditioning theory either blandly disregards such simple facts as that the conditioned response is different from the unconditioned response or else introduces such complications into the theoretical model as to bring into serious question its greatest alleged virtue, the parsimonious explanation that it offers.

The issue of parsimony is relevant to my entire argument in a more fundamental sense. The principle states that explanatory constructs should not needlessly be multiplied, that is, it tells us to stay as close as we can to available data. But how is needlessly to be assessed? Does it require the bringing to bear of all relevant data or does it apply to limited sets of data? Let me try to illustrate the point. Whatever else I know about learning, I know that cognitions play an important role in my own learning processes. For me to take noncognitive learning theories seriously, I must assume that there are, in all other creatures, learning processes that look just like my own but that are really quite different. That is, for what are manifestly quite similar processes, I must assume that different principles of learning operate: one set of principles that apply to me and another set that apply to all other creatures. Simply on the grounds of parsimony, therefore, and Lloyd Morgan's canon notwithstanding, I must assert that the burden of proof rests on the anticognitive theorists — especially so when some of the latter have privately confessed to me that they, too, sometimes operate with cognitive maps. The latter, incidentally, are not scientific scoundrels — or, at least, not exceptionally so. They justify their manifest dereliction on the basis of a sharp distinction between private knowledge and that which, on philosophical grounds, properly belongs in the domain of science. The derailment and misconstruction of the behaviorist revolution that is involved in their position is an issue to which I will return later.

Note that I have absolutely nothing against any psychologist setting out to determine whether there are dependable stimulus-response relationships when cognitive and the like processes are disregarded. The point, if any, at which my quarrel with him begins is when he starts pretending that what he has disregarded does not exist or is not a proper concern of the scientific enterprise and when he remains obtusely oblivious to the fact that, having ignored cognitive and like factors, he is in no position to say anything about the variation or lack of variation in these factors under the conditions of his observations and, hence, that he is equally in no position to judge whether and how the dependability of the relationships he discovers itself depends on the status of the variables he has ignored. The principle of parsimony was never intended as a license to achieve simplicity by ignoring the unparsimoniousness of nature. The simplicity demanded by the principle is of the explanation, not of the explicandum. Note my emphasis on needlessly in my statement of the principle and the phrase 'except by necessity' in Occam's original statement.

At any rate, my immediate concern is not with the deficiency of the conditioning model *per se* but with its effect on the tone and scope of psychological thinking in general, namely, in the sanction that it gives to the image of Man as a robot.

The second major way in which we go astray is in the distribution of psychological research effort. There may be good reason for such a distribution apart from our metatheoretical frames of reference, for instance, our tendency to follow available research techniques rather than to pursue rationally derived problems. The question, however, is whether we are justified in a sense of contentment about that distribution and the course it is likely to take or whether we ought to be worried about it. In terms of the prevailing image of Man, I think we may well rest content. In terms of the active image, I think we should be worried about our failure to generate imperatives in the upcoming generation of psychologists (to bypass the issue of our own doings) to confront problems we ourselves avoid.

It follows, then, that though my charge of flagrant disregard of relevant fact may have some bearing on the work and thought of individual psychologists, it is with the totality of our scientific enterprise that I am concerned.

Notes

1 S. Koch, 'Psychological science versus the science-humanism antimony: intimations of a significant science of Man,' *American Psychologist*, 16 (1961): 624, 629, 631; and generally see pp. 629–39.

2 See R. R. Holt, 'Freud's mechanistic and humanistic images of Man,' in *Psychoanalysis and Contemporary Science*, vol. 3, ed. Leo Goldberger et al. (International Universities Press, 1974).

Issues in the Philosophy of the Social Sciences

Introduction

Tony Walton

In the first article of this volume, Alan Ryan raised questions about the problem of how far the social sciences can claim to be scientific in the sense in which the natural sciences are. Whether the study of society is or is not a science has long been an issue of interest and deep controversy. A particularly contentious issue which stems in part from the question of the appropriateness of the methods of the natural sciences in respect of the study of society is that of whether the social sciences can be value free. Not all proponents of a scientific — or *naturalistic* — approach to the study of society have thought that value freedom is a necessary condition for the scientific study of society, but there exists a major tradition — generally referred to as *positivist* — which asserts, among other things, that properly scientific explanation is free from the intrusion of values. Thus, the logic of explanation is taken to be independent of the values prompting the investigator. Hence the well-known positivist insistence on the distinction between factual and evaluative statements, and the claim that scientific explanation should be confined to the former and free from the latter.

Philosophers writing in the positivist tradition have not always denied that value judgments affect explanation in the social sciences. Ernest Nagel, in the extract included in this volume, is prepared to recognise that what the social scientist selects for study is affected by his values. And he does not deny that the values and moral judgments of social scientists invariably colour their conclusions. But there are two points that need to be noted about Nagel's view which indicate that he is firmly rooted in the positivist tradition. First, he regards the intrusion of values as a difficulty which makes reliable scientific knowledge difficult to achieve in the study of society. Second, he insists that, at least in principle, 'there is a relatively clear distinction between factual and value judgements' and that it is the task of social scientists to strive to give expression to this distinction in their work.

393

This view has, however, been questioned and issued in conceptions of explanation which claim that value judgments are not so much an unfortunate intrusion but are, rather, partly constitutive of explanation and should be recognised as such. The idea of an objective and value free social enquiry is thus rejected. In the article by Steven Lukes the point is made that 'moral and political positions are . . . also at issue in theoretical disputes'. It is the existence of this evaluative dimension which, according to Lukes, goes some way to explaining the widespread existence of controversy between rival theoretical positions.

Lukes refers to the importance of moral and political positions in explanations as part of a more general account of the *underdetermination* of theory by factual evidence. That is, he addresses the question as to why it is that the same empirical evidence can be interpreted in different ways by incompatible theories, and why a knowledge of the available empirical evidence does not unambiguously determine which theory is true.

In his discussion of underdetermination Lukes also draws attention to the importance of the fact that social reality is in part constituted by social actors' theories. That is to say, social reality is already pre-interpreted by social actors, and the social scientist has the complex job of getting to grips with a reality which is not only pre-interpreted, but which is pre-interpreted in different ways by different social actors. Consequently, a complex relationship exists between actors' and observers' (social scientists') theories. Actors' theories often conflict, and observers' theories may conflict with actors' theories. Moreover, observers' theories may conflict with one another. In the absence of wholly determinate empirical evidence these conflicts are inescapable. By drawing attention to the respects in which social reality is partly constituted by actors' theories, Lukes is taking up the perennially controversial issue of the significance of the *meaning content* or *conceptual* aspect of social action. The importance for explanation of the conceptual aspect of social action has long been a source of disagreement among philosophers of the social sciences, and the Lukes article provides a helpful re-posing of this difficult issue.

The character of explanation inevitably raises the question of the practical usefulness of the social sciences. How far does the knowledge generated by the social sciences provide the basis for rational decision-making? Can social scientific knowledge be used to improve society? With the aid of social science can we predict and control the social world just as natural scientific knowledge makes possible control over the natural environment?

The famous twentieth-century philosopher, Sir Karl Popper, an extract of whose work is included here, has claimed, although with a degree of caution, that the social sciences can generate knowledge which is properly scientific and that this can form the basis for 'piecemeal social engineering'. In Popper's view, the social sciences can be used as an aid to bringing about reforms in society, although he rejects the claim that scientific technocratic thinking should become a substitute for moral and political debate. According to Popper, the social sciences, and indeed also the natural sciences, can never tell us which goals we ought to pursue, but they can tell us the technically most rational means of achieving whatever goals we choose to pursue, the latter being established through free democratic processes.

The article by Brian Fay takes issue with the view that there can ever be a reliable social technology, even of the cautious Popperian kind, which can provide technical solutions to practical social problems. Writing in a tradition in which the well-known German social theorist Jürgen Habermas is prominent, Fay rejects the view that the social sciences can produce the kinds of scientific explanation which would enable us to predict and control the social environment in the light of criteria independent of value presuppositions. Central to Fay's analysis is the claim that what purports to be an objective and value free (positivist) conception of social explanation and control actually derives from a set of values and presuppositions about man and society which are not self-evidently true and easily verified. Namely, a set of presuppositions according to which people in society are treated as manipulable objects of scientific interest and political domination.

Following Habermas, Fay extends his analysis into a more general critique of the increasing scientisation of the political process and the associated tendency towards the greater power of bureaucrats and technocrats. He argues that the idea of a 'policy science' of the kind which stems from the Popperian notion of 'social engineering' legitimates the increasing influence of technical experts and provides a rationalisation for the diminishing role of genuine political processes.

29   Fact and theory in the social sciences

Steven Lukes

I start from the general thesis that theories may be underdetermined by data: that is, that theories may be incompatible with each other and yet compatible with all possible data. Theories may conflict yet be empirically equivalent, that is compatible with all the observations that not merely are but could be made. In this article, I shall suggest some reasons why the underdetermination of theories by data may be more acute in the social than in the natural sciences,[1] and I shall seek to support this suggestion by citing as an example conflicting theories of the modern state held by marxists and liberal pluralists.

In arguing for the underdetermination thesis, in relation to physical theories, the philosopher Quine writes that he expects wide agreement about it 'if only because the observational criteria of theoretical terms are commonly so flexible and fragmentary'.[2] This comment already suggests a first reason why underdetermination should be more acute in the social than in the natural sciences. If it is true of physical theories that 'the observational criteria of theoretical terms are commonly so flexible and fragmentary', how much more likely is it to be true of social theories? There are probably few terms in the social sciences whose expunging from the lexicon has not been advocated by somebody, on the grounds of persistent disagreement and confusion over definition and application. Consider, more or less at random, say, 'social system', 'class', 'deviance' and 'rôle' in sociology; 'political system', 'state', 'political culture' and 'power' in political science; 'religion', 'symbol', 'culture' and 'kinship' in social anthropology; and 'capital', 'value', 'utility' and 'consumer surplus' in economics. Often such disputes are an unsatisfactory surrogate for properly theoretical disagreements, and often the lament is heard that, if only the conceptual questions could be solved, one could get on with the real business of theorizing.

Source: article commissioned for this Reader, prepared on the basis of his earlier essay, 'The underdetermination of theory by data', Aristotelian Society, *Supplementary vol.* LII, 1978, pp. 93–107. Steven Lukes is Fellow in Politics and Sociology, Balliol College, Oxford.

This situation arises not just because of the less rigorous and less developed state of the social, as compared to the natural, sciences – whether this be due to the intractability of many social phenomena to scalar measurement, to their complexity or their instability, to the inherent difficulties of replication and experimentation, to the openness of systems, to ineradicable experimental interference with the data, or whatever. Social theories are themselves partly constitutive of the very reality being theorized about, so that the actors' beliefs and actions are themselves already going to embody theories with which other actors' theories and the observer's theory and indeed other observers' theories may well conflict. Hence the observational criteria are going to have to include decision rules for adjudicating between such contending theories, and how can these be definitively established?

The old behaviourist way out of this dilemma was to narrow down the notion of 'observable data' to events and processes which were separable from and neutral between contending interpretations. But few could now seriously maintain that this is a genuine way out. The data of the sciences of man are already pre-interpreted and their observation necessarily involves a further process of interpretation, which raises an inevitable problem of indeterminacy. Here let it suffice to observe that the fixity and the completeness of the observational criteria of theoretical terms is jeopardised, first by the fact that, among other things, they are themselves in dispute, among actors, among observers and between actors and observers, and, second, by the fact that observation of social phenomena, involving agents' desires, beliefs and actions, always and ineradicably involves interpretation on the part of the observer.

The second reason for holding that underdetermination is more acute in the case of social theories has to do with the divergent interests of those who espouse them. Social theories come in overall packages, involving methodological and epistemological but also moral and political positions, which are therefore also at issue in theoretical disputes. This is why social scientists so frequently seem to be examining the roots, rather than reaping the fruits, of their own and others' work. One central difference between the social and the natural sciences is that the history of the latter suggests what one might call a 'filtering process' by which contending theories and positions are filtered out, leaving one, or in some few cases, a small number of contenders in the field. Perhaps one reason for this is that they typically share background assumptions in a way that the social sciences do not, because they have a common cognitive interest in the prediction and control of the object world – in knowing how to bring about or avoid the explanandum.[3]

Mary Hesse has made this point most persuasively, writing of the 'pragmatic criterion of predictive success'[4] which, as successful prediction accumulates, filters out both simplicity criteria and other value judgments, overriding all other possible criteria of theory choice. There is thus a 'filtering-out mechanism' which 'has been powered by universal adoption of one overriding value for natural science, namely the increasingly successful prediction and control of the environment'.[5] The method of natural science is, on this view, like a computer programme 'designed to process environmental data and to learn to make successful predictions'.[6] The criteria of success of such a device can be made independent of the computer's language system.

If this argument is plausible, then the absence of such a filtering device in the social sciences (perhaps because 'there will be some environments and some types of data which do not permit learning by any computer of limited capacity'[7]) cannot be attributed to their immaturity. Contending theories will be governed by different, though not exclusive (indeed complementary) interests.[8] On this argument, underdetermination may be explained by the argument that the interest-relativity of all explanation reveals continuing disagreement in the social as opposed to the natural sciences because of persisting differences among students of social life as to what requires and what constitutes explanation. Hesse suggests that 'There are not at present, and perhaps can never reasonably be expected to be, general theories in the social sciences that satisfy the pragmatic criterion . . . namely, theories that can provide increasingly successful prediction and control in the social domain'.[9] Perhaps so, or perhaps, rather, the very possibility that such theories may be developed itself represents a doom-laden prospect, that of a kind of one-dimensional object-world, or Weberian iron cage, an interest in whose avoidance is central to the social scientist's task.

The third reason why social theories might be held to be subject to underdetermination in ways in which natural science theories are not is, unlike the first two, a matter of degree, not of kind. It is this: that in so far as the incompatibility between theories lies in their divergences over counterfactual claims, this raises quite peculiar problems of validation in social inquiry. I am assuming here that the counterfactual claims are taken to be part of the theories, rather than part of the observational data. This is reasonable enough where the theoretical disputes occur precisely over what is claimed to be possible but does not happen, that is over the scope of the constraints upon and enabling conditions of what occurs, and whence they derive.[10]

Recall the story Lakatos tells of the pre-Einsteinian scientist's manoeuvres to save Newtonian theory in the face of planetary misbehaviour, which makes the general point that *ceteris paribus* clauses are infinitely substitutable for one another.[11] This situation is, of course, far worse, in practical terms, in the social sciences, even than for the astronomer (who, along with the meteorologist, is in the worst position in the natural sciences), just because the non-replicability of initial conditions makes for the possibility of indefinite and rationally sustainable disagreement about counterfactual claims. At least, the natural scientist has, through experiment, a practical, if not theoretically conclusive, way of making the counterfactual factual.

Let us, then, look for examples of the underdetermination of social theories. If the reasons for their underdetermination suggested above have any plausibility, it will of course be open to an objector to reject any suggested case of social scientific underdetermination, because the theories lack the kind of rigour in the specification of their theoretical terms and of their falsification conditions that would make them sufficiently well formed to be labelled incompatible with one another. But this very objection itself presupposes as an ideal for social theories an end to the essential contestability of theoretical terms, a consensus about cognitive interests and a practically effective way of establishing the truth-value of counterfactual claims. This ideal may for many, perhaps most, areas of social science be unattainable, or, rather, unattainable in any world in essential respects familiar to us.

Consider, as an example of theoretical underdetermination, ranging across sociology, politics and economics, different theories of the nature and rôle of the state. I choose this example, partly because it brings out well the force of all three of the reasons for the underdetermination of social theories proposed above. Contending theories of the state quite generally illustrate the theme of the underdetermination of social theories, exhibiting disputes about the observational criteria of theoretical terms (not least 'the state' itself), strikingly opposed interests governing alternative doctrines of explanation, and contending and perhaps irresolvable counterfactual claims.

No empirical evidence is going to decide between, for example, the view, classically expressed in the Ancient World by Aristotle and in the modern by Hegel, that the state is *natural*, the embodiment of the human good and of justice, the condition of a life lived in accordance with virtue, that is, for the realization of ethical life; and, on the other hand, the view, common to the Sophists, the Stoics, the Christian Fathers, medieval philosophers before Aquinas, the theorists of the Social Contract and the utilitarians, that the state is a *conventional institution*, an artifice, a human contrivance, a means of attaining certain ends. No evidence will enable us to decide between Hegel's view of the state as inevitable and beneficent, standing above and outside civil society, restraining the conflicting passions that arise within it, and resolving the conflicts between its various components; and Marx's view of the state as only conditionally necessary and of its nature oppressive, a creature of civil society, reflecting the conflicting interests and tensions within it, guarding and protecting a hierarchical class structure, and, however much its rôle may be mystified, furthering the interests of the ruling class. No evidence is going to decide the issue between Bosanquet's Rousseauian theory of the state and Hobhouse's critique of it, or between contemporary theories of totalitarianism which see it as the conquest of society by the state and those who see it as the destruction of the state, seen as a legal structure of rules protecting individuals, by an all-powerful elite.[12] Evidence cannot decide between contemporary liberal theories, such as those of Galbraith and Milton Friedman, or among recent neo-marxist theories, such as those of Miliband, Poulantzas and Habermas. The theoretical packages involved in these disputes are both too inclusive and too internally coherent for it to be possible that neutral evidence could simply decide between them. Which theory is true, if any, is not, in cases such as these, empirically decidable.

To make this example a little more specific, consider the opposition between so-called liberal-pluralist and marxist theories of the liberal-democratic state in capitalist societies. Summarizing drastically then, first picture the state as a sort of political market place, a neutral arena in which the autonomously generated demands expressing the interests of the various sections and groups within the population are articulated and aggregated. On one view of the matter, the conflicting interests are mediated through party competition, with politically neutral state agencies responsive to the outcomes of that competition; in another version, the state agencies are directly accessible to the play of interest groups, and their competition within the state either reinforces or supplants party competition. The general claim is made that the liberal-democratic state is diverse, open and penetrable by any dissatisfied group seeking a political voice. On this view, the state is conceived as a set of constraining and enabling conditions favourable to open political competition, generated elsewhere; any group not currently in the political arena or trying to get in, thereby manifests a low level of dissatisfaction. This implies the counterfactual claim that, if that level were to rise, such a group would both try to enter the arena and succeed in defending its interests within it.

Contrast this with the neo-marxist view which, in various different versions, combines a number of theses about the state: that it is an instrument of class rule (a 'committee for managing the common affairs of the bourgeoisie'),[13] a condition for the reproduction of capitalism and the class relations within it, a form of illusory and alienated life, and itself an object of class struggle. In *The State in Capitalist Society*,[14] Ralph Miliband stresses the instrumentalist thesis, arguing that the

most important political fact about advanced capitalist societies . . .
is the continued existence in them of private and ever more concentrated economic power. As a result of that power, the men — owners
and controllers — in whose hands it lies enjoy a massive preponder-
ance in society, in the political system, and in the determination of
the state's policies and actions . . . the state in these class societies is
primarily and inevitably the guardian and protector of the economic
interests which are dominant in them. Its 'real' purpose and mission
is to ensure their continued predominance, not to prevent it.

In his more recent *Marxism and Politics,*[15] Miliband offers a more
nuanced view that is still, however, basically instrumentalist, arguing
that

the character of [the state's] leading personnel, the pressures exercised by the economically dominant class, and the structural constraints imposed by the mode of production — constitute the Marxist
answer to the question why the state should be considered as the 'instrument' of the 'ruling class'.

Other recent marxist writers offer more 'structuralist' and indeed 'func-
tionalist' accounts of the rôle of the capitalist state, but all agree that
the idea of diverse, open and penetrable politics is an illusion, itself
serving to conceal the continual reproduction of class relationships. On
this view, the state is seen as a set of conditions which constrain and
enable continued class domination, partly by concealing it, diffusing or
defusing it at the political level. In contrast to the counterfactual claims
implicit in the liberal-pluralist position, marxists and neo-marxists see
the activities, ideology and forms of organization characteristic of the
state as (perhaps indefinitely?) deflecting, defusing or postponing crises
of capitalist relations of production and the development of forms of
class consciousness and class action both responsive to and generative of
such crises.

Liberal-pluralists and neo-marxists offer contrasting accounts of the
increased rôle of the state in contemporary capitalist economies. Thus
Galbraith, in his *American Capitalism*, saw it as in large part associated
with the development of countervailing power:

In fact, the support of countervailing power has become in modern
times perhaps the major domestic peacetime function of the federal
government. Labour sought and received it in the protection and
assistance which the Wagner Act provided to union organisation.

Farmers sought and received it in the form of federal price supports to their markets – a direct subsidy of market power. Unorganised workers have sought and received it in the form of minimum wage legislation.

For Galbraith 'a large part of the state's new activity . . . is associated with the development of countervailing power' and 'supports or supplements a normal economic process'.[16] By contrast, the marxist Ernest Mandel discusses the way in which the role of the 'bourgeois State as a weapon of capitalist class interests, is concealed from both the actors and from the observers and victims of this tragi-comedy by the mystifying image of the State as an arbiter *between* classes, a representative of the "national interest", a neutral and benevolent judge of the merits of all "pluralist forces"' – and he cites Galbraith's *American Capitalism* as 'a good example of such mystifying theses'.[17] For Mandel, by contrast, the typical political decision of the state reflects

> the class interests of the bourgeoisie in the sense of promoting or consolidating the general conditions for the valorization of capital, though it may simultaneously endanger particular interests of even important sections of the bourgeois class.

Indeed, the very 'structure of the bourgeois state' results in 'the permanent prevention of any direct exercise of power (self-administration) by the mass of the working-class'.[18]

Particularly instructive from our point of view is the way in which 'evidence' is used by opposite sides of this argument. Mandel takes as an illustration 'an account of the origins of economic programming in Great Britain provided by a leading liberal-bourgeois journalist, and naïvely presented by this commentator as proof of the "conversion" of capitalism into a "mixed economy" in England'. The journalist, Samuel Brittan, wrote as follows:[19]

> When Selwyn Lloyd entered the Treasury, he already thought that long-term planning of government expenditure was, like other things he believed in, 'common sense'. He was converted to the belief that planning has something to offer for the private sector as well by a conference of the Federation of British Industries, held at Brighton at the end of November 1960, to consider 'the Next Five Years' . . . The Brighton Conference was attended by 121 leading businessmen and thirty one guests, including the heads of government departments and of the nationalised industries, and a few economists . . . During the course of 1960, some of the more active minds in the Treasury

had, quite independently of the FBI, become interested in new ideas for adding some zip to British industry . . . there were a very small number of officials who thought it was worth putting together the forecasts and plans on which individual industries were already working, to see if they fitted together.

Mandel's comment on this passage is this: 'It would be difficult to find a more obvious confirmation of the marxist account of the functions of the late bourgeois State than this candid report of strategic decisions suggested by "leading businessmen", empathised by high civil servants, and implemented by bourgeois politicians'.[20]

. An adequate discussion of the precise respects in which these contending theories are indeed offering theoretically alternative but empirically equivalent accounts would involve unravelling a whole host of knotty and specific issues. But I hope that enough has been said to show (1) that the issue of how 'the state' is conceptualised and its operations identified through observation is essentially in dispute among both actors and observers; (2) that alternative interests govern different theoretical packages yielding incompatible theories; and (3) quite opposite counterfactual claims about what would occur but for the operations of the state are at issue.

For liberal theories (of which, over the last three centuries there have, of course, been many varieties), the state is outside or above, and neutral between, the conflicting interests of civil society: hence the images of a constitutional and institutional framework, of the night-watchman or traffic-policeman (note the difference between these: only the latter is functionally indispensable to the activity he regulates), of a political market-place or a bureaucratic machine. Its workings are observed (that is, interpreted) in the form of political, economic and social policies which are themselves interpreted in the light of a particular theory of the socio-economic order (which may be called capitalist, or 'post-capitalist'). For marxist theories (of which there have been, similarly, many versions) the state is, by contrast, an intrinsic part of the capitalist order, central to its relations of production and never neutral between the conflicting, or rather contradictory, interests generated within it though it may be relatively autonomous from any particular interests at any given time: hence the images of instrument and condition of class rule, alienated life-form, and object of class struggle. Its workings are observed (that is, interpreted) in the form of political, economic and social policies which are themselves interpreted in the light of a particular theory of the capitalist mode of production.

These alternative sets of theories are at odds at many levels, including the methodological, epistemological, moral and political: indeed, one might even say that one issue between them is the question of what is real and what apparent. For the marxist, liberal pluralism conceals the reality of capitalist domination; whereas, for the liberal, marxist theory postulates exploitation and contradictions where none exist.

Clearly, one central form that their rivalry takes is over the question of non-events or counterfactuals. For the liberal, the role of the state is explained against the background assumption of the normal working of a capitalist economy, though liberals have differed widely over how and to what extent the state either helps or hinders that normal working. For the marxist, however, one central role of the state is to contribute to the prevention of crises, of the development of class consciousness and eventual social revolution, and the socialist order that it would make possible. Some might suppose that the arrival of that revolution might finally decide the matter, but, needless to say, both liberals and marxists would then have competing and incompatible accounts of why it came about, just as they now have such accounts of its continuing non-arrival.

Conclusion

The examples of social theories that I have cited are far from conclusive. They are certainly not examples of the best that the social sciences can offer in the way of rigour, sophistication and explanatory power. But they do, I think, illustrate the three reasons I have singled out why social theories are likely to conflict and remain for ever persuasive to their adherents, even where the evidence fails to decide between them.

Notes

1   In the text of this article I leave aside a deep and worrying question which I mention here only for the benefit of footnote readers seeking to add to their perplexities. To speak of the underdetermination of theories by data is to assume that there are unambiguously interpretable data of which it can truly be said that they are neutral as between rival theories which are underdetermined by them. But can this supposition be sustained for all the data of the social sciences? Is there always a determinate answer to the question of how agents' desires, beliefs and actions are to be interpreted?

2   W. v. O. Quine, 'On the reasons for the indeterminacy of translation', *Journal of Philosophy*, 1970, p. 179.

3   I owe this idea to Mary Hesse: see her paper, 'Theory and value in the social sciences', in C. Hookway and P. Pettit (eds), *Action and*

Interpretation, Cambridge, 1978. See also my paper, 'On the relativity of power', in S. Brown (ed.), *Philosophical Disputes in the Social Sciences*, Harvester Press, Hassocks, 1979.

4 Ibid., p. 4.

5 Ibid., p. 2.

6 Ibid., p. 6.

7 Ibid., p. 7.

8 See K. O. Apel, 'Types of social science in the light of human cognitive interests', and my 'On the relativity of power', in S. Brown (ed.), op. cit. Cf. J. Habermas, *Knowledge and Human Interests*, Heinemann, London, 1972. On the interest–relativity of explanation, see also H. Putnam, *Meaning and the Moral Sciences*, Routledge & Kegan Paul, London, 1978, pp. 41 ff.

9 Op. cit., p. 7.

10 For examples, see my *Essays in Social Theory*, Macmillan, London, 1977, ch. 1.

11 I. Lakatos, 'Falsification and the methodology of scientific research programmes', in I. Lakatos and A. Musgrave (eds), *Criticism and the Growth of Knowledge*, Cambridge University Press, 1970, pp. 100–1.

12 See the writings of Hans Buchheim, Leonard Schapiro and Franz Neumann.

13 K. Marx and F. Engels, *The Communist Manifesto*.

14 R. Miliband, *The State in Capitalist Society*, Weidenfeld & Nicolson, London, 1969, pp. 265–6.

15 R. Miliband, *Marxism and Politics*, Oxford University Press, 1977, pp. 73–4.

16 J. K. Galbraith, *American Capitalism*, Hamish Hamilton, London, 1957, pp. 136, 151. Galbraith's more recent writings on the state have shifted to a more bureaucratic theory, in which the market is supplanted by the 'planning system', within which the corporations and the state form co-operating partners, both increasingly run by the 'technostructure'.

17 E. Mandel, *Late Capitalism*, New Left Books, London, 1975, pp. 494–5, 495 fn., 490–1, 495.

18 Ibid., p. 495.

19 S. Brittan, *The Treasury under the Tories*, London, 1964, pp. 216, 217, 219, as quoted in Mandel, op. cit., p. 495.

20 Ibid., p. 495.

30   The value-oriented bias of social inquiry

Ernest Nagel

We turn [. . .] to the difficulties said to confront the social sciences because the social values to which students of social phenomena are committed not only color the contents of their findings but also control
their assessment of the evidence on which they base their conclusions.
Since social scientists generally differ in their value commitments, the
value neutrality that seems to be so pervasive in the natural sciences is
therefore often held to be impossible in social inquiry. In the judgment
of many thinkers, it is accordingly absurd to expect the social sciences
to exhibit the unanimity so common among natural scientists concerning
what are the established facts and satisfactory explanations for them.
Let us examine some of the reasons that have been advanced for these
contentions. It will be convenient to distinguish four groups of such
reasons, so that our discussion will deal in turn with the alleged role of
value judgments in (1) the selection of problems, (2) the determination
of the contents of conclusions, (3) the identification of fact, and (4) the
assessment of evidence.

1   The reasons perhaps most frequently cited make much of the fact
that the things a social scientist selects for study are determined by his
conception of what are the socially important values. According to one
influential view, for example, the student of human affairs deals only
with materials to which he attributes 'cultural significance,' so that a
'value orientation' is inherent in his choice of material for investigation.
Thus, although Max Weber was a vigorous proponent of a 'value-free'
social science – i.e., he maintained that social scientists must appreciate
(or 'understand') the values involved in the actions or institutions they
are discussing but that it is not their business as objective scientists to
approve or disapprove either those values or those actions and institutions. [. . .]
   It is well-nigh truistic. to say that students of human affairs, like

Source: *The Structure of Science*, London, Routledge & Kegan Paul,
1961, extracts from pp. 485–96, 498–502.

students in any other area of inquiry, do not investigate everything, but direct their attention to certain selected portions of the inexhaustible content of concrete reality. Moreover, let us accept the claim, if only for the sake of the argument, that a social scientist addresses himself exclusively to matters which he believes are important because of their assumed relevance to his cultural values. It is not clear, however, why the fact that an investigator selects the materials he studies in the light of problems which interest him and which seem to him to bear on matters he regards as important, is of greater moment for the logic of social inquiry than it is for the logic of any other branch of inquiry. For example, a social scientist may believe that a free economic market embodies a cardinal human value, and he may produce evidence to show that certain kinds of human activities are indispensable to the perpetuation of a free market. If he is concerned with processes which maintain this type of economy rather than some other type, how is this fact more pertinent to the question whether he has adequately evaluated the evidence for his conclusion, than is the bearing upon the analogous question of the fact that a physiologist may be concerned with processes which maintain a constant internal temperature in the human body rather than with something else? The things a social scientist *selects for study* with a view to determining the conditions or consequences of their existence may indeed be dependent on the indisputable fact that he is a 'cultural being.' But similarly, were we not human beings though still capable of conducting scientific inquiry, we might conceivably have an interest neither in the conditions that maintain a free market, nor in the processes involved in the homeostasis of the internal temperature in human bodies, nor for that matter in the mechanisms that regulate the height of tides, the succession of seasons, or the motions of the planets.

In short, there is no difference between any of the sciences with respect to the fact that the interests of the scientist determine what he selects for investigation. But this fact, by itself, represents no obstacle to the successful pursuit of objectively controlled inquiry in any branch of study.

2   A more substantial reason commonly given for the value-oriented character of social inquiry is that, since the social scientist is himself affected by considerations of right and wrong, his own notions of what constitutes a satisfactory social order and his own standards of personal and social justice do enter, in point of fact, into his analyses of social phenomena. [. . .]

It is surely beyond serious dispute that social scientists do in fact often import their own values into their analyses of social phenomena. It is also undoubtedly true that even thinkers who believe human affairs can be studied with the ethical neutrality characterizing modern inquiries into geometrical or physical relations, and who often pride themselves on the absence of value judgments from their own analyses of social phenomena, do in fact sometimes make such judgments in their social inquiries. Nor is it less evident that students of human affairs often hold conflicting values, that their disagreements on value questions are often the source of disagreements concerning ostensibly factual issues; and that, even if value predications are assumed to be inherently capable of proof or disproof by objective evidence, at least some of the differences between social scientists involving value judgments are not in fact resolved by the procedures of controlled inquiry.

In any event, it is not easy in most areas of inquiry to prevent our likes, aversions, hopes, and fears from coloring our conclusions. It has taken centuries of effort to develop habits and techniques of investigation which help safeguard inquiries in the natural sciences against the intrusion of irrelevant personal factors; and even in these disciplines the protection those procedures give is neither infallible nor complete. The problem is undoubtedly more acute in the study of human affairs, and the difficulties it creates for achieving reliable knowledge in the social sciences must be admitted.

However, the problem is intelligible only on the assumption that there is a relatively clear distinction between factual and value judgments, and that however difficult it may sometimes be to decide whether a given statement has a purely factual content, it is in principle possible to do so. [. . .] Accordingly, the undeniable difficulties that stand in the way of obtaining reliable knowledge of human affairs because of the fact that social scientists differ in their value orientations are practical difficulties. The difficulties are not necessarily insuperable, for since by hypothesis it is not impossible to distinguish between fact and value, steps can be taken to identify a value bias when it occurs, and to minimize if not to eliminate completely its perturbing effects.

One such countermeasure frequently recommended is that social scientists abandon the pretense that they are free from all bias, and that instead they state their value assumptions as explicitly and fully as they can. The recommendation does not assume that social scientists will come to agree on their social ideals once these ideals are explicitly postulated, or that disagreements over values can be settled by scientific inquiry. Its point is that the question of how a given ideal is to be realized, or the question whether a certain institutional arrangement is an effective way of achieving the ideal, is on the face of it not a value question, but a factual problem — to be resolved by the objective methods of scientific inquiry — concerning the adequacy of proposed means for attaining stipulated ends. Thus, economists may permanently disagree on the desirability of a society in which its members have a guaranteed security against economic want, since the disagreement may have its source in inarbitrable preferences, for different social values. But when sufficient evidence is made available by economic inquiry, economists do presumably agree on the factual proposition that, *if* such a society is to be achieved, then a purely competitive economic system will not suffice.

Although the recommendation that social scientists make fully explicit their value commitments is undoubtedly salutary, and can produce excellent fruit, it verges on being a counsel of perfection. For the most part we are unaware of many assumptions that enter into our analyses and actions, so that despite resolute efforts to make our preconceptions explicit some decisive ones may not even occur to us. But in any event, the difficulties generated for scientific inquiry by unconscious bias and tacit value orientations are rarely overcome by devout resolutions to eliminate bias. They are usually overcome, often only gradually, through the self-corrective mechanisms of science as a social enterprise. For modern science encourages the invention, the mutual exchange, and the free but responsible criticisms of ideas; it welcomes competition in the quest for knowledge between independent investigators, even when their intellectual orientations are different, and it progressively diminishes the effects of bias by retaining only those proposed conclusions of its inquiries that survive critical examination by an indefinitely large community of students, whatever be their value preferences or doctrinal commitments. It would be absurd to claim that this institutionalized mechanism for sifting warranted beliefs has operated or is likely to operate in social inquiry as effectively as it has in the natural sciences. But it would be no less absurd to conclude that reliable knowledge of human affairs is unattainable merely because social inquiry is frequently value-oriented.

3   There is a more sophisticated argument for the view that the social sciences cannot be value-free. It maintains that the distinction between fact and value assumed in the preceding discussion is untenable when purposive human behavior is being analyzed, since in this context value judgments enter inextricably into what appear to be 'purely descriptive' (or factual) statements. Accordingly, those who subscribe to this thesis claim that an ethically neutral social science is in principle impossible, and not simply that it is difficult to attain. For if fact and value are indeed so fused that they cannot even be distinguished, value judgments cannot be eliminated from the social sciences unless all predications are also eliminated from them, and therefore unless these sciences completely disappear. [. . .]

We shall not attempt a detailed assessment of this complex argument, for a discussion of the numerous issues it raises would take us far afield. However, three claims made in the course of the argument will be admitted without further comment as indisputably correct: that a large number of characterizations sometimes assumed to be purely factual descriptions of social phenomena do indeed formulate a type of value judgment; that it is often difficult, and in any case usually inconvenient in practice, to distinguish between the purely factual and the 'evaluative' contents of many terms employed in the social sciences; and that values are commonly attached to means and not only to ends. However, these admissions do not entail the conclusion that, in a manner unique to the study of purposive human behavior, fact and value are fused beyond the possibility of distinguishing between them. On the contrary, as we shall try to show, the claim that there is such a fusion and that a value-free social science is therefore inherently absurd, confounds two quite different senses of the term 'value judgment': the sense in which a value judgment expresses *approval or disapproval* either of some moral (or social) ideal, or of some action (or institution) because of a commitment to such an ideal; and the sense in which a value judgment expresses *an estimate* of the degree to which some commonly recognized (and more or less clearly defined) type of action, object, or institution is embodied in a given instance.

It will be helpful to illustrate these two senses of 'value judgment' first with an example from biology. Animals with blood streams sometimes exhibit the condition known as 'anemia.' An anemic animal has a reduced number of red blood corpuscles, so that, among other things, it is less able to maintain a constant internal temperature than are members of its species with a 'normal' supply of such blood cells. However, although the meaning of the term 'anemia' can be made quite clear, it is not in fact defined with complete precision; for example, the notion of a 'normal' number of red corpuscles that enters into the definition of the term is itself somewhat vague, since this number varies with the individual members of a species as well as with the state of a given individual at different times (such as its age or the altitude of its habitat). But in any case, to decide whether a given animal is anemic, an investigator must judge whether the available evidence *warrants* the conclusion that the specimen is anemic.* He may perhaps think of anemia as being

* The evidence is usually a count of red cells in a sample from the animal's blood. However, it should be noted that 'The red cell count gives only an estimate of the *number of cells per unit quantity of blood*,' and does not indicate whether the body's total supply of red cells is increased or diminished. – Charles H. Best and Norman B. Taylor, *The Physiological Basis of Medical Practice*, 6th ed., Baltimore, 1955, pp. 11, 17.

of several distinct kinds (as is done in actual medical practice), or he may think of anemia as a condition that is realizable with greater or lesser completeness (just as certain plane curves are sometimes described as better or worse approximations to a circle as defined in geometry); and, depending on which of these conceptions he adopts, he may decide either that his specimen has a certain kind of anemia or that it is anemic only to a certain degree. When the investigator reaches a conclusion, he can therefore be said to be making a 'value judgment,' in the sense that he has in mind some standardized type of physiological condition designated as 'anemia' and that he *assesses* what he knows about his specimen with the measure provided by this assumed standard. For the sake of easy reference, let us call such evaluations of the evidence, which conclude that a given characteristic is in some degree present (or absent) in a given instance, 'characterizing value judgments.'

On the other hand, the student may also make a quite different sort of value judgment, which asserts that, since an anemic animal has diminished powers of maintaining itself, anemia is an undesirable condition. Moreover, he may apply this general judgment to a particular case, and so come to deplore the fact that a given animal is anemic. Let us label such evaluations, which conclude that some envisaged or actual state of affairs is worthy of approval or disapproval, 'appraising value judgments.'* It is clear, however, that an investigator making a characterizing value judgment is not thereby logically bound to affirm or deny a corresponding appraising evaluation. It is no less evident that he cannot consistently make an appraising value judgment about a given instance (e.g., that it is undesirable for a given animal to continue being anemic), unless he can affirm a characterizing judgment about that instance independently of the appraising one (e.g., that the animal is anemic). Accordingly, although characterizing judgments are necessarily entailed by many appraising judgments, making appraising judgments is not a necessary condition for making characterizing ones. [. . .]

Consider [now] the claim that the sociologist of religion must recognize the difference between mercenary and nonmercenary attitudes, and that in consequence he is inevitably committing himself to certain values. It is certainly beyond dispute that these attitudes are commonly distinguished; and it can also be granted that a sociologist of religion

---

* It is irrelevant to the present discussion what view is adopted concerning the ground upon which such judgments supposedly rest — whether those grounds are simply arbitrary preferences, alleged intuitions of 'objective' values, categorical moral imperatives, or anything else that has been proposed in the history of value theory. For the distinction made in the text is independent of any particular assumption about the foundations of appraising value judgments, 'ultimate' or otherwise.

needs to understand the difference between them. But the sociologist's obligation is in this respect quite like that of the student of animal physiology, who must also acquaint himself with certain distinctions — even though the physiologist's distinction between, say, anemic and nonanemic may be less familiar to the ordinary layman and is in any case much more precise than is the distinction between mercenary and nonmercenary attitudes. Indeed, because of the vagueness of these latter terms, the scrupulous sociologist may find it extremely difficult to decide whether or not the attitude of some community toward its acknowledged gods is to be characterized as mercenary; and if he should finally decide, he may base his conclusion on some inarticulated 'total impression' of that community's manifest behavior, without being able to state exactly the detailed grounds for his decision. But however this may be, the sociologist who claims that a certain attitude manifested by a given religious group is mercenary, just as the physiologist who claims that a certain individual is anemic, is making what is primarily a characterizing value judgment. In making these judgments, neither the sociologist nor the physiologist is necessarily committing himself to any values other than the values of scientific probity; and in this respect, therefore, there appears to be no difference between social and biological (or for that matter, physical) inquiry.

On the other hand, it would be absurd to deny that in characterizing various actions as mercenary, cruel, or deceitful, sociologists are frequently (although perhaps not always wittingly) asserting, appraising as well as characterizing value judgments. Terms like 'mercenary,' 'cruel,' or 'deceitful' as commonly used have a widely recognized pejorative over-tone. Accordingly, anyone who employs such terms to characterize human behavior can normally be assumed to be stating his disapprobation of that behavior (or his approbation, should he use terms like 'nonmercenary,' 'kindly,' or 'truthful'), and not simply characterizing it.

However, although many (but certainly not all) ostensibly characterizing statements asserted by social scientists undoubtedly express commitments to various (not always compatible) values, a number of 'purely descriptive' terms as used by natural scientists in certain contexts sometimes also have an unmistakably appraising value connotation. Thus, the claim that a social scientist is making appraising value judgments when he characterizes respondents to questionnaires as uninformed, deceitful, or irrational can be matched by the equally sound claim that a physicist is also making such judgments when he describes a particular chronometer as inaccurate, a pump as inefficient, or a supporting platform as unstable. Like the social scientist in this example, the physicist is characterizing certain objects in his field of research, but, also like the social scientist, he is in addition expressing his disapproval of the characteristics he is ascribing to those objects.

Nevertheless — and this is the main burden of the present discussion — there are no good reasons for thinking that it is inherently impossible to *distinguish* between the characterizing and the appraising judgments implicit in many statements, whether the statements are asserted by students of human affairs or by natural scientists. To be sure, it is not always easy to make the distinction formally explicit in the social sciences — in part because much of the language employed in them is very vague, in part because appraising judgments that may be implicit in a statement tend to be overlooked by us when they are judgments to which we are actually committed though without being aware of our commitments. Nor is it always useful or convenient to perform this task. For many statements implicitly containing both characterizing and appraising evaluations are sometimes sufficiently clear without being reformulated in the manner required by the task; and the reformulations would frequently be too unwieldy for effective communication between members of a large and unequally prepared group of students. But these are essentially practical rather than theoretical problems. The difficulties they raise provide no compelling reasons for the claim that an ethically neutral social science is inherently impossible. [. . .]

4   There remains for consideration the claim that a value-free social science is impossible, because value commitments enter into the very *assessment of evidence* by social scientists, and not simply into the content of the conclusions they advance. This version of the claim itself has a large number of variant forms, but we shall examine only three of them.

The least radical form of the claim maintains that the conceptions held by a social scientist of what constitute cogent evidence or sound intellectual workmanship are the products of his education and his place in society, and are affected by the social values transmitted by this training and associated with this social position; accordingly, the values to which the social scientist is thereby committed determine which statements he *accepts* as well-grounded conclusions about human affairs. In this form the claim is a *factual* thesis, and must be supported by detailed empirical evidence concerning the influences exerted by a man's moral and social values upon what he is ready to acknowledge as sound social analysis. In many instances such evidence is indeed available; and differences between social scientists in respect to what they accept as credible can sometimes be attributed to the influence of national, religious, economic, and other kinds of bias. However, this variant of the claim excludes neither the possibility of recognizing assessments of evidence that are prejudiced by special value commitments, nor the possibility of correcting for such prejudice. It therefore raises no issue that has not already been discussed when we examined the second reason for the alleged value-oriented character of social inquiry. [. . .]

A [further] form of this claim is the most radical of all. It differs from the first variant mentioned above in maintaining that there is a necessary *logical* connection, and not merely a contingent or causal one, between the 'social perspective' of a student of human affairs and his standards of competent social inquiry, and in consequence the influence of the special values to which he is committed because of his own social involvements is not eliminable. This version of the claim is implicit in Hegel's account of the 'dialectical' nature of human history and is integral to much Marxist as well as non-Marxist philosophy that stresses the 'historically relative' character of social thought. In any event, it is commonly based on the assumption that, since social institutions and their cultural products are constantly changing, the intellectual apparatus required for understanding them must also change; and every idea employed for this purpose is therefore adequate only for some particular stage in the development of human affairs. Accordingly, neither the substantive concepts adopted for classifying and interpreting social phenomena, nor the logical canons used for estimating the worth of such concepts, have a 'timeless validity'; there is no analysis of social phenomena, which is not the expression of some social standpoint, or which does not reflect the interests and values dominant in some sector of the human scene at a certain stage of its history. In consequence, although a sound distinction can be made in the natural sciences between the origin of a man's views and their factual validity, such a distinction allegedly cannot be made in social inquiry; and prominent exponents of 'historical relativism' have therefore challenged the universal adequacy of the thesis that 'the genesis of a proposition is under all circumstances irrelevant to its truth.' [. . .]

Historical research into the influence of society upon the beliefs men hold is of undoubted importance for understanding the complex nature of the scientific enterprise; and the sociology of knowledge — as such investigations have come to be called — has produced many clarifying contributions to such an understanding. However, these admittedly valuable services of the sociology of knowledge do not establish the radical claim we have been stating. In the first place, there is no competent evidence to show that the principles employed in social inquiry for assessing the intellectual products are *necessarily* determined by the social perspective of the inquirer. On the contrary, the 'facts' usually cited in support of this contention establish at best only a contingent causal relation between a man's social commitments and his canons of cognitive validity. For example, the once fashionable view that the 'mentality' or logical operations of primitive societies differ from those typical in Western civilization – a discrepancy that was attributed to differences in the institutions of the societies under comparison – is now generally recognized to be erroneous, because it seriously misinterprets the intellectual processes of primitive peoples. Moreover, even extreme exponents of the sociology of knowledge admit that most conclusions asserted in mathematics and natural science are neutral to differences in social perspective of those asserting them, so that the genesis of these propositions is irrelevant to their validity.Why cannot propositions about human affairs exhibit a similar neutrality, at least in some cases? Sociologists of knowledge do not appear to doubt that the truth of the statement that two horses can in general pull a heavier load than can either horse alone, is logically independent of the social status of the individual who happens to affirm the statement. But they have not made clear just what are the inescapable considerations that allegedly make such independence inherently impossible for the analogous statement about human behavior, that two laborers can in general dig a ditch of given dimensions more quickly than can either laborer working alone.

In the second place, the claim faces a serious and frequently noted dialectical difficulty – a difficulty that proponents of the claim have succeeded in meeting only by abandoning the substance of the claim. For let us ask what is the cognitive status of the thesis that a social perspective enters essentially into the content as well as the validation of every assertion about human affairs. Is this thesis meaningful and valid only for those who maintain it and who thus subscribe to certain values because of their distinctive social commitments? If so, no one with a different social perspective can properly understand it; its acceptance as valid is strictly limited to those who can do so, and social scientists who subscribe to a different set of social values ought therefore to dismiss it as empty talk. Or is the thesis singularly exempt from the class of assertions to which it applies, so that its meaning and truth are not inherently related to the social perspectives of those who assert it? If so, it is not evident why the thesis is so exempt; but in any case, the thesis is then a conclusion of inquiry into human affairs that is presumably 'objectively valid' in the usual sense of this phrase – and, if there is one such conclusion, it is not clear why there cannot be others as well.

To meet this difficulty, and to escape the self-defeating skeptical relativism to which the thesis is thus shown to lead, the thesis is sometimes interpreted to say that, though 'absolutely objective' knowledge of human affairs is unattainable, a 'relational' form of objectivity called 'relationism' can nevertheless be achieved. On this interpretation, a social scientist can discover just what his social perspective is; and if he then formulates the conclusions of his inquiries 'relationally,' so as to indicate that his findings conform to the canons of validity implicit in his perspective, his conclusions will have achieved a 'relational' objectivity. Social scientists sharing the same perspective can be expected to agree in their answers to a given problem when the canons of validity characteristic of their common perspective are correctly applied. On the other hand, students of social phenomena who operate within different but incongruous social perspectives can also achieve objectivity, if in no other way than by a 'relational' formulation of what must otherwise be incompatible results obtained in their several inquiries. However, they can also achieve it in 'a more roundabout fashion,' by undertaking 'to find a formula for translating the results of one into those of the other and to discover a common denominator for these varying perspectivistic insights.*

But it is difficult to see in what way 'relational objectivity' differs from 'objectivity' without the qualifying adjective and in the customary sense of the word. For example, a physicist who terminates an investigation with the conclusion that the velocity of light in water has a certain numerical value when measured in terms of a stated system of units, by a stated procedure, and under stated experimental conditions, is formulating his conclusion in a manner that is 'relational' in the sense intended; and his conclusion is marked by 'objectivity,' presumably because it mentions the 'relational' factors upon which the assigned numerical value of the velocity depends. However, it is fairly standard practice in the natural sciences to formulate certain types of conclusions in this fashion. Accordingly, the proposal that the social sciences formulate their findings in an analogous manner carries with it the admission that it is not in principle impossible for these disciplines to establish conclusions having the objectivity of conclusions reached in other domains of inquiry. Moreover, if the difficulty we are considering is to be resolved by the suggested translation formulas for rendering the 'common denominators' of conclusions stemming from divergent social perspectives, those formulas cannot in turn be 'situationally determined' in the sense of this phrase under discussion. For if those formulas were so determined, the same difficulty would crop up anew in connection with them. On the other hand, a search for such formulas is a phase in the search for invariant relations in a subject matter, so that formulations of these relations are valid irrespective of the particular perspective one may select from some class of perspectives on that subject matter. In

*   Karl Mannheim, *Ideology and Utopia*, Routledge & Kegan Paul, 1954, pp. 300–1.

consequence, in acknowledging that the search for such invariants in the social sciences is not inherently bound to fail, proponents of the claim we have been considering abandon what at the outset was its most radical thesis.

In brief, the various reasons we have been examining for the intrinsic impossibility of securing objective (i.e., value-free and unbiased) conclusions in the social sciences do not establish what they purport to establish, even though in some instances they direct attention to undoubtedly important practical difficulties frequently encountered in these disciplines.

31   Social science and social progress

Karl Popper

1   The technological approach to sociology

Although in this study my topic is historicism, a doctrine of method with which I disagree, rather than those methods which, in my opinion, have been successful, and whose further and more conscious develop ment I recommend, it will be useful to deal briefly with the successful methods first, so as to reveal to the reader my own bias and to clarify the point of view that underlies my criticism. For convenience, I shall label these methods *'piecemeal technology'*.

The term 'social technology' (and even more the term 'social engineering' which will be introduced in the next section) is likely to arouse suspicion, and to repel those whom it reminds of the 'social blueprints' of the collectivist planners, or perhaps even of the 'technocrats'. I realize this danger, and so I have added the word 'piecemeal', both to off-set undesirable associations and to express my conviction that 'piecemeal tinkering' (as it is sometimes called), combined with critical analysis, is the main way to practical results in the social as well as in the natural sciences. The social sciences have developed very largely through the criticism of proposals for social improvements or, more precisely, through attempts to find out whether or not some particular economic or political action is likely to produce an expected, or desired, result. This approach, which might indeed be called the classical one, is what I have in mind when I refer to the technological approach to social science, or to 'piecemeal social technology'.

Technological problems in the field of social science may be of a 'private' or of a 'public' character. For example, investigations into the techniques of business administration, or into the effects of improved working conditions upon output, belong to the first group. Investigations into the effects of prison reform or universal health insurance, or of the stabilization of prices by means of tribunals, or of the introduction of

Source: *The Poverty of Historicism*, London, Routledge & Kegan Paul, 1961, extracts from pp. 58–70.

new import duties, etc., upon, say, the equalization of incomes, belong
to the second group; and so do some of the most urgent practical questions of the day, such as the possibility of controlling trade cycles; or
the question whether centralized 'planning', in the sense of state management of production, is compatible with an effective democratic
control of the administration; or the question of how to export democracy to the Middle East.

This emphasis upon the practical technological approach does not
mean that any of the theoretical problems that may arise from the
analysis of the practical problems should be excluded. On the contrary,
it is one of my main points that the technological approach is likely to
prove fruitful in giving rise to significant problems of a purely theoretical
kind. But besides helping us in the fundamental task of selecting problems, the technological approach imposes a discipline on our speculative
inclinations (which, especially in the field of sociology proper, are liable
to lead us into the region of metaphysics), for it forces us to submit our
theories to definite standards, such as standards of clarity and practical
testability. My point about the technological approach might perhaps
be made by saying that sociology (and perhaps even the social sciences
in general) should look, not indeed for 'its Newton or its Darwin',* but
rather for its Galileo, or its Pasteur.

This and my previous references to an analogy between the methods
of the social and the natural sciences are likely to provoke as much opposition as our choice of terms like 'social technology' and 'social engineering' (this in spite of the important qualification expressed by the
word 'piecemeal'). [. . .] Nevertheless, I do not see why we should not
make use of this analogy as far as it is fruitful, even though we recognize
that it has been badly misused and misrepresented in certain quarters.
[. . .]

A *prima facie* objection against what we call the technological approach is that it implies the adoption of an 'activist' attitude towards
the social order and that it is therefore liable to prejudice us against the
anti-interventionist or 'passivist' view: the view that if we are dissatisfied
with existing social or economic conditions, it is because we do not
understand how they work and why active intervention could only make
matters worse. Now I must admit that I am certainly out of sympathy
with this 'passivist' view, and that I even believe that a policy of *universal* anti-interventionism is untenable — even on purely logical grounds,
since its supporters are bound to recommend political intervention aimed

---

* See M. Ginsberg, in *Human Affairs* (ed. R. B. Cattell and others,
Arno, 1937), p. 180. It must be admitted, however, that the success of
mathematical economics shows that one social science at least has gone
through its Newtonian revolution.

at preventing intervention. Nevertheless, the technological approach as such is neutral in this matter (as indeed it ought to be), and by no means incompatible with anti-interventionism. On the contrary, I think that anti-interventionism involves a technological approach. For to assert that interventionism makes matters worse is to say that certain political actions would not have certain effects — to wit, not the desired ones; and it is one of the most characteristic tasks of any technology to *point out what cannot be achieved.*

It is worth while to consider this point more closely. As I have shown elsewhere,* every natural law can be expressed by asserting that *such and such a thing cannot happen*; that is to say, by a sentence in the form of the proverb: 'You can't carry water in a sieve.' For example, the law of conservation of energy can be expressed by: 'You cannot build a perpetual motion machine'; and that of entropy by: 'You cannot build a machine which is a hundred per cent efficient.' This way of for-mulating natural laws is one which makes their technological significance obvious and it may therefore be called the *'technological form'* of a natural law. If we now consider anti-interventionism in this light, then we see at once that it may well be expressed by sentences of the form: 'You cannot achieve such and such results', or perhaps, 'You cannot achieve such and such ends without such and such concomitant effects.' But this shows that anti-interventionism can be called a typically *tech-nological doctrine.*

It is not, of course, the only one in the realm of social science. On the contrary, the significance of our analysis lies in the fact that it draws attention to a really fundamental similarity between the natural and the social sciences. I have in mind the existence of sociological laws or hypotheses which are analogous to the laws or hypotheses of the natural sciences. Since the existence of such sociological laws or hypotheses [...] has often been doubted, I will now give a number of examples: 'You can-not introduce agricultural tariffs and at the same time reduce the cost of living.' — 'You cannot, in an industrial society, organize consumers' pressure groups as effectively as you can organize certain producers' pressure groups.' — 'You cannot have a centrally planned society with a price system that fulfils the main functions of competetive prices.' — 'You cannot have full employment with inflation.' Another group of examples may be taken from the realm of power politics: 'You cannot introduce a political reform without causing some repercussions which are un-desirable from the point of view of the ends aimed at' (therefore, look out for them). — 'You cannot introduce a political reform without

* See my *Logic of Scientific Discovery* (1959; Hutchinson, 1968), section 15. (Negated existential propositions.) The theory may be con-trasted with J. S. Mill, *Logic*, Book V, ch. V, section 2.

strengthening the opposing forces, to a degree roughly in ratio to the scope of the reform.' (This may be said to be the technological corollary of 'There are always interests connected with the *status quo.*') – 'You cannot make a revolution without causing a reaction.' [. . .] Nothing is here assumed about the strength of the available evidence in favour of these hypotheses whose formulations certainly leave much room for improvement. They are merely examples of the kind of statements which a piecemeal technology may attempt to discuss, and to substantiate [. . .]

2 Piecemeal versus Utopian engineering

Notwithstanding the objectionable associations which attach to the term 'engineering', I shall use the term 'piecemeal social engineering' to describe the practical application of the results of piecemeal technology. The term is useful since there is need for a term covering social activities, private as well as public, which, in order to realize some aim or end, consciously utilize all available technological knowledge. Piecemeal social engineering resembles physical engineering in regarding the *ends* as beyond the province of technology. (All that technology may say about ends is whether or not they are compatible with each other or realizable.) In this it differs from historicism, which regards the ends of human activities as dependent on historical forces and so within its province.

Just as the main task of the physical engineer is to design machines and to remodel and service them, the task of the piecemeal social engineer is to design social institutions, and to reconstruct and run those already in existence. The term 'social institution' is used here in a very wide sense, to include bodies of a private as well as of a public character. Thus I shall use it to describe a business, whether it is a small shop or an insurance company, and likewise a school, or an 'educational system', or a police force, or a Church, or a law court. The piecemeal technologist or engineer recognizes that *only a minority of social institutions are consciously designed while the vast majority have just 'grown', as the undesigned results of human actions.* But however strongly he may be impressed by this important fact, as a technologist or engineer he will look upon them from a 'functional' or 'instrumental' point of view. He will see them as means to certain ends, or as convertible to the service of certain ends; as machines rather than as organisms. This does not mean, of course, that he will overlook the fundamental differences between institutions and physical instruments. On the contrary, the technologist should study the differences as well as the similarities, expressing his results in the form of hypotheses. And indeed, it is not difficult to formulate hypotheses about institutions in technological form as is shown by the following example: 'You cannot construct foolproof institutions, that is to say, institutions whose functioning does not very largely depend upon persons: institutions, at best, can reduce the uncertainty of the personal element, by assisting those who work for the aims for which the institutions are designed, and on whose personal initiative and knowledge success largely depends. (Institutions are like fortresses. They must be well designed *and* properly manned.)'

The characteristic approach of the piecemeal engineer is this. Even though he may perhaps cherish some ideals which concern society 'as a whole' — its general welfare, perhaps — he does not believe in the method of re-designing it as a whole. Whatever his ends, he tries to achieve them by small adjustments and re-adjustments which can be continually improved upon. His ends may be of diverse kinds, for example, the accumulation of wealth or of power by certain individuals, or by certain groups; or the distribution of wealth and power; or the protection of certain 'rights' of individuals or groups, etc. Thus public or political social engineering may have the most diverse tendencies, totalitarian as well as liberal. [. . .] The piecemeal engineer knows, like Socrates, how little he knows. He knows that we can learn only from our mistakes. Accordingly, he will make his way, step by step, carefully comparing the results expected with the results achieved, and always on the look-out for the unavoidable unwanted consequences of any reform; and he will avoid undertaking reforms of a complexity and scope which make it impossible for him to disentangle causes and effects, and to know what he is really doing.

Such 'piecemeal tinkering' does not agree with the political temperament of many 'activists'. Their programme, which too has been described as a programme of 'social engineering', may be called 'holistic' or 'Utopian engineering'.

Holistic or Utopian social engineering, as opposed to piecemeal social engineering, is never of a 'private' but always of a 'public' character. It aims at remodelling the 'whole of society' in accordance with a definite plan or blueprint; it aims at 'seizing the key positions' and at extending 'the power of the State . . . until the State becomes nearly identical with society', and it aims, furthermore, at controlling from these 'key positions' the historical forces that mould the future of the developing society: either by arresting this development, or else by foreseeing its course and adjusting society to it.

It may be questioned, perhaps, whether the piecemeal and the holistic approaches here described are fundamentally different, considering that we have put no limits to the scope of a piecemeal approach. As this approach is understood here, constitutional reform, for example, falls well within its scope; nor shall I exclude the possibility that a series of piecemeal reforms might be inspired by one general tendency, for example, a tendency towards a greater equalization of incomes. In this way, piecemeal methods may lead to changes in what is usually called the 'class structure of society'. Is there any difference, it may be asked, between these more ambitious kinds of piecemeal engineering and the holistic or Utopian approach? And this question may become even more pertinent if we consider that, when trying to assess the likely consequences of some proposed reform, the piecemeal technologist must do his best to estimate the effects of any measure upon the 'whole' of society.

In answering this question, I shall not attempt to draw a precise line of demarcation between the two methods, but I shall try to bring out the very different point of view from which the holist and the piecemeal technologist look upon the task of reforming society. The holists reject the piecemeal approach as being too modest. Their rejection of it, however, does not quite square with their practice; for in practice they always fall back on a somewhat haphazard and clumsy although ambitious and ruthless application of what is essentially a piecemeal method without its cautious and self-critical character. The reason is that, in practice, the holistic method turns out to be impossible; the greater the holistic changes attempted, the greater are their unintended and largely unexpected repercussions, forcing upon the holistic engineer the expedient of piecemeal *improvization*. In fact, this expedient is more characteristic of centralized or collectivistic planning than of the more modest and careful piecemeal intervention; and it continually leads the Utopian engineer to do things which he did not intend to do; that is to say, it leads to the notorious phenomenon of *unplanned planning*. Thus the difference between Utopian and piecemeal engineering turns out, in practice, to be a difference not so much in scale and scope as in caution and in preparedness for unavoidable surprises. One could also say that, in practice, the two *methods* differ in other ways than in scale and scope — in opposition to what we are led to expect if we compare the two *doctrines* concerning the proper methods of rational social reform. Of these two doctrines, I hold that the one is true, while the other is false and liable to lead to mistakes which are both avoidable and grave. Of the two methods, I hold that one is possible, while the other simply does not exist: it is impossible.

One of the differences between the Utopian or holistic approach and the piecemeal approach may therefore be stated in this way: while the piecemeal engineer can attack his problem with an open mind as to the scope of the reform, the holist cannot do this; for he has decided beforehand that a complete reconstruction is possible and necessary. This fact has far-reaching consequences. It prejudices the Utopianist against certain sociological hypotheses which state limits to institutional control; for example, the one mentioned above in this section, expressing the uncertainty due to the personal element, the 'human factor'. By a rejection *a priori* of such hypotheses, the Utopian approach violates the principles of scientific method. On the other hand, problems connected with the uncertainty of the human factor must force the Utopianist, whether he likes it or not, to try to control the human factor by institutional means, and to extend his programme so as to embrace not only the transformation of society, according to plan, but also the transformation of man.* 'The political problem, therefore, is to *organize human impulses* in such a way that they will direct their energy to the right strategic points, and steer the total process of development in the desired direction.' It seems to escape the well-meaning Utopianist that this programme implies an admission of failure, even before he launches it. For it substitutes for his demand that we build a new society, fit for men and women to live in, the demand that we 'mould' these men and women to fit into his new society. This, clearly, removes any possibility of testing the success or failure of the new society. For those who do not like living in it only admit thereby that they are not yet fit to live in it; that their 'human impulses' need further 'organizing'. But without the possibility of tests, any claim that a 'scientific' method is being employed evaporates. The holistic approach is incompatible with a truly scientific attitude.

* 'The Problem of Transforming Man' is the heading of a chapter of K. Mannheim's *Man and Society* (Routledge & Kegan Paul, 1940). The following quotation is from that chapter, p. 199 f.

32   Positivist social science and technological politics

Brian Fay

The role of social science in modern political life

What I write in this section ought to be quite familiar, for the general view I will give is not only to be found in the early development of mainstream social science, but has become one of the mainstays which supports the whole enterprise of social science in our own time. The general view which I propose to give is one that can be culled from the writings of Saint-Simon, Comte, Mill, Weber, and Durkheim, as well as such modern thinkers as Lasswell, Mannheim, Skinner, Lundberg, Robert Lynd, etc. Of course, these writers did not simply repeat each other over the years — indeed, subtle and important distinctions have been made by each of them; consequently, the general view I will present will not do full justice to any one of these thinkers in particular. Nevertheless, what has become a contemporary cliché is rooted in their writings, and what I say will be compatible with their major ideas.

One might begin by asking the question, why have social science at all? Now there are several answers which might be given to this question, but there is one which is strikingly predominant in the writings of social scientists themselves when they reflect on their own work; it is an answer that invokes the analogy with the natural sciences. For, it is claimed, just as the natural sciences have provided men with a certain kind of knowledge by which they can control their natural environment, thereby making it more hospitable and productive, so also the knowledge gained from social science will enable men to control their social environment, thereby making it more harmonious and congruent with the needs and wants of its members. Natural science gives to men an enormous power based on a knowledge of the workings of the external world, and it is this power which sustains and supports the entire undertaking; so also social science will permit men to control and order the social arrangements which structure their own lives.

Source: *Social Theory and Political Practice*, London, Allen & Unwin, 1975, extracts from pp. 18–23, 27–32, 37–43.

In fact, the need for a social science is actually perceived as far more urgent a task than I have so far made it out to be. For many social scientists would claim that it is not merely *desirable* that man's knowledge of his social world become scientific, it is *vital* that this transformation occur. For my purposes one of the most interesting reasons why this should be thought to be so has to do with the rise of industrial society. In the *Division of Labour in Society* Durkheim says that man can escape nature not merely by controlling it but also by creating another world where he himself is at home and secure; this 'world' is society. Underlying this observation is the perception that modern industrial society – which is itself partly engendered by the revolution in thinking and technique caused by the science of nature – is a society so dynamic, divisive, impersonal, and unstable that it cannot be properly governed by any of the traditional political methods. A recurring theme in the social scientific tradition is the necessity for the discovery and implementation of a social structure which is rationally organised so that it can cope with the displacement, the conflicts of interest and need, the rapid change in the forms of social organisation and individual private fortune that characterise a technological society. Therefore, it is argued, because of the social effects of mastering nature through science, technology, and industrial production, society itself must be mastered if social life is going to continue in an uninterrupted and unchaotic way.

Of course this is only part of the story. For another factor that must be taken into account – it was so most articulately by Comte – is that men's attitudes themselves change as a result of the spread of the conceptual assumptions inherent in natural science. For obvious reasons these changes make obsolete or ineffective the religion or magic or traditional justifications from authority which in pre-industrial societies had promoted order, established status, set communal goals, and legitimated authority. Science deprives men of the old faith by which they lived and thus helps to destroy their old social order; thus it can cause suffering and a sense of helplessness in the face of this suffering. It is for this reason that a new faith, one compatible with and arising out of the scientific spirit, must emerge from this chaos and lead men out of the void into which they had been thrown. Social science has a great weight to bear.

I will return to the connection between social science and industrial society at the end of the chapter, for enough has been said to indicate the sorts of concerns which support the efforts to analyse society scientifically. But why, we might ask, does this require a social *science*, conceived as the study of social institutions and social actions with essentially the same epistemology and methodology as employed in the natural sciences? The answer to this is twofold. In the first place, it is claimed, only a scientific study can give us the truly *objective* knowledge of how events or properties of systems are related, and thus it alone can provide us with the power requisite for the task of social control. Older, more traditional attempts at understanding society, particularly those found in political philosophy, are inferior because they mingled among their factual observations mere opinion, because they expressed subjective dispositions and preferences, and because they judged other theories in terms of some vague and unprovable conception of human needs and wants. One can grasp the laws which govern the world − social as well as natural − only if one throws off these adolescent habits of interpreting the world in terms of one's own needs and values, and adopts the mature stance of neutrality *vis-à-vis* one's social world, studying its workings as they are and not how one wishes them to be or how one thinks they ought to be. Only then will the mechanisms which determine this social world reveal themselves as they are. It is science, and only science, which adopts this stance, and it does so because it only employs concepts which are rooted in intersubjectively evident observations, because it employs techniques of experimentation which are reproducible, because it utilises reasoning processes which are rigorous and uniformly applicable, and because it accepts explanations only when they predict outcomes which are publicly verifiable. [. . .]

Only a social *science* will give an intersubjectively verifiable (or at least falsifiable) account of how the social world operates, and only a social science will give us causal explanations which are of the type that allow one to prevent the occurrence of an unwanted event, or permit one to bring about the occurrence of one that is desired: it is for this reason that only a social science, conceived as a body of knowledge analogous to that of the natural sciences, can satisfy the condition which modern society demands be satisfied if it is to continue without substantial suffering and ultimately without a total breakdown.

Earlier I mentioned the felt inadequacy of 'traditional political methods', and it seems appropriate at this point to translate what I have been saying into purely political terms, for it is in the political realm that the power promised by social science will be exercised. What sorts of political changes are suggested by such a promise? One might divide these changes into two areas: those dealing with the nature of political argument, and those dealing with institutional changes, specifically the rise of the policy scientist.

In the first place, it is thought that if it were to be the case that political decisions would be made on the basis of technical application of social scientific knowledge, then the character of political argument would drastically alter. The point here is that, at least in the ideal, the disagreements which arise in engineering or medicine are not expressed in terms of personal values or wishes, nor are they debated on the basis of the power or position which the disputants have in the social order to which they belong, nor settled in terms of subtlety of exposition or rhetorical power; rather, the issues are tangible, measurable, and testable, and debates about them are conducted in such a way that it is these objective features accessible to all which decide the matter at hand. In technical arguments one expects to reach mutually acceptable answers, and the reason for this is that it is assumed in such arguments that, given the publicly known parameters of the case, there is one best way to maximise whatever value is to be maximised. If politics were to become an applied science, it is argued, its conjectural, arbitrary, emotional and personal elements would drop out, and its arguments and decisions would assume the same neutral characteristics as those of engineering.

Of course, there are limits to the changes in political decision-making that are possible. In the first place, it does not follow from the argument I have been recounting that no political arguments would be left to divide men; arguments occur in engineering all the time. The point is rather that it is believed there would no longer be arguments as to the kinds of considerations that will be admitted as relevant to rational discussion, and, furthermore, that the criteria for truth would be explicitly accepted so that one would be able to determine clearly when they are satisfied, thereby eliciting automatic agreement and permitting conclusions to be transmitted to anyone trained to understand. In political arguments there would be, as there are in scientific arguments, reliable public standards of ascertainable truth, and therefore the possibility of a universally recognisable decisive solution to a particular problem. It is in this way that a social science would be able to eliminate the 'anarchy of opinion' which characterises modern political thinking. [. . .]

All through this exposition I have been speaking in the subjunctive mood because the ideas I have been putting forth are largely promissory. But one ought not to conclude that they are therefore not germane to the political affairs of our own day. Obviously, many of the changes that I have suggested are already occurring all around us: today it is plain to everyone that the central government has grown in importance; that technical decisions play an increasingly large part in our political life; that the experts claim an irrefragability for their recommendations based on their assertions that untrained men are incapable of judging their worth; and that the majority opinion is that it is only through increased planning that our pressing social and political problems can be solved. Now it would be utterly fantastic to claim that the doctrine I have been espousing is responsible for these changes — there are obviously socio-economic factors here which are of overwhelming importance. But what is true is that how one regards these changes, how one assesses responsibility, whom one desires to make political decisions, how one argues against specific decisions, how these sorts of issues are settled is a direct function of one's beliefs about the doctrine of a policy science.

What ought to be clear by now is that all of the political changes that I have enumerated are united by an underlying theme which one might call the sublimation of politics. For what these political changes amount to is an attempt to eliminate politics as we know it, overcoming its limitations and uncertainties by replacing it with a form of social engineering analogous to the applied physical sciences. [. . .]

Implicit in this belief that an applied science can perform the tasks now seen as political is the tacit presumption that science provides the paradigm example of proper thinking, and that as long as any human enterprise is not treated in a scientific way it is being treated in an imperfect way. It is this viewpoint which underlies the single most important element in the whole social engineering view of politics, which is that there is a *correct* way of proceeding in human affairs and that it is the responsibility of the decision-maker to discover what this way is. As in the building of a bridge or the repairing of a broken arm, so also in social affairs there is a right mode of operation which is inherent in the matter at hand and in the nature of the problem. Until now the unreliable intuitions and the muddled impressions 'based on experience' of the politicians have prevented men from going about finding the rational way to proceed, but the methods of science will overcome this disastrous manner of deciding what to do. At least with respect to instrumental questions, a policy science will be able to do clearly and accurately what politics has been fumblingly trying to accomplish all along; and with the maturation of such a science, truth, transcending the ignorance, the pettiness, and the self-interestedness of political men will finally prevail in the authoritative decisions which determine the way in which resources and values are allocated in a society.

Social science is indeed critical for politics. It will change the nature of much, if not all, of political argument, making it technical and therefore soluble; it will press the scientific expert to the fore, at last establishing authority on the grounds of competence and expertise rather than on the quite arbitrary and manifestly unsatisfactory basis of heredity, wealth, social status, or demagogic power. Thus, much of political life will be transformed into a rational activity in which policy is made on explicit, objective, impartial criteria of efficiency; in Saint-Simon's now famous phrase, government, in the sense of government of men by men, will be abolished in large measure, and in its place will be inaugurated 'the administration of things'. When this time arrives, a new period of man's history will dawn, for through the manipulative powers gained as a result of social scientific knowledge, and it alone, man will achieve the satisfaction of his desires and consequently the happiness for which he longs. All of this today has become commonplace. [. . .]

It is at this point that one must face directly the issue of whether there is in fact a conceptual connection between a view of how one ought to understand social life and a view of how this understanding is to be translated into action. Is there such a connection between a positivist *theory* of social knowledge and a social engineering conception of political *practice*? I think that there is, and that this can be demonstrated by examining, first, the conception of explanation which is at the heart of the positivist theory of science, and second, the conceptual assumptions which underlie the whole scientific enterprise, assumptions which themselves account for the theory of explanation within science. When I have finished making these essentially philosophical arguments, I then want to go on to make a few brief remarks, in the tradition of Max Weber, about the interconnections between science, rationalisation, control, and industrial society; I do this with the idea of setting the more philosophical remarks within a larger sociological framework, and thereby investing them with more historical significance.

In order to show the conceptual connection between science and control, a connection which is at the heart of my claim that a certain conception of social science implicitly contains a notion of how theory is related to practice, I must first demonstrate the interrelationship between scientific explanation and prediction; it is only then that I will be able to show that the possibility of control is a constitutive element in the scientific enterprise itself. I will start with a straightforward and oft repeated account of the structural identity of scientific explanation and prediction, and then go on to examine several objections that have been raised against this view.

Say that E is a state of affairs that the scientist wants to explain; how does he accomplish this task? It is generally said that he does so when he is able to indicate the determining factors or causes which produce E. Now discovering the causes of E is discovering those features of the situation which, taken together, invariably result in E; it is this notion of invariability which is crucial in an explanation, for we can say that we have explained E only when we can see that E had to happen given certain explanatory facts, which means to say that it is an instance of some general regularity of nature. Once we see this we understand that what once appeared as a puzzling event is not now puzzling at all. [. . .]

The question now is, what bearing does this discussion have on the question of the relation of theory to practice? Its relevance is neatly summed up in Comte's epigram, 'From Science comes Prevision, from Prevision comes Control.' For, precisely because scientific explanations are the obverse of predictions, they lay the foundation for the instrumental control of phenomena by providing the sort of information which would enable one to manipulate certain variables in order to bring about a state of affairs or prevent its occurrence. It is thus no accident that social science positivistically conceived is historically linked with a social engineering viewpoint, for it is in the very nature of the sort of understanding given to us by science that it underlies such a viewpoint.

But, our objector might retort at this point, even though science does provide the information which *would* enable one to control phenomena through technical manipulation, the scientist *need not* relate to particular phenomena in this way: it is up to him to decide whether he wants to use his knowledge in this way, and such a decision would be an extra-scientific one. So, the objector might continue, all the argumentation so far still has not met the principal objection voiced at the beginning of this discussion, namely, that just because there is a historical connection between a positivist conception of social theory and a social engineering conception of how this theory is related to practice, this does not mean that there is a conceptual connection between them. In effect, he might claim, all that has been shown in demonstrating that science lays the basis for manipulative control is why someone with an engineering sort of political theory would turn to the promise of such a social science; surely it has not been shown why this conception of social theory commits one to this sort of political theory.

But the basis upon which this objection rests is false, and an explanation of why it is false will enable me to demonstrate not merely that the positivist conception of social science underlies and supports the idea of a policy science — something which has admittedly already been done — but that it is conceptually connected with it. To begin with, it is inaccurate to assert that, in the context of practical decision-making, 'it is up to the individual scientist to decide whether he wants to use his knowledge in this way', for, given the form which scientific knowledge takes, there is no other way that such knowledge can be useful in making practical decisions *except in an instrumentalist manner.* Science provides us with objective causal laws in which a certain state of affairs or type of state of affairs is explained by showing how other states of affairs either produce or prevent it; if a man turns to science, therefore, in order to learn how to cope with a state of affairs, the only information that it provides is the means by which, through certain technical operations, he can produce or prevent it, or, in the case of systems over which he has no control, how he can prepare himself in order to mitigate its effects. Scientific explanations give man power to act in situations by giving him the knowledge by which he can control phenomena through the manipulation of a particular set of variables.

Moreover, and much deeper, is the fact that the connection between the form which scientific knowledge takes and an instrumentalist conception of theory and practice lies at the very heart of what the nature of the scientific enterprise is; for, I would argue, the possibility of technical control, far from having a contingent relationship to science, is indeed part of the framework which constitutes the very possibility of scientific activity. I now want to show why this is so.*

A good place to begin is with the question, why is it the case that in science to explain something is to potentially predict it? To understand an event or state of affairs is to know another event which will invariably produce or prevent it. But this is to say that *we understand a state of affairs scientifically only to the extent that we have the knowledge of what to do in order to control it, and it is thus that the ability to control phenomena provides the framework in terms of which scientific explanation proceeds.*

Of course this theory of understanding is itself rooted in a whole series of metaphysical assumptions as to the nature of truth and reality, but this is a topic far beyond the scope of this article. But even at a superficial level it ought to be apparent that for the scientist reality is comprised of observable objects and events which are related nomologically, i.e. they are related according to a series of general laws of the type, if X then Y under situation C, and that therefore, in line with this scientific assumption about reality, only statements which reveal the concrete forms which those general relationships take can be true statements. Science must view the world in this way in order for it to provide the kind of explanations it prizes, which is to say, in order for it to provide the control over the phenomena which is a sign of its having understood a phenomenon. Because science marks out the 'world' as a world of observable phenomena subject to general laws it thereby is *constituting this 'world' from the viewpoint of how one can gain control over it.* It is for this reason that possible technical control provides the framework within which the definition of reality and truth in science occurs.

Underlying and informing the theory of explanation which I have presented are deeper assumptions as to the nature of truth and reality,

---

* For an account of the sort of argument that I will now make, cf. G. Radnitzsky, *Contemporary Schools of Metascience* (Henry Regnery, Chicago, 1970), vol. 2, ch. 1 and vol. 3, ch. 1. He calls this type of analysis the 'philosophical anthropology of knowledge'. For the clearest and simplest account of this, cf. K. O. Apel, 'The *a priori* of communication and the foundation of the humanities', *Man and World*, vol. 5, no. 1, Feb. 1972. This thesis is discussed briefly in the Preface to the new edition of Lucien Goldman's *The Human Sciences and Philosophy* (Cape, London, 1969).

and these deeper assumptions are rooted in the notion of manipulative control. So the conclusion is not merely that scientific knowledge provides the basis for manipulative control, but also, and more importantly, that what can count as scientific knowledge is that which gives us the means by which one can in principle control phenomena.* The possibility of controlling variables is a factor in terms of which one distinguishes a cognitive enterprise as scientific, and thus technical control is a defining element in the scientific enterprise itself. [. . .]

What underlies the scientific conception of explanation is the assumption that to understand an event is to know the events which produced it — and not just any events either, but those natural events which preceded it in time and which invariably produce the event in question. The scientist says that he knows what happened when he knows the causes of the event, and he means by this when he knows the mechanism in terms of which he himself can in theory produce the event in an experimental situation. All of this means that the notion of understanding in science is intimately bound up with the notion of control, for it is our ability to control events, at least in principle, which constitutes one of the criteria in virtue of which one can be said to have given a valid scientific explanation. It is in this way that the possibility of control is a constitutive element of the scientific enterprise, and this

---

* It is important to emphasise that what I am saying here is that it is what *can count* as scientific knowledge that is defined by men, and not that what is *true* is simply decided by them. For the *truth* of a theory depends on the state of the world; it is what it *means* for a theory to be true that depends on human conventions.

It is of overwhelming importance to make this distinction between meaning and truth, as well as to distinguish between the related concepts of ethical neutrality and objectivity; for a failure to do so leads one into making such absurd statements as, 'whether some proposition is true or not is a subjective matter, up to the individual person', or 'because our knowledge is rooted in some ideological conceptions, there is no possibility of an intersubjective validation of a knowledge claim'. These statements are absurd because they do violence to the concept of 'knowledge' and 'truth'. They are made because the person fails to draw the distinctions I just mentioned; and, I would also submit, this failure is itself rooted in the further mistake of failing to differentiate between what can be said about the categories of our thought on the one hand, and about propositions uttered in terms of these categories on the other.

Even though what it means for a proposition to be true is a result of human conventions, and even though these conventions could have been otherwise than they are, and even though they contain ideological components, it does not follow that this proposition cannot be objectively true in an important sense. Thus, men decide what it means to say that 'it is raining outside', but men do not decide, given this meaning, whether this proposition is true, i.e. they do not decide whether it is raining — for *that* they have to look and see.

means to say that *it is its (instrumental) conception of the relation of theory to practice that gives the scientific conception of truth its meaning and therefore sets the conditions for the validity of a scientific explanation*. It is just this conclusion which supports my claim that a positivist conception of the knowledge of social life contains within itself an instrumentalist-engineering conception of the relation of this knowledge to social action: for one is committed to this engineering view of theory and practice in the very act of adopting the positivist view of theory — indeed, it is this engineering view which supports and gives meaning to this view of social theory. Thus it is no accident or contingent sociological fact that the notion of a policy science is one that is deeply ingrained in the development of positivistic social science itself; rather, the articulation of this notion and its ramifications is simply a drawing out of the consequences of adopting a certain conception of social theory, consequences which were inherent in this conception all along. [. . .]

Appendix
The Social Sciences Foundation Course (D102)

A Block and unit titles

Block 1 *Studying Society*
Unit 1 Vandalism: society in decline?
Unit 2 The energy to go on
Unit 3 Making sense of society
Unit 4 The social sciences

Block 2 *The Economy: a Social Process*
Unit 5 Modern Britain; the economic base
Unit 6 How is production organized?
Unit 7 How do we know what to produce?
Unit 8 Modern Britain; economic crises
Unit 9 Review A

Block 3 *The Production of Social Divisions*
Unit 10 Class divisions in modern Britain
Unit 11 Race and class
Unit 12 Gender and class
Unit 13 Review B

Block 4 *Politics, Legitimacy and the State*
Unit 14 Why do people accept the authority of the state?
Unit 15 Democracy and popular participation
Unit 16 The making of public policy
Unit 17 Competing theories of the state
Unit 18 Why do social scientists disagree?

Block 5 *Conformity, Consensus and Conflict*
Unit 19 Is conformity necessary for social cohesion?
Unit 20 How is social integration achieved?
Unit 21 Managing conflict, producing consent
Unit 22 Review C

Block 6 *Social Change, Geography and Policy*
Unit 23 Growth, welfare and conflict

435

B   The course team

David Potter (Chairman)
John Allen
James Anderson
Andy Blowers
Susan Boyd-Bowman
Peter Bradshaw
Duncan Brown
Hedy Brown
Frank Castles
Alan Clarke
John Clarke
Annie Clutterbuck
Tony Coe
Robert Cookson
Pat Coombes
Don Cooper
Jeremy Cooper
Neil Costello
Bernard Eccleston
Clare Falkner
Mike Fitzgerald
Michael Gurevitch
Stuart Hall
Laurence Harris
Carol Haslam
Peter Heatherington
Sue Himmelweit
Clive Holloway
Helen Lentell

Allan Macartney
Geoff Manser
Jo Mathieson
Marjorie Mayo
Jeremy Mitchell
Ines Newman
Andy Northedge
Carolyn Picton
Stella Pilsworth
Christopher Pollitt
Graeme Salaman
Roger Sapsford
Phil Sarre
Phil Scraton
Francis Seeley
Paul Smith
Richard Stevens
Barbara Thompson
Eleanor Thompson
Tony Walton
Chris Wooldridge

Tutor Panel
Joanna Bornat
John Bourn
Irvine Gersch
Jackie Penning-Rowsell
Maureen Taylor

Index

structural marxism 159, 200,
212–15, 401
structure: of industry 37, 71–8;
of power 161–81, 193, 198
structured communication of
events 269–89
success and class 257–8, 262
Suez crisis 165, 171, 175, 179
suicide 17
Sumner, H. 155
Sylvester, E. 259, 266

take-overs 74, 308–9
Tarkington, B. 153
tax 325, 333
Taxel, H. 384
teaching 142–3, 154; *see also*
education
technology 68; piecemeal 418–24;
and progress 425–34; scientific
60; and social sciences 13–14,
395, 418–21, 425–34; and
unemployment 80
television 67–8; commercial 166,
169, 171, 173–4; *see also* mass
media
Ten Hours Act *1847* 46, 48–9
textile industry: automation in
86–7; concentration in 63, 73;
decline of 51, 56–7, 65, 69,
294, 298, 300; development of
71; reforms in 48; *see also*
clothing
theory: and fact in social sciences
396–405, 433; meta- 387–9;
under-determination of 394,
396–404
Thomas, W. I. 374
Torney, J. V. 264, 267
Town and Country Planning Act
1946 166, 172, 174, 177
Town Development Act 335–6
Tracey, M. 287
trade: associations 63, 166–7;
free 45–6, 54, 62, 98; world 59
Trade Union and Trade Disputes
Act *1927* 188

trade unions 193, 207, 216, 253;
legislation 49, 188; in motor
industry 121–4; and policies
168–9; and politics 196–8,
265; and racialism 293, 339–
43; rise of 42, 47, 49–50, 115
transport 84, 322; *see also* railways
Tuchman, G. 288
Tullock, G. 219
Turner, R. 259, 268

ultimate values 255–6
underdeveloped countries 67, 88
underdetermination of theory
394, 396–404
understanding, lack of 189
unemployment 56–7, 80, 129,
299–302, 307, 322–5; and
crime 322, 325; and policy
316, 323; and racism 340–1
uneven geographical development
291, 292, 294–301, 309–11,
328–38
ungovernability of Britain 182–91
United States: automation in
79–89; clerical work in 140–55;
consensus in 255–63;
consumers in 66; crime and
violence in 202, 325;
depression in 51; income in
81–2; industry in 41, 43, 54,
61, 79–89, 291; investment by
Britain 43, 53, 59; loan to
Britain 165, 173; 'power élite'
in 203; research 68; women's
work in 140–55
unpredictability 22
upper class *see* élites
'Urban Development Corporations'
334
urban planning 327–38
Urry, J. 193
USSR, attitudes to 165, 173–4
Utopianism 242–3, 421–4

value system, central 241–54
value-commitment 256–63